Political Actors

D1596407

POLITICAL ACTORS

Representative Bodies and Theatricality
in the Age of the French Revolution

PAUL FRIEDLAND

Cornell University Press

ITHACA AND LONDON

First published 2002 by Cornell University Press
First printing, Cornell Paperbacks, 2003

Library of Congress Cataloging-in-Publication Data

Friedland, Paul, 1962–
   Political actors : representative bodies and theatricality in the age
of the French Revolution / Paul Friedland.
      p. cm.
Includes bibliographical references and index.
   ISBN 0-8014-3982-5 (cloth : alk. paper)—ISBN 0-8014-8809-5 (pbk. : alk. paper)
   1. France—History—Revolution, 1789–1799. 2. Theater--Political
aspects—France—History—18th century. 3. Actors—France—Political
activity. I. Title.
   DC158.8 .F75 2002
   944.04—dc21
                              2002001598

Cloth printing   10 9 8 7 6 5 4 3 2 1
Paperback printing   10 9 8 7 6 5 4 3 2 1

Contents

Acknowledgments

Like any book that has been a long time in the making, this one owes quite a bit, both intellectually and financially, to many institutions and individuals. A predissertation fellowship from the Council on European Studies and a Bicentennial Fellowship from the French American Foundation respectively funded a summer and a year of research in France. A Mellon dissertation write-up grant awarded by the University of California allowed me to transform my research into a dissertation. When I later began the long process of transforming the dissertation into a book, a Newberry Library–Loyola summer grant afforded me the opportunity to make use of the Newberry's extraordinary collection of medieval and early modern political texts. The National Endowment for the Humanities helped to fund a membership in the School of Social Science at the Institute for Advanced Study, and it was at this institution—a veritable scholar's paradise—that the book truly began to take shape. I am very much indebted to the permanent faculty at the School of Social Science and to my fellow members who shared the year with me for the exchange of ideas that took place there.

I would like to express my gratitude to the staff at the Archives nationales, the Bibliothèque de l'Arsenal, the Bibliothèque nationale de France, and to Noëlle Guibert and Jacqueline Razgonnikoff of the Bibliothèque de la Comédie-Française. In the United States I would like to thank the staff at the libraries of the following institutions: the University of Chicago, the University of California at Berkeley, the Institute for Advanced Study, and Princeton University. And I would especially like to thank staff members at the libraries of Bowdoin, Bates, and Colby Colleges who were extraordinarily helpful in procuring essential texts at a moment's notice.

Over the years, several individuals have shared their ideas with me. Members of the Berkeley French dissertation group, including Megan Koreman, Douglas Mackaman, Katharine Norris, Marc Roudebush, Vanessa

Schwartz, and Tamara Whited, provided moral support and intellectual ca-
maraderie. Dana Kostroun was kind enough to share her work on a related
subject with me. Lisa Cody-Forman was a constant source of encourage-
ment and was always willing to hash out improbable theories with me.
Joseph Zizek was invariably inspiring on our long walks with Hamilton the
Basset Hound through the California redwoods. James Swenson provided
endless food for thought during our many chats in many places. Jeffrey
Ravel helped me in innumerable ways at almost every stage of this process,
and I am truly grateful for his generosity. And David Bell took it upon himself to read my entire dissertation and to give me extensive comments that
proved enormously helpful when it came time to reconceptualize the project
as a book. Over the past several years, he has been a continual source of en-
couragement and advice.

Several scholars with whom I have studied have contributed to the making of this book. The initial crucible for many of the ideas expressed in these
pages was a research seminar at the University of Chicago co-taught by
Keith Baker and the late François Furet. Although I'm sure she doesn't remember it, I owe thanks to Jan Goldstein who managed to pluck the general
topic of this book from a rather dense and semiotically saturated master's
thesis on Rousseau's antitheatricality. And at Berkeley, Tom Laqueur's seminar on the history of the body came at a crucial time in my initial concep-
tualization of this project.

I am particularly indebted to three individuals who helped to make this
book possible. Keith Baker was involved with this project from the very beginning. And, after we had both coincidentally left Chicago for Northern
California, he graciously agreed to continue his association with it, although
we were no longer at the same institution. Those who are familiar with his
work will undoubtedly see the innumerable ways in which he has influenced
this book, even if I suspect he may not agree with all of its conclusions.

During my years at Berkeley, Susanna Barrows single-handedly created a
community of French historians and by her example taught her students the
meaning of intellectual generosity and collegiality. I could not have hoped
for a better advisor and friend.

Joan Wallach Scott deserves more kind words than I can possibly fit into
a paragraph. Over the years, she has read more drafts of this book than any
other individual, possibly including me. Without her invaluable insights, en-
couragement, and help, this book, in its current form, would not have been
possible. To me, and to her many former students to whom she gives so self-
lessly of her time and her energy, she is the very model of an intellectual men-
tor.

Selections from several chapters in part 1 appear in a different form in my
chapter "Parallel Stages" in *The Age of Cultural Revolutions: Britain and
France, 1750–1820*, edited by Colin Jones and Dror Wahrman (Berkeley:
University of California Press, 2002). Copyright © 2002 The Regents of the

University of California. I am grateful to the University of California Press for permission to use this material. I would also like to express my thanks to my copyeditor, Susan Tarcov, and to the staff at Cornell University Press, in particular Louise E. Robbins, for their help in transforming the manuscript into a book. I owe special thanks to my editor at Cornell, John G. Ackerman, whose unerring judgment and good humor made the entire publishing process surprisingly pleasant.

On a more personal note, I would like to thank my parents, Lawrence and Alice Friedland, for their financial support when times got tough (if not for their incessant reminders that law school was, and always will be, an option). I could not be blessed with a better friend than Ian Burney, who talked me through many a difficult moment and many an intellectual conundrum over the years. And I owe very much to Mlle Alice Ruez, who, as she helped to raise me, passed on to me a love for French language and culture, tempered, when appropriate, with a healthy disdain.

More than to anyone else, I owe thanks to my family. Alexander, Talia, and Lily Friedland have accepted the demands of their father's book for their entire lives without a complaint. And Page Herrlinger, although she did, in fact, complain, nevertheless gave of her time, her sage advice, and her love when they were needed most. For that, and for so many other things, I dedicate this book to her, my colleague, my companion, and the mother of our wonderful children.

Political Actors

Introduction

Il ne fallait au fier Romain
Que des Spectacles et du pain;
Mais au Français plus que Romain
Le Spectacle suffit sans pain.*

In the decades before the French Revolution, the Catholic Church expended a significant amount of effort in broadcasting the fact that theaters and the actors who performed in them were indecent and sinful and that no good Christian should have anything to do with either of them. To a certain extent, the church was preaching to the converted: actors in France were excluded from most aspects of political and civil life. And at a more informal, social level, actors suffered varying degrees of prejudice and ostracism.

This general repugnance associated with actors did not, however, translate into a distaste for the theater. On the contrary, throughout the eighteenth century theater was something of a national obsession in France—an obsession that was apparently shared with the rest of Europe. By the time of the Revolution, French-language plays were being performed all across the continent, and as one observer noted, "[T]hroughout Europe one finds French actors and French hairdressers."[1]

Even if we take into account, however, a long-standing infatuation with the theater (if not necessarily with the actors themselves), the theatricality of French society during the Revolutionary years is nonetheless remarkable. The increase in the number of theaters alone is astonishing: in two years, from 1789 to 1791 (the year in which theaters were deregulated and exclusive theatrical privileges abolished), the number of theaters in Paris tripled.[2] By 1792, the authors of the yearly theatrical almanac of Paris were so astounded by this rapid increase in theaters that they declared, "This multi-

---

* (The proud Roman needed only spectacles and bread [i.e., bread and circuses]; but for the Frenchman, more than Roman, spectacles without bread will do.) Cited in [L.-A. Beffroy de Reigny et al.], *Almanach général de tous les spectacles de Paris et des provinces, pour l'année 1791* (Paris, [1791]), 256.

plicity of spectacles is truly frightening. . . . Soon, in Paris, we will count one theater per street, one actor per house, one musician per basement and one author per attic."[3]

One particular aspect of Revolutionary theatricality especially struck contemporary observers: the strange and seemingly unprecedented intermingling of the worlds of theater and politics. If politics and theater had in some vague manner always resembled each other (in the sense, for example, of the elaborate court ceremonials of Louis XIV), theatrical and political actors had nevertheless always kept to their respective stages. After all, given their status as virtual pariahs, for actors to have anything to do with politics would hardly have been appropriate.

With the Revolution, however, the rules seemed to have changed almost overnight: dramatic actors, who only a few months before had been social and political outcasts in an old regime that officially regarded their craft as profane, were elected to powerful political and military positions. At the same time, politics seemed to have become infused with a new and different kind of theatricality: there were reports that deputies to the National Assembly were taking acting lessons and that claqueurs were being planted in the audience to applaud their employers on demand. There was, in short, a general merging of the theatrical and political stages, which suddenly made possible new theatrico-political hybrids that would have been unthinkable only a short time before: in the middle of the Palais-Royal, for example, in a circus pavilion, a mock National Assembly charged admission to spectators who wanted to act the part of political representatives.

Not surprisingly, this new theatricality that permeated Revolutionary politics proved deeply disturbing to many: pamphlets were written in which the entire National Assembly was unmasked as a troupe of actors in disguise and election results were printed in the form of a cast list. Invariably, denunciations of political figures sought to portray them as unscrupulous actors, deceiving the people with their all too believable performances. Edmund Burke's *Reflections on the Revolution in France* is only the most enduring of countless works in which France's new politicians were denounced as second-rate hams. Conversely, while politicians were being unmasked as actors, dramatic actors were themselves being denounced by both the political left and the right as being secret agents of the other. During the Terror, suspicions about actors' political allegiances would lead to the large-scale imprisonment of actors in Paris as well as in the provinces.

The French Revolution has long been portrayed as "dramatic" in a very general sense. Few, however, have focused explicitly on its theatricality—on the formal identity between the theatrical and political stages that seemed so striking to the Revolution's contemporaries.[4] And even among those who have taken note of Revolutionary theatricality specifically, a fundamental question has yet to be asked: How, when, and why did politics and theater become so intimately intertwined?

The answer to this question takes us farther afield than one might imagine. For the question itself cannot be addressed without tracing the logical development of both theatrical and political representation over the course of the centuries leading up to the Revolution. And what this genealogy of theater and politics reveals is not only a surprising conceptual identity between the two representative forms but a radical and simultaneous revolution that struck both in the second half of the eighteenth century, altering them as well as altering their relationship to each other. The argument made in this book is that the French Revolution is fundamentally related to a revolution in the theory and practice of theater, and that both revolutions are manifestations of an underlying revolution in the conception of representation itself. In fact, as I argue throughout this book, representative democracy and modern theatricality are not merely related; they are conceptual siblings.

This claim of a formal identity between representative democracy and theater is not my own; it is an overriding obsession among many texts of the Revolutionary period, particularly those texts (on both the right and the left) that were hostile to the moderates who ruled France in the early years of the Revolution. The argument presented here, then, is not motivated by a priori theoretical assumptions; rather, it is an argument inspired by the texts of the Revolutionary period themselves. And here, I think, it would be useful for the reader to come upon the connection between theater and politics just as I did.

About a dozen years ago, I chanced upon a pamphlet with a strange title: *Remarkable and Interesting Events on the Occasion of the Decrees of the August National Assembly Concerning the [Political] Eligibility of Messrs. the Actors, the Hangman, and the Jews.* Here, I thought, was a text that harbored some inside joke that I would never fully understand. Actors, executioners, and Jews? By what logic, I wondered, could these three groups be related?

As I soon discovered, the pamphlet was written in late December of 1789 or early in 1790 and was a satire that sought to ridicule the National Assembly for actions that it did indeed undertake in December of 1789, when it bestowed civil and political rights on executioners and actors (and considered bestowing such rights on Jews—something the representatives could not quite bring themselves to do for another two years). In the deputies' minds, the extension of civil and political rights to the old regime's outcasts was nothing but the rational, logical consequence of natural law, in contrast to which their exclusion had been irrational, illogical, and the result of prejudice. But the author of *Remarkable and Interesting Events* was not so easily convinced. Where the deputies saw the logical consequence of reasoned tolerance, essentially no different from the extension of political rights to Protestants, who had also suffered political restrictions in the old regime, our author saw the fruit of an illicit collusion. And in particular, the pamphlet insinuated a certain complicity between the nation's political representatives and theatrical actors.

The first part of this satirical pamphlet is largely devoted to parodying the debates within the National Assembly, with the political actors too swept up in the moment to hide their true colors. Here, a very theatrical comte de Mirabeau confesses not only that he himself has played on the theatrical stage but that "sixty, seventy" of his colleagues are actors as well. The second part of the pamphlet plays out the laughable, and yet at the same time deeply disturbing, consequences of the Assembly's decision to grant actors political eligibility. In a fictional town in France, the actors take control. The election results are detailed in the form of a cast list. And the actors, whom generations of townspeople had heckled as a natural right, suddenly finding themselves in a position of political authority, inform the townspeople that they will no longer tolerate being ill-treated: now *they* will be masters on both the theatrical and the political stages. When the parterre seems reluctant to accord them the respect they demand, the actor-politicians try to order the local military "to disperse the parterre or else to kill it."[5]

My initial impression was that the pamphlet was a bit disorganized and seemed to degenerate into silliness. The executioners and Jews quickly fall by the wayside, and the bulk of the rhetoric is directed at actors and the representatives to the National Assembly, with the pamphlet devoting the greater part of its energies to pointing out a complicity and even a conceptual identity between these two groups. The author, I thought, seemed unable to decide whether he was horrified by or scornfully dismissive of the events and processes he described. As I was soon to discover, however, the pamphlet was not at all unique in its half-mocking, half-horrified reaction to the intermingling of theatrical and political forms.

Initially, I was interested in discovering the logic according to which old regime France had ostracized actors, executioners, and Jews. Was there, I wondered, some connection between these three groups? Or were they simply linked by virtue of their all being denied a civil status, perhaps for very different reasons? And above all, I was interested in trying to understand why actors in particular seemed to elicit such a strongly negative response, especially when it was a matter of their possible connection to politics and politicians. The fact, of course, that Jews, actors, and executioners were denied a civil status because they were respectively non-Christian, excommunicated, and set apart from other Christians seemed to beg the question (at least with respect to the last two) of why their activities—which were, we should not forget, tolerated by the public and by the state—demanded that they be set apart from the Christian community.

As I made my way through an inordinate number of pre-Revolutionary antitheatrical tracts, as well as the far less common texts discussing executioners, I gradually became convinced that the status of these outcasts holds the key to a way of looking at the world that had prevailed for centuries and began to fade away in the second half of the eighteenth century. The very fact of these outcast groups, and the logic connecting them, revealed the existence of a conceptual vantage point that has since disappeared: a way of looking at the world in which all political and social phenomena were comprehended in terms of the nonvisible reality of corporate, mystical bodies.

The concept of the mystical body, or *corpus mysticum,* referred to bodies that had no tangible form but were nevertheless profoundly real. It was a term that had been borrowed from theology, originally referring to the body of the Christian community as well as to the body of Christ, which, since the Crucifixion, had been intangible except during those moments when it was made present within the Eucharist. By the early fifteenth century, the concept of the corpus mysticum had become a relative commonplace of political theory, describing the nonvisible body of the nation of which the three estates formed the trunk and limbs and the king the head. The nation, then, was a living communal body—a literal rather than a metaphoric body—that under normal circumstances possessed no tangible form and could not be seen and yet whose existence was nevertheless beyond doubt; the visible, tangible body of the individual was, by contrast, a relatively meaningless abstraction of the communal whole.

The great crime of actors, executioners, and Jews was to have—each in their own way—toyed with or negated the sanctity of the corpus mysticum, this most sacred of politico-religious principles. Although their presence and their activities were tolerated by the state, there is no question that the existence of these outcasts was profoundly problematic in premodern France. The actors' profession, as it was practiced prior to the middle of the eighteenth century, essentially called upon them to conjure the mystical, nonvisible body of characters within their own flesh. In other words, they used themselves as a vessel for the intangible body of the character that they literally re-presented within their own body—all of this for the amusement of a paying public, an act that could not help striking contemporaries as a kind of prostitution of the body. The task of the executioner was to mold the flesh of the criminal—often referred to as the *patient*—in order to create a living sculpture of the communal body wounded by the crime. The execution was a kind of healing spectacle in which the patient—the term itself shares an etymological root with the Passion—gave up his or her body so that the body of the community might be healed. And the Jews, who denied the sanctity of the various Christian mystical bodies—of Christ's body, of its re-presentation in the Eucharist, and of the body of the Church—must have seemed, by their very presence, to challenge the logic from which the political corpus mysticum had been derived. In short, all three of these groups were trudging on sanctified ground.

All of this changed, however, in 1789, when the Revolutionaries, finishing the work of a generation of political theorists who preceded them, killed off the mystical body in the political sphere. Within a remarkably short period of time, the relative importance of mystical and individual bodies was reversed; the abstract individual was posited as a reality, and the corpus mysticum was relegated to the realm of defunct mythology. Actors, executioners, and (later) Jews would no longer be civil outcasts, not so much because the Revolution was committed to the rights of man—a commitment that was more the result than the cause of the new civil inclusion—but because the mystical body that these outcasts had threatened was no longer deemed to exist (or at least was relegated to the now theoretically apolitical sphere of religion). Actors, executioners, and Jews could be citizens because their citizenship was not in the sacred corpus mysticum of the nation but rather in the newly articulated metaphoric body of hypothetically equivalent and undifferentiated citizens.

Although I was intrigued by the logic of ostracism in the old regime and the various commonalities between these groups of outcasts, I found myself particularly drawn to the question of the actors. And so, like the anonymous author of the pamphlet *Remarkable and Interesting Events,* I eventually left executioners and Jews by the wayside and focused on the peculiar conceptual affinity between politics and theater. How, precisely, I wanted to know, were political and theatrical representation related? And to what extent was this relationship unique to the Revolutionary period?

My research would eventually lead me to the conclusion that prior to the middle of the eighteenth century, theatrical representation and political representation were conceptualized in a virtually identical fashion: on both stages the actor was meant to embody or make present a mystical body (a character in a play or the corpus mysticum of the French nation) that had no visible or tangible presence of its own. In the decades after 1750, however, the task of actors on both stages underwent a parallel redefinition: Theatrical actors were prevailed upon to represent their characters abstractly, in a manner that *seemed realistic* to the audience, rather than a manner that the actors experienced *as real.* And, at the same time, political theorists were slowly articulating a comparable reconceptualization of political representation. This theoretical revolution would ultimately lead to the invention in 1789 of the revolutionary political body known as the National Assembly, marking the triumph of abstract representation on the political stage: unlike previous political bodies that had claimed to *be* the French nation, the National Assembly merely claimed to speak on the nation's behalf.

This extraordinary revolution in the conception of representation itself had important consequences on both the theatrical and the political stages. But it also greatly affected the relationship *between* these stages: although the representations of theatrical and political actors had always been conceptually identical, they had been practiced on stages that were respectively profane and sacred. The relationship between the two stages was, then, strictly parallel, never intersecting. Only when the theory and practice of representation changed—when it was no longer about the presentation of actual bodies—did the distinction between the sacred and the profane disappear. Only then did antitheatrical indictments of the theater as an abomination begin to lose their rationale. And only then did the walls separating the profane and the sacred begin to crumble, allowing for a kind of conceptual *métissage*—an intermingling of previously discrete forms.

The pamphlet *Remarkable and Interesting Events,* like many of the texts discussed in this book, is relatively obscure. But the obscurity of texts that have as their implicit or explicit purpose the unmasking of the inherent theatricality, the fraudulence of representative democracy should not surprise us. The canonicity of such texts has tended to be in inverse proportion to the success of the system of government that they condemn, a system that has spread throughout the world. One might, of course, point out that representative democracy has not been lacking in critics, and wonder why none of these availed themselves of the texts in question. But the logic employed in these texts lies so far outside modern modes of thinking that they are relatively incomprehensible to present-day readers, mixing categories that we are not used to seeing in the same place and drawing conclusions that can only strike us as absurd.

If many of the texts discussed in this book are relatively obscure, I should be very clear that I am not basing the claims presented here on strange pamphlets of uncertain authorship and no less certain readership. In fact these texts are important, at least in part, for what they have to teach us about the canon. For even the most obscure, unlikely text inevitably contains within it the preconceptions of its age. But more than that, such texts often highlight aspects of the particular historical context in which they were written that other texts, whether intentionally or unintentionally, have been content to gloss over. The obscure, somewhat paradoxically, often sheds a new and unexpected light on concepts that we have come to think of as clear and self-evident.[6] In this sense, then, the noncanonical helps us to find new ways of reading the canon.

In the following pages, the reader will find both strange texts by anonymous authors and more familiar texts by well-known authors; both the private correspondence of dramatic actors and the published debates of France's legislators. By forcing these unlikely pairs into dialogues, one begins to uncover something of the spirit of the age—a spirit, as I have suggested, that was in the middle of a profound transformation, much deeper and farther-reaching than the Revolution itself.

In many respects, this has not been an easy story to tell. The concept of a fundamental revolution in representation itself, combined with a now parallel, now intermingling relationship between theater and politics, seemed to call for both a long-term analysis that revealed the nature of change over time and a close-up, more textually based analysis that revealed the complex relationship between politics and theater at given moments in time. This combination of a diachronic and synchronic focus made a conventional narrative somewhat difficult to construct, and at times I have made use of certain terminological and narrative irregularities to help tell this ever-twisting tale.

For one, compromises had to be made between narrative and juxtaposition. If, for example, I had traced the entire evolution of representation within the world of theater, and then done the same for politics, such a narrative would, I think, have implied a causality that I did not want to suggest. If, instead, I had attempted to avoid altogether a coherent narrative of either theater or politics and had chosen to flit constantly back and forth between the two, I would have tried the reader's patience. And so, although much of this book does indeed follow a narrative line, there are times when theater and politics are juxtaposed chapter by chapter, and other times when they are juxtaposed within chapters. What to the reader may very well seem like a jarring intrusion of theater where one expected to find politics (or vice versa) is an admittedly inelegant formal solution to an intellectual dilemma: how to present the complex relationship between theatrical and political representation in a way that did not suggest the primacy of either and that nevertheless presented a coherent story.

Readers who are primarily interested in the political narrative may very well regard the sections on theatricality and on dramatic actors as something of an interruption. Readers who are primarily interested in the theater and theatricality of the period may well find the detailed chapters on political theory to be overly dense. But I would urge both to resist present-day disciplinary boundaries and to read the book as, I would claim, those who lived through the events described here experienced the world in which they lived—a world in which the political and the theatrical mirrored and eventually merged with each other. At the very least, I would urge even the most die-hard political theorists not to skip over the prologue, even if only to read it as political metaphor. And I would caution all readers that the argument presented here progresses from chapter to chapter, with each new chapter building upon the preceding. If, therefore, readers approach individual chapters out of context, the argument may very well lose whatever plausibility it might otherwise have had.

A second, somewhat inelegant solution to a narrative difficulty is my use of the presence and absence of a hyphen to distinguish between premodern and modern forms of representation. When I am referring specifically to the act by which an intangible body is literally made present in concrete form, I use the hyphenated form, *re-presentation;* this act of re-presentation is essentially analogous to the Catholic conception of transubstantiation in which the body and the blood of Christ are materially re-presented, or incarnated, within the bread and the wine of the Eucharist. I use the nonhyphenated form, *representation,* to refer to the process by which an intangible body is abstractly represented in spirit rather than in substance; this form is analogous to the various Protestant conceptions of the Eucharist in which the body and blood of Christ are symbolically referred to by the bread and the wine.

Finally, I would like to add a few words on the claims being made here with respect to other interpretations of the French Revolution as well as the relationship of these claims to the subject of representative democracy.

Every scholar who attempts an interpretation of the French Revolution must, in one sense or another, confront the powerful narrative bequeathed to posterity by the Revolutionaries themselves. From the siege of the Bastille onward, they saw themselves as participating in events with world-historical significance. They were ushering in the age of democratic revolution not only in France but in the world at large, an age in which despotism, injustice, and arbitrary privilege would be replaced by liberty, justice, and equality.

Skeptics, of course, might have pointed out that the Americans and even the English had managed to achieve a measure of liberty significantly earlier than the French, but the Revolutionaries were convinced that their Revolution was of unique importance. They had seemingly done in a few days what had taken generations for the British to accomplish. And, as far as the American Revolution was concerned, the French were convinced that a revolution in a "new" country with no history and relatively few inhabitants was hardly comparable to their own unprecedented feat of having shaken the foundation of the most formidable power in continental Europe. Two weeks after the fall of the Bastille, Duke Mathieu de Montmorency urged his colleagues in the National Assembly to draft a Declaration of the Rights of Man as soon as possible, declaring that the world was waiting for the French to set an example that the Americans, in their own small way, had set before them: "[The United States] have given a great example to the new hemisphere; let us give one to the universe; let us present it with a model worthy of admiration."[7]

To a remarkable extent, for more than two centuries now the French Revolutionaries have largely been taken at their word: this was a revolution that ended the reign of arbitrary despotism and brought the rational rule of liberty and democracy not only to France, but to the world at large. The nineteenth-century historian Jules Michelet declared, "Every nation, at the news of [the Bastille's] destruction, believed it had recovered its liberty," and he therefore urged that the anniversary of the Bastille's conquest "remain ever one of the eternal *fêtes* of the human race."[8]

Certainly, this master narrative has had its share of critics, none more important than Marx, who saw in the Revolution not the liberty of all but the replacement of one form of oppression by another. And yet, far from minimizing the importance of the French Revolution, Marx seized upon its fundamental importance as a crucial moment in the inevitable march of world history toward the final goal of communism. In the end, however, the Revolutionaries' version of the story has proved more enduring than Marx's. Just in the past generation, we have seen Marxist historiography wane, only to be replaced by two somewhat amorphous schools of thought that, whether by default or intentionally, have encouraged a resurgence of the Revolutionaries' master narrative.

One school of thought, that of the so-called revisionists, has sought to discover the internal logic of the Revolution and in so doing rescue it from decades of Marxist historiography that had done what was necessary to stuff the Revolution into its inexorable teleology. Although initially, the revisionists were content to poke holes in the presuppositions of Marxist historians, a later generation of revisionist historians was less concerned with Marx than with the Revolution itself. The Revolution, this more recent group has argued, must be considered on its own terms; in short, it should be read as a text, or body of texts, in its own right, divorced not only from Marx's narrative of class struggle but from all grand causal theories. One inevitably distorts the experience of the Revolution itself, they argue, if one is obsessed with uncovering its place in history and most especially the Revolution's relationship to the present.

This study is enormously indebted to the work of several revisionist historians and particularly to the method of close textual analysis many of them have employed. Nevertheless, the argument expressed in these pages proceeds from the central presupposition that the full import and meaning of the Revolution as a text cannot be understood divorced from its greater context. We risk missing what was truly at stake in the Revolution if we intentionally abstract it from long-term changes over time, from what came before it and what followed after it. In short, despite the invaluable contributions they have made to an understanding of the internal logic of the Revolutionary moment, those who took the "linguistic turn" may very well have led us to a dead end when it comes to understanding the *relevance* of the French Revolution. And, although most of the revisionist historians certainly did not subscribe to the Revolutionaries' master narrative and indeed made a point of saying that we must look beyond the intentions of the historical actors themselves, they nevertheless, almost by default, have allowed its resurgence. For in the absence of any clear discussion of how the French Revolution relates to the present, the Revolutionaries' own version of the story has seeped back in like water filling a hole in swampy ground.

In the wake of the Revolution's bicentennial, a historiography that championed the Revolutionaries' contributions to the field of human rights gained prominence, reminding modern society of the important debt that it owes to the French Revolution: at a time when France was at the very epicenter of Western civilization, the French people erected a political and social system based upon the fundamental recognition of the value of the natural rights of the individual and a commitment—inherited from the Enlightenment—to stamping out injustice and prejudice. As an essential part of this process of Enlightenment, the Revolutionaries bestowed a civil and political status on a range of individuals who had been deprived of these rights under the old regime. France, we are told, even if it continued to deny certain rights to women and to African slaves, was nevertheless becoming more democratic. For, after all, is not the extension of the franchise, the guarantee of the right to participate in the formation of ruling political bodies, one of the hallmarks of democracy? The answer, however, is not quite as apparent as it might seem, for it hinges on one's definition of democracy.

Democracy, as it has traditionally been defined and as it was defined in the eighteenth century, is a government in which the people have no need of representatives, in which the people themselves tend to all matters on their own behalf. Most political theorists of the eighteenth century argued that for a government to be truly democratic, the essential formulation and articulation of the nation's will ought to be the task of the entire body of citizens, although the citizenry might delegate certain technical responsibilities. Representative democracy, by contrast, was from its very inception a contradiction in terms, for the basic reason that a true democracy precluded representation. But as so many political theorists of the eighteenth century pointed out, it was practically impossible for a nation as large as France (or America or England) to assemble its citizenry to deliberate on all matters of importance, as had ancient Athens or, some argued, modern Geneva. And so representative democracy was put forward as the logical next-best-thing: if democracy were practically impossible, then the people's interests could be represented by deputies who had their constituents' interests at heart.

On some level, the distinction that I am drawing here (and, incidentally, that most pre-Revolutionary political theorists and commentators were careful to draw as well) between democracy and representative democracy may seem like terminological hairsplitting. Is representative democracy not democratic in spirit if not in actual practice? In fact, as I endeavor to prove in this book, representative democracy was never intended to be democratic in spirit. Even while the Revolutionaries sang the praises of "democracy," they constructed, brick by brick, a political edifice predicated on the *exclusion* from active political power of the very people in whose name their government claimed to rule. And it is a curious fact that the rhetoric of democracy reached a crescendo precisely when political practice was at its most despotic: the politicians of the Terror proclaimed the will of the people to be triumphant, and claimed to be acting in an almost transparent relationship with that will, even while the various avenues through which that will had previously made itself manifest were being shut down. "Democracy," as it was defined during the Terror, seemed to call for the people's complete acquiescence, rather than their direct participation. And here, far from being an aberration, the essential logic of the Terror is fully consistent with the other regimes of the Revolutionary period. Although many of the important political figures of the Terror may very well have criticized representative democracy and extolled the virtues of direct democracy, if one looks at its political practice rather than its rhetoric, the Terror was, like the regimes that came before and after it, a government in which political actors acted and political audiences watched, preferably in silence.

What was characterized by the Revolutionaries themselves as a straightforward choice between despotism and liberty, between irrational injustice and rational justice, was certainly the forsaking of one system for an entirely different one; but to argue that this particular choice was either inherently "rational" or an inevitable step in the march toward progress is to buy into the mythology of the mythmakers themselves. An infinity of political choices were available to eighteenth-century reformers, and they chose one particular path. The fact that we, more than two centuries later, still tend to see this path as rational and inevitable may say more about us than it does about rationality and inevitability. Representative democracy, in short, does not have a monopoly on reason and justice, despite the claims of those who put the system in place.

But, I should stress, my intention here is not simply to give the lie to the Revolution's claims to have inaugurated the reign of liberty in Europe. This is not, in other words, the story of how wily politicians hoodwinked the French people into believing that they were being freed, even as they laid the foundation for oppression. In fact, I am certain that no one was more convinced of the Revolution's rhetoric of liberty, justice, and natural rights than the very people who spoke the words. And as for those who found themselves excluded from a political process performed in their name, they seemed only dimly aware of the fact that they had been removed from the political stage. The problem, then, is decidedly more complex than the simple dynamic of oppressors and oppressed. This utter conviction on the part of the political actors that they were the servants of the people and were acting in their best interest; this willingness on the part of the political audience to sit back and partake vicariously in action from which they had been excluded; and the impenetrable yet invisible wall that divided these actors and these spectators—all of this seems to have very little to do with outright political subjugation. This is not oppression; this is theater.

The claim that I make in this book, then, is not that one group of people perpetrated an act on another. I am not, in other words, suggesting that we replace Marx's bourgeoisie with political actors and retell the story of the Revolution as the victory of the latter. Both actors and spectators alike were caught up in the new dynamic, and both were equally oblivious to the true nature of the change that was occurring at a much more fundamental and deeper level than either politics or theater. I am convinced that the revolutions in theater and politics were themselves manifestations of an underlying revolution in the very categories of perception, in the way that individuals made sense of the world around them.

The French Revolution was not, therefore, simply a moment in time. It was *the* moment when one of the most powerful and culturally influential nations in the world entered into political modernity—*our* modernity. The theory and practice of representation—both theatrical and political—that were invented in the eighteenth century are still the ones that reign today. And if we have come to regard them as entirely natural, it is my hope that this book will help contribute to a new vantage point from which to study them. By placing these now all-too-natural forms within the historical context of their coming into existence as novelties, I hope to encourage a fresh and critical approach to what has for a very long time been regarded as self-evident.

It is my contention here that the true import of the Revolution—both on its own terms and in terms of its relevance to the present day—lies in the greater process of which it was a part. This is not to minimize the importance of the Revolution. On the contrary, it is to recognize precisely *how* it was important: if the Revolution cannot be reduced to class, then neither can it be reduced to a moment. The Revolution is an integral part of a broader sea change in the way that people interacted with the world around them, in the way that they made use of signs and symbols to understand and communicate with others. This change was not inevitable, but neither was it random. It had a logic which can be traced through the very same tools of textual analysis that have previously been used to sever the French Revolution from its broader history. And when we trace this logic forward, we find ourselves holding the end of the thread.

I
THE REVOLUTION IN
REPRESENTATION

Prologue

A Parable: The Revolution in Theatrical Representation

Throughout the early modern period, in France as in much of Europe, theatrical actors constituted something of a people apart. Despite the monarchy's official patronage of the theater, the Catholic Church and a good portion of the public tended to regard actors, whether on or off the stage, as pariahs. Repeated official decrees declaring that the actor was not *infâme* seemed to do little to combat religious and popular hostility toward actors, a hostility that did not necessarily have an effect on theater attendance: it was apparently possible to attend plays and thoroughly enjoy the actors' performances while at the same time despising the actors for their profession.[1]

Most opponents of the theater were quick to cite the problematic *content* of the actor's performance as the basis for their disapproval. The seventeenth-century bishop Jacques-Benigne Bossuet, for example, although best remembered for his legitimization of absolutism and his arguments concerning the sacredness of royal re-presentation, devoted significant attention to the inappropriate passions re-presented on the theatrical stage. Bossuet argued that actors were rightly regarded as an object of prejudice because their craft involved the intentional dredging up, from their own memory, of shameful feelings that were more appropriately left in the recesses of the mind than resurrected and paraded around in front of an audience: "I ask you what an actor does when he wants to play a passion naturally: as much as he can, he recalls the passions that he has felt and that, as a Christian, he would have drowned in tears of penitence so that they might never return."[2] Such immoral feelings, which would be problematic enough if depicted in other art forms, were all the more problematic on the stage, Bossuet argued, because only there could they be truly brought to life, not only within the body of the actor, but also within the hearts and minds of the spectators who could not help being affected by the performance:

If nudes and immodest paintings naturally cause that which they express and have for this reason been condemned, . . . how much more are we touched by the expressions of the theater, where everything seems real *[effectif]*, where it is not at all lifeless characteristics and colorless complexions that are in operation but living characters, real eyes, whether ardent or tender and steeped in passion; real tears in the actors, who cause real tears to flow in those who look at them; in short, real movements that ignite the entire parterre and all the spectator boxes?[3]

Despite the fact that Bossuet and other opponents of the theater had a tendency to stress that their condemnation of the theater was primarily due to the immoral content of the passions presented on the stage, one cannot help noticing that the very act of theatrical re-presentation seemed troubling to them, regardless of its content. At the core of their hostility to theater, then, was not simply the *content* of the passions presented on the stage but also, and perhaps more important, the *form* in which those passions were re-presented: these passions were actually, literally, re-presented on the stage. Paraphrasing Plato, Bossuet argued that "in representing the passions, it was necessary to form inside that which one wished to bring to the outside expression and character."[4] Actors, in short, were not pretending to feel the passions of the character; they actually felt them.

Underlying much of the hostility to the theater, existing underneath protestations against illicit content, lay a more profound anxiety surrounding re-presentation itself and a deep-seated conviction that there was something inherently debased about the act of conjuring real passions within one's own flesh for the sole purpose of amusing a paying audience. As far as Bossuet was concerned, there was little that separated the actions of a prostitute and those of an actress who gave over her body to physical passions that were not properly her own: "What mother, I won't even say what Christian mother, but what mother with a modicum of decency, would not rather see her daughter in the tomb than on the stage? [The mother would inevitably ask:] Have I raised her so tenderly and with such care for [it all to end in] such opprobrium? Did I [guard] her day and night, under my wings with such care, in order to deliver her over to the public?"[5]

Although antitheatrical authors were loath to discuss it directly, the antipathy toward actors arose in part from the undeniable similarities between religious ceremony and dramatic performance. The scholar Jean-Marie Apostolidès has suggested that religious antitheatricality in the seventeenth century "is partially caused by a parallelism one can trace between the Mass and tragedy," claiming that the two shared certain "aesthetic preoccupations."[6] And it seems clear enough that the Catholic Church felt itself in direct competition with theatrical spectacles, endeavoring to avoid any contamination between the two spheres: theaters were closed on important religious holidays, and actors were forbidden to take Communion and were denied the right to be buried on holy ground.[7]

Something of the logic that underlay the marking of the actor as profane can be seen in the particular sensitivity of the church with respect to theater around Passion Week and Christmas. Actors, who so adeptly summoned passions at will and just as easily made them disappear the moment they walked off the stage, were so troubling to the church because they seemed to put into doubt the reality of Christ's Passion on the cross. As Bossuet argued in his sermon "On the Passion of Jesus Christ," the profundity of Christ's Passion lay in his *choosing* to feel it, for as the son of God he could have chosen to feel absolutely nothing. And here the similarities between Christ on the cross and the actor on the stage must have seemed painfully apparent to Bossuet:

> [Jesus] could have, in a single word, calmed the pain and left his soul untroubled; but he chose not to. He, who is eternal Wisdom, who arranges and undertakes all things in their ordained time, seeing himself arrive at the time of suffering, very much wanted to unbridle those sufferings and allow them to act with all their force. . . . His whole person was affected, and it felt to its very core, to the last frailty, if I can speak so, all the weight of anxiety, all the tremors of fear, all the dejection of sadness. Do not think, Christians, that the perseverance that we adore in the Son of God in any way diminished his sufferings; he overcame them, but he felt every last one of them; he drained the cup of Passion to the dregs; he did not allow one drop to be lost; not only did he drink, but he felt, he tasted, he savored drop by drop all the bitterness.[8]

So, Bossuet argues, here was Christ at a moment that he knew would come to pass, and he chose to allow his body to feel every last passion that the events demanded. For Bossuet, the parallel with actors on the stage must have been all too clear: they too chose to feel all the passions within their bodies; they too knew the script in advance. If the actor's performance could be said to bear a resemblance to Christ's Passion, then the danger, of course, was that Jesus himself might, by corollary, be taken for an actor.[9]

Apart from the Passion, actors challenged the uniqueness of Christ in another troubling manner: like Christ himself, actors were, in a sense, word become flesh. By lending their bodies to the words of the author and giving flesh to the spirit of the character, actors performed a profane version of Christ's Incarnation. An early-seventeenth-century pamphlet, for example, criticized those who had the indecency to wear masks around Christmas time, declaring that "metamorphosing themselves in this manner, . . . [they] strike against the mystery of the Incarnation."[10] Similarly, a century and a half later, an *abbé* from Auxerre declared in 1754, justifying that city's strict ordinances against theater, "Theater . . . leads to nothing less than rendering the suffering and death of J. C. useless; in one word, it directly attacks the point of the Incarnation."[11] The church, then, condemned theatrical re-pre-sentation, not because it was false, but because it was real. Actors attacked the Incarnation because they cheapened the miracle by which spirit had be-come flesh. They profaned the holy by prostituting their bodies, summoning forth passions within themselves for the amusement of the public.

Apologists of the theater differed in many ways from the theater's reli-gious opponents, arguing that the theater was at worst harmless and at best offered the potential for educating its audiences. Oddly enough, however, proponents of the theater shared with opponents a fundamentally identical view of the nature of theatrical re-presentation. The unchallenged rule of French acting theory prior to 1750 might very well be summed up by the fol-lowing maxim credited to the poet and critic Nicolas Boileau: "If you want me to cry, you must cry yourself."[12]

Acting textbooks up until the middle of the eighteenth century repeatedly stressed the importance of the verity of the actor's emotions because it was taken for granted that only real feelings could be perceived as real by spec-tators. Largely derivative of classical Greek rhetorical theory, French acting textbooks uniformly insisted that a successful performance depended upon the actor's experiencing the passions of the character, on the actor's literally becoming the character for the duration of the play.[13] Writing in 1639, Georges de Scudéry described theatrical re-presentation as a process of metamorphosis: "It is necessary, if possible, that [actors] metamorphose into the characters that they are representing."[14] Two decades later, the abbé d'Aubignac insisted that a character could be made present on the stage only if the actor "believed in [the character's feelings] even as he expressed them. . . . [I]t would be ridiculous to see him deliver a long speech either of lamentation or of joy, on a matter he considered to be false."[15]

Up until the mid-eighteenth century, the conviction that metamorphosis lay at the root of theatrical re-presentation remained largely unchallenged. In 1744, a century or so after Scudéry and d'Aubignac, a poem entitled "L'art du théâtre ou le parfait comédien" described the "perfect" actor in terms that would have made perfect sense to seventeenth-century theatrical theorists:

> Je veux donc qu'un Acteur, s'il gronde ou s'il plaisante,
> Soit véritablement ce qu'il me représente.
> [I wish that an actor, whether he screams (in anger) or he jests,
> Be in truth that which he represents to me.][16]

As late as 1747, acting textbooks were warning prospective actors that act-ing was a difficult process of metamorphosis, a process in which actors had to suspend their sense of self and become the characters they presented on the stage: "If you cannot lend yourself to these metamorphoses, do not venture upon the stage. In the theater, when one does not feel that which one wishes to make appear, one presents us with only an imperfect image."[17]

Around 1750, everything changed. The first crack in the monolith of French theatrical theory appeared in the form of François Riccoboni's *L'art du théâtre*. Riccoboni, a well-known actor in Paris, espoused a radically new conception of theatrical representation that directly challenged centuries of French theatrical tradition. Riccoboni called into question the cardinal rule that the representation of a character necessarily entailed the actor's actual physical experience of the character's emotions: "I am far from ever having shared this opinion, which is almost universally held, and it has always seemed evident to me that if one is unfortunate enough actually to feel that which one is trying to express, then one is not acting *[hors d'état de jouer]*."[18] Instead of insisting that actors present the real passions of the characters, Riccoboni called upon actors to present passions that seemed real—a performance that was not *vrai* (true) but rather *vraisemblable* (literally: resembling the true).

The fundamental novelty of Riccoboni's conception of representation cannot be overemphasized. Instead of a process in which the intangible body of the character was made incarnate within the body of the actor—a conception of acting that opponents and supporters had shared for generations—Riccoboni's conception of theatrical representation involved abstract appearances and the bifurcation of the actor's body into believable exteriors and false interiors; instead of transubstantiation, Riccoboni called for imitation. Over the next several decades, this new conception of theatrical representation would sweep the French stage. By the 1770s, a decidedly defensive tone had crept into the writings of those who still clung to the old belief of theatrical representation as metamorphosis. In 1772, for example, the playwright Jean-François Cailhava de l'Estendoux criticized the "crowd of actors who reduce to a purely mechanical state an art that can be sublime, & that [they] bring down to the [level] of a monkey's or a parrot's talent."[19] And the celebrated playwright and author Jean-Charles Levacher de Charnois was even more straightforward when, in 1788, he offered the following observation on Boileau's famous maxim: "If you want me to cry, you must cry yourself. Boileau did not say: pretend to cry."[20]

Riccoboni was by no means the lone progenitor of a revolution. His new method of acting, although undoubtedly revolutionary in itself, would ultimately form the core of a much more extensive project to transform the theory and practice of theater as a whole—a project whose most complete articulation is to be found in the works of Denis Diderot. At the heart of the *Paradoxe sur le comédien*, a text written some twenty years after Riccoboni's *L'art du théâtre*, Diderot offered a definition of acting virtually identical to Riccoboni's: "[The actor's] entire talent consists not in feeling, as you [the spectator] suppose, but in rendering the outward signs of feeling so scrupulously that you [the spectator] mistake them [for real] *[que vous vous y trompiez].*"[21] Much like Riccoboni, then, Diderot maintained that acting had nothing to do with the presentation of true passions but rather with the abstract or figurative representation of those passions in outward mannerisms, or what Diderot called "signs." Diderot reasoned that there were two ways to produce such signs. One method, the one employed for generations in the French theater, was the authentic production of external appearances as the natural by-product of real emotions by actors who subjected themselves to the grueling process of metamorphosis. Another method, clearly the one that Diderot preferred, might be termed the artificial method—external appearances could be manufactured by actors who, after spending some time in front of a mirror, could imitate the outward signs of passions with none of the inner turmoil: "The cries of his sorrow are recorded in his ears. The gestures of his despair are from his memory and were prepared in front of a mirror. . . . The actor is weary, and you are sad; he has thrashed about without feeling a thing, and you have felt without thrashing about."[22]

Diderot's vision of the actor as an unfeeling automaton, who somewhat paradoxically elicits a torrent of emotions from spectators, helps to explain the negative connotations associated with the actor's craft even after the actor could no longer be accused of profaning the Incarnation. If actors prior to 1750 were profane because they *were* what they re-presented on the stage, actors who were devotees of the new method were not profane but rather duplicitous precisely because they *were not* that which they pretended to represent. In the following passage, Diderot compared the "great" actor with the stock figures of duplicity in the eighteenth century:

> [The actor] cries like an unbelieving priest who preaches the Passion; like a seducer on his knees before a woman whom he does not love, but whom he wishes to deceive; like a beggar in the street or at the door of a church, who insults you when he loses hope of moving you; or like a courtesan who feels nothing, but who swoons in your arms.[23]

Eventually, Diderot's characterization of the actor's performance as eminently believable and yet profoundly untrue came to replace the problematic nature of metamorphosis as the basis of antitheatrical prejudice. Religious condemnations of the theater by no means disappeared in the latter half of the eighteenth century, but they had a tendency to rehash old and somewhat outdated arguments, often simply offering to their readers a compendium of earlier antitheatrical works. Newer prejudices against the actor revolved primarily around the actor's inherent untrustworthiness. And Jean-Jacques Rousseau's notorious *Letter to d'Alembert on the Theater* is perhaps best described as a work that stands at the crossroads between these two genres: Rousseau condemned the actors both for denaturing their own bodies and for their duplicity and the dangers that they presented to society as a whole.

Although Diderot's conception of the actor's craft differed little from Riccoboni's reconceptualization, Diderot pursued the logical ramifications far beyond Riccoboni's initial vision. Grasping a key component of the new method of acting that his predecessor had only dimly understood, Diderot effectively transformed what was essentially a reconceptualization of the actor's performance into something with much broader repercussions. The old system of metamorphosis had been entirely dependent on the actor's ability to believe himself transformed. But this new, artificial system depended, not on the actor's belief (it actually precluded the actor's belief), but rather on the *spectator's* belief—or, as we tend to refer to it today, on the spectator's suspension of disbelief. This fundamental shift in the burden of belief was the cornerstone of an entirely new conception of representation.

I would be tempted to say that the onus of belief was simply transferred from the actor to the spectator, but such a statement implies a simple shifting of burdens between two already existent entities, and this is not the case. It would be more accurate to say, then, that after redefining the role of the actor, the new theater set about *inventing* the modern spectator, to whom it then transferred the burden of belief. For it is crucial to understand that the passive and silent individual, seated in the darkness, obsessed with the action on the lighted stage, did not exist in the middle of the eighteenth century; that willing and pliant spectator had to be manufactured in theory and then meticulously sculpted in practice over a period of several decades.

Prior to the middle of the eighteenth century, the rigid differentiation of actors and spectators, a concept that would later become one of the fundamental principles of the modern theatrical space, was virtually unknown in the French theater. Instead, the relationship between actors and spectators was decidedly more carnivalesque[24] and permitted a great deal of fluidity between the representative space and the audience. On the stage itself, spectators who had paid for the privilege sat virtually in the middle of the actors who were attempting to perform. Down below in the lighted parterre, audience members wandered about, greeting one another, chatting, and occasionally commenting on the play, out loud, whenever they saw fit. Indeed, certain theatergoers seem to have made a part-time career out of intentionally upstaging the actors with performances of their own.[25]

We might think that the chaotic atmosphere of the premodern theater made it difficult for spectators to pay attention to the play, and this was undoubtedly the case. In his *Lettre sur les spectacles,* the playwright Prosper Jolyot de Crébillon painted the following portrait of the confusion that reigned on the early-eighteenth-century nondifferentiated stage:

One sometimes wasn't sure if the young gentleman who was in the process of taking his seat wasn't the love interest of the play who had just finished performing his part. [This situation] gave rise to the phrase:
We were waiting for Pyrrhus: [but] some jackass appeared instead!
The actor always missed his entrance; he appeared either too early or too late;

1. Spectators on the stage during a seventeenth-century performance. Photo: Bibliothèque nationale de France, Paris.

emerging from amongst the spectators like some ghost, he disappeared in the same manner, without one even noticing that he'd left.[26]

But the spectators of the eighteenth century hardly seemed to mind the confusion on the stage or the numerous offstage distractions vying for their attention. Perhaps we are even mistaken in labeling them "distractions," for as many observers of the French theater prior to the 1760s pointed out, spectators often behaved as if it were the *actors* who were distracting them. The real spectacle was the spectators themselves; the action on the stage was merely a sideshow.[27] In the *Persian Letters,* for example, Montesquieu cleverly satirized the inattention of French theatergoers by having his foreign visitors assume, in their first visit to the theater, that they were *supposed* to be watching the "actors" in the spectator boxes and the parterre and to be taking no notice of the professional actors on the stage.[28]

For those who hoped to revolutionize the nature of theatrical representation, the problem was clear: the burden of belief could hardly be transferred from the actor to the spectator if the latter only occasionally glanced at the stage. The new theories of acting called for rapt attention on the part of the spectator, and in order for this to be achieved, something had to be done to force the spectators to pay attention, to stop chatting amongst themselves, and instead to turn their (silent) attention to the professional actors on the stage. But how was this to be accomplished? How could these active and unruly individuals who seemed to think of themselves as participants in the theatrical spectacle be transformed into passive and attentive spectators? The answer lay in a series of practical innovations, each one of which was intended to remove spectators from the stage and to isolate spectators visibly and audibly from one another; as a result of these innovations, theatrical spectators in France were exiled and cordoned off from a newly delineated representative space and forced into the role of nonparticipatory observers.

The first task of the theatrical revolutionaries was to remove the most obvious intrusion into the representative space: the spectators seated on the stage itself. The reign of the carnivalesque stage came to an end beginning in 1759, when theatrical companies began removing spectator benches from the Parisian stages.[29] This act was immediately hailed by many theater critics and playwrights, who praised the remarkable effects of this simple innovation. In the following passage, the playwright Charles Collé describes his impressions upon first witnessing a performance on a stage cleared of spectators:

> I went to see the theater of the Comédie-Française, [where] people are no longer allowed upon the stage. God willing this will last! This produces the best effect in the world; I even think you could hear the actors' voices better. The theatrical illusion is actually whole; no longer does one see Caesar [accidentally] about to remove all the powder [from the wig] of some jackass seated in the front row of the stage seats, or Mithradates expiring in the midst of all of one's acquaintances.[30]

To sharpen the distinction between the stage and the audience down below, in 1759 (the very same year that spectator seats began to disappear from the stages) theater technicians began to experiment with ways of improving the chandeliers that up until then had bathed both actors and spectators indiscriminately in bright light.[31] By 1778, a device had been perfected that made it possible to illuminate the stage while hiding the sources of light and casting a shadow upon the audience.[32] Audience members who had always been so fond of looking at and displaying themselves to one another could now perceive one another only dimly, in contrast to the now brilliantly illuminated figures of the actors on the stage.

Perhaps the last tangible vestige of the undifferentiated theatrical space was the spectator boxes above and on both sides of the stage. In 1793, these began to disappear as well. And the rationale for this aesthetic reform was once again the enhancement of the illusion: an even clearer differentiation between the representative space and spectators could be achieved if spectators were cleared not only from the stage but from the sight lines of the audience as well. The *Moniteur* reported the rationale for this architectural innovation:

> The theater owners felt that in order to render the theatrical illusion more complete, there was need for a line of clear demarcation between the spectators and the action that was represented; and if it is necessary for the enchantment of the public that all of their senses focus entirely on the play, then the actor must, so to speak, be alone with his character upon the stage.[33]

I have mentioned only practical reforms to the theatrical space. But perhaps the innovation that was most fundamental to the creation of the realistic representative space was not a practical element of stage design but rather a theoretical concept that has come to be known as the "fourth wall." The fourth wall was a concept predicated on the conviction that no action on the stage would ever have the appearance of plausible reality *(vraisemblance)* if the actors betrayed any hint that they were aware of being watched. Instead of directing their performances toward the audience, actors should pretend that the open space between the stage and the audience was a fourth wall. Actors should behave, in short, just like real people enclosed in a defined space, without observers: they should direct their lines to one another and respond appropriately.

That the concept of the fourth wall seems so elementary today is testimony to the complete victory achieved by the practitioners of the new theater: until their ideas took hold, in the 1760s and 1770s, it was customary for French actors to direct their performances to the audience, comparatively ignoring those who shared the stage with them. Diderot, who more than anyone else was responsible for the rapid proliferation of fourth walls in theaters throughout France, can be credited with redirecting the attention of the actors toward one another; it was he who instructed actors to "think no more of the spectator than if he did not exist. Imagine, at the edge of the stage, a high wall that separates you from the parterre. Act as if the curtain never rose."[34]

And so, in the newly created void made possible by the physical separation of actor and spectator, an imaginary wall arose, conceptually separating the world inhabited by the actors from that inhabited by spectators. This wall was opaque on one side, translucent on the other, and permitted nothing to pass through it but the gaze of the spectator, a gaze that now focused on something that had never existed before: an entirely self-contained artificial reality. Before, there had been nothing but scattered performances in the midst of a crowd of spectators who could choose to devote their attention either to the performances on the stage or to one another. Now, there existed two completely separate worlds. Down below in the darkness were isolated spectators who could no longer communicate with one another and who formed a cohesive body *only* through their common experience of watching the action on the stage, not through their interactions with one another. And up above, the separate performances of the actors had been fused into a believable whole. As I quoted Collé above, after he had witnessed his first performance on a stage cleared of spectators, "The theatrical illusion is actually whole."

The fourth wall, therefore, made possible something greater than the sum of individual illusions produced by each actor's performance. A stage devoid of spectators suddenly made possible the creation of something that could never have existed before: a new world, purged of mundane reality, and made up entirely of realistic fictions; a universe physically and conceptually set apart from the world inhabited by spectators; a world existing in its own time and place, that took no notice of anyone or anything beyond its borders, and that to the spectators seemed somehow more interesting, more believable, more intoxicating than their own fragmented reality. This was the theoretical premise of the modern theater; it was also, as we shall see, the theoretical premise of modern representative politics.

The creation of this new self-contained artificial reality necessitated that all of the various practical aspects of the French stage be brought into line with the dictates of vraisemblance. Whereas such things as costume and scenery had always been tangential to the dramatic process, now such trappings became the centerpiece of theater, and theater critics applauded the fact that "[a]ll the Heroes of Rome no longer show up in white gloves, and with *coiffures à la française.*"[35] Each innovation in the movement to create a more vraisemblable theater seemingly spawned a new idea, as if once a blatantly unrealistic aspect of the stage was removed, other vestiges of the old theater suddenly became glaringly apparent. One critic, for example, insisted that the stiff tableaux of characters be replaced by more realistic domestic scenes: "Why . . . not . . . have the actors chat with one another around a fireplace. This would at the very least have an air of truth. Because I do not see anything as ridiculous as never letting people who are [supposed to be] in their own homes sit down."[36] Other implausibilities that drew the fire of theatrical critics included the "aside" (the widespread convention according to which it was somehow possible for characters to deliver lines directly to the audience, unnoticed by the other characters) and the practice of writing plays in verse, both of which became increasingly rare if not extinct toward the end of the eighteenth century.[37]

By the time of the French Revolution, the theater that had existed in France until 1750, replete with individual metamorphic performances and a carnivalesque mixing of spectators and actors, was almost nowhere to be found. In less than four decades, it had ceased to exist. In its place, two different worlds had come into existence. One was a world of artificial reality, where actors basked in the stage lights, seemingly oblivious to anything or anyone that lay beyond the representative space. The other world, on the opposite side of the fourth wall, was made up of individuals seated in the darkness. Unable to see one another, the spectators had as their only function to gaze in rapt attention at the actors who ignored them. Active participants in the representative process had been transformed into passive observers of the new realistic, representative spectacle. The following pages trace how this process was paralleled on the contemporary political stage.

1 *Embodiment*

Concrete Re-presentation in Premodern France

Embodied representation is a concept very familiar to historians of the old regime, and numerous studies have been written, particularly in recent years, focusing on the bodily nature of monarchical representation in medieval and early modern France.[1] These studies have served the very useful function of reminding us of the essentially representative nature of the king's body—a fact that had been somewhat obscured by a long-standing tendency, itself the legacy of the Revolution, to equate representation with political assemblies rather than individuals. But the historical evidence is clear: for medieval and early modern political theorists, monarchies were considered to be a form of representative government in which the political body was composed of one individual (in contradistinction to aristocracies and democracies, in which political bodies were composed of numerous individuals).[2] Indeed, the only form of government that was not properly thought of as representative was a pure democracy, usually idealized as a form of government in which all the people would gather in the public square to attend to affairs of state and would consequently have no need of representatives.

The classic study of monarchical representation in medieval and early modern Europe is Ernst Kantorowicz's *The King's Two Bodies*. Kantorowicz's brilliant analysis explores the distinction drawn in medieval Europe between the *king* as body natural (the mortal, individual, and human body of the king) and the *King* as body politic (the intangible, eternal office of king, represented successively by the natural bodies of individual monarchs). Kantorowicz's work, for example, helps to make clear what would otherwise be the nonsensical cry of the English Puritans: "We fight the king [body natural] in the name of the King [body politic]."[3]

Given the advanced state of the historiography on monarchical representation, I would be tempted to seize upon Kantorowicz's distinction between the king (body natural) and the King (body politic) as a prime example of embodied political re-presentation, conceptually analogous to the embodied re-presentation of the premodern theatrical actor. For, like the actor on the stage, the king's natural body physically incarnated the political body of the King. But there are important reasons why the comparison does not hold. For one, although the distinction between the natural and political bodies of the king seems very clear with respect to medieval political theory and practice, the relationship between these two bodies changed over time. With absolutism, in particular, the distinction between the king's natural and political bodies began to blur, and it ultimately disappeared entirely.

But there is another important respect in which the king's re-presentation of the political body within his own natural body does not quite offer a political parallel to the embodied re-presentation performed by premodern theatrical actors. Political bodies in premodern France were not the ultimate objects of the re-presentative process; political bodies were themselves re-presentations. Even for the most die-hard absolutists, the political body of the king was not so much the object of re-presentation as it was a kind of conceptual way station between the political actor and the true object of political re-presentation: the mystical body of the nation or the *corpus mysticum*.

The concept of the corpus mysticum was the fundamental organizing principle of premodern political re-presentation, and, for the purposes of the analogy being drawn here, constitutes the "fictional character" that was re-presented on the political stage. If, in other words, we are looking for an intangible body that was made present, or incarnated, within the body of a political actor (or actors), then the corpus mysticum was clearly that body. Originally, according to Kantorowicz and his student Ralph Giesey, the term *corpus mysticum* was used to refer to two distinct religious concepts that were conceptualized as bodies and yet possessed no visible, tangible form of their own: one of these mystical bodies was the Christian community, intangible because it was so massive that it could not assemble in any one place, and yet resembling a living body in the sense that it functioned with one will and was greater than the mere sum of the members that composed it; the other was the body of Christ, intangible except when it was made present or re-presented in the visible form of the Eucharist. By the twelfth century, the meaning of the corpus mysticum had changed somewhat and had come to be defined in contradistinction to the *corpus verum,* or real body of Christ; the corpus mysticum now referred to the mystical body of the church of which Christ was the head. This later meaning of corpus mysticum gradually made its way into secular spheres, becoming a well-recognized concept of medieval jurisprudence, and provided the basis for a distinction between the individual (corpus verum) and the corporation (corpus mysticum).[4]

By the thirteenth century, the concept of the corpus mysticum had found its way into vague conceptions of the political collective. And by the early fifteenth century, the mystical body of the nation had come to be defined in relatively precise terms as a body in which the three estates of France (together referred to as the Estates General) constituted the members and the king the head—a concept that owes a clear debt to earlier ecclesiastical conceptions. For the next several centuries, political theorists uniformly held that the king re-presented the head of the mystical body of the nation. But there seems to have been a fair amount of poetic license in describing which of the different estates made up which parts of the mystical body underneath the head. Jean Gerson, for example, writing in the early fifteenth century, characterized the knighthood as the chest and arms of the corpus mysticum ("for their vigor and strength"); the clergy as the stomach ("the stomach does not labor but it nourishes the other members"); and the bourgeoisie, merchants, and laborers as the legs and feet ("for their labor and humility in serving and obeying").[5] Writing almost two centuries later, Guy Coquille offered a somewhat different breakdown: the nobility was the heart of the mystical body ("the vivacity and vigor of the whole body"); the clergy was the brain ("the understanding and exercise of reason"); and the third estate was the liver ("the nourishment of the body").[6]

If the exact makeup of the mystical body seems to have been open to question, the purpose in invoking the corpus mysticum as a political concept was relatively constant. As the various peoples and territories in the French kingdom were being slowly forged into a modern nation-state, the concept of the corpus mysticum was instrumental to the expression of the ideal of the seemingly different and unrelated parts of the kingdom united in a living whole under the leadership of one king. Jean de Terre Rouge, who wrote in the early fifteenth century and was perhaps the first political theorist in France to evoke the corpus mysticum with regularity, maintained that the very essence of a mystical body was the unity of wills, without which there would be only a conglomeration of individual members: "[A] mystical body is united alone by the union of its will."[7] This simple statement should signal to us one of the most important legacies of the corpus mysticum: long after the term itself had fallen by the wayside, generations of French political theorists still assumed that the very concept of nationhood necessarily implied the existence of a solitary (general) will.

The corpus mysticum was not merely a metaphor for social organization. Terre Rouge did not claim, in other words, that society functioned *like* a body; rather, he claimed that society *was* a body and therefore ought to function like one. The various members of society ought to cooperate with one another and ought to function in concert with the head, whose sole will they were bound to follow. The mere mention of the corpus mysticum was tantamount to an injunction to the various groups who composed the French nation to behave as if they constituted a single body. The following "verities," written by Jean Gerson, are clearly intended as precisely such an injunction:

[1] Just as in nature all the members of a real body expose themselves for the safety of the head [*chief*], so must it be in the mystical body of real subjects with respect to their lord. But, on the other hand, the head [*chief*] must direct and govern the other members, because to do otherwise would be destruction, because a head without a body cannot survive. . . . [2] Just as corporally there is nothing more cruel, horrible, and hideous as seeing a human or animal [*naturel*] body torn apart or dismembered piece by piece or otherwise, so spiritually is it not less cruel, but rather much more cruel, in the mystical body if the parts have divided and persecute one another, as in the case of subjects to lords or lords to subjects.[8]

The mystical body was very literally a way of "organizing" the confusing mass of rivalries and allegiances that made up the French nation. Although the mystical body was intangible, it was somehow more concrete, more comprehensible than the disorganized chaos of the visible world. And just as the inhabitants of premodern France were often encouraged to see themselves as members of the Christian community rather than as independent individuals,[9] so too as political individuals were they meant to see themselves as part of the mystical body rather than as individual citizens of the nation.

But the mystical body was not *always* purely mystical. Under certain extraordinary circumstances, the entire mystical body of the French nation could be made visible, could be literally re-presented in a tangible, visible form. At the king's summons, ordinary individuals from the farthest reaches of the kingdom would gather at an appointed place and time to take part in the political spectacle of the re-presentation of the mystical body. With the king at their head (or literally *as* their head), these separate individuals would become, together with the king, the incarnation of the mystical body of France. This political spectacle, in which spirit took on flesh, in which political actors re-presented with their own bodies a mystical body that had no substance of its own, was the convocation of the Estates General.

Unlike modern representative assemblies, the Estates General were not routinely convened but rather were convened only under extraordinary circumstances in which the king was bound to consult the entirety of his people. Opinions differed as to precisely which circumstances necessitated the calling of the Estates General, but most agreed that the following situations constituted events in which the king was required to consult with the entire nation: the imposition of any kind of tax or subsidy; the alienation of any part of the realm; any unusual event in the line of succession such as rival claimants or the necessity of establishing a regency; and the undertaking of any fundamental legal or religious reforms.[10]

To the modern mind, of course, there is an essential difference between a representative assembly and the entirety of a nation assembled in one place, between the government and the people. But to the inhabitants of premodern France, the political body of the Estates General meeting in assembly with the king was synonymous with the entirety of the French mystical body. Such an "absorptive"[11] re-presentation was possible not because pre-Revolutionary French people failed in some way to differentiate between reality and representation; it was possible because they re-presented differently. Unlike modern representation, which attempts an approximation of a general majority consensus and, in theory, reflects the proportional breakdown of constituents' opinions, premodern re-presentation sought a holistic re-creation (in a different form) of the entire object that could not present itself. Just as the Eucharist gave material form to the body of Christ, which was not capable of showing itself, so the political body of the Estates General made visible and tangible the mystical body of France that was visible nowhere else.

A system of re-presentation in which the part could be taken for the whole, a system that was so transparent, so "absorptive" of the thing that it re-presented, was not—and could not have been—the result of simple political elections. The formation of the political body of France was a costly and time-consuming process through which the entirety of the French nation slowly and methodically transformed itself into a perfectly re-presentative political body.

The process began with the word of the king, the head summoning forth its own body. A letter from the king was copied out to each *bailliage* in France, detailing the reasons for the assembly, as well as the time and place where the three estates would convene. The notice of convocation was duly registered by the officials of the bailliage, whereupon the notice was reprinted and posted throughout the principal city of each bailliage. A third generation of copies was disseminated in smaller towns and parishes throughout each bailliage, and for those who could not read, town criers were often sent forth to trumpet the news, "lest no one claim ignorance" of the impending convocation.[12] In such a manner, like an original idea that is born in the head and is quickly transported to and acted upon by the rest of the body, the word of the king was spread to every member of the mystical body.

As soon as they had received word of the impending convocation, the people of France set about the arduous process of forming themselves into a political body—a body that, like the mystical body it would re-present, was composed of three separate but interdependent estates. From a modern vantage point, we might say something like the following: in the capital cities of each district, the three estates met separately to elect delegates to the national assembly of the three estates, where representatives from across the country would gather to decide upon important issues on behalf of their constituents. To say this, however, would be to miss the very point in forming the political body of the Estates General: the people of France did not gather together in local assemblies only to hand over sovereign authority to newly elected representatives. On the contrary, the selection of delegates was incidental to the process of re-presentation as they understood it. Infinitely more important than the deputy himself was the content with which the deputy was entrusted. To put it more suggestively: the political actor was merely a means to the much more important end of the transparent expression of the character to be expressed. And the character, in this instance, was the will of the people being re-presented.

From a modern perspective, all of this seems a bit implausible, and two questions immediately spring to mind: How was it possible for millions of people to arrive at a condensation of their various wills in such a manner that it could be coherently expressed at the national level? And even if such a condensation of wills were possible, how did this system ensure that the will of the people was not distorted in some manner by the people's representatives? The answers to these questions are surprisingly simple. The process of condensation was not some miracle whereby the wills of millions were instantaneously reduced to a manageable number. Rather, thousands of local assemblies were held whose fundamental purpose was to draft a local *cahier*, containing the written expression of the people's will. These local cahiers underwent several rounds of condensation before the final product was produced: one general cahier for each of the estates, containing a condensation of the members' will. And, to ensure that the will of the people was not distorted, the various local and regional cahiers were transported by delegates who had sworn a binding oath, known as the *mandat impératif* (imperative, or binding, mandate); each delegate swore that he would in no way alter the contents of the cahier or misrepresent the cahier in any way. Because the king's original letter of convocation had enumerated the specific items that would be on the agenda at the Estates General, members of the three estates had set down specific responses to that agenda in their respective cahiers. Every opinion to be expressed by the delegate was to be found in his cahier, and a delegate was therefore more analogous to a modern-day proxy or to someone who possesses a power of attorney than to a modern political representative.[13] Whereas modern representatives who violate the will of their constituents (if indeed that will is ever concrete enough to be known) might be voted out of office, delegates in premodern France who strayed beyond the bounds of their cahiers could be immediately disavowed and even sentenced to a fine or imprisonment.[14] The dual conventions, therefore, of the cahier and the mandat impératif ensured the transparent re-presentation of a consolidated national will.

Although the cahiers contained carefully worded responses to the king's agenda, they also contained whatever information the members of the estates considered worthy of being brought to the king's attention. The Estates General, as a political body, was expected to enter into a kind of carefully scripted conversation with the king, in which they would not only assent to (or, occasionally, dissent from) the king's proposals but also apprise the king

of the existing state of affairs throughout the realm. The cahiers were therefore intended as a kind of clearinghouse for the various problems and complaints that had not been expressed (at least by the people directly to the
king) since the last meeting of the Estates General—hence the full name of
the cahiers: *les cahiers des plaintes et doléances* (notebooks of complaints
and grievances). In theory, at least, there was a perfect transparency between
the deputies and those they re-presented, and between the cahiers and the
grievances of the people, such that it could be said that through the body of
the Estates General all the people of France met with their king. In his opening remarks to the Estates General in 1560, Chancellor L'Hospital declared:
"It is without doubt that the people benefit greatly from these estates [gen-
eral]; because [the people] has the good fortune to approach the person of
its king, to present its complaints, to present its requests, and to obtain reme-
dies and necessary provisions."[15]

The task of drafting the ideas and grievances of the millions of French
people and consolidating them into a form that could actually be presented
to the king was, needless to say, an enormous undertaking. And this task was
by far the most cumbersome for the third estate, which comprised the vast
majority (somewhere in the neighborhood of 95 percent) of the inhabitants
of France. Despite the overwhelming numbers of individuals who made up
the third estate, however, no shortcuts were taken in the formation of a general will of the third estate. In theory at least, by the time the general will
had been formed, every member of the third estate would have taken part in
its formation—a theory that in practice necessitated that thousands of preliminary assemblies throughout the country be held so that all rightful members of the third estate could participate in the drafting of cahiers.

In general, citizens of the towns tended to gather into preliminary assemblies, admission to which was often limited by such conditions as the pay-
ment of over a certain amount in taxes or a minimum length of residence.
Inhabitants of the countryside, by contrast, held comparatively open assemblies in which heads of families from the surrounding communities gathered
in assemblies. In certain areas, the term "head of family" was applied only
to the most prominent individuals from the most important families. In
other areas, however, *all* heads of families would attend, a rubric that did
not necessarily exclude women (or even minors), presumably in the absence
or after the death of the adult male head of the household.[16] Thus, although
women were not properly included in the re-presentative process in premodern France, neither were they explicitly excluded, as they would be from
the Revolution until the middle of the twentieth century.

In all of these preliminary assemblies of the third estate, whether the relatively restricted assemblies of the cities or the comparatively open assemblies of the villages and parishes, the same fundamental task was undertaken: those assembled painstakingly drafted a local *cahier de doléances*.
The various individuals composing the assembly would attempt to fuse to-

gether their separate complaints and opinions into one coherent document that ideally contained every idea worthy of being recorded. Redundancies and inanities were weeded out, and the final product would be a cahier representing a distillation of their ideas. They would then name a delegate or delegates to carry (literally) this cahier to the regional assembly in the district capital. This delegate was not necessarily a member of the third estate, and it occasionally happened that a prominent local notable or member of the clergy would perform the function of deputy for the local members of the third estate. Individual delegates were chosen less for their specific viewpoints than for their trustworthiness.

Finally, in the district capitals of France, deputies from the third estate from the various cities, towns, and villages of the district would gather together in a regional assembly of the third estate, where they would essentially reproduce the activities already undertaken at the lower level: they would consolidate their cahiers, crossing out redundancies, and occasionally attempting to remove articles that were deemed too specific or insignificant for the ears of the king. Once again, the specific views of the deputy selected were infinitely less important than the cahier itself. There is no better evidence of this fundamental difference between modern and premodern political re-presentation than the fact that no hard and fast rule existed that regulated the number of deputies to be selected, and it was often the case that an estate in a particular region would deputize numerous individuals to transport its cahier to the national assembly.[17] Above all, it was the *quality* of the cahier and not the *quantity* of deputies that would speak on behalf of those in the region.

Members of the first two estates generally joined into the political process at the level of the district assemblies. Given the comparatively small numbers of nobles and prelates, members of these estates usually proceeded directly to the district capital at the appointed date to form their separate assemblies.[18] Sometimes the three estates met at the same time and place, but perhaps in different rooms of the same building. Sometimes they met independently of one another. But the activities of all of the estates at this level were identical and repeated the actions taken by the more local assemblies: each of the three estates of a particular region fused the grievances and opinions of its respective members into one regional cahier (one for each estate) and named a delegate or delegates to carry the regional cahier of the estate to a higher convention, in this case the national assembly of the Estates General.

When the delegates from throughout the kingdom coalesced in the city where the Estates General was to be held, the first order of business was the crucial process of the co-verification of powers. In the assemblies of each of the three estates, the delegates would examine one another's papers, ensuring that they were the rightful possessors of duly executed powers and that the cahiers they carried had been properly confided to their care. Identities were checked; mandates were perused for irregularities. Only once this initial verification of powers had been completed could the official opening of the Estates General take place: the raw stuff of re-presentation was present. And at this point, the political process had come full circle: the word had gone forth from the king to his subjects, and his subjects had assembled in their entirety at the appointed time to present their cahiers, or as one witness to the events put it, "to bring the word" to the king.[19] The head had summoned, and the body had appeared. As a witness to the Estates General of 1588 reported, delegates from throughout France had gathered in the city of Blois, rendering that city nothing less than "a condensation *[abrégé]* of all France."[20] Now it only remained for this assemblage of individual political actors to be transformed into the political body of the Estates General.

On the official opening day of the Estates General, the king and the royal court would join together with the deputies of the three estates in a carefully orchestrated procession through the streets of the city, culminating in a ceremonial communion at the main cathedral of the city. The opening ceremonies, both the procession itself and the taking of communion, constituted nothing less than the incarnation of the corpus mysticum in its entirety. With this coming together of the head and the body, the corpus mysticum—a body that had existed only in the mystical realm since the last meeting of the Estates General—re-presented itself in the visible form of a political body.

The symbolic re-presentation of the mystical body of the nation in the opening ceremonies was immediately followed by a corresponding practical condensation of the nation's will. This final condensation took place exactly as it had at the more regional level: delegates fused their regional cahiers into one general cahier for each of the estates. And then, in an act by which the wills of millions of inhabitants of France were theoretically fused into one, the three estates met together to form one cahier, containing the condensed will of the entire nation, which they then presented to the king. By the act of receiving and determining how to answer and ultimately act upon this final *cahier général,* the king essentially merged his own will with that of the nation, and the corpus mysticum in its entirety could speak as one body with one will. Once the king had responded to the cahier of the nation, the will of the nation had been formed, and the Estates General could disband. One final ceremony would take place, during which the king would once again assemble with his court and the deputies of the three estates, exactly as they had done in the opening ceremony. After this final act of re-presentation, the political body would disband into its constituent parts, and the king would once again take on his role as the sole re-presentation of the corpus mysticum: the visible head of a mystical body.

Beginning with the Estates General of 1560, however, something changed. From this moment on, the fusion of wills in the form of common deliberations and the production of one general cahier never happened again. For complicated reasons, the three estates henceforth decided that it served their respective interests to deliberate as three separate orders and to present three separate cahiers to the king. Because each of the orders was further subdivided into twelve governments for the purposes of deliberation, the practical formation of the national will changed from a process in which one body arrived at one cahier to a process in which thirty-six deliberative units separately formed different parts of three different cahiers. The king would respond to each of these three *cahiers généraux* independently, and then a symbolic ceremony of closure would take place, much as it had before, in which the deputies, the court, and the king would meet one last time before disbanding.

Nowhere, then, after 1560, was the entirety of the nation visible as one body *except* in the symbolic opening convocation and in the ceremony of closing. It should not surprise us, therefore, that the ceremonies of convocation—that brief moment when the entire mystical body came together immediately before breaking apart for deliberation—should have taken on greater and greater significance with each of the successive assemblies after 1560. And so, in a fascinating twist on the mechanics of political re-presentation, what the three estates could no longer bring themselves to accomplish through the material condensation of their wills they now accomplished through ceremony. The events of the convocation were expanded so that there might be more opportunities to glimpse the formation of the political body of the entire corpus mysticum. A parade known as the *procession générale,* which had traditionally been a formality associated with the opening of the Estates General, now took on the attributes of a full-blown spectacle of political incarnation.

With each of the convocations of the Estates General after 1560, the *procession générale* became an increasingly elaborate and meticulously choreographed affair in which extreme precautions were taken to ensure that those taking part marched in the appropriate order. In 1576, for example, local church officials were the first to march through the streets, followed by the deputies of the three estates "in a confused order"; the deputies were followed by various bishops and archbishops, and the last to march was the royal house, headed by the king, the queen, and their relatives and attendants.[21] In 1588, a distinctly more organized procession took place: the deputies of the three orders were now clearly differentiated in such a way that the procession more nearly reflected each estate's prominence within the mystical body, in ascending order with feet first and head last. The third estate marched first, in rows of four, followed by deputies of the second estate, and lastly by members of the first estate. Directly after the high church officials, and immediately preceding the king himself, something new appears to have been added, or at least the sources mention it for the first time in conjunction with the general procession: "four knights of the Holy Spirit carried the pile [of velvet] underneath which the archbishop of Aix carried the Holy Sacrament."[22] The mystical body of Christ made visible therefore marched between the body and the head of the procession of the mystical body of the nation made visible.

The high point of the general procession as a political spectacle, however, was reached in the Estates General of 1614, the last meeting of the Estates General prior to the Revolution. Much greater care seems to have been taken in predetermining the order of marchers, with the magistrates of parlement even undertaking the task of researching how the procession had been organized in previous assemblies of the Estates General.[23] Despite this nod to historical tradition, the general procession of 1614 through the streets of Paris was decidedly more—well—theatrical than its predecessors. According to a royal script circulated three days in advance of the event, the procession would begin at nine o'clock in the morning in the convent of the Augustins and would make its way through the city of Paris, along a carefully chosen route, toward Notre-Dame Cathedral. Archers would be dispatched in advance of the procession, each with a torch in hand, to make sure that the way was clear. Instructions for the various categories of marchers were given in much more explicit detail than in previous processions, with groups being divided into subgroups and directed to march at the left or right of the main body. Once again, the deputies would march in order from the third to the first estate, all arranged in rows of four, with each deputy in each of the estates marching in a prearranged order. The deputies of the first estate would be followed by bishops, archbishops, and cardinals, who would march in rows of two. Then, "The Holy Sacrament will be carried by the bishop of Paris, having at his right and his left hand several from his order singing near the Holy Sacrament, in front of whom will be oboes, cornets, and sackbuts. The poles of the pile [of velvet] will be carried by the duc de Guise and the prince de Joinville, in front, and those behind, closer to the king, by monseigneur the brother of His Majesty, and monseigneur the prince de Condé." After the Holy Sacrament came the king and the entire court as well as the magistrates of parlement (an entity that was part of the royal administration of justice, having nothing but its name in common with the English representative institution). Everything was arranged in such explicit detail that every marcher would know not only whom to follow but whether to march on the left or the right. And, at the very end of the procession, lieutenants, ensigns, and archers of the *gardes du corps* would bring up the rear, "so that confusion might be avoided."[24]

In theory, at least, that was the way the procession was supposed to proceed. And everything started off well enough, as the various marchers assembled in the Church of the Augustins on the morning of 26 October 1614:

> The gentlemen of the three orders assembled at eight o'clock in the morning at the convent of the Augustins, each order in the hall in which the king had permitted them to assemble in order to deal with affairs; where, having stayed

there some time, monsieur de Rhodes, Grand Master of Ceremonies, came to fetch each order separately, & had white candles brought and distributed to each of them on behalf of the king; & after he put the gentlemen of the third estate in order, whom he arranged two by two according to a list that had been drawn up the previous Friday morning, in other words by bailliages, & the last [ones on the list] marched first. The gentlemen of the third estate having been arranged on one side of the cloister, all the gentlemen of the nobility . . . were called by rank, according to the above-mentioned list, and were put in order like the gentlemen of the third estate, and immediately after them. The same was done to the members of the clergy.

Once the deputies from the three estates had been properly arranged in the cloisters, various members of the royal administration, the court, and members of the parlement arranged themselves in the chapter house. Then the king arrived at the Augustins with the queen. For this first face-to-face encounter between the king and his estates, the interior of the church was lavishly decorated "with the smoothest of rich tapestries accentuated with gold and silk."

Once the king and queen had taken their respective seats, above which was "a canopy of green velour, brocaded with fleurs-de-lis in gold," the three estates were escorted (in the arranged order) into the church, where a formal procession-before-the-procession took place. Here, once again, those last on the list came in first:

> The three estate were brought in, and the gentlemen of the third estate were the first to come in, then the nobility with candles lit; the exempts of the guard had everyone pass in front of the altar master, and a gentleman who had been placed there let them know that the Holy Sacrament was on the altar, so that they could bow to it, and from there they went along the choir where the king and queen were seated, in between whom it was necessary to pass in order to exit the choir; they bowed to the king as they passed: and afterward the gentlemen who were there let them know that the queen was on the other side, so that they might bow to her as well.[25]

This preparatory spectacle inside the Church of the Augustins—a spectacle that, as far as the sources reveal, was devoid of spectators—seamlessly blended into the outdoor spectacle, as the carefully arranged groups exited the church onto the streets lined with spectators.[26] Here, at least for a time, the procession progressed as per the instructions of the king. But then, as so often happens with scripts, several of the actors involved soon expressed a certain dissatisfaction with their allotted roles:

> When [the procession] had advanced to the end of the pont Saint-Michel, the gentlemen of the third estate in front, the procession came to a halt as a result

of two different issues arising: one concerning the clergy who wanted to go no farther if the cardinals separated themselves from [the body of the clergy], as they wanted to do so as to put themselves near the king. [The clergy were] saying that, since they were all there as deputies, [the cardinals] could not separate themselves from the body [of the clergy]: they presented their case so well that the cardinals ceded the issue after having contested for quite some time. The other [issue] concerned the nobility, who did not want to march any further if the archers of the grand provost and the hundred Swiss Guards did not march first; [they contested] so strongly that a certain number [of the nobility] who had already progressed [outside] near the Augustins were made to return so that all these people [the archers and the Swiss Guards] could go first, not without apprehension of rain, which threatened the coats of velour and the feathers.[27]

What are we to make of the pettiness of those involved, holding up the entire procession so that no one less important than they was allowed to march behind them, closer to the king, even at the risk of wet feathers? The impulse to declare that these grown men were behaving like three-year-olds is only strengthened by the behavior of the deputies the following day at the official opening of the assembly of the Estates General, the proceedings of which were held up because "[the deputies] of the clergy and the nobility . . . were offended that the Gentlemen of the Council . . . were closer to the king than they were, and that they had been pushed back from the king by the length and the quantity of benches that had been set out for the Gentlemen of the Council."[28]

And what about the fussiness, the punctiliousness with which the various orders and officials had been arranged in the Church of the Augustins even *before* they were visible to spectators? For whose benefit was this spectacle staged? What did the various groupings symbolize, and for whom were these symbols intended? These questions, inevitable to the modern observer, say perhaps more about us and our preconceptions about the way symbols function than they do about the actors in this premodern political spectacle. The political spectacles of the general procession of 1614, both inside (in the Church of the Augustins) and outside (on the street before crowds of spectators), were not primarily intended to manufacture symbols for the benefit of others; these spectacles were first and foremost about the metamorphosis of political actors—or as we tend to phrase it today, the process by which actors "get into character."

Forming itself inside the church was a living tableau of the corpus mysticum: members were arranged here, organs there; the king and his court arranged themselves at the head. And the entire spectacle of the general procession was nothing less than the mystical body of the nation on parade. Marching feet first and head last, the corpus mysticum wended its way through the city of Paris, visible in its entirety for the first time since its incarnation at the previous assembly of the Estates General. The parade of a political body was not, however, unique to those years in which assemblies of the Estates General were convened; in the long intervening years, kings took it upon themselves to re-present the only permanent (portion of the) political body in spectacles of royal entry in cities throughout the kingdom.[29] But this general procession that took place during convocations of the Estates General was very different from spectacles of royal entry: the Estates General was an occasional political body, and its assembly constituted an extraordinary event which necessarily altered the role that the king played.[30] Whereas the king normally was the sole political body and thus the only legitimate mouthpiece for the national will, once the Estates General had been convened the king became much more specifically the head of the nation, a role with somewhat less clearly defined powers when it came to the formation of the national will.

The preparatory spectacle in the Church of the Augustins, then, was an organization—in the literal sense—of the various parts and members of the mystical body. But just as conceptions of the exact physical makeup of the *corpus mysticum* seem to have varied widely, so too was the order of the marchers in the general procession somewhat open to question. Various estates and groups jockeyed for better positions and resented those who, they felt, unjustifiably moved closer to the king, not because of a petty obsession with outward appearances and symbolic importance, but precisely because outward appearances and symbols were anything but petty: they were the central defining fact of identity in premodern France.[31] Deputies struggled to be as close to the king as possible, not because they wanted their position in the procession to reflect their social rank, but because their position in the procession *was* the determination of their social rank. To be forced to move farther away from the king was tantamount to a derogation of rank.[32]

As for the role of the Eucharist in the procession, its placement immediately before the king and immediately after the three estates (not to mention its status as an object of reverence placed next to the king inside the Augustins) would seem to be indicative of something more than simply the invocation of God's blessing. The Eucharist was the ultimate transubstantiated object, and its place between the estates and the king served the function of bridging the occasional and the permanent political bodies. Because the Eucharist is the miraculous transubstantiation of ordinary matter into an extraordinary body, it parallels the metamorphosis of deputies into the body of the nation. But because Christ is made present in the sanctified Host on a more or less routine basis throughout the day *somewhere* in the Christian world, the Eucharist has a permanence as a transubstantiated object that parallels the permanence of the king's re-presentation of the political body. Finally, we should not forget that the ultimate destination of the general procession, not only in 1614 but in previous assemblies of the Estates General, was the main cathedral where all who had taken part in the general procession would consume the transubstantiated Host in Communion—a communion that was not only a coming together as Christians but also a coming together of the head and the body of a Christian nation.

Even iconographically, the arrangement of the deputies and the king resembled a human body—a resemblance that seems particularly clear with respect to the seating arrangements for those occasions (i.e., the opening and closing addresses and the communal mass) when the entirety of the political body could be found in one room. A human body is perfectly symmetrical on the bottom (with the same number of toes, feet, and legs on each side), has both external symmetry and internal asymmetry in the middle (an arm, a hand, a breast on each side, but a heart, liver, and spleen only on one side), and has one head centered at the top. Similarly, in seating arrangements in three out of four of the Estates General from 1560 to 1614, the third estate was arranged symmetrically on both the right and left side and along the bottom; the nobility and the clergy were arranged inside the deputies of the third estate, symmetrically, in the sense that there was a roughly equal number of benches for each, but asymmetrically in the sense that the nobility was always seated on the king's left and the clergy was always seated on the king's right. At the head of the three estates, in the center, was the king, surrounded by his court.

Certainly, one can press the point and make far too much of the iconographic parallels between the organization of the political and the human bodies. And, for the purposes of this argument, this parallel is not indispensable—after all, the transubstantiated Eucharist bears no visible resemblance to the body and blood of Christ that it re-presents. Nevertheless, the curious arrangement of the deputies demands some explanation. In a society obsessed with outward appearances, in which great care was taken that every individual be in his proper place, why would the deputies of the third estate be arranged symmetrically on both the right and the left, and those of the first two estates divided into the left and the right, if there was not—at the very least on some unconscious level—some intent to re-present the members and organs of the human body to which these estates were so frequently compared? Whatever we might make of their seating arrangements from our modern vantage point, it seems clear that as time progressed the political actors themselves took greater and greater care in ironing out the particulars of arranging the various parts of the political body. And particularly as real divisions threatened to rend the political body, increasing importance was placed on these ceremonies of symbolic unity, making one's relative position within such ceremonies all the more meaningful.

These elaborate spectacles, which were intended to re-present the unity of the nation's body in the face of all too apparent religious and political differences, had another purpose as well: they not only reminded spectators of the fact that all members were part of the same body but also expressed the

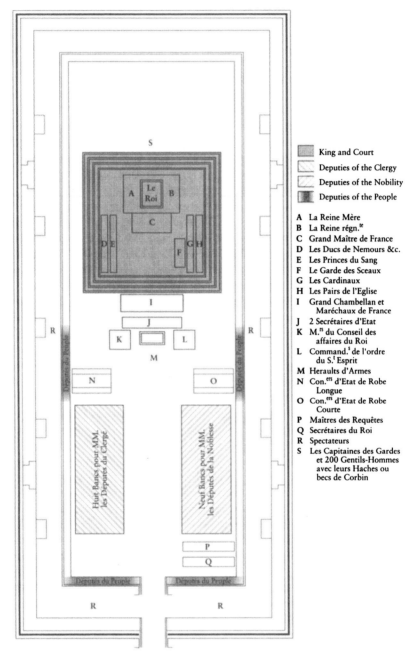

Key (right of diagram):

King and Court
Deputies of the Clergy
Deputies of the Nobility
Deputies of the People

A   La Reine Mère
B   La Reine régn.ᵗᵉ
C   Grand Maître de France
D   Les Ducs de Nemours &c.
E   Les Princes du Sang
F   Le Garde des Sceaux
G   Les Cardinaux
H   Les Pairs de l'Eglise
I   Grand Chambellan et
     Maréchaux de France
J   2 Secrétaires d'Etat
K   M.ʳˢ du Conseil des
     affaires du Roi
L   Command.ˢ de l'ordre
     du S.ᵗ Esprit
M   Heraults d'Armes
N   Con.ᵉʳˢ d'Etat de Robe
     Longue
O   Con.ᵉʳˢ d'Etat de Robe
     Courte
P   Maîtres des Requêtes
Q   Secrétaires du Roi
R   Spectateurs
S   Les Capitaines des Gardes
     et 200 Gentils-Hommes
     avec leurs Haches ou
     becs de Corbin

Labels within diagram:
S
A — Le Roi — B
C
D E — F — G H
I
J
K — L
M
N — O
R — Deputés du People — R
Huit Bancs pour MM. les Deputés du Clergé
Neuf Bancs pour MM. les Deputés de la Noblesse
P
Q
Deputés du People — Deputés du People
R — R

2. Table of seating arrangements at the Estates General of 1588. Based on a diagram in Lalourcé and Duval, eds., *Recueil de pièces originales et authentiques, concernant la tenue des États-Géneraux . . .* (Paris, 1789).

fundamental premise that the body and the head formed an indivisible union. For, unlike the merging of wills between the members of the estates, which was conceptualized as a more or less mechanical distillation of the cahiers, the precise manner in which the royal will and the national will were supposed to merge had never been properly spelled out. This potential for conflict between the estates and the king had always been a feature of convocations of the Estates General, and opening remarks had traditionally contained some sort of exhortation to the estates and to the king to strive toward unity. The following remark, for example, was addressed by the chancellor of state to the Estates General that met in Tours in 1484:

> Let not the members be in opposition to the head; let there be nothing keeping them apart; but let them get along all together and let them all strive for the life and the prosperity of the body politic. . . . It will be therefore up to your wisdom and your virtue, O illustrious *seigneurs,* to conserve without alteration that which is recommended to you: namely, the union, the pact of friendship, and the ties between the head and its members![33]

By the second half of the sixteenth century, however, as religious differences came into sharp relief, fewer and fewer individuals were prepared to content themselves with mere exhortations to unity. Guy Coquille was perhaps the last influential theorist of the time to cling to the notion of the harmonious whole: "The king is the head *[chef]* & the people of the three orders are the members, & all together they make up the political and mystical bodies, of which the ties & union are one and inseparable, & no part can suffer harm without the rest feeling and suffering the pain."[34]

In contrast to Coquille's calls for harmony, most political theorists of the late sixteenth century abandoned the notion of the final communing of wills between the estates and the king and came down definitively on one side or the other with respect to the question of who, in the last instance, possessed ultimate sovereignty. Sovereignty became something that resided in either the head or the body, but not both. The two parts of the mystical body therefore became enmeshed in a battle for primacy, the result of which would be the complete victory of one and the relegation of the other to the role of bodily appendage.

With respect to this relationship between the estates and the king, the Estates General of 1560 marks something of a watershed in the practicability of re-presenting the corpus mysticum. In contrast to the Estates General of 1484, in which the mystical communion of various deputies and the king in a unified whole still seemed within the grasp of those assembled, the Estates General of 1560 was marked by grave religious, political, and social cleavages that produced a clear incommensurability of wills.[35] Consequently, the traditional exhortation to harmony was replaced by somewhat more radical methods of achieving unity. In his opening speech to the deputies, Chancellor L'Hospital broached the idea of a kind of emergency surgery to save the corpus mysticum:

> Because if we are all like a body, of which the king is the head [*chief*], it is much better to cut off the rotten member than to allow it to ruin and corrupt the [other] members, and force them to die. If there were a man suffering from the plague or infected with leprosy, you would chase him from your city: there is even more reason to chase [away] the seditious.[36]

Unlike Terre Rouge and Gerson in the preceding century, whose invocations of the corpus mysticum had served as an injunction to the people of France not to forget that they formed a cohesive body with one will, L'Hospital here invokes the corpus mysticum as a means of excluding those who do not conform to the will of the vital center. L'Hospital, in other words, has rejected the presupposition that the people of France formed a cohesive body, and he has consequently rejected the notion that the will of the whole could be formed by the condensation of the parts. The will of the body, he claimed, was already present in the head and in those whose will conformed to that of the head: this was the vital center. After all, as L'Hospital reminded the deputies, "the king does not receive his crown from us, but from God."[37] As for those whose will did not conform, they were by definition not a vital part of the body, but rather "rotten" and diseased and a threat to the health of the whole.

In contrast to L'Hospital's conception of the vital center, which is unmistakably head-centered, several political theorists of the late sixteenth century began to articulate a notion of sovereign will that was body-centered, and these individuals consequently (and, from an organological point of view, somewhat illogically) declared the head to be a mere appendage of the body. Such important works as François Hotman's *Francogalia*, Innocent Gentillet's *Anti-Machiavel*, and Théodore de Bèze's *Du droit des magistrats*, all of which were published in the 1570s, insisted on the primacy of the estates. Gentillet, for example, pointed out that because the estates were not subject to the various inconveniences that might affect the natural body of the king (such as captivity, minority, or mental and physical incapacity), the estates constituted "the true and perpetual foundation for the maintenance and conservation of the kingdom."[38] Other authors, Hotman in particular, went so far as to conduct extensive historical research in an attempt to locate the original act by which the sovereign people had given themselves a king—research which, as the historian J. G. A. Pocock has written, "forced [them] into a kind of historical obscurantism [and] compelled [them] to attribute their liberties to more and more remote and mythical periods in the effort to prove them independent of the will of the king."[39] Their explicit intention was to prove not only that the people, rather than God, had created kings but also that the people, in giving themselves a king, had merely intended to delegate the *exercise* of sovereignty rather than sovereignty itself. In short, sovereignty, as exercised by the king, was more a long-term lease than a proper transfer of title; in the final instance (whether it be an interruption in the succession, a king who was incompetent or a minor, or a king whose will was at odds with the will of the people) sovereignty reverted back to the people themselves. As Bèze put it, "In all conventions that are contracted by mutual consent, those who initiated the contractual obligation can also undo it with just cause; thus they have the power to depose a king who had the power to create him."[40]

For obvious reasons, historical myths of the original election of a king and the retention of sovereignty by the people tended to be most attractive to those individuals whose will was at odds with the royal will, most importantly those whose religion differed from that professed by the king. Although most of the political theorists who embraced this position were indeed Huguenots threatened by theories of royal sovereignty in a country headed by a Catholic king, there was nothing inherently "Protestant" about this position. When Catholic France was faced with the prospect of a Protestant king in Henri of Navarre, Catholics began towing the line formerly held by Protestants. In 1590, for example, a pamphlet with the title *De la puissance des roys,* which was published anonymously, stated in unmistakable terms the conviction that the vital center of the *corpus mysticum* was the body and that the head was nothing more than an appendage, and an expendable appendage at that. In terms that recall L'Hospital's amputation of the rotten members of the mystical body, the anonymous author proposed a form of amputation somewhat more radical than that suggested by L'Hospital:

> [T]he king is the head [*chef*] of the estates, the deputies are his counselors, who are the members of these same estates. Everything must be published in the name of the king as head, & not in the name of the estates, who are but members. The head will not order, nevertheless, anything against the advice of the latter, because the head should not be in disagreement with the members. . . . The estates received . . . power from God, and then transferred it to the prince, so that he might use it in a legitimate fashion for their defense and protection. As long as he uses it thus, the members will never separate themselves from their head; but, as soon as [the head] is no longer healthy, but infected and rotten, in evident danger of corrupting the rest of the body, the body will separate itself: because it is not a head born naturally, but one voluntarily imposed.[41]

Some two centuries after Gerson had based his political theories on the seemingly incontrovertible notion that "a head without a body cannot survive," certain segments of the population were willing to entertain the idea that a body without a head *could* survive. And so, half a century before the English beheaded their king (body natural) but could not bring themselves to dispense with their King (body politic),[42] and a century before Locke would justify the right of the English people to replace its head with a more suitable one, French political theorists were already beginning to speak of the survivability of a body without a head—a proposition that sheds a great deal of light on the Revolutionary iconographic obsession with heads severed from bodies two centuries later.

One cannot imagine a clearer contrast between two different positions: Advocates of royal sovereignty maintained that the will of the king was primary and that those whose will was intractably opposed to that of the sovereign were no longer part of the corpus mysticum. Advocates of popular sovereignty maintained that the will of the people was primary and that kings merely exercised the sovereign will that resided in the body of the people.

The apparent opposition between these two positions, however, masks a shared assumption that is extremely important: advocates of royal sovereignty and popular sovereignty unanimously rejected the notion that had been current before the latter half of the sixteenth century, that the will of the corpus mysticum could be produced through a coming together of the deputies with the king. For both these groups, sovereignty was now indivisible: it resided either in the head or in the body, but it could not reside in both. The almost universal acceptance of the idea of the indivisibility of sovereignty by the late sixteenth century left only two possible paths for France's political future: the tyranny of the head or the tyranny of the body. By the last decades of the sixteenth century, France's path had been narrowed to a choice between absolutism and revolution.

Nowhere is the principle of the indivisibility of sovereignty articulated more clearly than in the writings of the late-sixteenth-century political theorist Jean Bodin. In his earlier writings, Bodin suggested that the principle of indivisibility did not necessarily mandate one particular form of government over another: as long as the political body possessed sovereignty absolutely, that body could be an assembly of the people, an aristocratic senate, or a king. Eventually, however, the deteriorating political situation in France, and the St. Bartholomew's Day Massacre of 1572 in particular, seem to have persuaded Bodin that absolute and indivisible sovereignty could truly exist only in a monarchy. Only a political body composed of one natural (i.e., human) body could, by its very nature, guarantee a unitary will. And, as his firsthand experience as a deputy to the Estates General had proved to Bodin, political bodies composed of more than one individual inevitably tended toward factiousness rather than the coherent expression of a unitary will.[43]

By maintaining that the indivisibility of sovereign will could be assured only if the political body were composed of one individual, Bodin and other advocates of royal sovereignty were espousing a theory of royal sovereignty that, in effect, reversed the traditional "flow" of the will of the corpus mysticum.[44] Instead of a process in which the will was gathered from the many and condensed into a single whole, absolute royal sovereignty presupposed the will to be already present in the body of the monarch. Instead of *condensation* from the periphery to the center, therefore, absolutism necessarily implied a *radiation* of sovereign will from the center to the periphery. Absolutist theorists, in effect, relieved the French people of the cumbersome process of drafting cahiers and selecting proxies; there was no need to condense the will of the nation or to form a political body when that will and that body were already present in the body of the king.

Although absolutism made the formation of the sovereign will an exclusive function of the monarch, thereby usurping the traditional role of the Estates General, there was no reason why the Estates General could not continue to perform its iconographic role in the process of re-presentation. In fact, Bodin argued that a purely ceremonial Estates General, stripped of any substantive powers, served the purposes of absolutist monarchy very nicely; the assembly of deputies could be a spectacle of homage, a purely formal appearance of the national body to show its approval of the royal will: "We conclude therefore that the sovereignty of the monarch is in no way altered or diminished by the presence of the estates, and on the contrary, His Majesty is much more grand and more illustrious seeing all his people recognizing him as their sovereign."[45] Bodin, therefore, did not challenge the right of the Estates General to assemble; he did, however, state very clearly that their right of assembly did not imply that one was particularly obligated to listen to what the estates had to say:

> With respect to general and particular customs, . . . we are not accustomed to changing anything, without having properly and duly assembled the three estates of France in general, or of each bailliage in particular, not that it is necessary to pay much attention to their opinion, or that the king cannot do the opposite of what they ask, if natural reason and the justice of his will have aided him [in coming to his decision].[46]

If, in theory, absolute royal sovereignty did not necessarily imply a monopoly on iconographic re-presentation, in practice there was no reason why the king could not also arrogate this function as well. After all, an individual human body is in many ways better suited to the re-presentation of a unified mystical body than is an assemblage of several hundred deputies who cannot refrain from jockeying amongst themselves for position. After 1614, spectacles of royal entry and public appearances by the king would fulfill the function formerly performed by the Estates General: the king himself had become not only the repository of sovereign will but also the iconographic re-presentation of the mystical body.

So if the Estates General never met again from 1614 until the eve of the Revolution in 1789, does this mean that absolutism marked a break in the conception of political re-presentation? Yes and no. Unquestionably, absolutism changed the process of re-presentation in a variety of important ways. I have already mentioned the reversal in "flow" that resulted from the positing of sovereign will to be already present in the body of the king, and the transformation of political re-presentation from a process of condensation and contraction (from the periphery to the center) to radiation and dissemination (from the center to the periphery). This new dynamic of a radiating re-presentation is clearly related to the plethora of solar metaphors associated with the reign of Louis XIV in particular. But absolutism brought other important changes to the process of re-presentation as well: for one, political re-presentation became a continuous function, rather than a rare event. Whereas the corpus mysticum had previously been re-presented in its entirety only when the king met with his estates, now the entire mystical body of the nation was held to be permanently re-presented in the political body of the king alone. Like a Eucharist that no longer needed to be transubstantiated and was in a state of continuous re-presentation, the process of political re-presentation became a function of permanent display rather than extraordinary metamorphosis.

In addition, absolutism altered the traditional relationship between the king's two bodies: because the king now re-presented the political body in its entirety (rather than its head alone), there was no longer any practical reason to differentiate formally between the king's body natural and the King as body politic. For all intents and purposes, the king's body natural was the nation itself, a concept so elegantly summed up by the phrase that Louis XIV may or may not have uttered: *l'état c'est moi*. The theoretical relationship between the body of the king and the body of the nation seemed so perfectly transparent that, at least in the eyes of absolutist theorists, the king merely needed to *be* in order for the nation to be re-presented. As the historian of political theory Raymond Carré de Malberg characterized this view, "The king is, according to the claims of the absolutist monarchy, the state itself. He is not a representative of the state; he is the direct organ of the state."[47]

The personalization of power that resulted from absolutism was not without its unintended consequences. Whereas preabsolutist political theory had had a tendency to immortalize the notion of kingship by linking the body of the king to the eternal body of the corpus mysticum, the personalization of power had the opposite effect of rendering the political body of the nation mortal. Because the body of the nation became so closely associated with the (natural body) of each monarch, the inevitable death of that body natural ultimately raised questions about the durability of the political body. Absolutism, as Ralph Giesey put it, "made sovereignty itself into something mortal. Because, if this celebrated little phrase *[l'état c'est moi]* was intended to mean that the body natural of the king possessed the immortal quality of his mystical body, time would soon prove otherwise."[48]

Despite the practical changes that did result from absolutism, however, one cannot say that the fundamental conception of re-presentation itself was markedly transformed. The essential purpose of political re-presentation remained the visible and tangible incarnation of a mystical body. France remained a mystical body with one head and three estates, and although the king now performed the incarnation of the mystical body entirely with his own body (whereas previously he had formed only the head of the re-presentative body), the form of re-presentation was still embodied and concrete. The play of political re-presentation therefore remained relatively unchanged, even if the number of actors on the political stage had been reduced to one.

For almost a century and a half, the absolutist model of representation would rule. Toward the middle of the eighteenth century, however, the perfectly absorptive, one-to-one correspondence between the king and the nation as a whole began to encounter difficulties. A new, abstract entity, which came to be known as "public opinion," began to set itself up alongside the nation, seemingly independent and almost incognizant of the body of the king. Articulating, at least initially, notions of "good taste" in the arts, in literature, and in the theater, public opinion gradually, almost imperceptibly, began making pronouncements on political, social, and judicial concerns, measuring the status quo according to abstract principles of "universal reason." Almost before anyone was fully aware of its existence, public opinion had positioned itself as the true representative of the will of the nation, a position that inherently implied that the king was not (and perhaps had never been) the true arbiter of the nation's will or the legitimate re-presentation of its body.

2 A New Political Aesthetic

Public Opinion and the Birth of the Modern Political Audience

Throughout the first half of the eighteenth century, France was still in most respects an absolutist state: the will of the king was the will of the nation. And the nation could not properly be said to exist outside the body of the king. As Louis XIV had put it, "In France, the nation does not constitute a body [unto itself]; it resides in its entirety in the person of the king."[1] Such a one-to-one correspondence between the body of the king and the body of the nation necessarily obviated the need for any form of re-presentation other than the king's body. In fact, the only national political re-presentations apart from the king's body itself (in spectacles of royal entry and sessions of the *lit de justice,* for example) were iconographic re-presentations of the king's body (in the form of portraits, medallions, and so on).[2] And there was, of course, no need to gather together the will of the nation, as the king had only to consult himself in order to know the nation's will.

In recent years, several historians have traced the erosion of absolutist rule to the rise of "public opinion" in eighteenth-century France, arguing that the very concept undermined the authority of absolutism in profoundly important ways. Not only did public opinion imply the existence of a will that lay outside the body of the king, it also raised a troubling question: If public opinion could claim to re-present the will of the public, then whose will, exactly, did the king re-present other than his own?

Most recent studies that have focused on the rise of public opinion in the eighteenth century have traced a common trajectory. From roughly 1720 to 1750, public opinion—literally the right of "the public" to make its views known on a particular subject—carefully restricted itself to topics that were ostensibly unrelated to politics. Only after 1750 or so did the public gradually dare to apply its newfound authority to issues with clear political relevance. But, such studies have often argued, the seemingly apolitical debates of the earlier part of the century served as a kind of practice run for the less frivolous, more consequential political developments of the latter half of the eighteenth century.

No work has been more influential to the study of the development of public opinion than Jürgen Habermas's *The Structural Transformation of the Public Sphere*. Habermas traces the origins of the "public sphere," laying out the argument that public opinion developed initially with respect to the arts, the theater, and literature and only later came to assert itself in the political realm. In what Habermas refers to as the development of a "public sphere in apolitical form," an ascendant bourgeoisie began to manifest a desire to see itself (and the "patriarchal conjugal family" in particular) as the subject matter for literary and artistic works.[3] This desire on the part of the bourgeoisie to see itself represented in fiction and on the stage was ultimately fulfilled in the proliferation of domestic dramas revolving around bourgeois family crises, psychological novels often written in epistolary form in which the innermost thoughts of the protagonists are revealed, and paintings in which unspectacular, average subjects are intently absorbed in their private thoughts.[4]

With artistic and literary works increasingly focusing on the private bourgeois as a subject, Habermas argues, the entire mechanism for judging the merit of such works underwent a transformation: Who better to determine the talents of the artists than those who could recognize themselves in these representations? Whereas previously, Habermas writes, "a circle of connoisseurs had combined social privilege with a specialized competence,"[5] the shift in subject matter now gave the individual bourgeois a right to claim a special competence of his own, a competence based not on familiarity with the art form but on personal experience with the subject matter. Increasingly, critiques of the arts, literature, and drama revolved around the extent to which a given work was true to life or *vraisemblable;* the best works of art were those that most easily allowed the observer to imagine himself as the subject.[6] Now paintings, plays, and novels were the province of all; as art critic La Font de Saint-Yenne declared in 1747, "A painting on exhibition is like a printed book seeing the day, a play performed on the stage—anyone has the right to judge it."[7]

In Habermas's view, this apolitical public sphere was the "training ground" for a public opinion that would slowly begin to assert its competence within the political public sphere.[8] If what constituted "good" art and drama could appear self-evident to the reasoning individual, then perhaps so too could the concepts of "just" law and government. In the place of the "arbitrary" will of the king, public opinion slowly began to substitute its own self-evident reason.[9] As La Font had remarked with respect to the work of art, so too could one say with respect to the work of state: "Anyone has the right to judge it." Applied in the political realm, this simple principle with its implied objectivity was inimical to the principles of absolutism: if the state and everything in the state were *interior* to the body of the king, then there could be no objective vantage point from which to judge them. Public opinion, when it began to assert its right to judge within the political sphere, posited a critical vantage point *outside* the body of the king, or perhaps more to the point, *inside* the body of each reasoning individual. A re-presentation that had been wholly contained within the body of the political actor now seemed subject to the judgment of a newly posited political audience, composed of separate, reasoning individuals.

Although Habermas writes that the literary and political spheres "blended with each other in a peculiar fashion" and that "in the educated classes the one form of public sphere was considered to be identical with the other," he nevertheless implicitly divides the two spheres: public opinion *first* expressed itself in the realm of the arts, and *later*, in politics; the former was the "training ground" for the latter. An unfortunate consequence of this general claim is that it has tended to encourage a reading of public opinion in the arts as if it were veiled political metaphor. With respect to studies on the theater, there is a certain tendency to read the various spectator-actor-dramatist dynamics (accusations of tyranny and despotism leveled against dramatic actors in their relations with the public, an equation of the theatrical parterre with the nation, and so on) as somehow imbued with political culture, or as prefiguring the political drama that was about to unfold. And there seems to be a general consensus among historians that questions of theater and theatricality were gradually superseded by more pressing, less frivolous concerns of serious philosophy and political theory: theatrical culture gave way to more serious print culture, and indeed theatricality would eventually become synonymous with the old regime, with its inherent showiness and artifice.[10]

If we resist, for the moment at least, the unquestioned primacy of the political in the pre-Revolutionary and Revolutionary periods, it becomes possible to ask an interesting question: If public opinion honed its skills on the proving ground of the arts, revolutionizing the understanding of what constituted "good" representation and who was qualified to judge it, then is it not possible that certain aesthetic preoccupations carried over into the political realm when public opinion turned its attention there? In other words, if we are used to asking whether discussions of artistic taste and the behavior of the parterre might have been playing out questions of national sovereignty before such questions could be asked outright, is it not equally plausible (and, from a chronological standpoint, perhaps even more plausible) to ask, To what extent were later debates over national sovereignty playing out questions of representation and relations between (political) actors and audiences—questions that had first been raised in the realm of the arts?

But let me be clear: I am not arguing for a reversal of our present-day understanding of the metaphoric relationship between theater and politics; I am *not* suggesting that politics is merely theater and that one ought to read political culture as theatrical metaphor. What I am suggesting, however, is that, given the equal plausibility of the two claims, we would do better to abandon the notion of metaphor altogether. Theater was not "really" about politics any more than politics was "really" about theater. Instead, theatrical and political representation were particular manifestations of the same underlying representative process. The fact that they should mirror each other in their rhetoric and their practice, then, is not an indication that each was secretly or metaphorically about the other. Rather, it expresses a conceptual commonality between the two.

As I have already suggested, theatrical representation was, by the middle of the eighteenth century, in the throes of a profound theoretical and practical transformation. If theater and politics really are conceptually identical, then one might expect to find the same transformation on the political stage. And indeed one does, with the important difference that this transformation was, at least for the moment, more or less restricted to theory, practical innovations being decidedly more difficult to effect on the political stage. But at the level of theory, the revolution in representation that took place in political thought in the middle of the eighteenth century parallels developments in theatrical theory to a startling degree: here too, a system of re-presentation that depended upon the political actor's (the king's) belief in his own performance as an embodied re-presentative was in the process of being replaced by a representative system that instead looked to the critical judgment of the political spectator (the reasoning individual) for its legitimacy. And, here too, a political audience was invented (the public) and established as the raison d'être of representation, only for that audience to be kicked off the representative stage and transformed into passive observers of a realistic political spectacle performed on its behalf, but without its direct participation.

In the first half of the eighteenth century, public opinion had yet to extend its sphere of influence beyond the literary and artistic realms. The period from 1720 to 1750 saw the proliferation of journals that judged works of art, plays, and novels by the standards of the average spectator devoid of any particular expertise, a phenomenon that can be seen in the number of journals that used the words *spectateur* and *spectatrice* in their titles.[11] Beginning at mid-century, however, this three-decade trend, in which critics increasingly claimed to speak on behalf of a public audience and in which, correspondingly, artists, playwrights, and novelists increasingly catered to what they perceived to be "public" taste, gradually began to make itself felt in the political sphere.

At mid-century, tensions between the magistrates of the parlement of Paris and ecclesiastical authorities erupted over the issue of the refusal of sacraments to Jansenists. The issue itself was by no means new; the magistrates of parlement and the ecclesiastical hierarchy had been battling over essentially the same questions since the promulgation of the papal bull *Unigeni-*

tus in 1713, which had put into effect a variety of repressive measures against Jansenists. The *parlementaires* had resisted *Unigenitus* not only because several of the magistrates were themselves Jansenists but also because an even greater number of gallican magistrates resented the intrusion of papal influence in French domestic affairs.[12]

When the Jansenist controversy erupted once again around 1749, it was largely in response to a newly imposed crackdown by church authorities who seemed intent on denying Jansenists the sacraments of the Catholic Church, and the last rites in particular. According to new regulations, all Catholics in the process of dying would be required to present a *billet de confession*, signed by a duly certified confessor who had sworn allegiance to *Unigenitus*, before they would be allowed to receive last rites and be buried in consecrated ground. In retrospect, it seems clear that the *billet de confession*, even if it might have scared a few Jansenists into going straight, ended up being a public relations disaster for the ecclesiastical authorities and a dream come true for their opponents. Public opinion was outraged when, for example, the former rector of the University of Paris was denied the last rites on his deathbed, simply because he could not produce a *billet de confession*. Several thousand people attended his funeral in protest.[13]

After numerous well-publicized cases in which individuals had been denied last rites, the magistrates of parlement were finally emboldened, in April of 1752, to issue a decree forbidding the refusal of sacraments to the dying. The public response was overwhelming. Voltaire wrote, "More than ten thousand copies of the decree were purchased in Paris, and everyone was saying [as they pointed to the decree,] 'Here's my *billet de confession*.' "[14] Although the decree was nullified several months later, the magistrates clearly felt that public opinion was behind them and that they had won a moral victory.

In what way, then, is this squabble between the parlementaires and the church new? As David Bell has shown, prominent individuals in the legal community, not to mention the ordinary barristers who followed their lead, had engaged in a significant degree of political pamphleteering since at least the original promulgation of *Unigenitus* in 1713.[15] What makes the events of the early 1750s so interesting for our purposes, however, is the fact that the magistrates of parlement were not content merely to ride a wave of public opinion: in scattered remarks sprinkled through the various parlementary remonstrances of the early 1750s, one discerns the beginnings of a campaign to have themselves recognized as the rightful interpreters or the representatives of that opinion. The sheer audacity of this claim by a political body that possessed little historical justification for making it marks the crisis of the 1750s as the beginning of a break in the traditional conception of political representation.

Historically, the parlement of Paris and the regional parlements had never been perceived as an independent political body, much less a body that could lay claim to any aspect of national representation. Instead, the parlements had always been considered appendages of the royal body: the magistrates of parlement had personified royal justice, and through the various local parlements of the realm they dispensed justice to all in the king's name. In royal funeral processions, it was the four presidents of the parlement that marched closest to the body of the king,[16] and in the general procession of the Estates General, the magistrates had always marched with the king and his court and not with the deputies of the nation.

Beginning with the so-called Grand Remonstrances of April 1753, however, one finds the rudiments of a new conception of parlement's role and indeed of a new, decidedly nonabsolutist conception of the French constitution as a whole. Drawing upon Montesquieu's *Spirit of the Laws*,[17] which had been published in 1748, the magistrates began to articulate the claim that the various parlements throughout the realm constituted a single and intermediary body between the nation and the king, a body that translated the king's will to the nation and the nation's will to the king. The magistrates declared that they were "essentially entrusted [with the task of] representing the very person of Your Majesty to your subjects, . . . [and] of representing your subjects before the eyes of Your Majesty."[18] The radically anti-absolutist nature of this claim is twofold: On the one hand it posits the existence of a nation and a national will that are presumably separate from or incompletely re-presented by the body of the monarch—a proposition that inherently contradicted the central tenets of absolutism. And on the other hand, the parlementaires claimed for themselves, as an independent political body, the role of the nation's unmediated representatives.

King Louis XV had little patience for such claims, and in May of 1753 he exiled the magistrates of the parlement of Paris, scattering them throughout the realm as if to offer convincing proof that they did not constitute a single body as they had claimed. But this was an old response to a very new challenge: the claims to legitimacy that the parlementaires were making had very little to do with their physical presence and therefore could not be effectively quashed merely by fragmenting them physically. On the surface, parlement seemed to be claiming a right to national representation similar to the right exercised by the Estates General prior to the reign of absolutism—a right that had indeed been curtailed by physically preventing the Estates from gathering. In fact, however, parlement was claiming the right to a very different kind of political representation—one that had nothing to do with physical presence and the concrete embodiment of the national will. Unlike the Estates General, which had been invested with the tangible will of the nation in the form of *cahiers de doléances* to which the deputies were bound by the principle of the mandat impératif, parlement was laying claim to a moral right to represent the nontangible, abstract will of public opinion. It was almost as if the magistrates of parlement were borrowing from the repertoire of the absolutist monarchs, who had claimed the right to represent the nation without any legitimacy other than their having said it, and without any tangible means of gathering the national will comparable to those employed by the Estates General.

The physical fragmentation of the parlementaires had little effect on their newfound moral authority, for theirs was not a physical but an abstract legitimacy. Not only did they continue to correspond with one another, but their Grand Remonstrances, which the king had refused to receive, proved to be an overnight publishing sensation. More than sixteen thousand copies were snapped up immediately; they were followed by several reprintings, not to mention a variety of clandestine editions, which were purchased not only throughout France but throughout Europe as a whole.[19]

According to the traditional logic, the publication of the remonstrances was not only illegal but nonsensical: the words of the parlement, which constituted a part of the political body of the king, were intended only for the king's ears. Justice was not a public matter; it was the *secret du roi*.[20] Now, not only were the parlementary remonstrances being disseminated beyond the ears of the king, but the locus of authority was clearly shifting: a parlement whose very existence was tied to the body of the king was now directing its remonstrances over the king's head, to a new body—a political audience whose opinion would increasingly be the arbiter of legitimacy.

In September of 1754, the monarchy decided to put an end to this unprecedented freedom of debate. No sooner was the parlement of Paris recalled from exile than it was asked to register a "law of silence" on the question of the Jansenists. The magistrates of parlement, to whom the concept of political public opinion was apparently becoming more and more self-evident, purported to have difficulty understanding what the king meant by a "law of silence," going so far as to ask for a clarification of the word *silence*.[21] Even after they had been prevailed upon to register the law, they attempted to use it to their own purposes: in 1755, the magistrates attempted to "silence" the *Unigenitus* and prevent its enforcement within the boundaries of France, presumably on the pretext that it spoke about Jansenists.[22]

During the 1750s and the early 1760s, after the controversy over the Jansenists had subsided somewhat and the parlementaires had turned their attention to other issues such as the liberalization of the grain trade, strange novelties continued to make their way into parlementary remonstrances. Sandwiched between innumerable expressions of loyalty and devotion, and the obligatory references to Bossuet, appeared several radical assertions that, as a whole, constituted an attempt on the part of the parlementary magistrates to arrogate, on behalf of the parlements, the functions, duties, and status of the defunct Estates General. The arguments of the magistrates were increasingly based not on the abstract theories of Montesquieu but on the "real" history of France, or at least the history of France that Louis-Adrien Le Paige had claimed was real, in his recently published and extremely influential treatise *Lettres historiques sur les fonctions essentielles du parlement*.

According to Le Paige, the parlements could trace their origins to the national assemblies of the Franks. Far from being a national assembly by default in the absence of the Estates General, therefore, the parlements were, in Le Paige's view of history, the only political body that could claim to speak on behalf of the nation. It was the Estates General that was the fraudulent political body with no real, historical claim to national representation; as Keith Baker summarizes Le Paige's views, "The Estates General were summarily dismissed from the pages of the *Lettres historiques* with a categorical denial that this body had any link with the Frankish national assemblies of a kind that could make it the legitimate representation of the national will."[23]

No doubt with Le Paige's history in mind, the magistrates began to characterize the constitutional relationship between the parlements and the king in terms that recall the traditional characterization of the relationship between the Estates General and the king, as the respective body and head of the French nation. In the remonstrance of 27 November 1755, for example, the magistrates declared, "Our sovereigns and their parlements have [always] composed one and the same body [which is] also indivisible; this august body exists today: you are, Sire, *its head,* and the magistrates of your parlement are its members."[24] In addition, in 1764, the magistrates spoke of the role of all the parlements not only as the representative of the king's justice before the people but as the representation of the people before the king—a representation that they chose to summarize in terms that could not fail to recall the *cahiers des plaintes et doléances* of the Estates General: "[T]he magistrates represent . . . the people by carrying to the throne the testimony of [the people's] submission and their love and the expression of their complaints *[plaintes]* and their claims *[reclamations].*"[25]

A significant clue, however, that the representative role that parlement envisioned for itself was fundamentally different from the role performed by the deputies of the Estates General was the fact that, immediately after laying claim to the right to present complaints and claims to the king on behalf of the people, the magistrates invoked the concept of parlementary "inviolability." The magistrates argued that the concept of inviolability had been developed in order to protect the magistrates from the possible consequences of their exercising the punitive powers of the king's justice:

> It was necessary . . . to cover [the magistrates] with a dignity that was respectable to the people in whose eyes [the magistrates] represented the sovereign . . . ; it was necessary to render their persons sacred and inviolable, to assure them . . . a liberty independent of the caprice of those whose ambition the laws frustrate, a liberty [that] alone [is] capable of maintaining the confidence of the people.[26]

Here, in rudimentary form, is the germ of the principle of representative inviolability, a concept that would later be taken up by the representatives of the National Assembly in 1789, and a concept that is fundamentally at odds with the manner in which the Estates General functioned. Unlike the deputies of the Estates, who had been legally bound by the cahiers entrusted to them and who were subject to stiff penalties if they violated the instructions given them by their constituents, the magistrates of parlement were beginning to formulate a conception of representatives who not only had no cahiers but who claimed themselves to be inviolable. The form of representation that they envisioned was *representative* only in an abstract sense; in actual practice, the magistrates' representation of public opinion would be free from interference by any actual, tangible members of the political audience they claimed to represent. Just as theatrical reformers were, at the very same time, articulating the concept of the fourth wall in the dramatic theaters of France, so parlementary magistrates were beginning to formulate the idea that in the best interest of the nation itself, for the purposes of more effective representation, representatives ought to be alone with their representation on the political stage, free from the interference of those for whose benefit they were claiming to perform.

The magistrates of parlement were clearly fashioning something of a representational hybrid: from absolutism, they had borrowed the notion of an abstract national will that existed nowhere outside of the body that represented it; from absolutism as well, they had borrowed the concept of a representative body that was sacred and inviolable. From the Estates General, the magistrates had taken such concepts as a political body that could be independent from the body of the king but that nevertheless constituted along with the king's body the whole of the mystical body of France; and, also from the Estates General, the magistrates had taken the concept of a political body that could claim to be gathering the grievances of the people, a claim that effectively equated their own voice with the voice of the nation.

The importance of this strange hybrid of an absolutist/representative body lies more in its theoretical foreshadowing of the National Assembly of 1789 than in anything the parlementaires would themselves accomplish. In fact, the parlementaires cannot really be said to have formulated a coherent ideology so much as scattered assertions that were somewhat randomly tossed into their remonstrances. Paradoxically, the most coherent expression of parlementary political thought can be found not in the remonstrances themselves but rather in the royal denunciation of parlementary arrogance of March 1766, known as the *séance de la flagellation*, which, in the words of Keith Baker, "gave parlementary doctrine a radical coherence that it had yet to achieve in the remonstrances."[27]

Among the radical political concepts that the king imputed to the magistrates in the *séance de la flagellation* were the following:

> [That] the parlements compose but one and the same body, distributed among several classes; that this body, necessarily indivisible, is the essence of the

monarchy and serves as its foundation; that it is the seat, the tribunal, the voice *[organe]* of the nation; that it is the protector and the essential depository of [the nation's] liberty, of its interests, of its rights . . . ; [and] that it is a judge between the king and his people.

And, in the face of "such pernicious novelties," Louis XV saw fit to reiterate the central tenets of absolutism, chastising "his" magistrates for their having seemingly "forgotten" the true nature of the French constitution:

> As if it were possible to forget that it is in my person alone that sovereign power resides . . . ; that it is from me alone that my courts derive their existence and their authority; that the plenitude of this authority, which they exercise only in my name, rests always with me; . . . that public order as a whole emanates from me and that the rights and the interests of the nation, which some would dare to make a body separated from the monarch, are necessarily united with my [rights and interests] and repose only in my hands.

The king then concluded the *séance de la flagellation* by reminding his magistrates that remonstrances were meant to be a form of secret correspondence between the king and his parlements, and he therefore ordered the magistrates "that, in their decrees and in their remonstrances, they should restrict themselves within the bounds of reason and the respect that is due to me; that their deliberations should remain secret."[28]

One can hardly imagine a more clear repudiation of the new importance of public opinion in the political sphere and of the parlements' claims to represent that opinion. And yet, around this time, in direct contradiction to this royal injunction to return to the discreet politics of the past, the king and his ministers began toying with the idea of beating the parlementaires at their own game. Largely the brainchild of Jacob-Nicolas Moreau, who for several decades would oversee the project, a royal propaganda campaign was launched with the aim of discrediting the parlementary magistrates in the eyes of the public and presenting the king as the one true representative of the nation. Royal propaganda, formulated with the explicit intention of influencing public opinion, began modestly in the early 1760s and eventually ballooned into something of a government industry.[29]

One might very well argue that a government that still subscribed to absolutism in theory, and yet which found it necessary to justify itself to the public at large, was no longer absolutist in practice. For the parlement to play to public opinion was one thing, but for the political actor of the king, whose legitimacy had always been a self-evident consequence of re-presentational embodiment, to turn to the political audience for legitimacy signals a turning point in the history of political representation—a turning point that is in many respects parallel to the (contemporaneous) redefinition of theatrical representation in which the burden of belief was transferred from the actor to the spectator. The king's playing to public opinion marks the moment in which a system whose legitimacy rested upon the king's conviction in the truth of his re-presentation was superseded by a system in which the legitimacy of the king's representation ultimately depended upon the public's willingness to find his representation credible. A politics of embodiment was gradually beginning to cede to a politics of vraisemblance.

Although the king and the parlementaires were now both engaged in attempts to win over public opinion by means of propaganda, they had by no means forsaken direct confrontations with each other. Escalating tensions between the parlements and the king reached a critical juncture in late 1770, culminating in a "disciplinary" edict in November. The king noted with particular displeasure, in a prologue to the edict, that "one of the most pernicious effects [of the parlements' claim to constitute a single body] was to persuade our parlements that their deliberations thereby carry more weight, and already several [of the parlements], believing themselves to have become more powerful and more independent, have established maxims hitherto unknown: *they have declared themselves the representatives of the nation, the necessary interpreters of the public wills of kings.*" In response to these parlementary claims, the king declared that the time had come to take action against his parlements: "We owe it to the good of our subjects, and to the very interests of the magistracy, even more to [the good] of our royal power, to smother the germ of these dangerous novelties."[30]

The magistrates of parlement professed to be horrified by the edict and took aim directly at Chancellor René-Nicolas Maupeou and his colleagues, whom they took to be the real authors. They declared that their real duty was to the king, warning him that if only he "judged [the matter] with that wisdom which is natural to you, . . . you would recognize, Sire, in the culpable authors of such an edict, an all too real project, hidden under false appearances, to light from a single spark a widespread fire, . . . so that [the authors of the edict] might profit from this violent crisis." The parlementaires consequently refused to register the edict because, as one of the magistrates would later declare, "the registration would cover [parlement] with shame in the eyes of the people today, and in the eyes of the sovereign himself one day in the future."[31]

The king stood by Maupeou and proceeded to force through the registration of the edict of discipline in a *lit de justice,* which he held on 7 December 1770. Parlement responded three days later by suspending its operations. The king, in turn, ordered the magistrates to return to service, which they did briefly, only to resume their strike a week later. At this point, Chancellor Maupeou and the king took more extreme measures: on 19–20 January, a pair of musketeers was sent to the houses of each of the members of the parlement, to awaken the magistrates in the middle of the night with an ultimatum from the king. They were handed a *lettre de cachet* written by the king, which asked them point-blank whether or not they would resume their service immediately and promise no further interruptions. Recipients were instructed to answer "with a simple declaration of yes or no, your acquiescence, or your refusal, signed by your hand."[32]

The majority of the magistrates refused to be intimidated by what they interpreted as Maupeou's middle-of-the-night power play, and they answered "no" to the king's letter. The very next day they received word that they had been dispossessed of their offices, and furthermore that they would be exiled—some to their estates, and some (those whom Maupeou particularly disliked) to the farthest reaches of France. When the magistrates who had initially agreed to the terms of the king's letter heard what had happened to their colleagues, they too resigned their positions and were in turn exiled as well.[33]

With all of the magistrates shipped off to various parts of France, Maupeou seized the opportunity to have done with magistrates once and for all: he dismembered the parlement of Paris, dividing its jurisdiction into six Conseils supérieurs that would be staffed by individuals who were subservient to the crown and whose duties would be strictly limited to dispensing justice. This act of fracturing the very core of the parlements of France, referred to by contemporaries as the Maupeou "coup" or "revolution," effectively obliterated the parlementary magistrates' claims to the representation of national sovereignty.

The Maupeou coup proved surprisingly successful in removing the parlements as a contender for national representation. Although the original parlements would be restored some four years later in a gesture of goodwill by Louis XVI at the beginning of his reign, the parlements would never again hold pride of place in the eyes of public opinion. The ease with which they had been swept aside by the king and his ministers seemed convincing proof that the magistrates were no match for the king's sovereign authority.

Indeed, contemporaries responded to the Maupeou coup in a way that Maupeou himself could hardly have anticipated. The sudden disappearance of the parlements provoked an immediate revelation among those who had embraced the magistrates as the true representatives of the nation: they had placed all of their hopes in a chimera, which could be made to disappear at the wave of a royal hand. The movement of the parlementaires had somehow given the impression that France was not really absolutist; and now many felt as if they had been duped. In the words of the comtesse d'Egmont, people had been taken in by a "simulation of liberty [that] had made [men] believe that they were not subject to an arbitrary authority."[34] Another observer noted that the illusion of parlement as a representative body had created a situation in which the king "had, at one and the same time, the credit [in the eyes of the public] of a limited power and the capabilities of an absolute power."[35] The political theorist abbé Gabriel Bonnot de Mably seized on the moment to declare that Maupeou had, in a sense, done the nation a favor by lifting the veil that had concealed the "secret of empire."[36] And Diderot remarked that "a spider's web upon which the multitude adored a great image of liberty" had suddenly been "torn away," with the result that "tyranny stands openly revealed."[37]

The Maupeou coup, in short, prompted contemporaries to reexamine the very foundation of monarchy itself—a subject that had been decidedly off-limits since the advent of absolutism. All of a sudden, according to one observer, "everyone wants to probe the constitution of the state; heads will become overheated. Theories are being put into question about which one never would have dared to think."[38] Dinner parties were suddenly transformed into "miniature estates-general where women, transformed into legislators, spouted maxims of public law."[39]

One might almost describe the reaction to the Maupeou coup as an instantaneous shift of paradigms: public opinion had imagined that the parlements had constituted an intermediary body between the nation and a reasonable king; suddenly, public opinion had come to the stark realization that the nation stood unrepresented before a king possessed of unlimited powers. This revelation spurred an unprecedented barrage of anti-Maupeou pamphlets,[40] the vast majority of which espoused an entirely new view of national representation. Gone were the smug assurances of the magistrates that the parlements could form a representative body that was superior to the defunct Estates General. For the first time in more than a century and a half there was a sudden groundswell of support for the reestablishment of the Estates General as the only viable organ of the nation.

Although it is true that public opinion still stood by the exiled magistrates and demanded their reinstatement, the parlements were now almost universally characterized as a temporary expedient. This sentiment was expressed within weeks of the Maupeou coup, most notably in the remonstrances of the Cour des aides, a fiscal court attached to the parlements that had yet to experience the wrath of Maupeou. Unlike previous parlementary remonstrances, the remonstrances of the Cour des aides characterized the role of the parlements as the last hope of a nation deprived of other, more legitimate forms of representation: "The [parlementary] courts are today the only protectors of the weak and the unfortunate; the Estates General has for a long time not been in existence . . . : all [political] bodies except the courts have been reduced to a mute and passive obedience. . . . The courts are therefore the only [bodies] to whom it has been permitted to raise a voice in favor of the people, and Your Majesty does not want to remove this last resource of the distant provinces." Implicitly assailing the absolutist notion that the monarch could, by himself, perfectly represent the interests of the nation, the remonstrances boldly declared the nation to be without representation in the wake of the Maupeou coup:

By whom, now, will the interests of the nation be defended against the [machinations] of your ministers? By whom will the rights [of the nation] be represented before you *[vous seront-ils représentés]* when the courts will no longer exist and will have been replaced by tribunals abhorred from the very moment of their creation? The scattered people have no voice to make themselves heard.[41]

The king, far from being the perfect representative of the nation, is here characterized as a body before whom the nation must be represented.

Although the remonstrances of the Cour des aides paid lip service to the concept of divine right, assuring the king that "[y]ou owe [the crown] to God alone," they also (and in apparent contradiction) immediately afterward asked of the king: "Do not refuse us the satisfaction of believing that you are also indebted for your power to the voluntary submission of your subjects." And then the remonstrances went so far as to claim that "[t]here exist in France, as in all monarchies, some inviolable rights that belong to the nation."[42] This concept, of a nation endowed with inviolable rights—inviolable, presumably, even by the king—constituted a direct repudiation of absolutism.

The author of the February remonstrances of the Cour des aides, Chrétien-Guillaume Lamoignon de Malesherbes, the first president of the court, made sure that the remonstrances were disseminated to the public in clandestine editions even before the king had seen them. Virtually overnight, Malesherbes became the hero of the opposition, and his remonstrances were widely acclaimed. The *Mémoires secrets* reported that "[t]he remonstrances of the Cour des aides have enjoyed prodigious success in the public, and copies have multiplied to such an extent that there is not a house where one does not find this manuscript. All good Frenchmen want to read them and to see their author, not just as the defender of the magistracy, but as the titulary God of the Fatherland."[43]

It is important to note that Malesherbes and his fellow magistrates of the Cour des aides had stopped short of explicitly calling for the Estates General in the remonstrances, contenting themselves with merely pointing out that the Estates General had not been in existence "for a long time." Public opinion, however, preferred to ignore the magistrates' reticence, slowly convincing itself that Malesherbes and the Cour des aides as a whole were martyrs in the struggle for the restoration of the Estates General.[44] And if the Cour des aides had been reserved, the provincial parlements, taking their initial cue from the Cour des aides, grew bolder and bolder in their calls for the Estates' restoration. On 8 March 1771, the parlement of Toulouse, the oldest provincial parlement in France, respectfully declared to the king that "if the court [of Toulouse] were not strongly convinced that the execution of such dangerous projects [i.e., Maupeou's coup] . . . would find an invincible obstacle in the wisdom and the goodness [of the king], the court would have perhaps no other resource than to respectfully request the king to order a convocation of the Estates General."[45] Some two weeks later, the magistrates of Rennes were decidedly more direct, enumerating the following truths:

> that the constitution of the state has been clearly violated; . . . that it appertains to the nation alone to change the conditions of the kind of contract that the fundamental law of the state forms between the prince and his subjects; that never has a more important occasion merited the general assembly of the nation; that the magistracy is bound by its estate to inform the king of this, because it is the sole organ that the nation has retained during such time as it is not assembled.[46]

Even if the Estates General were not explicitly named, there was no mistaking the meaning of the nation "assembled."

Although the success of the remonstrances of the Cour des aides and the public acclamation of its president would eventually prompt Maupeou to dissolve the Cour des aides and exile Malesherbes to his provincial estate in April of that year, in the intervening months Malesherbes managed to gather around himself a circle of like-minded individuals to discuss the present state of affairs. Participating in Malesherbes's circle were such individuals as Jacques-Mathieu Augeard, André Blonde, and Guy Target, all of whom would be at the forefront of the coalition against Maupeou—a coalition of individuals who came to refer to themselves as *patriotes*.[47]

The *patriotes* were defined less by any particular ideology than by a general sense that the nation had been deprived of its voice by a tyrannical government, and by the conviction that this situation could no longer be resolved simply by restoring the parlement. The idea would quickly take hold among the *patriotes*—and by 1775 it would be a virtual commonplace of public opinion—that the nation would not be in full possession of its rights until its legitimate representation had been restored to it in the form of the Estates General, a body that had not met since 1614. Maupeou's coup, therefore, intended to restore the practical mechanics of absolutism, had in a remarkably short amount of time paradoxically resulted in an almost universal conviction that the Estates General was the only legitimate national representative body.

One of the more prominent political theorists who argued for the restoration of the Estates General was the abbé Mably, whose *Observations sur l'histoire de France* was self-consciously written as the definitive repudiation of pre-Maupeou parlementary representative ambitions, and of Le Paige's *Lettres historiques* in particular. As Baker has written, in Mably's history of France the "political failure to constitute the Estates General as a national assembly became the essential drama . . . —a drama, indeed, in which the parlementary magistrates played the villain's role."[48] Very far from calling for the restoration of the old parlements as a voice of the people, Mably implicated the magistrates in the despotic plot to rob the nation of its sovereignty, noting that the parlement had "seen its prestige and authority augmented by the total suppression of the Estates General."[49]

Although Mably went further than most in his repudiation of parlement, by 1775 (the year in which Louis XVI, having recently acceded to the throne, restored the parlements and exiled Maupeou in an attempt to garner public support for his reign) even the magistrates themselves had abandoned any illusions that parlement might become the permanent representative body of the nation. Malesherbes, who in 1771 had refrained from explicitly calling for the Estates General, was no longer so restrained when drafting the remonstrances of the restored Cour des aides in May of 1775. As he had done in 1771, Malesherbes characterized the king as a political body before whom the nation must represent itself; but in 1775 he left little doubt as to the most legitimate form in which such a representation might take shape:

> How is it possible to establish a relationship between the king and the nation that would not be interfered with by all those who surround the king? We must not hide the truth from you, Sire; the most simple and the most natural method, the one that is most in conformity with the constitution of this monarchy, would be to listen to the nation itself assembled, or at the very least to permit the assemblies of each province: and no one must have the cowardice to tell you otherwise: no one must let you ignore [the fact that] the unanimous wish of the nation is to obtain either the Estates General or at least the Provincial Estates.[50]

By 1775, as Malesherbes noted, the call for the convocation of the Estates General had indeed become "unanimous." Even Le Paige, the very architect of parlementary representative ambitions, whom Mably had found it so necessary to refute—the same Le Paige who had once characterized the Estates General as merely an "imperfect copy" of the ancient parlementary assemblies—now reluctantly admitted the necessity of the Estates' convocation.[51] And Gabriel-Nicolas Maultrot and Claude Mey, two barristers who along with Le Paige had collaborated on a variety of parlementary texts, also abandoned the parlements for the Estates General as the representative body of choice in their *Maximes du droit public français;* this work, one of the most influential works of political theory of the Maupeou period, even went so far as to claim, in its second edition of 1775, that the nation had a right to convene itself if the king refused to do so.[52]

Many of the anti-Maupeou authors thought of themselves as acting within a broad historical context: they were not merely combating the status quo; they were reversing more than a century of absolutist rule that had deprived the nation of its right to represent itself. Malesherbes, in 1775, boldly denounced the historical "despotism" of royal administrators (if not of monarchs themselves) of the previous century whose first despotic act had been "the destruction of all the representatives of the nation" (206–7). Malesherbes therefore explicitly linked the struggle against Maupeou to the century-long struggle against (ministerial) despotism, referring to the current political system as "these politics [that were] introduced a century ago by the jealousy of ministers, [and] that reduced to silence the Orders of the state, excepting only the magistracy" (172).

As a consequence of this self-consciously anti-absolutist stance, much of the anti-Maupeou literature bears more than a passing resemblance to the texts written toward the end of the sixteenth century that railed against the increasing authority of the king and his court and their perceived encroachment on national sovereignty. Thus, for example, just as Hotman and like-minded political theorists of his time sought historical evidence for primeval assemblies between the king and his people,[53] Malesherbes waxed nostalgic about "the days of our earliest ancestors . . . [when] kings personally rendered justice to the nation assembled on the Champ-de-Mars with a splendor *[éclat]* and an authenticity that have seen no counterpart in modern times" (270–71).

In many respects, no text of the period is more reminiscent of preabsolutist conceptions of political representation than Guillaume-Joseph Saige's *Catéchisme du citoyen*, which appeared in the same year as Malesherbes's remonstrances of the restored Cour des aides (1775). Not unlike Malesherbes, Saige reminisced about the days when the entire nation assembled before their king who—at least in Saige's rendition of the events— would not dream of doing anything without the consent of the nation.[54] But Saige went further than Malesherbes by explicitly locating sovereign authority within the body of the nation, which was the true "proprietor" of the kingdom, and in contrast to which the king himself was but a mere "administrator" (16). In a sense, Saige asked the very same question that had predominated political discourse in the half century or so prior to the triumph of absolutism: Was the body or the head the more essential part of the corpus mysticum? And Saige, like Hotman, Gentillet, and Bèze before him, had no trouble answering the question:

Question: But in this contest between the will of the king and the estates with respect to legislative power, which is the more necessary of the two? Is it the one that forms the essence of sovereignty?
Answer: It is the will of the estates; . . . [There exist] circumstances in which the estates can act without the consent of the king; but there are no [circumstances] in all matters pertaining to legislation in which the king can act without the consent of the estates. To [the estates] alone belongs [the right] to consent to laws proposed by the government, to accord and establish taxes, to judge the succession of the Crown, and to replace by a new election the reigning house when it has been extinguished, or to give at such time, if it so wishes, an entirely new constitution. (16)

Saige, in fact, was so convinced of the nation's sovereign right that he argued that the nation did not need to wait for the king's summons to be convened and that if the nation so wished, it could assemble on its own authority:

> Although it has been a rather long time since the last convocation of the Estates, their legislative right is not, and cannot be, extinguished. It is inherent in the very nature of the political body, & the essence of sovereignty resides always in the nation, whether assembled or not. [The nation] can still, if necessity demands, assemble itself legitimately by its own will, without waiting to be convened by any magistrate [i.e., executive authority]: it is from [the nation] that all political authority flows; & it is [the nation's] consent, whether tacit or express, that can alone render legitimate all power that is exercised in society. (96)

A cursory reading of Saige's work might easily lead the reader to the conclusion that Saige was advocating a simple return to preabsolutist conceptions of political re-presentation. And there is much in Saige's work that lends itself to such a reading. Saige, for example, is adamant in his support for a strict, binding mandate as a bulwark against the ambitions of deputies. But even in his advocacy of this staple of traditional re-presentation, certain conceptual novelties are mixed into the old formula:

> *Question:* The power that municipalities give to their deputies, does it extend as far as putting, without any restriction, their interests in the hands of these deputies, in such a manner that they can vote in all matters of legislation without consulting their constituents?
> *Answer:* No, & this [scenario] would be the greatest absurdity, & would be absolutely repugnant to the essence of civil society; in such a case, legislative power would no longer reside in the nation, & it would no longer be the general will that directed the state; but sovereign authority would find itself concentrated in the body of these deputies whose will would be but a particular will, & [whose] interest [would be] but a private interest: a veritable despotism would result, because despotism exists in all states controlled by another will than the general will & the latter resides essentially and exclusively in the collective of all the citizens. Therefore, . . . deputies of communities are obliged to consult [those communities] in all matters relating to the general interest & cannot conclude anything without the express consent of their constituents, the lack of which would render all operations invalid and contrary to the constitution. (60)[55]

As we can see from the above passage, Saige's conception of the process of re-presentation differs in important ways from the traditional conception. Prior to the advent of absolutism, the ties between the deputy and the locality had been of paramount importance; the unified will of the nation as a whole was the *end product* of a long process in which the wills of constituents in all of the localities were gradually distilled into one general will. Saige, by contrast—and it is an important difference—speaks of a "general will" as if such a will were in existence *prior to* the act of re-presentation. The will Saige speaks of is, in a sense, not unlike the absolutist conception of the national will: it exists prior to the re-presentation, and makes use of re-presentation to make itself known to the nation at large (through radiation outward as opposed to distillation inward).

Saige's conception of the general will is undoubtedly borrowed from Rousseau's *Social Contract*. And, not unlike Rousseau, Saige struggled to find a way in which the general will might be articulated without being distorted by representatives. For Saige, perhaps more than for Rousseau,[56] a strict binding mandate seemed to guarantee that the will re-presented in an assembly of deputies was truly the general will rather than the will of the representatives themselves:

> *Question:* These powers accorded to deputies [to the Estates General], are they so broad that they can act on all occasions without consulting their constituents?
> *Answer:* This must never be; otherwise the nation would find itself at the mercy of a few men who could abuse its confidence, & it is to be feared that their decision would not always be the expression of the general will. That is why, in important cases, in everything relating to legislation and to the general interests of the political body, it is essential that the deputies must not make a decision without having communicated the matter to their principals & having been endowed with their consent. (24)

In the end, Saige seems caught between two very different—perhaps even mutually exclusive—paradigms of representation: one paradigm ties the will of the deputy to that of his particular constituents expressed in the form of written cahiers; the other makes the general will paramount and effectively relegates the will of constituents, taken separately from the nation as a whole, to the status of mere particularizations of the general will. When it came to articulating the will of the nation, Saige's deputy was beholden to two very different masters: the individuals who composed his constituency and the body of the nation as a whole.

If the legislative assembly, in Saige's system, was bound by conflicting loyalties, the obligations of the executive government were surprisingly unambiguous.[57] Here, it was the dictates of the general will that prevailed above all else:

> *Question:* But since the social body is composed of individuals, & the laws must be applied to them, and [since] sovereign authority has only a general view, is it necessary that there be an agent charged with particularizing such views and applying them to the members of society?
> *Answer:* Such an agent exists in every society; it is what we call executive power or the government, and the depositories [of this power] are in general called

magistrates. . . . Magistrates being purely the instruments of the general will must act only in its name; it is only as a consequence of this quality that they have the right to demand the obedience of members of society. (69–70)

Although Saige was careful to divide his politicians between legislative deputies with dual loyalties and executive magistrates with loyalties to the general will alone, we are not very far here from a conception of political representation in which the representative is paramount—a representation bound to the general will of the nation as a whole, in contrast to which the wills of individual constituents are comparatively meaningless.

Saige, as I have said, was careful to bind his legislative deputies both to the mandate of constituents and to the general will without recognizing the potential conflict between the two. Although he seems to have been almost unaware of it, his very juxtaposition of the binding mandate and the general will raised a pressing question that would become the late-eighteenth-century counterpart to the turn of the seventeenth century's obsession with whether the head or the body of the corpus mysticum held precedence: political discourse from 1775 until well into the Revolutionary period would incessantly ask whether political representatives were truly beholden to the constituencies that had elected them or to the nation as a whole, to their mandate or to the general will. The Revolutionaries would ultimately answer this question rather definitively by abolishing the binding mandate as an impediment to the representation of the general will. Representatives would, in effect, sever the bond between themselves and their constituents and relegate the latter to the passive role of spectators to a representative process performed on their behalf. If Saige did not himself take this step, he nevertheless helped to open the door to a new kind of representation that others would walk though.

Saige's *Catéchisme du citoyen* was not alone among the texts circulating around 1775 in its subtle introduction of theoretical novelties into the discourse of representation. Although decidedly less audacious than Saige's *Catéchisme* on the surface, the text of Malesherbes's remonstrances of 1775 similarly conceals bold and revolutionary innovations behind an ostensibly benign fondness for the days when the early kings of France personally rendered justice on the Champ-de-Mars.

One of the purported goals of Malesherbes's remonstrances was to bring to the attention of the new, inexperienced King Louis XVI the manner in which the French monarchy had functioned in its halcyon days. Addressing the young king directly, Malesherbes expressed his hope that the image of Charlemagne meeting with his nation on the Champ-de-Mars might serve as an example: "We have recalled to you the example of these former kings who did not consider their authority injured by the liberty given to their subjects to come and plead for their justice in the presence of the nation assembled. It is for you to judge, Sire, if it would weaken your power to imitate Charlemagne in this respect." And Malesherbes went on to suggest that by imitating Charlemagne, Louis could restore the rightful constitution of the French nation: "It is in following his example that you can still reign at the head of a nation that will, in all its entirety, be your council" (275).

Despite the invocations of such familiar images as a king reigning at the head of the entire nation assembled, the remonstrances, in truth, could not be farther from calling for a return to the personal dispensation of justice before the nation assembled in its entirety. What Malesherbes and his fellow magistrates were proposing was not a restoration of the original Champ-de-Mars but something very different, something whose very conception would have been unthinkable only a few years earlier: they were proposing the creation of what we might call today a "virtual" Champ-de-Mars.

No one debated the fact that the French nation was simply too large to assemble all in one place, as they were supposed to have done in the days of Charlemagne. And the remonstrances clearly regarded the traditional Estates General as an acceptable substitute for the assembly of the entire nation on the Champ-de-Mars, declaring the restoration of the Estates to be, as we have seen, the "unanimous wish of the nation." But alongside this— now conventional—position, the remonstrances broached new conceptual territory: decrying the centuries of "clandestinity" that had overtaken the justice system in the years after Charlemagne (when justice had become the province of those few who could read and interpret the complex legal codes), the remonstrances seized upon the printing press as the novel means by which publicity could be brought back into affairs of state. Yes, it was true that the nation could not assemble in one place. Yes, everyone wanted a convocation of the Estates General, where deputies would re-present their constituencies by proxy as they had done before the reign of absolutism. Nevertheless, Malesherbes and his colleagues were convinced that the age of printing, combined with the increasing literacy and enlightenment of the French people, could usher in an era in which politics might approach—in the abstract, if not in actual practice—the publicness and the immediacy of the assemblies under Charlemagne: "The art of printing has therefore imparted to writing the same publicity that the [spoken] word had in earlier times, in the midst of the assemblies of the nation" (273).

What Malesherbes and his colleagues were proposing was a national assembly that would be, for all practical purposes, *like* the assemblies on the Champ-de-Mars, and yet an assembly that would be relieved of the burdensome task of actually assembling: this was a national assembly existing purely on an abstract plane, a political public based upon the educated reading public and the theatrical public that had developed in France at mid-century. Just as literary and dramatic taste had been wrested from the hands of experts and proclaimed the province of all, so the dispensing of justice would be a public affair, accessible to everyone. One could now say about politics what La Font de Saint-Yenne had declared almost three decades before with respect to other representative forms that fell under the purview of public opinion: "A painting on exhibition is like a printed book seeing the day, a play performed on the stage—anyone has the right to judge it." And just as literary and dramatic representations had begun to cater to public taste, so public opinion would become the most important arbiter when it came to issues of justice and legislation. As Malesherbes put it,

> Knowledge having spread as a result of printing, written laws are today known by all the world; each individual can understand his own affairs. Legal scholars have lost that empire which the ignorance of other men had bestowed upon them. Judges can themselves be judged by an informed public; and this censure is much more severe and more just when it can be exercised in a dispassionate *[froide]* and thoughtful reading than when voting is swept up in a tumultuous assembly. (272–73)[58]

We should pause for a moment to consider Malesherbes's use of the phrase "dispassionate and thoughtful reading," which he contrasts to a "tumultuous assembly." Malesherbes implicitly assumes here that the sum of numerous dispassionate readings will somehow result in a coherent public opinion, one that is more studied and more reasonable than a decision produced by a "tumultuous assembly." As Roger Chartier points out, "Malesherbes converted the congeries of particular opinions that emerge from solitary reading into a collective and anonymous conceptual entity that is both abstract and homogenous."[59] The production of public opinion is abstract because, unlike the manner in which the nation came to a decision on the Champ-de-Mars (or even, for that matter, in the Estates General), one cannot see the process by which the will of the many is consolidated into the unified and coherent will of the nation. As Chartier puts it, Malesherbes's abstract political process produced a "uniform opinion that, unlike that of the ancients, had no physical location in which it could express or experience its unity."[60]

Precisely how the solitary experiences of individual citizens/readers/spectators would be formed into a collective and presumably unified opinion was a somewhat thorny issue for theoreticians of public opinion. Malesherbes seems to have resolved this question in a manner that is extraordinarily suggestive for our purposes here. Explaining why so many years had passed between the invention of the printing press and the possibility of constructing a new, public-minded political order, Malesherbes maintained that it had been necessary for the French people to become more literate and for a cadre of "gifted" individuals to have developed capable of expressing public opinion on behalf of the public:

But several centuries were necessary before the discovery of this art had had its full effect on mankind. It was necessary for the entire nation to form the taste and the habit of instructing itself through reading, and that enough individuals gifted in the art of writing had been formed who could lend their abilities to the public, and could take the place of those who, gifted with a natural eloquence, let themselves be heard by our forefathers on the Champ-de-Mars or in public proceedings. (273)

Here, in this concise passage, is the crux of Malesherbes's conception of how abstract political opinion finds expression. Although the remonstrances clearly demanded greater "publicity" in government, Malesherbes and his colleagues were not in any way proposing that the public assume control of political affairs; rather, they were proposing that political representation ought to regard the public as its primary audience. Far from transforming the public into political actors, Malesherbes was proposing the creation of a nation of political spectators; the public would relinquish active participation to expert representatives, uniquely gifted in the art of expressing themselves. In short, a government based upon the principle of *publicité* did not mean a government in which the public played a greater role; it meant a government whose functioning was visible to the public.

On the threshold of a new political age, Malesherbes clearly envisioned a politics that, although it catered to the public in the abstract, would nevertheless exclude the public in reality as active participants. Just as in the world of theater, the reasoning individual had been discovered and posited as the raison d'être of representation, while at the very same time the collective audience had been declared a meaningless abstraction.[61] The lone, quietly attentive spectator would replace the vocal audience; the individual citizen would replace the national body. And, because there were simply too many such individual citizens to re-present themselves in assembly, each citizen was required to relinquish his active rights to experts gifted in the art of representation.

At times it is difficult to discern whether the remonstrances are speaking in very general terms about men of letters as the leaders of public opinion (as Malesherbes had suggested three months before the publication of the remonstrances, in a speech before the Académie française),[62] or whether the remonstrances are hinting at the implementation of specific political reforms, based upon artistic and literary conceptions of public opinion. And indeed, if one looks carefully, one finds a curious little political scheme inserted into the remonstrances almost parenthetically, a scheme that Malesherbes is quick to minimize as a temporary expedient that could function "while waiting [for the moment when] it pleases the king to convene [the Estates]" (282). Claiming that his conception of the political deputy is based upon the historical *élu* of the *pays d'élection*,[63] Malesherbes argues that his representative system is not an innovation but rather the restoration of an aspect of France's traditional constitution: "What we are proposing to Your Majesty is not at all, Sire, an innovation, because it is the ancient constitution of the kingdom that we are imploring you to restore, in according to each province that which is accorded to every individual, the right to be heard before being judged" (233).

Malesherbes's political system, despite his assurances to the contrary, was indeed innovative, and one wonders as well—once again, despite his assurances to the contrary—whether he did not believe his own system to have certain advantages over the traditional re-presentation by Estates General. Malesherbes repeatedly stresses the cost-effectiveness of his system, insisting that because his deputies would remain in one place, constituencies would not be required to bear the burden of their representatives' traveling expenses, an issue that was a significant feature of re-presentation by Estates General. How, then, would Malesherbes's deputies represent the interests of local constituents to the central government if they never traveled? His answer is as follows:

> This system would not necessarily be costly to the province, and it is possible to avoid [such expense], because it is not absolutely necessary that these deputies should come to appear and to personally plead [their positions] in the capital. This function could be performed by the elected officials that we have proposed to reestablish, and it would be by means of *mémoires* addressed to the court that they would stipulate the interests of their provinces. One could also have at the same time two kinds of representatives that would cost nothing to the province, and who, being in constant communication with each other *[dans une relation continuelle]*, would exercise conjointly their functions. The first kind [of representatives] would live in the province and would know more about the true interests [of the province] than those who reside near the court, and these [representatives] would incur no expense in performing their function because they would stay in the same place. The other [kind of representatives], brought by their own personal affairs to the capital, would take on the responsibility, at no charge, of following the affairs of the province, and would deem it an honor to be responsible [for such things]. (283)

Here, in a rather rudimentary form, is an abstract system of political representation. The constituency would be spared the expense and inconvenience of gathering together its tangible will in the form of a cahier and of entrusting it to a deputy to re-present in some distant assembly. Instead, a representative who lived semipermanently in the capital would represent the interests of those back home. But Malesherbes is not yet ready to cut the cord completely between the representative and the represented and to embrace a system in which all links between the two were intangible; hence, Malesherbes stresses the "constant communication," presumably written, between the representative in the capital and the representative back home whose proximity to the represented constituency would enable him to "know more about the true interests" of the province. We should note, however, that the will of the people would be inferred rather than scrupulously ascertained. And, in Malesherbes's system, there is of course no talk of a binding mandate: after all, one can hardly bind a representative to a will that is expressed only in a vague intangible form.

In Malesherbes's political system, the representative plays a much greater role (particularly with respect to determining the content of the representation) than traditional deputies of the Estates General, and the role of the constituency is comparatively diminished; indeed, the constituency would seem to have no practical role in the representative process apart from the act of voting, an act constituents undertook as individuals rather than as a collective. In such a system, the will of the people verges on an abstraction, while the will of the representative becomes paramount.

The traditional form of re-presentation had been based upon the premise that the re-presentative body, taken as a whole, reincarnated the entirety of the mystical body, rendering that body visible, albeit in a different form. Malesherbes's system of representation, by contrast, had nothing to do with reincarnation (in fact, for him the body of the nation verges on an abstraction); the task of his deputies was merely, as he put it, to "stipulate the interests of their provinces." In the older system, constituents themselves had gathered together at the local level to debate and discuss the formulation of their communal will. In Malesherbes's system, the formulation of will happens at the level of representation. Not unlike the spectators in the newly reconfigured theaters of France, Malesherbes's constituents would cease communicating with one another and turn their (silent) attention to the professional representatives who performed for their benefit.

In these remonstrances of the Cour des aides of 1775, many of the theoretical building blocks were already in place that the National Assembly would eventually use to craft its political legitimacy in 1789: the concepts of an abstract national body, united virtually by the written word, and represented in reality by professional representatives who spoke on behalf of their constituents without deeming it necessary to gather their will in any tangible form, and who consequently were free to act without any specific mandate from them—all of these concepts were present in Malesherbes's remonstrances.

Although, on the whole, Malesherbes's representative system is certainly novel, many aspects of his thinking can be found diffused throughout the pamphlet literature of the period. In particular, Malesherbes's characterization of public opinion as being formed from the "dispassionate and thoughtful reading" of lone individuals ought to be seen within the context of a broader, long-term trend toward the positing of the autonomous individual, abstracted from the whole, as the foundation upon which any collective was built. Almost two decades earlier, for example, Anne-Robert-Jacques Turgot had written that "the general good must be the result of the efforts of each individual in his own interest."[64] Turgot had been among the earliest authors to attack France's traditional organic structure that had bound individuals to one another in the form of estates (and estates to one another in the form of the nation); instead, Turgot had argued that "[c]itizens have rights, and rights to be held sacred, even by the body of society—they exist independently of society, they are its necessary elements; they enter into society only to place themselves, with all their rights, under the protection of these same laws which assure their property and their liberty."[65]

As to the problem of how the private will of innumerable individuals could be forged into a unified whole—an almost universal preconception that was no doubt the legacy of organic conceptions of the nation as one body possessing one will—many authors fixed upon the same solution as Malesherbes: they regarded men of letters and other "gifted" individuals as those who were uniquely capable of forging a unified opinion out of what otherwise would have been a multiplicity of different opinions. As Voltaire had written in the wake of the Calas affair, "Opinion governs the world, and in the end the philosophes govern men's opinions."[66] Often implicit in such a view was a distinction between the rational opinion of the enlightened "public" and the instinctive opinion of the multitude. In an article that focuses largely on this particular distinction, Mona Ozouf cites several examples in which Malesherbes's contemporaries lauded public opinion at the expense of what was often termed "popular" opinion. D'Alembert, for example, wrote that the historian "often tends to distinguish the truly enlightened public, which must guide his pen, from that blind and noisy multitude," and Condorcet wrote that "[w]hen one speaks of opinion, one must distinguish three species: the opinion of enlightened people, which precedes public opinion and ultimately dictates to it; the opinion whose authority sweeps along the opinion of the people; popular opinion, finally, which remains that of the most stupid and the most misery-stricken part of the people."[67]

We should be careful, however, not to characterize pre-Revolutionary conceptions of public opinion as homogeneous; in truth, the subject was constantly debated, and one finds a significant range of views on the question. Mably, for example, was one of the few to hold that public opinion need not necessarily be uniform.[68] And even Condorcet, who compared popular opinion so unfavorably with enlightened public opinion in 1776, would in later writings seek to prove that the will of the majority ought in most instances to be obeyed, not necessarily because it was sovereign but because it had a greater probability of being rational than the will of any individual.[69]

As to the formal mechanics of how enlightened opinion was to be expressed, Malesherbes was not alone in hatching schemes of abstract representation in 1775—a year that witnessed not only the publication of Malesherbes's remonstrances and Saige's *Catéchisme* but also the drafting (if not publication) of Turgot's *Mémoire* on the subject of local government. Turgot, who was briefly comptroller general at the beginning of Louis XVI's reign, offered in his *Mémoire* a rather detailed plan for a representative system that, like Malesherbes's system, seemed primarily intended for the collection and disbursement of tax revenues—a material basis for what was essentially an abstract system. Although loosely based on the Estates General, replete with a "whittling down" of deputies from the local to the national level, Turgot's system is decidedly within the framework of abstract representation and contains a variety of novelties worthy of our attention.

One of the cornerstones of Turgot's system was a concept of citizenship based upon wealth rather than orders. A citizen in the countryside was defined as an individual who possessed land that earned 600 livres in income, and any individual who possessed land that earned less than 600 livres was, in Turgot's words, "not a whole citizen, if one can speak in such terms; he is a greater or lesser fraction of a citizen."[70] Each citizen, rather than being a qualitative part of an organic whole (in the sense that each citizen was an integral part of a particular organ of the social whole), was instead a quantitative part of a mathematical whole: those who earned 300 livres in income on their property were half citizens, and by corollary, those whose property earned 1,200 livres in income constituted two citizens, for as Turgot explained, "there is nothing repugnant in looking at a man who has two shares of citizenship as two citizens" (33).

In the towns, the requirement for citizenship was even more restrictive, being set at the equivalent of 18,000 livres in landed wealth. Although Turgot rationalized this figure as being "roughly equivalent" to 600 livres in income in the countryside, the unmistakable net effect of this requirement for citizenship would be effectively to disenfranchise vast numbers of urban dwellers—or, in Turgot's words, to render them "fractional citizens." And indeed, this appears to have been Turgot's aim: strict property qualifications for active citizenship would ensure dignified assemblies that "would take place without tumult; reason could be spoken there. For it is an important matter, in all deliberations in which a large number of persons have interests and rights, to get rid of the chaos of the multitude, while ensuring the rights and interests of each of its members" (61–62).

Turgot's system was therefore designed to manufacture rational public opinion (as opposed to the popular opinion of the multitude). In contrast to Malesherbes, however, who was careful to describe his system as a temporary expedient in lieu of the Estates General, Turgot proudly boasted of the superiority of his municipal assemblies, whether local, regional, or national: "They would have all the advantages of the assemblies of the Estates & none of the disadvantages: neither confusion, intrigues, nor corporatism nor the animosities and prejudices of one order against another" (95).

If Turgot's assemblies lacked the "confusion" and the "corporatism" of the Estates General, they also lacked other characteristics of the Estates General: namely, cahiers, binding mandates, and a system of re-presentation intended to condense the will of the nation without divesting it of its sovereignty. Instead of cahiers detailing the will of his constituents, each of Turgot's deputies would arrive at the assembly bearing a "statement" detailing "the number of parishes forming the district from which he was sent, & the number of citizens' votes [determined by wealth] included within them" (78). The stuff of representation, the document that assured the legitimacy of the representation, was not the concrete will of a locality being re-presented but rather the number and wealth of inhabitants it possessed (a factor that would be used to determine the relative rank of the deputy). If, as Turgot claimed, the aim of his system was "to establish a chain by which the most remote places might communicate with Your Majesty" (69), it was a chain of elections, each link of which further removed the representative from the will of his constituents. In short, the effect of Turgot's system was the progressive delegation of sovereign authority, as opposed to the unadulterated transmission of the sovereign will of the nation.

Turgot's system was one in which the representatives reigned supreme. Rather than whittling down the opinions of their constituents into one coherent document, their task was to vote among themselves, with the majority of their votes substituting for the will of the nation. And, in contrast to the traditional Estates General in which the quantity of representatives was inconsequential in comparison with the quality of the cahier, Turgot's system very clearly stipulated that each region should be represented by a single deputy. Although each deputy would be allowed an assistant and the assistants could "attend the assemblies as spectators," they were expressly deprived of the right to participate or vote (81). The role of the assistant, like that of the constituents back home, was to observe without participating. Here, very simply, was a system of representation in which professional representatives alone were entitled to act, while all others were relegated to the role of "spectators," as Turgot so aptly termed them.

Turgot was removed from his position as comptroller general in May of 1776, and his plans for a new representative system would, like Malesherbes's, never be implemented. Turgot's dismissal had been largely at the behest of the magistrates of the recently restored parlement, who did not appreciate his various schemes that stratified by landed wealth rather than by estate and that as a whole tended to chip away at the privileges of the nobility. Indeed, the magistrates' agitation for Turgot's dismissal was a clear indication that they regarded the interests of the privileged orders as a primary concern—an essential fact that had for a time been masked by the common agenda pursued by the anti-Maupeou coalition during the years of the Maupeou parlements. The fundamental differences among the various individuals who had struggled together against the "despotism" of Louis XV and his ministers would gradually become apparent over the next several years and would coalesce into two almost antithetical revolutionary agendas: those, on the one hand, who wanted a restoration of the nation's sovereignty along the lines of preabsolutist France and who clung to the conception of the national body as an organic, qualitatively differentiated body; and those, on the other hand, who wanted sovereignty restored to the nation according to radically new definitions of nationhood, citizenship, and sovereignty.

Although Turgot's vision of a new representative system was never implemented, both he and Malesherbes had attempted to find a political solution to the vexing question of how to give the public a voice and prevent that voice from being commandeered by the multitude; both, in short, had offered a vision of a representative system that spoke on behalf of, but without the participation of, political spectators.

The various texts examined in this chapter were, from a practical standpoint, failures. None of the reformers and theorists examined here—either those in positions of authority, such as the magistrates of parlement, Malesherbes, and Turgot, or radical theorists such as Saige—succeeded in transforming their ideas into reality. Practical failure, however, in no way minimizes the extraordinary importance of these texts: if we recall that in 1750 the body of the king was the sole national re-presentative political body, then the political discourse a quarter century later seems all the more remarkable. For by 1775 the king's body had been all but excised from conceptions of national representation, and in its place was something profoundly different. By 1775 political representation, in the minds of many, would have nothing to do with embodiment or with the distillation of the will of constituents. Political representation would henceforth be the articulation of public opinion—a concept that seemed to exist nowhere in any tangible form and yet was somehow accessible to the enlightened or gifted few. Representatives, from this point onward, no matter how much they might have spoken about the will of constituents, would in the last instance see themselves as representatives of a higher cause to which they alone seemed to have privileged access. In theory if not yet in actual fact, the people, in whose name representation was predicated, had been cleared from the stage.

Entr'acte
Public Opinion and the Theater

In the preceding chapter I drew several parallels between political and theatrical representation, with the implication that the conception of political public opinion as it was developed from the 1750s to the 1770s inherently carried with it a certain actor/spectator dynamic that was the hallmark of the newly reformed theater. But I do not wish to imply in any sense that theater was primary and that political representation was merely aping developments on the stage. For one can just as easily and just as plausibly reverse the relationship between theater and politics: particularly with respect to the tone of the reformers, one can certainly make the claim, as I do in this brief entr'acte, that theatrical debate was infused with political rhetoric. Not only that, many of the key players in these debates on the nature and import of the theatrical audience had played significant and sometimes central roles in analogous debates in the world of politics.

In 1773, for example, Louis-Sébastien Mercier, who had already expressed his political disapproval of the Maupeou regime through his playwriting,[1] turned his attention to the theatrical regime itself, launching a revolt against the "tyranny" of the Comédie-Française—a revolt that in many ways offers a striking parallel to contemporary political developments. Although Mercier's equation of the power of the Comédie-Française with political tyranny may seem somewhat hyperbolic to modern ears, Mercier had a point. After all, the Comédie-Française, otherwise known as the Théâtre-Français, not only had been founded by Louis XIV but had been established by him in his own image, as an absolutist enterprise. Just as political absolutism held the nation to be more perfectly re-presented by the sole body of the monarch than by any combination of political bodies, so Louis had gathered together several individual troupes into one corporation, proclaiming that "henceforth there [will] be a single [theater] company in order to render more perfect the performance of plays."[2] In homage to the king who had created them, the actors of the troupe were called the Comédiens du roi, and as a sign of their importance, they were under the direct supervision of the Gentlemen of the Bedchamber—those same individuals whose proximity to the king was ceremonially manifested in their participation in the dressing rituals that Norbert Elias detailed in his book *The Court Society*.[3]

From their incorporation in 1680 until the "liberty of the theaters" was proclaimed in 1791, the Comédiens du roi enjoyed an absolute monopoly over the right to perform serious (nonfarcical and nonmusical) dramas within the French capital—a privilege they guarded jealously.[4] In various legal briefs intended to shut down their competitors, the Comédiens du roi vigorously defended themselves against all those who dared to encroach upon their monopoly. In 1680, for example, the very year in which they were incorporated, the Comédiens complained that competing theatrical troupes were, by the simple act of performing, engaging in an activity "that might even be called a revolt against the decrees of the court."[5] And, as late as 1789, the Comédiens du roi published a mémoire accusing the Spectacle du faubourg Saint-Antoine of having embarked upon "a kind of insurrection." In this same mémoire, the Comédiens du roi offered a defense of theatrical absolutism that almost bears comparison to Louis XV's *séance de la flagellation*:

> Public opinion is furthermore convinced of the advantages that result from this presence of many talents in the same place, in the same play, on the same stage. . . . [The art of theater] could only degenerate in the face of competition [among different theaters], which would not produce any more talent, & which would [instead] weaken that which [the theatrical arts already] possess by scattering [those talents]. . . . In a word, never has a privilege been as acknowledged, as public, and as authentic as that of the Comédie-Française.[6]

Mercier's attack against the Comédiens du roi in 1773 was motivated not so much by the Comédiens' monopoly per se as by the net effect of this monopoly on public expression. In his scathing indictment of the theatrical status quo entitled *Du théâtre, ou Nouvel essai sur l'art dramatique*, Mercier criticized the closed sessions in which a few privileged actors somehow had the right to determine which plays would be performed and which would be relegated to oblivion. Casting the playwright—or rather *poète dramatique*—in the role of the "legislator" and the "public orator of the oppressed," Mercier declared that the Comédiens, in silencing the voice of the public, were "vile instruments of despotism [who should] be struck down dead."[7]

Because *Du théâtre* had been published anonymously, the Comédiens had refrained for the moment from retaliating against Mercier in any overt manner. In 1775, however, Mercier demanded to know why none of his plays had been performed at the Théâtre-Français. The Comédiens responded by accusing Mercier of having authored *Du théâtre* and declared that they would have no more dealings with him, remarking that "[t]he theater would in fact deserve the odious imputations of M. Mercier if it weakened and dealt with this worm of an author." Mercier in turn responded by hiring a lawyer with whom he drafted two legal mémoires against the actors. In addition, Mercier continued to excoriate the actors in defamatory articles that he published in his *Journal des Dames,* repeatedly calling for the establishment of a second theatrical troupe so that the "indolent despots" of the Théâtre-Français might be overthrown.[8]

By June of 1775, not only the actors but the administrative overseers of the Théâtre-Français, the Gentlemen of the Bedchamber, had had enough of Mercier's provocations. The duc de Durat, who headed the governing board of the Comédie, issued a *lettre de cachet* ordering Mercier's arrest and imprisonment. Mercier sought the protection of the newly restored parlement, an act that prompted Durat to rescind his *lettre de cachet* and replace it with an *arrêt du conseil* that condemned Mercier's writings against the Comédiens for their "scandalous rantings disrespectful of His Majesty's authority."[9] Furthermore, the Gentlemen of the Bedchamber accused Mercier of having "believed that he could bring about a revolution," claiming—Mercier would later say, erroneously—that he had even made use of that expression in his mémoire.[10]

Whether or not Mercier had explicitly called for a "revolution," it would seem that he sparked one. Several pamphlets followed Mercier's mémoires, one of which demanded that the public, not the Comédiens, ought to decide which plays were performed.[11] And the playwright Palissot de Montenoy, in filing suit against the Comédiens du roi that same year, praised Mercier for having had the courage to fire the opening salvo in the "revolution" against the "humiliating despotism" of the theatrical tyrants. He declared: "A universal cry has arisen against the audacious conduct of the Comédiens. . . . Mercier's complaint has paved the way for this revolution."[12]

To the modern ear, the rhetoric of those involved in the dispute between Mercier and the Comédiens seems overblown: the claim on one side that Mercier had embarked upon a "revolution," and the charges of "despotism" on the other side, hardly seem suited to what was, after all, nothing more than a dispute between playwrights and a theater company. For that matter, my discussion of Mercier's squabble with the Comédiens du roi might seem to be a digression from the political narrative of the previous two chapters. And yet, an essential fact is abundantly clear from the evidence: the participants involved in this dispute did not regard political and theatrical absolutism to be separate issues. Indeed, when Mercier, in the wake of his run-in with Durat, filed a formal *requête au roi*—a personal appeal to the king for justice—he and his attorneys condemned the Gentlemen of the Bedchamber in words that might just as easily have been written by the anti-Maupeou magistrates in their condemnation of political despotism: the *requête au roi* declared that the Gentlemen of the Bedchamber were exercising a "combination of executive power and legislative power, . . . [which is the] complement of the most absolute authority."[13]

But the common rhetoric shared by condemnations of political and theatrical despotism need not alone convince us of the parallels. The words that condemned theatrical "despotism" sound so similar to the words that condemned political despotism in part because those who associated themselves with Mercier's case were intimately involved in the political struggles of the day. In fact, only months before he took on Mercier's case and drafted the *requête au roi,* Mercier's lawyer, Pierre-Paul-Nicolas Henrion de Pansey, had been selected to deliver the oration before the *avocats au parlement* on the occasion of the Paris Parlement's restoration. And Malesherbes himself, now triumphantly installed as the minister of the Maison du roi, was said to have taken a special interest in Mercier's case.[14] Thus, at the height of his prestige and political clout, Malesherbes chose to ally himself with Mercier's cause, no doubt because he recognized in Mercier's condemnation of the Comédiens du roi and of their secret meetings determining the theatrical agenda the very same antipathy for absolutism and "clandestinity" that he himself had expressed in his remonstrances.

Theatrical and political struggles had more in common, however, than their common struggles against the tyranny of the present. They also shared a common vision of the future, of a new regime founded upon rational public opinion. And, inevitably perhaps, they both became preoccupied with the same fundamental question that the prospect of rule by public opinion necessarily engendered: To what extent would the public, in whose name public opinion was invoked, be included in the formation of that opinion? Would public opinion, in other words, be formulated *on behalf of* the public, or *by* the public?

Although calls for a true democracy of the people were relatively rare within political discourse, within the context of the theater advocates of what might be called "theatrical democracy" were somewhat more common. There were those, in short, who held that theatrical public opinion was nothing other than the opinion spontaneously formed by the public, without the need of any interpreter or mediator. Indeed, it became increasingly common in the 1770s to endow the theatrical parterre with a kind of politico-theatrical general will. Mercier, for example, claimed that the spectator possessed both a particular will and a general will, the first of which each spectator "put aside" in order to judge the play fairly: "Every spectator judges as a public man and not simply as a private individual; he puts aside both his interests and his prejudices; he is just toward himself, and it is a fact that in the long run the people are the fairest judges."[15] And Jean-François Marmontel, writing in 1777, in the entry "Parterre" in the supplement to the *Encyclopédie,* similarly endowed the parterre with a kind of instinctive common sense, untainted by the fashions of the moment:

[T]he parterre . . . is commonly composed of the citizens who are the least rich, the least mannered, and the least refined in their customs [*moeurs*], of those [citizens] for whom [what is] natural is the least polite, but also the least altered, of those [citizens] in whom opinion and sentiment owe the least to the passing fancies of fashion, to the pretensions of vanity, to the prejudices of education; of those [citizens] who commonly have the least enlightenment, but perhaps also the most common sense, & in whom the most healthy reason and the most naive sensibility form a taste [that is] less delicate but more sure than the light and whimsical taste of a world in which all sentiments are artificial or borrowed.[16]

This passage, which lauds the instinctive and natural common sense of the parterre (presumably in comparison to the artificial taste of the *loges*) recalls Rousseau's comparison of the unspoiled Genevans and the debauched Parisians in his 1758 *Letter to d'Alembert on the Theater*, with the important distinction that Marmontel, unlike Rousseau, did not believe that the theater was inherently corrupting; on the contrary, Marmontel believed, as he had declared in his 1759 rebuttal to Rousseau's *Letter*, that the theater had the potential to be a "school of citizens."[17]

Although Marmontel and Rousseau did not see eye to eye on the inherent evils of the theater, Marmontel's theatrical ideology nevertheless seems derivative of Rousseau's political writings. For example, Marmontel endowed the parterre with the ability to reduce the mass of particular opinions into a kind of uniform will, a process not unlike Rousseau's description of the formation of the general will in the *Social Contract*: "[T]he pluses and the minuses . . . [of the particular, individual wills] cancel each other out, and the general will remains as the sum of the differences."[18] Marmontel, although he divided the spectators between those of the parterre and those of the loges, nevertheless uniquely credited the parterre with the ability to reduce the mass of opinions to a unitary whole: "I am persuaded that if the parterre, such as it is, did not captivate public opinion, & did not reduce it to one by bringing it around to its [opinion], there would be more often than not as many different judgments as there are loges in the theater, & that for a long time the success of a play would be neither unanimously nor absolutely decided."[19]

Even at a distance of more than two centuries, one can hardly fail to notice the political resonance of Marmontel's theatrical opinions. And indeed Marmontel's writings are typical of contemporary writings on theatrical aesthetics in that they betray their author's awareness that when one was speaking of theatrical aesthetics one was also, at the very same time, pronouncing judgment on corresponding political issues. As Jeffrey Ravel has recently shown in his definitive account of the eighteenth-century parterre, from the 1770s onward an invocation of the parterre was often tantamount to an invocation of the nation itself. As Ravel writes, "[W]riters and readers began to understand the assembly of parterre spectators, diverse in its composition yet imperious in its judgment, as a metaphor for the nation whose political sovereignty was gaining momentum."[20]

Although invocations of the parterre in the late eighteenth century can plausibly be read as metaphoric invocations of the nation, we would do well to resist the temptation to push this metaphor too far—to assume, in other words, that when individuals held forth on the theory and practice of the theater or even on the explicit politics of the parterre, what they *really* meant to do was talk about politics.[21] By the 1770s, there was a considerable amount of freedom of expression, whether legitimate or illegitimate, and it seems implausible that anyone would have felt compelled to mask a political stance in theatrical terms, particularly in view of the numerous radically innovative and explicitly political texts that had already found their way into circulation.

Rather than thinking of debates in theatrical politics as a simple political metaphor, we would do better to look upon the discourses of *both* theatrical and political representation as two branches of a broader, general discourse of representation. But we should also not lose sight of an important fact: only theatrical representation was, at least for the moment, susceptible to innovation. New methods of theatrical representation and new power relationships in the realm of theatrical politics could be put into practice immediately in the theater, rather than remaining eternally at the level of theory, as threatened to happen in the world of politics.

Can we conclude, then, that innovations within the theater were, whether on a conscious or unconscious level, anticipating a new political mise-en-scène? The answer to this question is yes, I think, if we are speaking on a very general level of a sea change in the theory and practice of representation; but no, if we are speaking of a more conscious, explicit attempt to change the political world through the theater. One could challenge the archaism of a mode of re-presentation that called upon actors to embody their characters; but this did not mean that one was attacking the political body of the king as the embodiment of the nation. One could challenge the despotism of the actors; but this did not mean that one was at the same time attacking the despotism of political actors. Did these two viewpoints often go hand in hand? Yes. Were they meant to be interchangeable expressions of the other? No.

If we accept, however, on a general level the premise that theatrical discourse and political discourse were two specific manifestations of a broader discourse of representation, then questions concerning the role of the parterre—the "people" of the theatrical realm—have particular importance for the story being traced in these pages. And specifically, Ravel's analysis of attempts by theatrical reformers in the late 1770s and early 1780s to subdue the parterre, to quash calls for theatrical "democracy," is extraordinarily interesting for our purposes here. When the playwright and critic Jean-

François de La Harpe complained about the "shameful indecency of our tumultuous performances, which have been abandoned to the jeering cabal while decent sorts are silent," he was articulating, in theatrical terms, a more general viewpoint on the behavior of the multitude when left to their own devices. And when La Harpe proposed a simple solution to this problem of the "tumultuous mob," he was expressing in theatrical terms a solution that echoed the sentiments of those writing about the danger that political representation would be commandeered by the multitude. And La Harpe's solution, despite its simplicity, marks a milestone in the history of representation: "[T]here is only one way to prevent the absolute decadence of the theater: this is to seat the parterre."[22]

La Harpe, along with the many others who joined his campaign to seat the parterre of Paris's foremost theaters, was essentially proposing that the last breach in the fourth wall be closed: to seat the audience would have the effect of minimizing spectator interaction. Separated from one another in their seats, prevented from forming into groups, spectators would be less prone to spontaneous outbursts, and the actors could proceed with their representation uninterrupted by the "tumult" of the parterre. And spectators, for their part, would be free to form their own individual opinions, unmolested by the coercion of the parterre. As the architect Claude-Nicolas Ledoux reflected in 1775 on the anticipated effect of seating the parterre in the theater of Besançon, which he had designed, "[T]he cabal will end, and we will judge authors more rationally once we have destroyed what is incorrectly called the enthusiasm of the parterre."[23]

Ledoux's claim that a seated parterre would enable spectators to judge "more rationally" should remind us of Malesherbes's conception of public opinion, which was based upon the model of the solitary reader; judgment, he claimed, is "much more severe and more just when it can be exercised in a dispassionate *[froide]* and thoughtful reading, than when voting is swept up in a tumultuous assembly."[24] And the schemes Ravel cites to price the new seating in the parterre out of the range of the poorer sections of society, in the hope that they would take the cheap seats in the upper reaches of the theater while leaving the choice seating in the parterre for the more upstanding segments of society[25]—these strategies bear a striking resemblance to Turgot's scheme to stratify the public according to wealth, the end result of which would be, he believed, a more ordered (electoral) assembly: "[I]t would proceed without tumult; reason could be spoken there. For it is important . . . to rid oneself nevertheless of the chaos of the multitude."[26]

Marmontel, whose article in the *Encyclopédie* under the heading "Parterre" was conceived as a rebuttal to La Harpe and the others, saw in the scheme to seat the parterre an attempt to impose an "aristocracy" on what was in his view a theatrical "democracy." Speaking of the inevitable consequences that would result from seating the parterre, Marmontel wrote, "[T]his sort of republic that constitutes our theaters would change its nature, and . . . the democracy of the parterre would degenerate into an aristocracy: less license and tumult, but also less liberty, ingenuity, warmth, frankness, and integrity."[27]

One last parallel between theatrical and political discourse is worth exploring—a peculiar attribute shared by Marmontel's democratic parterre and Rousseau's ideal citizenry: its maleness. The parterre had traditionally been off-limits to women, and Marmontel, within the context of a defense of democracy, sought to justify the continued exclusion of women from the parterre. He believed that the inherent common sense of the parterre could only be tainted by the presence of women, whose well-known taste for artificiality and powers of seduction would necessarily distort the pure formulation of the simple truth: "[I]n [the parterre], there being no women, there is no seduction: the taste of the parterre is less delicate [because of this], but also less capricious, & above all more male & more firm."[28]

Marmontel was far from the only writer to support the continued exclusion of women; Levacher de Charnois, who, unlike Marmontel, was an advocate of seating the parterre, nevertheless hoped that women would continue to be excluded from the parterre after seating had been installed.[29] In the decades before the Revolution, within the context of theatrical representation, those who disagreed on the extent to which "the public" should be active or passive participants in the process of representation were strangely in accord on the necessity of excluding women. Whether they excluded them because of their artificiality and powers to seduce, or because of their perceived inability to think in that rational, *"froide"* manner of Malesherbes's solitary reader, individuals who were otherwise opposed to one another nevertheless agreed on the essential maleness of the public. There is, perhaps, no clearer parallel than this one between the pre-Revolutionary discourse on theatrical representation and the Revolutionary discourse on political representation.

As Ravel informs us, the parterre of the Comédie-Française was seated in 1782, and that of the Comédie-Italienne, in 1788. A seated parterre did not, however, immediately translate into a silent one, and as I will discuss in a later chapter, parterre disturbances continued well into the Revolutionary period. Nevertheless, despite these occasional disturbances, some observers thought that they could discern a new "apathy" on the part of spectators; one anonymous author described the newly seated parterre as sitting with "their eyes wide-open, mouths gaping, quite apathetic, even snoring as though at a private audience or a sermon."[30]

I am tempted to see in the birth of this new apathetic audience a parallel and a chronological precursor to the new political audience brought into existence by the advent of representative democracy. Yes, the parterre would continue to be an active presence: like the popular rebellions that occasionally interrupted the imposition of representative democracy, the parterres of Paris occasionally rose in rebellion. But the trend toward passivity had begun, and theatrical and political audiences were well on their way to becoming the passive observers that they are today.

The historian James Johnson began his recent study of musical audiences in France with the "simple question" that inspired his book: "Why did French audiences become silent?"[31] One might ask the same question of the French people, who after their triumphant forays onto the political stage were so often content to sit back and let others represent on their behalf. Marie-Hélène Huet, in her book *Rehearsing the Revolution*, has, as I have attempted to do here, explored certain parallels between Revolutionary theater and politics. And, in a sense, she has asked Johnson's question with respect to political audiences. She finds a "profound and secret violence" to be inherent in the constitution of the theater itself and claims that the coercive actor-spectator relationship also describes the power relations on the political stage:

> [T]he Revolution's constant concern with making the people into a public did not necessarily correspond to any form of political liberalism; that this objective was political in nature is beyond doubt, but it was inscribed in a tradition that consists in repressing by means of spectacle. To make a spectator of the people, while making sure that the possibility of a spectator-actor reversibility remains carefully controlled, is to maintain an alienation that is the real form of power.[32]

The Revolutionary period is remarkable for its popular uprisings. But it is also remarkable for its general public acquiescence to regimes that provided no concrete method for public participation in the formation of the sovereign will. A Revolution that was enacted in the name of the public effectively excluded the public from the process of national representation. Surprising, therefore, are not only the various popular rebellions of the Revolutionary period but also the willingness with which the political audience so quickly resumed their seats after taking the political stage and suspended their disbelief while a National Assembly or a Committee of Public Safety (or a Napoleon for that matter) acted in their place, with virtually no tangible input on their part.

The various regimes of the Revolutionary period, from 1789 until 1815, for all of their differences, shared a common political aesthetic: a representation that purported to be for the public's benefit but that nevertheless mandated a rigid separation of actors and spectators, with minimal participation by the latter in the representation of the national will. If the history of France is marked by repeated political revolts, the general trend over time—in France as elsewhere in the modern world—is one in which political audiences have become increasingly used to letting others act on their behalf, without their meaningful participation. The following chapters explore the moment when the *political* theory of rule by public opinion and the *theatrical* practice of removing the spectator from the representative process became the political reality of representative democracy, or what might more accurately be called rule by political actors.

3 *The Resurrection and Refashioning of the Estates General*

In November of 1787, after years of forestalling what had come to seem like the inevitable, and after attempts to garner public support for such substitute bodies as the Assembly of Notables as well as provincial assemblies of the Estates, the king and his ministers finally reconciled themselves, in principle, to the convocation of the Estates General. Although historians of the French Revolution have characterized the decision to convene the Estates as momentous primarily because of the dramatic chain of events that it initiated, we should not lose sight of the extent to which the Estates General's convocation was, in its own right, "revolutionary": for the first time in living memory, a French monarch had publicly acknowledged his willingness to entertain the notion that certain aspects of national sovereignty did not lie absolutely within the body of the king. The act of calling the Estates General therefore signified not only the tacit end to a century and a half of absolutism but also the reestablishment of a form of government that had not existed since the earliest decades of the seventeenth century. The language of the official announcement of the convocation makes very clear that the king and his ministers envisioned precisely such a re-volution back to a previously existing state:

> His Majesty will always seek to stay as close as possible to earlier practices, but when [such practices] cannot be ascertained, [His Majesty] does not wish to fill in the silences of the old records without asking the views of his subjects before making any decision, so that their confidence may be all the greater in an assembly that is truly national in its composition as well as in its results.
>
> Consequently, the king has resolved to order that all possible researches be effected in all the archives of every province, pertaining to the above matters. Let the results of these researches be put at the disposal of the provincial estates and the provincial and district assemblies of each province, which will let their

wishes be known to His Majesty by *mémoires* or *observations* that they can address to him.[1]

The royal appeal for "all possible researches" provoked an almost instantaneous deluge of enthusiastic pamphlets on the subject of the once and future Estates General. One of the most striking aspects of the torrent of political literature that greeted the announcement of the Estates' convocation is the degree to which these texts were virtually unanimous in their enthusiastic support for the king's decision. A century and a half of official absolutism had come to a de facto end without anyone to step forward to lament its demise. On the contrary, political commentators scrambled to put their hasty reflections into print on the subject of the Estates General, publishing "instant" histories with titles like *Coup d'oeil rapide, ou notice historique sur les assemblées des états généraux du royaume.* Authors of such pamphlets invariably invoked political expediency as an excuse for the somewhat slapdash quality of the final product. One such author prefaced his text with the following modest disclaimer:

> Despite the rapidity with which this work has been prepared and published, despite the faults with which it would perhaps be wrong to reproach the author too sharply because he recognizes them better than anyone, [the author] plucks up the courage to publish it; & ought not vanity to silence itself when public utility has spoken?[2]

This enthusiastic and universal embrace of the concept of a resurrected Estates General masked, at least for a time, the fact that two very different agendas lay behind this apparent unanimity. In the euphoria of the moment, public opinion had convinced itself that the resurrection of the Estates General was somehow in keeping both with France's historical precedent and with the enlightened principles of universal reason. The once and future Estates General was painted at one and the same time as France's true historical political body and the realization of enlightened aspirations. Only later did these contradictory premises begin to sort themselves out into two coherent and extremely different positions.

Everyone agreed in principle that absolutism was finished and that the rights of the nation to representation ought to be restored. But when it came to the constituent terms of this vague principle there was no consensus: What exactly was "the nation" and what did it mean to "represent" it within a political body? Was the nation an actual body composed of qualitatively different organs and members? Or was it a metaphoric body composed of citizens who were equal in rights? Was the nation to be re-presented by deputies who were bound to the tangible will of their constituencies in the form of written cahiers? Or was the nation to be represented by political representatives who were elected locally for the purpose of serving nationally—representatives who were bound not to the particular will of their constituencies but rather to the general will of the nation in its entirety?

For some, the Estates General was clearly the actual resurrection of the historical political body of the nation, brought back to life after one hundred and seventy-five years of suspended animation. For others, the Estates General seemed to promise the opportunity to move forward, a political body that might be fashioned according to the abstract principles of Reason and natural law. Toward the end of 1788, as the divisions between these two political ideologies were becoming increasingly apparent, an anonymous pamphleteer attempted to articulate the split within public opinion:

> The rights which belong to the nation in the administration of the public welfare are so obvious and so universally recognized today that there seems no longer to be need of further proofs. However, we are still divided when it comes to one question . . . : What is the form in which the Estates General should be convened? Should we follow that [form] which was practiced in preceding assemblies, particularly during the last Estates of 1614, or can we diverge from [previous practice] in order to adopt other forms that might seem more in keeping with the public good? . . . A nation can be considered according to two different respects, either according to the particular constitution that has thus far been proper to it, & that forms that which we call *its* public right, or according to the dictates of that primitive right which must serve as a basis for all social institutions, & which we can call for this reason the *universal* public right.[3]

These two different positions constitute a fork in the history of representation. One path led logically to a form of government in which the political body was composed of proxies beholden to their particular constituencies. The other path, the one eventually taken by the Revolutionaries of June 1789, led to a system of representation in which the political body was composed of representatives each of whom could claim to speak on behalf of the nation without formally consulting any actual constituents—the form of government that we today call representative democracy. A careful reconstruction and juxtaposition of the logic of both of these opposing theoretical camps reveal something that has been almost entirely obscured by the rhetoric of the inevitability and of the inherent rationality of representative democracy: how profoundly and radically novel was this new theory of representation.

The Importance of History: The Revolution as Restoration

Much like the king, who had encouraged his subjects to conduct historical research into France's past assemblies, many authors who wrote on the subject of the Estates General implicitly assumed that answers to questions concerning the Estates' proper formation and its role within the government were to be found in the history of the previous assemblies of the Estates General. These authors were certainly aware that other, less historically based arguments were finding their way into public discourse. But as far as they were concerned, any argument that did not take historical precedent as its guide was in danger of substituting philosophical whim for France's historical reality:

> Rather than presume [*prétendre*], like so many frivolous political commentators, to present fantasy as ideas, or to indicate plans that must be followed, or projects to be executed, . . . ; rather than fashion the state to our liking, & remake [*créer de nouveau*] the monarchy; let us content ourselves with indicating historically what from their origin until our own time, the motives, goals, utility, and forms of the various general assemblies of the nation.[4]

Although such a historically based position was ostensibly objective, the very assumption that past assemblies could have relevance for the upcoming assembly inherently implied a particular political outlook. Put simply, such an assumption betrayed a perception that the Estates General was not being convened so much as reconvened after an exceptionally long hiatus.[5]

For those who looked to France's past for the answers to France's future, the resurrection of the Estates General was not, however, a simple matter of taking a political body from the early seventeenth century and inserting it directly into the political context of the late eighteenth century: for the first time in one hundred and seventy-five years, France was faced with the prospect of two political bodies, each of which had a historical claim to national representation. And so the crucial question that had been left unresolved at the turn of the seventeenth century (or rather had been resolved de facto by the advent of absolutism) would now be, once again, of pressing concern: What was the relationship between the king and the Estates General, between the head and the body of the *corpus mysticum*? This time, however, such authors were determined that the question be answered very differently. France would choose the road that it had not taken—that it had not been allowed to take. Sovereignty would be declared the inalienable possession of the nation, and the king would be cast in the decidedly supporting role of chief executive.

Not surprisingly, the historically minded texts of 1787–89 reproduced many of the same arguments that had been articulated by champions of national sovereignty two centuries earlier. Just as Hotman and his contemporaries had delved into the recesses of French history for evidence that the French people had historically been full participants in affairs of state, so too did many of the pamphleteers of 1787–89 paint idealized portraits of France's age-old assemblies, portraying their ancestors, like classical republicans, as having attended to public affairs themselves without need of representatives. In one of the most widely read pamphlets of the immediate pre-Revolutionary period, *Mémoire sur les états généraux,* the comte d'Antraigues looked back wistfully to "the earliest days of monarchy, [when] the nation itself discussed its interests."[6]

The pamphlet literature of 1787–89 was very much following in the footsteps of its anti-absolutist predecessors, therefore, when it delved into the recesses of the past for proof that the nation's leaders had historically never been entitled to decide upon matters of great importance without the consent of the nation. Speaking ostensibly about the national assemblies of the Germains, forefathers of the Gauls, a pamphlet from 1787 declared—with obvious import for the present state of affairs—that "[m]atters of little consequence were summarily decided upon by the leaders of the country. For [matters] that were more important, the gathering and consent of the entire nation was necessary." And then, as if to make clear that the struggle of the nation in the 1780s was the same struggle that had been waged in the sixteenth century (while at the same time, nevertheless, reassuring the king that an Estates General, far from harming his authority, would actually enhance it), the pamphlet offered the following quotation from the sixteenth-century jurist Guy Coquille: "When the king takes the council of his people, he in no way diminishes his majesty, but on the contrary, he renders it more respectable and magnificent."[7]

One of the most striking aspects of the pamphlet literature surrounding the Estates' convocation was the fact that although virtually all pamphlets made a point of drawing a distinction between the nation and the political body of the king, they invariably did not draw such a distinction when speaking of the political body of the Estates General. Indeed, they often used the words "nation" and "Estates General" interchangeably in contradistinction to the king, who was clearly a body apart. A history of the Estates General published in 1788, for example, begins with the following statement: "Almost two centuries have gone by since the nation was assembled in order to deliberate her own interests for herself. The moment has arrived when all those who are animated by patriotism . . . will have the right to declare their opinions freely to a monarch worthy of hearing them."[8]

Clearly, an implicit distinction was being drawn between two very different types of political bodies. On the one hand, there was the political body of the Estates General, which these authors regarded as the concrete embodiment of the nation, a body whose will was a condensation of the actual will of the members of the estates; here, the historically minded authors were invoking the political body of the nation that they found in the writings of their preabsolutist predecessors. On the other hand was the political body of the king. And yet the political body of the king that these authors invoked was decidedly *not* the king of the sixteenth century—the head of a nation whose body was composed of the three estates and who participated in the formulation of the will of the nation by helping to condense the cahiers into one sovereign will. The king that they invoked was instead the political body of the king that was the legacy of absolutism: rather than being the indispensable head of the nation's body, the king was a body unto himself, whose will was formulated separately from the nation's and then—theoretically, at least—superimposed upon it. But whereas Louis XIV, and to a lesser extent Louis XV, had succeeded in having their bodies and their will accepted as those of the nation, Louis XVI had no such success: his was simply a body apart. It was almost as if, from the moment that the Estates General was resurrected in the postabsolutist world, the body of the king—the head of the ancient mystical and political body of the nation—was already expendable.

Despite the general enthusiasm surrounding the convocation of the Estates General, several of the pamphleteers who were particularly mindful of the all too recent heyday of absolutism were wary of all forms of political representation, even that of the Estates General. Such authors worried that the resurrection of the political body of the Estates General might be interpreted as a sign that the nation, on the verge of being restored to sovereign authority, wished immediately to delegate that authority to a new political body rather than exercise that authority on its own. Did not the existence of a political body made up of representatives, a body the nation clearly regarded as the most perfect re-presentation of itself, signify in some sense that the nation desired to delegate sovereignty after all? Did not the very fact of representation signify on some level the people's intent to abdicate their sovereignty?

No! came the resounding response from many political theorists who argued that the advent of representation had been not a choice on the part of the nation but rather a function of practical necessity. Political representation had been born out of the historical impracticability of direct democracy. Once nations progressed from tribes to city-states to nation-states, the self-presentation of the entire populace became increasingly difficult if not impossible; the nation became so large that it simply could not gather in one place, and consequently representatives had to be chosen to speak on behalf of a nation that could no longer speak on its own behalf. Among the more historically inclined pamphlets in particular, the advent of political representation was almost always portrayed as the sad but inevitable expulsion from the political Eden of the people's self-representation. D'Antraigues's comments on the subject are typical of such characterizations:

> As soon as the size of an empire and its immense population place an insurmountable obstacle in the way of a people's gathering, it becomes necessary that [a people] elect representatives to make decisions in its name and according to its will on every subject that is of interest to the republic. The existence of great empires is no doubt unfortunate. They become the scourge of their neighbors, subjugating them and corrupting them. They are equally [a scourge] to their own people, whose first misfortune is to be forced to confide to another their most precious interests. But it is a necessary evil.[9]

If political representation was a practical necessity, about which the nation had little choice, it followed that the existence of representative government in no way implied that the people had renounced its sovereignty: the nation had not *chosen* to abdicate responsibility for its government but had been *forced* by practical necessities to do so. Consequently, the nation had delegated only those tasks it was physically incapable of performing, retaining in theory every other aspect of sovereignty apart from its exercise. Again, to quote d'Antraigues,

> Never can a people be deprived of any rights other than those it is physically impossible for it to exercise. All [rights] which it can exercise it retains; & that is what constitutes its inalienable sovereignty. So a numerous [*grand*] people cannot make laws itself, because it cannot gather together on the public square. From this impossibility is born representation. So that which the people cannot do, it does through its representatives. But from the fact that the people has itself represented, it does not follow that it renounces its existence, its intelligence; it does not follow that it wishes to give itself masters. It follows only that it is through delegates that it wishes to manifest its will.[10]

Perhaps more than any other writer on the eve of the Revolution, the comte d'Antraigues had thought through the implications of the Estates General's resurrection with respect to issues of sovereignty and representation. Although his writings were certainly complex, they were by no means obscure. In fact, d'Antraigues's pamphlet *Mémoire sur les états généraux* was perhaps second only to the abbé Sieyès's infamous *What Is the Third Estate?* in the number of editions that it went through in the period immediately preceding the Revolution.[11] And yet, although d'Antraigues's and Sieyès's pamphlets were both embraced by public opinion, they could not have been more different. For a central tenet of d'Antraigues's work, which as we will see is conspicuously absent in Sieyès's pamphlet, is the fundamental conviction that the *only* aspect of sovereign will that the people had delegated was the *expression* of its will. In short, for d'Antraigues the impending convocation of the Estates General promised an assembly of the nation in which the will of the nation would be re-presented by deputies with virtually no distortion.

Given d'Antraigues's stance on the nation's retention of all aspects of sovereignty apart from its expression, it is not surprising that he seized upon the same device as his preabsolutist predecessors in his struggle to ensure the identity of the nation's will with the re-presentation of that will in a political body. The only way to prevent the despotism of kings from being replaced by the despotism of representatives was, d'Antraigues reasoned, to ensure that representatives were bound by the "law" of the mandat impératif, the age-old practice according to which deputies were limited in their expression to the will mandated by their constituents:

When the national assembly in estates general could meet only through its representatives, a law was formed at the same time that, I dare say, is the guarantor of our liberties. It is that the nation itself remains the possessor of all its powers; and that it is in the [primary] assemblies in which it elects its representatives that [the nation] pronounces its will. Its representatives are simply the bearers of the orders of their constituents, & they can never stray from them. From that time onward, the rights of the Estates General have been the rights of the nation itself.[12]

The binding mandate was so important to d'Antraigues's political outlook that he would devote an entire text to the subject in 1789 entitled *Mémoire sur les mandats impératifs*. But even in 1788, d'Antraigues was clearly aware that public opinion had not sufficiently grasped the fundamental import of the mandat impératif, and he warned his compatriots against the dangers of representatives who strayed from their mandates. In the following passage, from *Mémoire sur les états généraux*, d'Antraigues holds up the inhabitants of fourteenth-century Sens, who disowned their representatives after the latter had violated their mandate, as an example worthy of emulation:

The deputies of the bailliage of Sens [in 1382], having on their own [authority] consented to a tax, were disowned by their constituents, & the tax never took effect. When all of my efforts, when [the efforts] of all good citizens, have no other goal & no other effect than that of strongly engraving into all minds this conservative principle, that our deputies to the Estates General have not been created so that they might decide the fate of the republic, that they are simple mandatories, agents of proxy *[fondés de procuration]* on behalf of their constituents; that in no case, under any pretext, can they stray from the instructions that they have received in their cahier; that if they stray from it they become liars and traitors, & that their constituents have the right to disown them—when, I say, all the *bons esprits* of this century have established only this principle, they will have saved the republic.[13]

Such passionate rhetoric in defense of the sovereignty of the nation helps to explain the enormous popularity of d'Antraigues's pamphlet. In fact, his popularity was such that, within months of writing this pamphlet, d'Antraigues would be elected as a noble deputy to the Estates General. Somewhat more difficult to explain, however, is his stunning fall from grace in the eyes of public opinion. Within a month of the Estates General's official convocation, d'Antraigues had been branded a traitor to the patriotic cause. By February of 1790, this former leading light among the political theorists of the pre-Revolutionary period had emigrated to Switzerland. He would eventually continue on to Italy, where he would be a linchpin of counterrevolutionary propaganda and espionage.

During the Revolution itself, as well as within the subsequent historiography, d'Antraigues's career as a leading counterrevolutionary has tended to overshadow his earlier notoriety as one of the leading "patriotic" political theorists on the eve of the French Revolution. We tend to forget that d'Antraigues's pamphlet *Mémoire sur les états généraux* was second only to Sieyès's *What Is the Third Estate?* in its readership. We tend also to forget that when the Estates General first met in 1789, d'Antraigues was among the better known and most respected members of the assembly.

So what happened? Did d'Antraigues have a change of heart, as many of his contemporaries have suggested? Perhaps, and there is good reason to suspect that his initial enthusiasm with respect to the Revolution was quickly transformed into pessimism. But we should be careful not to assume that this pessimism was based upon blind nostalgia for the old regime. In fact, d'Antraigues's change of heart may say more about transformations within the political realm than about shifts in his own political outlook.

In truth, d'Antraigues's popularity and subsequent vilification may help us to understand important aspects of political discourse in the earliest moments of the Revolution. At the very least, his rise and fall tend to problematize the term "counterrevolutionary," with its inherent implication that those who were branded with this appellation had no ideas of their own beyond blind opposition to the Revolution.[14] Furthermore, his transformation into an enemy of the Revolution affords us a glimpse beneath the rhetorical veneer of the Revolutionaries themselves. For all their protestations against despotism and tyranny, the true victim of the Revolutionaries was not the political body of the king, for in many respects that body was already dead. The true victim of the Revolutionaries was the political body of the Estates General, as it was traditionally conceived, composed of proxies bound by a duly sworn oath to their constituents.

Far from merely opposing revolution, d'Antraigues's texts reveal a conception of national re-presentation that is surprisingly "democratic." In the following passage, for example, d'Antraigues defends the freedom of the forthcoming assembly against the anticipated efforts on the part of the king's ministers to quash its exuberance: "But, the ministers cry out, a numerous assembly is tumultuous; a disorder reigns there that inhibits the course of deliberations; the ardor of speaking there inhibits each individual from developing his opinion; & it is necessary, in order to render the national assembly useful, to establish rules for its interior order." To which objections d'Antraigues replies:

> The assembly of an immense nation is not a [sultan's] divan. Formalities of silence would not be appropriate to it. With respect to the tranquillity being demanded from it, one would think that [the assembly] was supposed to hold its sessions next to the bedchamber of a dying king. I have always said that this taste for silence, this love of severe formalities . . . is the taste of absolutist states . . . such as Turkey . . . where the sovereign is surrounded by the imperturbable silence of tombs.

> Hey! Let these sovereign assemblies do what they like. . . . It is in the heat of
> discussions that citizens achieve clarity; & there is perhaps no instruction more
> profitable than that which they gain from the free and ardent discussion of two
> eloquent men who hold opposing viewpoints.[15]

If we add to this defense of "tumult" d'Antraigues's declaration that "[t]he
third estate is the people & the people is the foundation of the state," he
hardly seems like the typical counterrevolutionary painted for us by the
Revolutionaries.[16]

My point in offering these quotations from d'Antraigues is not to show
that he was an atypical counterrevolutionary. My point, rather, is to make
the claim that counterrevolutionaries were not—or at least did not start out
by being—what we, in the ensuing two centuries, have understood them to
be. With respect to the body of literature produced from 1787 until the convocation of the Estates General, the one essential fact that separated future
counterrevolutionaries from future Revolutionaries was *not* allegiance to
the old regime; neither was it the steadfast defense of the privileges of the
first two orders, or even the desire to relegate the third estate to an ancillary
role.[17] The most important factor separating the two camps—the one that
functions as the most reliable litmus test predicting the future political allegiance of a range of individuals—was faithfulness to the principle of the
binding mandate. As d'Antraigues wrote unequivocally, "[T]he liberty of my
nation is tied to the use of the *mandats impératifs,* and should she renounce
them, then, instead of the tyranny of one, I believe that she would be af-
flicted and dishonored by the tyranny of many."[18]

Because of their nearly unanimous antipathy toward absolutism and their
defense of the sovereignty of the nation, those who were soon to oppose the
Revolution of 1789 were much more apt to quote Rousseau than Bodin or
Bossuet. Rousseau, in fact, despite his purported influence on the Revolutionaries, seems to have been the philosopher of choice for many of the Revolution's critics, particularly because of his anxieties about various forms of
representation.[19] In fact, d'Antraigues prefaced his pamphlet on the binding
mandate with the following epigraph taken from Rousseau's *Considerations
on the Government of Poland:* "I can but admire the negligence, the carelessness, & I dare say the stupidity of the English nation, which after having
armed their deputies with supreme power, applies no brake to regulate the
use that they might make [of that power]."[20]

In truth, one would be at great pains to discern significant differences between Rousseau's practical discussion of representation in his *Considerations on the Government of Poland* and d'Antraigues's views on the subject.
Both looked upon political representation as a sad but inevitable consequence of a nation's physical growth. We might compare d'Antraigues's remarks on the subject, quoted above, with Rousseau's comments that "[o]ne
of the greatest disadvantages of large states . . . is that legislative power . . .

can act only by deputation. This has its advantages and disadvantages, but the disadvantages win out."[21]

Rousseau, unlike so many of the Revolutionaries who would claim to be influenced by him, was as wary of representative tyranny as practiced by assemblies as of tyranny practiced by individual kings. On this point, d'Antraigues was fully in agreement:

> Wherever sovereignty exists outside the people, there is tyranny, because tyranny is nothing other than sovereignty exercised by someone other than the people. The representatives of the people are but the *mandataires* of the people; they do not possess even the slightest portion of sovereignty. [Sovereignty] resides essentially in the people who send [the representatives], without it being possible for the people to place its sovereignty outside itself.[22]

For both Rousseau and d'Antraigues, the binding mandate was of paramount importance and served as the most important bulwark against tyranny by assembly. As Rousseau warned the people of Poland, in addition to assuring the frequent assembly of their Diet, it was necessary to "compel representatives to follow their instructions exactly and to render a strict account to their constituents of their conduct in the Diet."[23]

Despite their insistence on the importance of the binding mandate, however, both Rousseau and d'Antraigues differed from sixteenth-century champions of the binding mandate in their insistence that the deputy's allegiance to his constituency must never stand in the way of the formation of the general will; in the event that the will of the constituency did not prevail in the general assembly and ultimately differed from the general will, then both the deputy and the bailliage whose will he re-presented were bound, in the interest of the nation, to bow to the will of the whole.[24] Nevertheless, both d'Antraigues and Rousseau were adamant that the bond must never be broken between the deputy and his constituency: in the event that their particular will did not coincide with the general will, the deputy and the bailliage were supposed to bow together as an indissoluble unit.

Does all of this mean, then, that in contrast to Rousseau and d'Antraigues and other defenders of the binding mandate, future Revolutionaries were loudly calling for the death of the binding mandate prior to the convocation of the Estates General? Not quite. The politicians of the Revolution were certainly savvy enough to know that outright attacks on the binding mandate would not have been well received in an age that paid such homage to public opinion. (And it would certainly not have made for a clever campaign strategy for candidates to proclaim: Vote for me and I will ignore you.) The manner in which the binding mandate was rendered obsolete was much more subtle, and—to be fair—undoubtedly less self-conscious: self-proclaimed disciples of Rousseau, citing the paramount importance of the general will, would alter the structure of the bonds that united the locality to the representative and the representative to the political body, positing the *latter* bond as unbreakable. The abbé Sieyès and others would for the first time stake the position that each deputy was an integral part of the political whole. In other words, if for Rousseau and d'Antraigues the deputy was bound in an indissoluble unit with his constituency, for Sieyès the deputy was bound with other deputies within the indissoluble unit of the political body of the nation. Sieyès's deputy was a deputy not of any individual locality but of the nation as a whole. And in his extraordinarily influential and widely read pamphlet *What Is the Third Estate?* Sieyès would articulate a profoundly innovative position that would ultimately lead to the justification of a political body bound not to its constituents but to itself—for where else could one find the general will except within the body of the nation's representatives? In contrast to d'Antraigues and Rousseau, then, who regarded sovereignty outside the people to be tyranny, Sieyès regarded sovereignty *outside the political body* to be a particularization of the general will. Sieyès would offer to France a vision of a national assembly of deputies who were at one and the same time endowed with a theoretical mandate from the nation and freed from the particular mandates of constituents—representatives who were, in short, free to do as they pleased in the name of the nation.

The Revolution before the Revolution: Theoretical Novelties of the Winter of 1788–89

The surprising thing about the pamphlets written by those who were soon to usher in the Revolution is how much they shared in common with the pamphlets written by their soon to be enemies. Virtually all pamphlets written during the years 1787–89, regardless of whether they were written by authors who would ally themselves with the Revolution or against it, were united in their calls for the reclamation of the nation's sovereignty and their attacks on a despotic form of government that had robbed the nation of its rights. But beneath this common rhetoric, there is undoubtedly a specific body of texts that contain a variety of radical theoretical novelties that cannot be found in the more historically focused texts. These novelties would soon find their way into the mouths of political actors in the summer of 1789—a fact that is not surprising, given that the pamphleteers and the political actors were often one and the same, many of them having been elected on the basis of the notoriety they had achieved through their writings. It is with reference to both these characteristics—their radical theoretical departure from previous political texts and their authors' future allegiance to the Revolutionary cause—that I term this body of texts "revolutionary."

The novelties expressed in the revolutionary pamphlets were not invented overnight but rather built upon two centuries of theoretical innovation that had slowly transformed both the conception of the national body itself and the conception of the process by which the national body represented itself in political form. Revolutionary pamphlets drew different strands of thought from the previous two centuries of representative theory to produce a new, synthetic political fabric. In common with their future adversaries, revolutionary theorists drew from the rhetoric of anti-absolutist theorists of popular sovereignty at the turn of the seventeenth century, who had privileged the body of the nation over its head, relegating the latter to the status of an appendage; but, in direct contrast to the theorists of popular sovereignty, the revolutionaries borrowed from absolutist representation a notion of proprietary representation by which a political body that exercised sovereignty was also deemed to be in possession of sovereignty itself. And, even if they were to pay lip service to the continuing right of the monarch to rule alongside the Estates General (and later the National Assembly), the revolutionaries also seem to have inherited an unquestioned belief in the indivisibility of sovereignty that had been current among both absolutists and advocates of popular sovereignty at the turn of the seventeenth century. Finally, the revolutionaries had inherited from the relatively recent discourse of the anti-Maupeou theorists of the 1770s a notion of professional representatives who could legislate on behalf of their constituents in a representative body from which the latter had been excluded and relegated to the role of spectator—a body that spoke on behalf of the nation without its tangible input. To these disparate strands of representative theory, the revolutionaries were to add two innovations: they would reformulate the national body into a homogeneous body of equivalent citizens, and they would sever the ties between deputy and constituency so completely that the only substantial bond between the two would be reduced to the moment of election. By sole virtue of election, the National Assembly would be able to proclaim as a political body, in the tradition of absolutism, *l'état c'est nous.*

The definitive historical resource on the pamphlet literature surrounding the convocation of the Estates General remains Mitchell Garrett's 1935 book *The Estates General of 1789,* which contains careful summaries and long excerpts from several hundred of the more important works produced in the years 1788–89. From Garrett's discussion of the literature, it quickly becomes clear that many of the pamphlets, regardless of their political bent, begin with brief journeys through the history of ancient France. This common point of departure is not at all surprising, given the fact that both the historically minded texts and the more radical, "revolutionary" texts took inspiration from the late-sixteenth-century advocates of popular sovereignty. Like all good enemies of royal claims to sovereignty, therefore, the revolutionary authors began with an often-told tale: Once upon a time the people had governed themselves, and only when they became too numerous or too widespread were they forced to delegate the exercise of their sovereignty to representatives. Mirabeau recited the lines from the familiar story as follows: "When a nation has no representatives, each individual expresses his will by himself. When a nation is too numerous to reunite in a single assembly, [the nation] creates many [assemblies] & the individuals of each particular assembly give to one individual the right to vote for them."[25]

For all its similarity to the story presented by the more historically minded pamphleteers, however, we should be careful to note a decided lack of pathos in Mirabeau's version of the birth of representative government. Indeed, for many of the revolutionary authors, if there was anything to be lamented in society's transition from its earlier state it was not the advent of representation, but rather the loss of the communal, nonhierarchical character of France's original national body. As an anonymous pamphlet published in December of 1788 told the story, France had originally been an orderless society, and it had only been the pernicious novelty of the feudal regime that had destroyed this "pure" state through the introduction of social orders:

> By going back to earlier times, we shall find the pure source of our constitution. We can reestablish it as it was under Pharamond and Clovis . . . [when] the nation in its assemblies formed but a single body. . . . It is evident then that the distinction of the three orders has not always existed in France, that this abusive constitution originated at a time when the true principle of government was destroyed, that our veritable constitution is to have assemblies formed of the nation, and that it is the only constitution admissible.[26]

As in d'Antraigues's writing, there is a kind of fall from a better, more natural state within some of the revolutionary pamphlets; however, it is a very different kind of "fall." D'Antraigues had lamented the advent of representation, calling it a "necessary evil," and had insisted that representation must be accompanied by strict adherence to the principle of the binding mandate if representatives were not to become tyrants. For many of the revolutionaries, however, the "fall" came not with representative government but with the advent of social stratification.

The revolutionary pamphlets, then, although partially seeking to recover the sovereignty of the nation from royal usurpation, also sought a historical justification for a society without the qualitative distinction of separate orders. What did they make, then, of the centuries of recorded history that afforded ample proof that the constitution of the French national body had been composed of separate but interdependent estates? In sharp contrast to those pamphlets that had presented archival research undertaken in response to the king's call, when it came to anything more recent than Pharamond or Clovis, the revolutionary pamphlets were often proudly ahistorical. As J. P. Rabaut Saint-Etienne declared in a popular pamphlet, "They lean upon history, but our history is not [the same thing as] our code [of laws]. We must defy this mania for proving what must be done according to what has been done; because it is precisely what has been done about which we are complaining."[27] And what did he propose instead? On what could France's social and political constitution be based if not on historical precedent? Rabaut answers: "[L]aws must be based upon fundamental principles. These principles are reason, equity, public peace, [and] public welfare."[28] As another revolutionary author put it, those searching for the "title-deeds of nations" should consult not historical archives but rather "the archives of reason."[29] And yet another author went so far as to suggest that "if all these traces of our antique representations had found themselves in one single depository, a fire might have consumed them, and we would no longer risk losing our reason among them. Our unhappiness comes, therefore, from having conserved these old archives."[30] Each of these authors almost seems to be rendering his own version of a master script; and indeed, the idea that the archives of history were ultimately irrelevant in determining the proper form of the Estates General, and that instead Reason should serve as a guide, occurs almost without exception in the pamphlets of the revolutionaries.

But what did revolutionary pamphleteers mean by "Reason"? The historian Ernst Cassirer has suggested that Reason, as it was understood within the context of the eighteenth century, was less a body of beliefs or principles than an impetus to deconstruct received truths into their component parts and then construct an entirely new system of thought:

> The whole eighteenth century understands reason . . . not as a sound body of knowledge, principles, and truths, but as a kind of energy, a force which is fully comprehensible only in its agency and effects. What reason is, and what it can do, can never be known by its results but only by its function. And its most important function consists in its power to bind and to dissolve. It dissolves everything merely factual, all simple data of experience, everything believed on the evidence of revelation, tradition and authority; and it does not rest content until it has analyzed all these things into their simplest component parts and into their last elements of belief and opinion. Following this work of dissolution begins the work of construction. Reason cannot stop with the dispersed parts; it has to build from them a new structure, a true whole.[31]

Cassirer's characterization certainly seems apt in the context of the convocation of the Estates General: those who declared themselves to be the standard-bearers of Reason were calling for the destruction of France's traditional national and political bodies and their reconstitution according to a new logic, based upon ideals that were self-evident and abstract rather than historical and tangible.

The divide between those who based their arguments on historical precedent and those who based theirs on abstract reason is most clearly visible in the invocation of the word *constitution*—a term that had enormous importance for everyone, and yet a term that was invoked in profoundly different ways by the two sides of the debate. To the historically inclined political philosophers, the word *constitution* could mean one of two things: it referred either to the bodily constitution of the nation, whether assembled or mystical, or to the form in which the nation's government was constituted, as in the phrase "the constitution of France is monarchical." As far as the revolutionary pamphleteers were concerned, however, the word *constitution* almost invariably referred to a rational body of laws based upon Reason and natural law (in contradistinction to actual historical laws, which were not necessarily reasonable or rational).

From the revolutionary vantage point, a constitution based upon Reason rather than history promised a kind of nonarbitrariness and rationality that the turbulent history of France could never offer as a foundation. As Constantin-François Volney, the author of *Des conditions nécessaires à la légalité des états généraux,* declared, "I open the collections of our laws, and I see there only antiquated and barbarous ordinances, inapplicable to our times, or [I see] modern edicts and statutes that contradict one another and nullify one another. . . . I go through our history, and I see in the life of the nation only trouble, change, and eternal variation." The constitution, if one defined it as a rational, constant system of organization, did not exist. And, Volney argued, even if one could show somehow that France had at some point in the past possessed a stable constitution, that did not mean that present-day French citizens ought to be bound by the decisions of their ancestors: "But suppose that we did have a constitution, [and] suppose that our ancestors consented to or [at least] endured a particular form of government, does it follow that we are compelled to retain it, to abide by it? Certainly not: because it is public law in all the nations that no one can bind another; and it is at one and the same time unjust and absurd that the dead can bind the living, and that one generation can contract on behalf of another." Instead of obliging the living to follow the inconsistent dictates of the past, Volney proposed a different standard to be followed: the eternal, rational, unchanging constitution that exists not in the past but in abstract natural law: "The days of old are uncertain; conventions were accidental; circumstances vary incessantly; the sole essential rights of men, their natural relations within society, these are the eternal bases of all forms of government, here is the indefeasible and constant model, present in all places and at all times."[32]

For those who searched the archives for France's historical constitution, this repudiation of the past and this invention of a new constitution in accordance with abstract ideals seemed like a violent assault upon France's historical body. The comte de Serrant lashed out against Volney's pamphlet in a pamphlet of his own, in which he proclaimed that France most definitely had a constitution, one that was "written in the hearts of the French; it is to be found . . . in the formulas of the royal coronations, and in the most respectable documents of history."[33] The widely respected parlementaire Jean-Jacques Duval d'Eprémémil fumed: "There are some rather imbecilic individuals or at least mean-spirited enough to proclaim that the kingdom has no constitution; this absurdity, however shocking it may be, must nevertheless be refuted very carefully because it has achieved too great a success among superficial minds for it not to be very dangerous to allow it to propagate itself further."[34] And in the remainder of the pamphlet, d'Epréménil went on to show that France indeed had a constitution—one that was not aristocratic or democratic but rather monarchical.

In this debate as to whether France possessed a "constitution," one cannot help noticing that the two sides were speaking a very different language. D'Epréménil's demonstration, for example, that France's constitution was monarchical must have seemed like something of a non sequitur to revolutionary authors who were asking, not how France's government had traditionally been constituted, but rather upon what (written) basis it *ought* to be constituted so as to be stable, rational, and reasonable. As Volney wrote, "Unless I am mistaken, by *constitution* one means *any form of government, expressed in writing, or determined by custom [usage]*, but always with the condition that it be *clear in its principles, identical in its spirit, without equivocation and without contradiction in the clauses of the political contract.*"[35] Whereas pre-Revolutionary society, in order to show the constitution of France, would have produced the political body itself in a general procession (or in a ceremony of royal entry during the reign of absolutism), Revolutionary society would produce instead a written document.[36]

So in contrast to those for whom the constitution was based upon historical precedent, the revolutionaries based their constitution on Reason. And Reason, as I have suggested, demanded the dismemberment of France's historical body; Reason demanded that everything that had existed in the past (apart from the revolutionaries' utopian vision of the earliest days) be branded irrational. But, as I quoted Cassirer above, "Reason cannot stop with the dispersed parts; it has to build from them a new structure, a true whole." What then, for the revolutionaries, was a society based upon Reason? And here the political discourse of the revolutionaries is rather difficult to pin down in concrete terms. The careful reader sometimes feels like the victim of a shell game in which cups are overturned to reveal nothing; abstract terms are often defined by other abstract terms. Reason is anything that is in accordance with natural law. Natural laws are immutable and rational. Rational is anything that is in accordance with Reason. But if we turn over all of the cups at once, we have a better chance of determining what lies behind these terms—what, in short, forms the logical foundation of France's constitution within the revolutionary pamphlet literature on the eve of the Revolution itself.

As I have suggested, the idea that historical precedent should be sacrificed in the name of Reason occurs in virtually every revolutionary pamphlet, although few pamphlets thought it necessary to define precisely what they meant by "Reason." When, however, the Assembly of Notables had been called for the second time in November and December of 1788, to determine once and for all the proper "constitution" of the Estates General, several pamphleteers marshaled Reason to the forefront of their arguments, using the term in rather precise ways. In the following three examples, all written within a few weeks of one another, the authors began with the obligatory attack on the historical form of the French constitution (or lack thereof) and then spelled out precisely what Reason would demand within the specific context of the Estates General's convocation. Their characterizations of Reason, even given the close time frame in which they wrote, are surprisingly specific and uniform.

The first example of a passage that offers a "reasonable" basis for the constitution of the government is from an anonymous pamphlet written around the beginning of December 1788:

> But let us leave aside this whole Gothic collection of dated arguments and worn-out deeds—& this whole useless mass of superstitions. Reason reigns today; it is she who said that it is not good that millions of men should be subject to the arbitrary will of one [man]; and it is she who says furthermore that it would not be good if millions of men were subject to the private interests of several men.[37]

The second example is from a pamphlet entitled "Petition of the Citizens Living in Paris," drafted in mid-December by Joseph-Ignace Guillotin, a respected physician who was soon to be famous for his attempt to bring "Reason" to the realm of justice by encouraging his fellow legislators to invent a "humane" decapitating machine. In the "Petition," however, he is uniquely concerned with the proper constitution of the Estates General:

> If we were to consult simply the natural right of every citizen, [then] within an assembly of the Estates General composed of six hundred members & which would be truly representative of the nation, twelve would be of the clergy, twelve of the nobility, & five hundred and seventy-six of the third estate. Such would be justice. But would it be appropriate? We do not believe so. This justice would seem rather severe, especially to the two privileged orders. . . .
> We demand that our representatives of the Estates General be at least equal in number to that of the other two privileged orders taken together; we wish no longer to be degraded or downtrodden. Thus speaks the third estate. This language is certainly the language of reason, & we cannot prevent ourselves from adopting the principles that form the basis of [this language]."[38]

And finally, the following excerpt is from a pamphlet that was apparently published within a few days of Guillotin's petition:

> It is not, Sire, in the *procès-verbaux* [of the past], which support only force and usurpation, that the composition of the Estates General of your kingdom

should be sought. It is in reason; it is in the proportional population & possessions of the three orders. It is repugnant that an order composed of eighty thousand individuals whose revenues amount to one hundred and ten million should be equal in number within the Estates General to an order composed of twenty-four million individuals whose revenues amount to four hundred and ninety million. . . . The great superiority of our numbers, and the [fact that] our possessions are almost double, entitles us to demand that our deputies form at least two-thirds of the Estates General. But this demand would tend to give us a decided preponderance, and this would not be fair. We will content ourselves, Sire, with asking that our deputies to the Estates General be equal in number to those of the clergy and the nobility combined.[39]

What, then, was the *reasonable* basis for the constitution of the nation? The answer given by all three of the above authors is ostensibly simple: Reason would dictate that the constitution of the representative body be in proportion to the population (or some agreed-upon formula of population and wealth within the population) of the three orders of the nation, and that therefore the third estate would make up the overwhelming majority of the political body. But the apparent simplicity of this answer masks a series of complex assumptions that are left unsaid, and we must be careful to draw them out one by one.

The first and most important assumption that lay behind the argument for a political body that was more nearly representative of the population and wealth of the respective orders was the following simple supposition: it was possible to count individuals from all of the three estates, as if they were essentially comparable units. To the sixteenth-century political theorists from whom many of these writers derived inspiration, this simple act of counting across estates would have been without meaning—the equivalent, perhaps, of comparing the relative weight of the brain and the legs. It could be done very easily, but the fact that one weighed more than the other was meaningless and entirely missed the point that the *qualitative* difference between these two parts of the body could not be expressed in *quantitative* terms.[40]

After calculating the population of each of the three orders, revolutionary pamphleteers often could not help inveighing against the "frightful disproportion" between the population and possessions of each of the orders and their relative influence within the Estates General.[41] And here the pamphleteers assumed the rhetorical high ground: this was not a matter of opinion; this was indisputable mathematical fact. As the author of the last of the three texts quoted above fumed, it was "repugnant" that "an order composed of eighty thousand individuals whose revenues amount to one hundred and ten million" could be equated with "an order composed of twenty-four million individuals whose revenues amount to four hundred and ninety million." The numbers, it would seem, spoke for themselves; the sheer mass of the third estate in comparison with the first two in and of itself exposed the absurdity of the traditional thinking on the question. Throughout the reformist literature, the repetition of population figures took on something of the quality of an incantation, as if the inherent rationality of numbers would expose the irrationality of the existing political system. The anonymous author of the pamphlet *Le tout est-il plus grand que la partie?* (Is the whole greater than the part?)—whose very title played up the inherent mathematical rationality of one side in contrast to the stubborn irrationality of the other—asked his readers what seemed a simple question: "[I]s it not absurd and monstrous to divide a nation [evenly] into three classes, one of which would contain twenty-four million individuals, and the other two only four hundred thousand?"[42]

The assumption, then, behind these repeated cries of disproportion was that the representation of the three orders should be *more* in proportion to their population and wealth. The logic of the revolutionaries demanded, in short, that if the third estate possessed the overwhelming share of population and wealth, then it should have the overwhelming share of representation. But, interestingly enough, very few of the pamphleteers pushed their argument as far as it ought to have been pushed according to their own logic. More commonly, as is evident in the examples quoted above, their carefully constructed arguments trailed off into something of a compromise. The following excerpt from a popular pamphlet by Target is typical of this reluctance to push the argument to its logical conclusion: "There are a million individuals in the two first orders, but there are twenty million in the third estate. I do not propose to distribute the deputies according to this ratio, but it is necessary that the nation have at least as much force as the two privileged orders combined."[43]

Revolutionary pamphleteers therefore made the point that previous assemblies of the Estates General had been wildly out of proportion to the true makeup of the body of the nation.[44] They therefore called for a more equitable system of representation that would more rationally reflect the population and wealth of the three orders. For them, it was a matter of simple mathematics. As Mirabeau put it, "In arithmetic, one does not represent large numbers and individual units with the same sign. In political economy, when one has respect for men, one does not class one hundred individuals with ten individuals."[45]

But is there not an inherent contradiction here? The desire for proportionality among the orders reflects the acceptance of two fundamentally irreconcilable conceptions of representation—one based upon quantifiable and equivalent units, and the other based upon a qualitative breakdown of society into distinct and incomparable parts. To count members of the three orders for the purpose of representation was, in short, to count the population of mystical entities. By the revolutionaries' own definition of Reason, the act made little sense. On the one hand they were assuming a fundamental equality of parts, and on the other hand they were accepting an inherent inequality.

Clearly, many of the revolutionaries were still caught between two very different paradigms. They had begun to conceptualize the national body according to mathematical principles whereby each unit was the equivalent of another, and yet at the same time they spoke of a political body that very much reflected traditional qualitative distinctions. It was almost as if, when they considered the national body, they saw it through the eyes of modern conceptions of natural law, and when they considered the political body, they could not yet entirely bring themselves to abandon the traditional notion of the French bodily constitution. They were willing, therefore, more often than not, to accept a compromise between what Reason dictated and what they somehow felt would be appropriate. In other words, even if it was *reasonable* to argue that the third estate should be accorded the number of deputies that would reflect their preponderant population (and wealth) within the nation as a whole, it was at the same time somehow *unreasonable* to assume that the third estate's share of the political body should be truly preponderant.[46]

We commonly think of the political debate that surrounded the convocation of the Estates General as one that centered on the question of whether the Estates would vote by head or by order. And the participants in the debate themselves certainly saw this as the central question. Once the king decided, in January of 1789, to mollify public opinion by according to the third estate twice as many deputies as the other two combined, in recognition of the third's far larger population, the question of whether the assembly would vote by head or by order became of crucial practical concern. If a vote were taken by order, then the doubling of the third estate's representation would be purely symbolic. If a vote were tallied by head, then the doubling of the third estate's representatives would translate into a doubling of the third estate's influence in the Estates General. And those who advocated voting by head and those who advocated voting by order appeared at the time (as well as in subsequent historical accounts) to be espousing antithetical positions that threatened to create a political impasse. As one pamphlet declared with respect to the debate,

> Entire provinces whose opinion is divided on this important point have already entrusted their deputies with a will that is at one and the same time binding and contradictory, with the effect that the assembly will not be able to choose any position without causing a defection that will immediately paralyze it. . . . [T]he end result will necessarily be that there will be no deliberations at all; . . . [and] we will offer to Europe the most ridiculous and the most shameful of spectacles.[47]

But what the participants in the debate and the subsequent historiography have not recognized is the extent to which, for all of their differences, adherents of *both* positions occupied a liminal space between the early modern and the modern. I have already suggested how the proponents of voting by head were arguing for a political body that offered a proportional and quantitative reflection of a qualitatively distinct mystical body. But the proponents of voting by order were also, despite their rhetoric to the contrary, and most likely unaware of the fact themselves, very much caught up in new ways of conceptualizing the process of political representation. Their obsession with how the orders would vote betrays the fact that they too seem to have lost sight of the traditional reduction of wills through the distillation of the cahiers. They too had implicitly come to accept a theory of representation that privileged the representative over the cahier. They seem to have forgotten that in previous assemblies of the Estates General, the number of deputies had been virtually meaningless, and that often the bailliages would decide for themselves how many representatives to send: it was almost entirely the *quality* of the cahier that mattered, not the *quantity* of deputies entrusted with the task of carrying it.[48] But the fact that so many members of the privileged orders were caught up in the debate over head versus order would indicate that among those arguing for historical tradition, there were many who did not understand that deputies to the Estates had not traditionally "voted" in the modern sense of the word.

One of the few not to have subscribed to this modern logic was the comte de Lauraguais, who, writing before the king had doubled the number of the third's deputies, declared the third estate's quest for more representatives to be meaningless, in that it missed the point that sovereignty was not expressed in the representative's vote and that "the sovereign will of the people of the three estates exists absolutely and only within the cahiers formed in each chef-lieu, & after the compilation and the rewriting of the cahiers of each jurisdiction."[49] And Lauraguais also took note of something else that he seemed to think was eluding the grasp of many of his contemporaries: although the revolutionary pamphleteers claimed that an increase in the number of representatives of the third estate was tantamount to an increase in that estate's influence, one could also argue the opposite. One could point out that, far from furthering the influence of the third estate, such a redefinition of representation (from cahier-centered to representative-centered) instead *lessened* the representation of the third estate in that it "tend[ed] to remove sovereignty from the constituents, and give it to the deputies: & here is what is being patriotically proposed for the good of the people, & that [is being done] in the name of the enlightenment of this enlightened century!"[50]

Lauraguais was, however, a relatively obscure pamphleteer. And his voice reminding his fellow citizens of an age-old process of writing and rewriting cahiers stands almost alone in a sea of voices that (regardless of their ostensible political position) seemed convinced that representation was essentially a process in which constituents voiced their will through the act of electing deputies, and the deputies in turn voiced their will by voting within an assembly. If Lauraguais was one of the few among the more historically minded pamphleteers to resist the internal contradictions of the moment, individuals began to appear on the other side of the political debate who similarly struggled to disengage themselves from the tortured contradictions of the dominant debate.

In November and December of 1788, individual revolutionary pamphleteers were slowly daring to venture into wholly uncharted territory, broaching the possibility that the body of the nation might actually not be composed of three different orders—or at least three *vital* orders. Such individuals did not reject the principle of qualitative distinctions so much as argue for a reconceptualization of their relative importance. Not unlike their sixteenth-century predecessors who argued for the greater importance of the body with respect to the head, certain pamphleteers were beginning to break down the national body into vital components, on the one hand, and what were beginning to seem like useless appendages, on the other. The first sallies in this direction are a curious mix of audacity and reserve: they tend to stop just short of boldly declaring the redundancy of the privileged orders, leaving it to the reader to take that last fateful step. In October of 1788, for example, Jérôme Pétion offered the following thoughts on the true constitution of the French national body: "The third estate people the church, the magistracy, the army; it occupies all the positions which give life and movement to the body politic; it mans the workshops, the factories, commerce; it cultivates and fertilizes the fields; it produces all the goods and services necessary to mankind; to it is due the prosperity of the nation; it is the broad and solid basis—we were about to say that it alone is the nation."[51]

Several different authors had a rather interesting way of making the same point—that the third estate comprised the entire vital portion of the nation—without actually saying it explicitly: in passages that are reminiscent of the sixteenth-century theoretical amputations of the mystical body,[52] these authors indulged in the hypothetical dissection of the national body as a means of determining which portion constituted the vital center. What better method could there be to determine the true organic constitution of the nation, they reasoned, than to suppose a division of the nation along the lines of the three estates and then to ask the loaded question, Which of the parts contains sufficient vital force to live on its own, separated from the other two? Rabaut Saint-Etienne expressed this radical thought in his pamphlet as follows: "Cut off, by supposition, the two hundred thousand people of the church that there might be in France, and you still have the nation. Cut off even the whole nobility, again by supposition, you still have the nation; because a thousand nobles can be created by tomorrow, as was done on the return from the crusades. But if you cut off the twenty-four million Frenchmen known by the name of the third estate, what would you have left? Some nobles and some people of the church? But there wouldn't be any nation anymore. Therefore, it is evident that the third estate is . . . the nation minus the nobility and the clergy."[53] As a pamphlet purportedly written by the citizens of Tarbe put the question somewhat less delicately in a petition to the king: "If the clergy and the nobility should disappear from the face of the earth, you would still have, Sire, a nation of faithful subjects who cherish and admire your virtues; but if the third estate should disappear you would have nothing left."[54] If we add to this the example of another pamphlet, which in the course of asking the same question urged its readers to "[d]estroy by supposition the 400,000 individuals of the two first orders,"[55] we can safely say that even while many were arguing for greater representation within the traditional political body, others were broaching the (ostensibly hypothetical) possibility of dismembering the traditional national body altogether.

While some, then, seemed caught between two contradictory paradigms and insisted on a quantitatively proportional representation of each qualitative estate in the political body, others were clearly more prepared to reject the traditional logic entirely: Why count the members of the various orders, when one could conceivably eradicate the privileged orders as extraneous appendages and have done with the question altogether? It was only one logical step further to argue, as the abbé Morellet did in late December of 1788, that if the nation itself could exist without the privileged orders, then the *political body* of the nation could function very nicely without them as well. In a pamphlet in which he imagined the king's response to the privileged orders' threat that they might secede from the Estates General if it were not constituted to their satisfaction, Morellet declared on behalf of the king:

> Twenty-three or twenty-four million people will not believe themselves to be despoiled of the right to concern themselves with their affairs because two or three hundred thousand nobles or ecclesiasts of the upper clergy (because the clergy of the second rank has all its interests in common with the third estate, to which it actually belongs) do not want to attend the national assembly. I will still have therefore an assembly of the nation [*Assemblée de la Nation*].[56]

Here, in this simple (yet purely hypothetical) proposition, we have the essence of Sieyès's *What Is the Third Estate?* almost a month before the latter was published: a political body composed entirely of the third estate could dare to call itself a national assembly.

Sieyès's *What Is the Third Estate?*—which appeared on the streets of Paris in late January or early February of 1789—is undoubtedly the most widely read of all the pamphlets published on the subject of the Estates General's convocation.[57] Although Sieyès's pamphlet had an extraordinary impact at the time and has been celebrated in the subsequent historiography of the Revolution as well, our overview of the various theoretical novelties prior to

1789 will enable us to see which of its aspects were truly innovative and which followed upon theoretical insights already well established in public opinion. For Sieyès's importance lies not only in his innovative theories on political representation but also in his ability to weave together the disparate strands of existing political thought into a synthetic and rhetorically powerful whole.

Like everyone else, regardless of their political bent, Sieyès made an effort to ground his political philosophy in the past. Sieyès's past was not, however, a concrete historical past but rather a past not unlike Rousseau's state of nature. Sieyès's past was an ur-past, devoid of historical details, perhaps even common to all nations. Sieyès divided the history of political society into three different epochs. In the first epoch, there had been an assemblage of individuals who wished to gather together but had not yet clarified a method for doing so; this epoch was therefore characterized by "a play of *individual* wills." In the second epoch, the individuals gathered together to come to decisions pertaining to the public welfare:

> One sees that here [in this second epoch] power belongs to the public. Individual wills are certainly still the origin and form the essential elements [of this public power]; but considered separately, their power would be nil. It resides only in the whole. The community must have a common will; without *unity* of will [the community] would not be able to achieve a willing and active whole. (123–24)

Here, following Rousseau, Sieyès argues that in the act of coming together individuals merged their particular wills into a unified general will. Sieyès's second stage, in particular, bears a close resemblance to the same old anti-absolutist tale told by so many of his contemporaries: once upon a time the people was in possession of its own sovereignty. And, once again, like so many of his fellow pamphleteers, Sieyès describes the next phase of political society—the advent of representation—as the result of practical necessities:

> Let us make our way through time. The members of the community *[associés]* are [now] too numerous and spread out across too great a surface for them to exercise their communal will easily. What do they do? They detach all that is necessary in order to watch over and attend to public needs and they confide the exercise of this portion of the national will—and consequently of [national power]—to several individuals among them. Here we are at the third epoch, which is to say [the epoch] of *government exercised by proxy [procuration]*.

Sieyès is careful to insist that in giving itself representatives, the community "in no way deprives itself of its right to will; that is its inalienable property; [the nation] can delegate only the exercise [of its will]" (124–25).

We should note that Sieyès's matter-of-fact tone with respect to the advent of representation puts him squarely in the revolutionary camp, which was much more likely to locate the fall from the state of nature not in the birth of representation but in the birth of qualitative distinctions within the national body. On this point, however, Sieyès seems to differ slightly from many of his fellow revolutionary pamphleteers. Some, as we have seen, argued for a kind of hybrid system that allowed for qualitative differences within the political body as long as such differences more nearly approximated the quantitative, proportional breakdown within society; others were so bold as to suggest outright that the privileged orders were theoretically expendable and that a political body could conceivably be formed without them. But Sieyès takes a different tack. Summarily discounting the clergy as an estate,[58] he reserves the bulk of his comments for the nobility, arguing that not only is the nobility extraneous to the national body but it actually functions like a parasitic organism, detracting from the overall health of the whole. Sieyès declares, "[The nobility] is truly a people apart, but a false people who, not capable of existing on its own as a result of a lack of useful organs, attaches itself to a real nation like a fungus *[tumeurs végétales]* that can live only by the sap of those plants that it uses up and sucks dry" (39).

This characterization of the nobility as not only not *of* the national body but actually inimical to it pushed the envelope of revolutionary political discourse. That same January, for example, Mirabeau seemed exceptionally bold to repeat in a public forum the hypothetical dissection of the national body then current in some of the more radical pamphlets. He referred to the third estate as "that order which is so important that without it the first two orders certainly do not form the nation, and which alone, without the first two orders, still presents an image of the nation."[59] But Sieyès, having dismissed the clergy and revealed the true nature of the nobility, argues that the third estate, far from being *enough* of a national body to continue to exist on its own, could actually claim to be *more* of a national body without the order of the nobility: "Who then would dare to say that the third estate does not contain within itself all that is necessary to form a complete nation? . . . If one removed the privileged order, the nation would not be something less but rather something more" (37).[60]

Given his characterization of the nobility as harmful and his dismissal of the clergy as a nonexistent order, one might wonder how Sieyès could reconcile himself to the demands of the third estate that it share power equally with the other two orders in the Estates General. He certainly does not hide the fact that he finds these demands not only insufficient but outdated: "I can not stop myself from repeating: the timid insufficiency of this demand smacks of the old days" (69). Despite such reservations, however, Sieyès forces himself to indulge in the same head counting as so many of his contemporaries: "With respect to the population, the immense superiority of the third estate over the first two is well known. Like everyone else, I do not know the true ratio. But like everyone else, I will allow myself to make my own calculations" (71). Estimating that there are 81,400 "ecclesiastical heads" and 110,000 "noble heads," resulting in a grand total of "not even two hundred thousand," he declares that the figures speak for themselves: "Compare this number to that of twenty-five to twenty-six million souls, and judge for yourself" (73–74).

The claim, then, that these twenty-five million or so should continue to be outvoted two-to-one by the proportionally minuscule numbers of the privileged orders was, for Sieyès, patently absurd; it was a violation of simple mathematical truths: "If therefore one pretends that it is part of the French constitution that two hundred thousand individuals form, as against some twenty million citizens, two-thirds of the communal will, what can one reply except that they are maintaining that two plus two equals five?" (142).

But, one might ask, if Sieyès insists on pointing out that the ratio of two hundred thousand to twenty-five million does not equal two-thirds, then how can he maintain that the same two hundred thousand to twenty-five million equals one half—one of the purported goals of his book? And this is precisely what makes Sieyès's text so clever. As William Sewell has pointed out, Sieyès intentionally undermines the very argument he purports to be defending: "In fact, by the time the reader has finished the chapter [in which he argues for the demands of the third estate], Sieyès has undermined the position for which he ostensibly has been arguing almost as effectively as he has refuted the arguments of the Parlement and the privileged orders."[61]

So what, then, is Sieyès really after, if he does not mean to defend the common position of double representation and voting by head? By reproducing step-by-step the logic of the third estate's demands, he has revealed, as he himself puts it, that it "smacks of the old days." He has shown that it suffers from the same mathematical absurdities as the logic of the revolutionaries' opponents. His ultimate aim is to prove that the ratio of two hundred thousand to twenty-five million equals two hundred thousand to twenty-five million—that *real* proportionality essentially renders the privileged orders statistically meaningless. Real proportionality, in short, demands the eradication of representation by orders; real proportionality demands the dismemberment of the mystical body of the nation into equal, individual units:

Individual wills are the only elements [that compose] the communal will. One cannot deprive the majority of the right to participate in the formation of it, nor decree that ten wills are worth only one as opposed to ten others that are worth thirty. This is a contradiction in terms, true absurdities. . . . The representative body is always, for that which it must perform, standing in for the nation itself. Its influence must conserve the same *nature*, the same *proportions*, and the same *rules*. (142–43)

Despite his claims to be defending the modest demands of the third estate, therefore, Sieyès's ultimate ends are in truth more radical, leading him to the conclusion that an assembly composed only of the deputies of the third estate could "without error speak in the name of the entire nation" (161). And to those who might dare to point out that an assembly composed solely of deputies of the third estate could never claim to be the Estates General in its entirety, Sieyès retorts by proposing a rechristening of the political body that was to prove prophetic: "Well! So much the better! [The third estate] will form a National Assembly" (155). Just as he argued that the national body, stripped of parasites, would "not be something less, but rather something more," so he argues that an assembly devoid of the privileged orders would be superior to one that included them. Not long after the publication of Sieyès's pamphlet, this same idea was expressed rather bluntly by the anonymous author of *Le tout est-il plus grand que la partie?* (who clearly had a penchant for rhetorical questions): "[Is] it not a fact that the third estate forms a more complete national assembly than one in which the two [other] orders would interfere & in which it would have but one vote?"[62]

Our reading of Sieyès's text makes clear that, in his eyes at least, the Estates General was being constituted in an illegitimate manner; regardless of whether the third estate was granted one-third or one-half of the votes in the assembly, any political body constituted according to the inherent disproportion of orders could not claim to be a legitimate representative body. But this brought up a practical question: How was it possible for the nation to determine the proper constitution of a political body without first constituting itself as a political body? Several pamphlets had already put forward the idea that only the Estates General could change the nation's constitution, and they therefore argued that the Estates should assemble according to traditional forms, after which it would then have the legitimate authority to alter the preexisting constitution.[63] But, as Target had pointed out, there was something of a logical problem with this line of reasoning:

> To say that it is for the nation itself to will and ordain the composition of the Estates General is to suppose that the nation can be assembled before it assembles, that it can speak before being able to speak, or that many or a few deputies sent at random according to the fancy of each district will form the nation rather than deputies sent from all parts of the kingdom according to wise rules and in just proportion.[64]

Sieyès, too, was troubled by this question. The idea that the Estates must be assembled before it could be reorganized seemed to him deeply flawed in its logic:

> To whom therefore does [the right] belong to decide? To the nation, independent as it must necessarily be, of all positive forms. Even when the nation will

have its regular sessions of the Estates General, it will not be for this constituted body to decide upon a dispute that touches upon its [own] constitution. There would be something of a begging of the question in this, a vicious circle. (134)

For Sieyès, there seemed to be only one way out of this logical trap. If, like the proverbial conundrum of the chicken and the egg, a legitimate assembly of the nation could not come before a new constitution, and a new constitution could be agreed upon only by a legitimate national assembly, the only answer was to invent an entirely new chicken. In the following passage, which is so important for our purposes that it deserves to be quoted at length, Sieyès puts forward the profoundly radical notion that France must make use of a new type of representation, what he calls *extraordinary* representation:

> *Extraordinary* representatives would have such new powers as the nation pleases to give them. Since a great nation cannot in reality assemble itself every time that circumstances out of the ordinary might demand, [the nation] must confide the necessary powers to extraordinary representatives on such occasions. If the nation could assemble before you and express its will, would you dare to dispute it because it did not exercise it in one form instead of another? Here reality is everything, form is nothing.
>
> A body of extraordinary representative takes the place of *[supplée à]* the assembly of this nation. [The body] does not need to be invested with the *plenitude* of the national will; it needs only a special power, and in rare cases; but it replaces the nation in its *independence* from all constitutional forms. It is not necessary in this case to take so many precautions to prevent abuse of power; these representatives are deputized only for a specific matter and only for a period of time. I say that they are not at all bound by the constitutional forms upon which they are to decide. (1) This would be contradictory, as these forms are undecided; it is for them to determine. (2) They have nothing to say on matters upon which positive forms have been fixed. (3) They are put in the place of the nation itself, having to determine the constitution. They are independent like [the nation]. It is enough for them to will as individuals will in the state of nature; whatever the manner in which they are deputized, in which they assemble, and in which they deliberate, so long as it is not possible to ignore (and how could the nation that appointed them ignore it?) that they act in the capacity of an extraordinary commission of the people, their communal will shall be equivalent to *[vaudra]* that of the nation. (135–36)

It is no exaggeration to say that here if anywhere is the script for the French Revolution. In the above passage, Sieyès lays out his vision of a system of representation in which the representatives are themselves endowed with the right to will on behalf of the people, becoming for all practical purposes the nation itself. Of course, the Estates General had traditionally been regarded as the equivalent of the nation itself, but only by virtue of the cahiers that the representatives carried, bearing the concrete will of the constituents to whom they had sworn a binding oath. The legitimacy of political representatives had therefore rested on this concrete mandate from their constituents. The traditional political body had had the right to re-present the physical being of the nation, and the mandate to voice the nation's will, but it had never possessed the right to determine that will.

Sieyès's political body, by contrast, is possessed of a very different kind of mandate, what we might call a *theoretical mandate* rather than a concrete mandate. The representative has a mandate from the nation not only to *be* the nation for all practical purposes of voicing its will but actually to *formulate* the general will. Possessed therefore of both the nation's *being* and its *will*, the political body is essentially indistinguishable from the national body: "[Extraordinary representation] is subject to no particular formal constraint *[forme]*: it assembles and deliberates just as the nation itself would deliberate if, being composed of just a small number of individuals, it wanted to give a constitution to its government" (137). The representative body, then, far from being beholden to the nation, takes on the nation's moral authority. For all practical purposes, it must be regarded as the nation itself, and the question that Sieyès asked with respect to the nation assembled in its entirety is therefore equally applicable to this political body: "Would you dare to dispute it because it did not exercise [its will] in one form instead of another?"[65]

One cannot help but notice the remarkable similarities between Sieyès's extraordinary representation and absolutism with respect to the manner in which the political body represents. Both political systems endow the political body, irrespective of the natural body or bodies that compose it, with the right not only to exercise the will of the nation but, most importantly, to formulate that will. Sieyès's representative body, far from being composed of *mandataires,* proxies, of the nation, is composed of independent individuals who are endowed with the right to decide on the nation's behalf without formal constraints: "It is enough for them to will as individuals will in the state of nature."

Certainly, there are differences between Sieyès's political body and the absolutist version: unlike the absolutist body of the king, Sieyès's representative body had very little if anything to do with the physical embodiment of the nation. And there were also important differences with respect to not only the number of natural bodies composing the political body but also the manner in which those natural bodies were selected. Nevertheless, it seems difficult to deny a fundamental similarity between the two systems with respect to the formation and representation of sovereign will. And if we are loath to describe Sieyès's representative system as a form of absolutism because of the difference in the manner in which the bodies are constituted, then perhaps "elective absolutism" would be more appropriate.

Sieyès was careful to maintain that he was advocating this extraordinary representation only with specific respect to the determination of the nation's constitution. Perhaps he had the recent American constitutional convention of 1787 in mind, as he seemed to regard this extraordinary body as an exceptional meeting rather than an ongoing legislative body. And he insisted that what he called *ordinary* representatives would continue to function within the bounds of the existing constitutional framework. The two types of representatives could therefore function, at least for a time, in conjunction with one another. Sieyès even went so far as to maintain that the same individuals could perform both types of representative functions:

> I do not want to say that a nation cannot give to its ordinary representatives the new commission of which I am speaking here. The same persons can without doubt participate in the formation of different bodies and exercise one after the other, by virtue of special mandates *[procurations]*, powers that by their nature ought not to be confused. (136–37)

Although Sieyès seems to have escaped the liminal world in which so many of his fellow pamphleteers were caught with respect to the social composition of the political body, judging by this coexistence of ordinary and extraordinary representation one is tempted to say that he too was caught between two different types of political representation. He put forward a profoundly radical conception of political representation, and yet he seems reluctant to dispense completely with the old system, suggesting that they might function simultaneously. A similar ambivalence can be seen in his characterization of the content of each representative's mandate: Is the representative beholden to the constituency that entrusted him with his cahier, or does each representative represent the nation as a whole? Sieyès seems to think the answer is *both*: "[T]he deputies of a district are not only the representatives of the bailliage that appointed them, they are also called to represent the generality of citizens, to vote for the kingdom" (69). Sieyès's representative, at least in January of 1789, seems bound both to his locality by a *mandat impératif* and to the nation at large by a theoretical mandate. As we shall see, his views were soon to change.

One last point is worthy of mention with respect to Sieyès's new representative system, as it helps us to situate him within the context of those who had previously written on the subject of political representation: he seems to have had very clear ideas as to who was suited to play the role of representative. In the following passage, objecting to the argument that the third estate might not have enough qualified members to serve as representatives, Sieyès reveals certain preconceptions as to the type of individual most suited to the position:

> Consider the class of people who are *available* within the third estate; and along with everyone else I call "available class" *[classes disponibles]* that [category within the third estate] in which a kind of comfort level *[aisance]* permits men

to receive a liberal education, to cultivate their reason, and finally to interest themselves in public affairs. This class of people have no other interest than that of the rest of the people. (68)

What might appropriately be termed Sieyès's elitism would be a constant refrain throughout his writings and speeches in the years to come. As several scholars have pointed out, the writings of Adam Smith, and in particular Smith's conception of the division of labor, seem to have been largely responsible for Sieyès's conviction that the job of political representative was uniquely suited to certain individuals; the ideal society was one in which every function—including political representation—was performed by skilled professionals.[66]

In arguing that political representation was best performed by an exclusive class of individuals within the third estate, Sieyès took his place alongside several political theorists who came before him and who had been careful to draw precise distinctions between enlightened public opinion and raw popular opinion. Malesherbes, for example, as we saw in a previous chapter, had spoken of a cadre of "gifted" individuals who "could take the place of those who, gifted with a natural eloquence, let themselves be heard by our forefathers on the Champ-de-Mars." And indeed a whole range of political theorists from Montesquieu forward had been anticipating a time when uniquely suitable individuals might perform the role of representatives on behalf of the nation as a whole.[67] Sieyès's political system, while it theoretically included all eligible citizens (itself a restricted category) in its perfectly proportional system of election, nevertheless excluded from the representative stage all but professionals.

Conclusion

By late 1788, the stage was set for a battle between two revolutionary camps. On one side were individuals who regarded the upcoming Estates General as the restoration of France's legitimate political body. And on the other side were individuals who saw in the Estates General an extraordinary opportunity to fashion a new regime based upon rational principles. To the historical actors themselves, as well as to subsequent historians, the divide between these two camps was epitomized by the debate as to whether the Estates General would vote by order or by head. A vote by order would ensure that the political body reflected the social character of France's traditional, national mystical body. A vote by head would ensure that the political body would be more nearly representative of the proportion of the estates within the general population.

As I have argued in this chapter, however, the two opposing camps, rather than espousing antithetical positions, were both caught in a liminal space between the early modern and the modern. Historically minded pamphleteers who insisted on voting by orders, although they did indeed seek to protect the qualitative aspects of premodern re-presentation, had forgotten that this logic had very little to do with the number of deputies and formal voting procedures, and everything to do with the drafting and redrafting of the cahiers expressing the will of their constituents. And revolutionary pamphleteers, for their part, were insisting on a rational and proportional representation of what was essentially a nonrational and disproportionate conception of the nation as a mystical body.

Within the ensuing months, however, revolutionary theorists would increasingly shake off the logic of the old regime and begin to insist, as did Sieyès, that *true* proportionality was a concept that was incompatible with a logic that divided the national body into qualitatively different parts; a truly representative political body, they would argue, was one that perfectly represented the social and economic makeup of the nation, according to each eligible citizen one and only one vote. Truly proportionate representation, in short, would demand the death of the mystical body and its dismemberment into individual citizens who were regarded as equivalent units for the purposes of representation.

This reconceptualization of the national body was to have a profound impact on the nature of representation itself. For in a national body that has been broken down into individual wills, where each individual is the exact equivalent of another, regardless of what social class or geographical region that individual might belong to, the only corporate entity that has a right to exist is the political body that represents these individual wills, a political body that now has a monopoly on corporate being and expression. Whereas under the old system constituencies were themselves regarded as corporate entities with a right to will, under the new system constituents are individuals, whose wills are inevitably regarded as inferior to the will of the whole. Such a system of representation, for all its claims to give the nation a voice, essentially borrows from absolutism a deep-seated conviction in the infallibility of the representative and a corresponding devaluation of the worth of constituent opinion. Proportionality in the name of the people effectively renders the people speechless, or at least renders their opinions unworthy of being heard. Instead, it is the political actors who make up the representative body, possessed of a monopoly on corporate expression, who are henceforth regarded as the only ones worth listening to. In the following chapter, I trace how this logic, which one can see in its nascent form in the pamphlet literature of 1787–89, was translated from theory into practice during the summer of 1789.

4   Praxis
The Birth of the National Assembly and the Death of the Binding Mandate

In the winter and spring of 1789, elections were carried out all over France in preparation for the first assembly of the Estates General in one hundred and seventy-five years. Although it had been several generations since the traditional political body of France had been formed, the king and his ministers made every effort to re-create the authentic character of previous assemblies. In a note that accompanied the royal regulations concerning the procedures of convocation, the king addressed the third estate, invoking the age-old image of a king approaching his people with the desire to communicate with each one of them:

> His Majesty has desired that every individual from the extremities of his kingdom and the least known dwelling places be assured of having his wishes and complaints reach [His Majesty]. His Majesty can often reach by his love alone that portion of his people that the breadth of his kingdom and the various requirements of the throne [*l'appareil du trône*] seem to make distant from [His Majesty], and who, outside the reach of his gaze, nevertheless rely on the protection of his justice and the foresighted attention of his goodness. His Majesty has therefore recognized, with true satisfaction, that through the means of the gradual assemblies decreed throughout France for the representation of the third estate, [His Majesty] will thus have a sort of communication with all of the inhabitants of his kingdom, and that [His Majesty] will move closer to their needs and their wishes in a manner that is more certain and more immediate.[1]

For the most part, the regulations concerning the convocation stipulated that the members of the three estates should begin the process of forming themselves into a political body in the traditional manner. Primary assemblies of three estates were convened much as they had been in the past, and the instructions given to them for drawing up and then consolidating their cahiers were not unlike instructions given in previous assemblies. Certain aspects of the traditional estates that no doubt contradicted the prevailing definition of Reason were retained. In the principal cities of the realm, for example, the third estate was assembled by various occupational corporations rather than as individuals.[2] In assemblies of the nobility, widows and children who were fief holders, although unable to participate directly, were nevertheless entitled to select proxies to re-present them in their estate's regional assembly.[3] And when all three estates gathered in the district capitals, they were instructed to form a single body according to the traditional manner (clergy on the right, nobility on the left, and the third estate underneath them) in order to receive instructions from the presiding authority, after which time they would separate into their respective estates.[4]

Alongside this very determined effort to re-create the traditional political body of the French nation, the king and his ministers also made concerted attempts to appease those who insisted on a more "rational" system of political representation. Although the question of whether the general assembly of the Estates General would vote by head or by order was studiously avoided, every effort was made to placate both the advocates of tradition and those of Reason when it came to determining how the deputies would be selected.[5] In the following passage from the preface to the regulations concerning the Estates' convocation, the king confesses the numerous difficulties involved in his attempts to reconcile the dictates of traditional qualitative disproportion with those of rational proportion:

> The king, in determining the order of the convocations and the form of the assemblies, has wanted to follow the ancient customs as much as possible. His Majesty, guided by this principle, has retained for all the bailliages that had direct representation in the Estates General in 1614 this [same] privilege consecrated by time, on the condition that they have not lost the character for which this distinction was initially accorded. . . . A result of these arrangements has been that certain small bailliages will have a number of deputies greater than that which would have been accorded to them in a division exactly proportionate to their population; but His Majesty has lessened the negative effects [*l'inconvénient*] of this inequality by assuring to other bailliages a deputation relative to their population and their importance; and these new arrangements will have no effect other than to raise by a little the general number of deputies. However, the respect for ancient customs and the necessity of reconciling them with present circumstances, without harming the principles of justice, have rendered the overall organization of the upcoming Estates General, and all preliminary arrangements, very difficult and often imperfect. This unfortunate result [*inconvénient*] would not have existed if an entirely free course laid out only by reason and equity had been followed; but His Majesty believed himself to be better responding to the wishes of his people, by leaving for the assembly of the Estates General the task of remedying the inequities that one could not avoid and of preparing a more perfect system for the future.[6]

This tortured attempt to appease two irreconcilable constituencies is fascinating in its seemingly genuine embrace of fundamentally incommensurable systems of representation. Like most of the political pamphleteers obsessed with the question of head versus order, the king himself seems to have been caught between the early modern and the modern. Like the advocates of Reason, he too was accepting the proposition that entities that were essentially qualitative could be translated into quantitative terms—that the "character" of each of the bailliages and of each of the estates could be represented in more nearly proportional terms. And like the advocates of tradition, the king believed himself to be following the ancient forms of convocation even while he seemed overly preoccupied with the *number* of deputies. Throughout the regulations, there are precise rules for determining the exact number of deputies allowed at each stage of the process, from preliminary assemblies to the final general assembly. But such rules were wholly out of keeping with instructions disseminated in conjunction with previous convocations of the Estates General, which had tended to leave such decisions up to the localities involved. Apart from the practical considerations of housing hordes of deputies, the number of deputies who actually carried the cahiers from one assembly to the next had in the past seemed relatively incidental to the process.[7]

Toward the end of April 1789, against this confusing backdrop of tradition and "rational" reform, the designated deputies from every bailliage and sénéchaussée in the kingdom, from each of the three estates, had begun to make their way toward Versailles, hoping to arrive in time for the official opening ceremony scheduled for 27 April. One of these deputies, the marquis de Ferrières, deputy of the nobility from Saumur, wrote a series of letters to his wife in which he described both the general political mood and the specifics of the Estates' convocation. Ferrières's letters are remarkable in that they capture France at the precise moment when the political tides were changing, when conflicting currents seemed to be rushing in opposite directions and isolated eddies still swirled in circles, oblivious to the sea change.

The signs of general agitation are very much in evidence in Ferrières's letters, with instances of active unrest occasionally flaring up just beyond his immediate purview. In his letter of 10 April, for example, while relating to his wife the details of his journey toward Paris, he makes note of a recent disturbance in the area: "There was a revolt at Saint-Maure; they were obliged to send in a hundred men from the regiment at Anjou. Bread at Tours costs 5 sols the pound; at Blois it costs 5 sols and a half; the people are alarmed and are afraid of dying of hunger."[8] A few days later, having arrived in Paris, he finds the city in a state of "great fermentation" (29). He seems particularly struck by all the rumors of political schemes afoot in Paris and thinks that they bode ill for the upcoming assembly: "My dear companion," he writes to his wife, "you cannot imagine [the state of this] miserable country. No one wants good [for her]; no one loves her. Our poor Estates will be very stormy" (30).

Despite this "general ferment," Ferrières nevertheless manages to indulge in the traditional pastimes of the aristocracy. He spends the lion's share of his time in Paris attending various dinner parties, and what time is not spent socializing seems to be spent at the theater. Shortly after his arrival in Paris, for example, after a "light" meal at the house of the marquis de Châtre consisting of a dozen or so dishes, he heads for the Théâtre de Monsieur. From his letter to his wife, it is clear that he thought of himself as a relatively sophisticated critic of the arts: "They were performing the *Serva padrona* by Paisiello. What a difference from the one by Pergolesi! No song, no intentionality, no finesse. I was bored; there was practically no one there; and to top off my disappointment, that same day Mme de Todi was giving a concert, but I found out too late"(30–31).

French audiences of the eighteenth century sometimes took as much delight in bad performances as they did in good ones, primarily because of the fodder they could provide for conversation (not to mention the fun of whistling at the actors). Unfazed by his less than satisfactory experience at the Théâtre de Monsieur, Ferrières informs his wife that he plans that evening to attend an opera performance of *Aspasie* "about which very nasty things are said"(31). And then, as if the mention of the opera reminds him of his own upcoming performance, he launches immediately into the subject of the costume he will soon wear at the opening *procession générale* of the Estates: "Let us talk about my wardrobe. My garment of velvet is very becoming; I had it padded. My garment of cloth, with steel buttons, is very smart; I'll add breeches of cashmere, the black garment, and that's it for the ceremony" (31).

That same evening, presumably as he is returning home from the theater, Ferrières passes by the Palais-Royal, the official residence of the duc d'Orléans who has thrown the square open to the public, allowing it to become the center of Parisian street life. At the Palais-Royal, Ferrières encounters a spectacle such as he has never seen before:

> This evening, at the Palais-Royal: one can hardly imagine the people of every type who gather there. It is truly an astonishing spectacle. I saw the circus [pavilion]; I entered into five or six cafés, and there is no comedy of Molière's that rivals the different scenes that lie before one's eyes: over there is a man who is reforming and correcting the Constitution; another who is reading a pamphlet out loud; at a table another is putting the ministers on trial; everyone is talking; everyone has his audience who listens to him very attentively. I stayed until ten o'clock; if I wasn't staying so far away, I would go every evening. (32)

And outside the Palais-Royal, the streets of Paris seem to present their own ongoing spectacle, which, Ferrières seems to suggest, is related to the excitement concerning the upcoming convocation of the Estates General:

Crowds of girls and young people stroll along the streets. The bookshops are filled with men who leaf through [books], read, and buy nothing. Everyone goes to the cafés—everyone suffocates in the cafés, to be precise. Everyone is sure that the Estates will not open on Monday. There will be a beautiful procession. The women of the court will be radiant, covered in diamonds. (32)

Ferrières's next letter to his wife is sent from Versailles, where he has arrived in anticipation of the opening of the Estates only to discover that the opening has been delayed. Almost as if to console himself, Ferrières returns to the subject of his costume, discussing it once again in detail:

And so, my dear companion, our Estates General are not opening. We do not even know exactly when the procession will be. Everything in this country is an object of spectacle. The women of the court will be covered [in jewels], radiant. Here is the costume. *Nobility*: Black garment, silk or cloth; trimming of a more or less magnificent material; coat of silk lined with the same material as the trimming; a vest similar to the trimming: gold or silver brocade. Hat with plumes like that of the knights of the orders; cravat of lace. . . . My crimson vest will be superb; I still need the trimming for the garment and for the coat. But the hat is expensive. The cheapest cost one hundred and twenty livres. (34)

He discusses the official costume of those who happen to be in "ordinary mourning" and those in "great mourning," musing playfully that perhaps he and his fellow deputy of the nobility from Poitiers might be able to come up with "some grandfather or other dead for twenty years" so that they could have an excuse to wear the elaborate costume of those in "great mourning."

And then something odd happens. Ferrières seems to step outside of himself for a moment, as if he were observing himself from a critical distance, as he glories in his costume. And it is clear that he finds something almost tragically superfluous about his ability to ponder his "superb" crimson vest and his other accouterments, while various forces are at work plotting the downfall of the very production for which he is so eagerly preparing. Interestingly enough, despite his fears of popular unrest, Ferrières sees the reactionary nobility as the source of greatest danger:

My dear companion, this [costume] is the amusing and almost ridiculous side of our mission. But how many disturbing things [lie] underneath this envelope of futility: the most damnable intrigues; hate, rage against that poor Necker; a universal plot by the grandees, the parlements, and finance; all that the most vile passions could invent; all the resources of wickedness. (34)

And then, after a few more words about the dire political situation and his sympathy for the unenviable position of the king, Ferrières returns to his next favorite subject: he was not impressed by the music at the Opéra, but found the ballets "delicious" and the scenery "charming" and "voluptuous" (35).

3. Official costume of a noble deputy to the Estates General of 1789. Photo: Bibliothèque nationale de France, Paris.

At Versailles itself, he tells his wife, "we have comedy as well as comic opera; I'll go tonight. Although I'd just as soon make some acquaintances." And finally, at the close of his letter, he returns to the subject of the costumes for the opening ceremony: "I forgot about the costume of the third estate: garment, vest, breeches of black cloth; coat of silk that falls down the front of the garment; cravat of muslin. The legal profession, in lawyer's robes. Isn't that funny? And doesn't it seem like Sganarelle in the *Mariage forcé?* Take a look at the engraving" (36).

In his next letter, Ferrières informs his wife that the opening of the Estates has finally been set for Monday, 4 May. And then he tells her about recent disturbing events in the city of Paris. He traveled to Paris from Versailles to attend a performance at the Opéra. He was thoroughly moved by the production, but upon exiting the theater discovered that, on the other side of Paris, a spectacle of a very different sort had been taking place:

> They were performing *Iphigénie en Aulide* at the Opéra; I wasn't going to miss such a wonderful opportunity. I arrived after the overture; the hall was filled. Oh! My dear companion, what a delicious sensation I experienced; what gripping music. Never have I heard anything that gave me a more lively and profound pleasure.
>
> While I was giving myself over to the tender emotions that moved my soul, blood was flowing in the faubourg Saint-Antoine. Five or six thousand workers, roused by an infernal cabal that hopes to get rid of Necker and prevent the Estates [from meeting], gathered at ten in the morning, armed with sticks, and threw themselves like madmen at the house of a man named Réveillon. . . . [Réveillon's] house was superbly furnished: mirrors, books, chests of drawers, paintings, everything was shattered, thrown out the windows. The Gardes-Françaises discharged several shots, but this served only to excite the mutineers. They climbed on the houses and threw rocks at the soldiers. The Gardes-Françaises came in with cannon; there were many people killed. The tumult lasted until four o'clock in the morning; the number of dead rose to seven or eight hundred. . . . [Some mutineers] were stopping everyone who passed by, asking them if they were of the third estate, and insulted or roughed up those who were of the nobility. (37–38)

The trouble, Ferrières tells his wife, spread beyond the borders of the poorer eastern half of Paris, and several of his noble acquaintances were accosted by the crowd:

> Du Tillet was stopped twice in his carriage; they asked him if he was of the third estate, he responded that he was; they threatened to throw him in the river, saying that he was lying and that he was of the nobility. The duc de Luynes was also stopped coming back from the races and forced to shout, "Long live the king and the third estate!" (39)

The "mutineers," Ferrières is convinced, were put up to this by various parties who encouraged them and even bribed them to take to the streets:

"[T]he abbé Roy is one of the instigators of this awful tumult. It is said that he gave money to the mutineers"(39). Once again, as with the events near Orléans, Ferrières concludes that there will be trouble in the Estates General: "May Providence protect the king and M. Necker. The pretext is the dearness of bread, which is however cheaper in Paris than in the provinces. The Estates will be stormy. Animosity is strong among the orders. They have too much intoxicated the third [estate]; it hardly knows itself anymore"(40). And, finally, no letter to his wife would be complete without a quick report of his latest visit to the theater: "The Comédie de Versailles is good; it's comic opera; the first *loges* are 3 livres. You see that this will be one of my principal resources [in Versailles]. Society consists of retired aides, practicing aides, officers of the king, of the queen and the princes. These kinds of people are not very likable" (41).

So here we are on the eve of the Estates General, and swirling around this aristocratic deputy from the provinces, recently arrived in Paris, are so many different kinds of theater and spectacle that one can disentangle them from one another only with difficulty. Ferrières moves easily between two subjects that are an obvious source of delight to him: the theatrical performances in Paris and Versailles and his own upcoming performance in the opening *procession générale* of the Estates General. He uses words like "delicious," "charming," and "voluptuous" when he describes the former, and words like "becoming," "superb," "radiant," and "beautiful" when speaking of either his own costume or other aspects of the upcoming procession. He is not, however, undiscriminating. He finds the first performance that he attends in Paris to be lacking in "intentionality" and without "finesse," and he is equally unimpressed by the costume for the third estate: "Isn't that funny?" he asks his wife.

The theater is clearly a familiar subject to Ferrières, and he thinks of himself as a knowledgeable critic. The Estates General, of course, is not at all familiar to him. And yet, given the fact that an eighteenth-century aristocrat was in some sense always on stage, performing the various formalities associated with a noble life, it seems fair to say that if he had not yet performed the role of nobleman at the Estates General, he had spent a lifetime rehearsing for the part.

But alongside these more familiar modes of spectacle, Ferrières is clearly aware of something else, and his characterization of the scene in the Palais-Royal is fascinating in this respect. Here is an "astonishing spectacle" that is more, well, *spectacular* than anything he has ever seen before: "No comedy of Molière's . . . rivals the different scenes that lie before one's eyes." But it is almost as if there is too much here for him to take in. He mentions several different scenes being performed simultaneously, each with its own attentive audience. And yet, in spite of (or perhaps because of) the fact that the scene is almost too much for Ferrières to take in, he confesses to his wife that he "would go every evening" if he lived nearby.

And, finally, there is another spectacle taking place, but offstage, in the wings: in the eastern section of Paris, crowds of unruly "mutineers" are turning everything upside down, as if they are performing the rites of some out-of-season carnival. They have destroyed the "superbly furnished" house of Réveillon. And they have poured outside their accustomed districts and accosted personal acquaintances of Ferrières. These aristocrats have been caught in the act of performing quintessentially noble functions (what could be more perfect than returning from the races?); they have been intercepted by these "mutineers" and, in a sense, forced into a different play. Some immediately learn to say the new lines: Du Tillet says he is of the third, but his lines do not ring true, and he is threatened with being tossed out of the production and into the river. By contrast, the duc de Luynes is forced against his will to shout the line "Long live the king and the third estate!" And, as if to compound the theatricality of these disturbing events, all of those involved are apparently not acting on their own behalf but rather have been paid to perform by the abbé Roy and other behind-the-scenes orchestrators of the events.

Amidst this confusing convergence of various forms of theater, both spontaneous and rehearsed, Ferrières and his fellow deputies prepared to perform in the last great political spectacle of the old regime—the age-old metamorphosis of political actors into the living corpus mysticum of the French nation. As the deputies donned their costumes and set out to perform the ritual of the *procession générale,* they were no doubt aware of the forces that threatened the political body that they formed. But the greatest threat to France's traditional bodily constitution did not lie in the eastern section of Paris or in the starving provinces. The greatest threat sat among them, in the form of a significant number of pamphleteers become deputies who, even while they went through the motions of the historic ritual of the act of constituting the nation's political body, had already dismembered that body in theory if not yet in fact.

What is remarkable about the *procession générale* is that, despite the fact that it had not been performed in more than one hundred and seventy-five years, it nevertheless managed to elicit the response that it had for centuries been intended to produce. Ferrières, who fancied himself an enlightened, liberal noble, found himself moved beyond words. He experienced that mystical forgetting of self—that giving of oneself over to something larger and outside oneself—that had always been such a crucial part of political (and theatrical) re-presentation, but that in the modern world would become the exclusive province of religion. His account of his experience in the procession, dutifully related to his wife shortly afterward, is a textbook case of the traditional (political) actor's giving over of his individual body to the mystical whole of the nation's body:

> I love my wife and my children too dearly not to share with them the delicious
> sensations that I experienced [at the opening ceremony].

Monday, 4 [May] we presented ourselves at seven in the morning at the Church of Notre-Dame; they did the roll call of the bailliages. At ten o'clock the king arrived; the fifes, the tambours, the trumpets announced his entry. The chancel was covered in rich cloth. The king placed himself on the right side of the choir screen, on a throne that had been erected. Monsieur [the comte de Provence], M. le comte d'Artois, the princes, the grand officers of the realm, the ministers were seated beneath the king, on benches of velvet embroidered with fleurs de lis. The queen sat [vis-à-vis] the king, on the other side; Madame, Mme Artois, the princesses, and the ladies of the palace, magnificently adorned and covered in diamonds, formed a superb cortege.

The deputies of the three orders, a candle in hand, [marched] two by two. The third estate dressed in black, coat of silk, cravat of batiste; the nobility in garments of black silk, vest of gold brocade, coat of silk, trimmings of gold brocade, hat with plumes, turned up à la Henri IV; the clergy in cassock and square bonnet; filed out before [the king], made a sign of reverence, and, turning toward the queen, did it again. The streets were festooned with tapestries from the furniture repository of the realm, the regiment of the Gardes-Françaises and the Gardes-Suisses formed a line from Notre-Dame all the way to Saint-Louis. An immense crowd of people watched us in respectful silence. The windows, filled with elegantly adorned ladies, offered a truly unique portrait; cries of "Long live the king!" mixed together continuously with the clapping of hands, plunged one's soul into sweet ecstasy. Choruses of music, arranged at intervals, the image of joy and happiness and satisfaction. Soon I lost sight of the spectacle that I had before my eyes; thoughts that were more intoxicating and yet at the same time melancholy came to offer themselves to my spirit. This France, my fatherland, showed itself in all its splendor. And what?—I said to myself— muddled minds, ambitious, vile men, for their own interests, are trying to dismember [désunir] this whole, so great, so respectable, and this glory will dissipate like a light smoke dissipated by the wind? Love for my country, you have made yourself felt very powerfully in my heart. I was not aware just how far the mutual ties extended that unite us all to this soil, to men who are our brothers; I understood it in that instant. Yes, I will swear an oath: cherished thing, France . . . never will I betray the honorable confidence that has been bestowed upon me by placing your interests in my hands; never will anything foreign to goodness, to the advantage of all, determine my judgment or my will. (42–43)

As was the custom, the holy Sacrament accompanied the deputies and the members of the royal court as they made their way though the streets toward the Church of Saint Louis, where all were to take part in a Mass of the Holy Spirit. The meaning of this procession, which was at one and the same time about the spirit of Christ become flesh and the transubstantiation of the corpus mysticum into the flesh of the political body, was not lost on Ferrières; all at the same time, he saw himself subsumed within the greater whole of the nation, and the nation subsumed within God:

> I see here the king, the queen, the powers of the century, render, at least in word, homage to the King of Kings, and say to all, by these exterior signs of respect: We are nothing, God alone is great; to Him alone belongs glory and empire.

I. ACCOMPLISSEMENT DU VOEU DE LA NATION

Vue de la Procession de l'ouverture des États-Généraux sortant de Notre-Dame pour aller à St Louis.

Prise de la Place Dauphine, à Versailles le 4 May 1789.

4. The *procession générale* of 4 May 1789. Photo: Bibliothèque nationale de France, Paris.

Who can, without emotion, hear the melodious songs that precede the triumphal march of the creator Being and the protector of the universe. . . . My heart was penetrated by the most delightful emotion, tears flowed from my eyes. My country, my fellow citizens, the monarch, God himself, everything transformed itself into me. . . . I existed in them, and they existed in me. The same sentiment penetrated all souls; and, far from growing weaker in disseminating itself, it acquired a force that was difficult to resist. (43–44)

On the following day, the Estates convened in the Salle des Menus-Plaisirs, and Ferrières continued to find the whole production worthy of praise: "The assembly was truly imposing, and worthy of a powerful empire; the hall was decorated with nobility, although with simplicity" (45). But the more mundane events of the convocation were certainly not of the sort to inspire the out-of-body experience of the previous day, and Ferrières found his critical faculties returning. Although he found the king's speech "noble and wise," he found Necker's three-hour speech (a large portion of which was delivered by an aide after Necker lost his voice) to be "very mediocre, and very much beneath what one might have expected from a man who enjoys such a great reputation" (45).

If there had been a mystical aura to the events of the *procession générale,* it seemed clear that the aura was rapidly dissipating. In fact, to those who had been less inclined to be swept away by the majesty of the spectacle, signs of discord had been apparent even during the procession. Gouverneur Morris, an American who witnessed the events of 4 and 5 May, perceived a somewhat different spectacle than the festival of oneness in which Ferrières saw himself participating. Referring to the *procession générale,* Morris wrote, "The Procession is very magnificent, thro a double Row of Tapestry. Neither the King nor the Queen appear too well pleased. The former is repeatedly saluted as he passes along with the Vive le Roi but the latter meets not a single Acclamation. She looks, however, with Contempt on the Scene in which she acts a Part and seems to say: for the present I submit but I shall have my Turn."[9]

Morris described the convocation of the Estates the following day in the Salle des Menus-Plaisirs in similarly theatrical terms, calling it a "spectacle more solemn to the Mind than gaudy to the Eye" and referring to the elevated platform upon which the king and queen sat as "a kind of Stage." After a detailed description of the seating arrangements and the costumes of the deputies and the court, Morris offered his judgment on the events; it was, he thought, at one and the same time the final scene of the old regime and the first of the new: "Here drops the Curtain on the first great Act of this Drama in which Bourbon gives Freedom. His Courtiers seem to feel what he seems to be insensible of, the Pang of Greatness going off."[10]

In his account of the Estates General's opening ceremonies, Morris seems struck by certain tensions between the old and the new: "[T]he different

Members are brought in and placed, one Baillage *[sic]* after the other. . . . An old Man who refused to dress in the Costume prescribed for the Tiers and who appears in his Farmer's Habit, receives a long and loud Plaudit. Mr. de Mirabeau is hissed, tho not very loudly." But it was what happened at the conclusion of the king's speech that seemed to Morris a significant indication that the seamless celebration of traditional ceremony was not nearly as seamless as the various orchestrators and many of the participants might have liked:

> After the King has spoken he takes off his Hat and when he puts it on again his Nobles imitate the Example. Some of the Tiers do the same, but by Degrees they one after the other take them off again. The King then takes off His hat. The Queen seems to think it wrong and a conversation seems to pass in which the King tells her he chuses to do it, whether consistent or not consistent with the Ceremonial; but I would not swear to this, being too far distant to see very distinctly, much less to hear. The Nobles uncover by Degrees, so that if the Ceremonial requires these Manoeuvres the Troops are not yet properly drilled.[11]

Was this "incident of the hats" merely the bumbling of political actors inadequately prepared for their roles? Or was it instead the willful resistance of the third estate to a mise-en-scène that required them to sit bareheaded before their betters? The incident was open to both interpretations.

Succeeding events would seem to indicate, however, that the moments in which the spectacle stumbled were due more to discord than to inexperience. The celebration of the united corpus mysticum rather quickly degenerated into a spectacle of disunity. And even Ferrières himself, who had been so carried away by the majesty of the spectacle on 5 May, had in a matter of a mere ten days lost all illusions: "Our Estates General do nothing. We assemble every day at nine o'clock; it is four thirty when we leave; time passes in useless talking, in shouting to the point that no one can hear each other. Everyone wants to shine and make great speeches. The [local] assemblies of Poitiers were tranquil and civilized compared to these. Noise, confusion."[12]

The Estates General that had convened in Versailles that May was, in truth, two Estates General. One was marked by the pomp and splendor of tradition, with deputies who dressed according to their rank and who marched and were seated in a manner befitting the bailliage and the estate of their constituents. This Estates General reflected the organic composition of France's bodily constitution, with its qualitative distinctions between estates as well as between geographic regions. It was essential that the three estates that composed *this* Estates General meet in separate chambers, for if the deputies were to meet in common, then the qualitative distinctions that defined them would be blurred and the political body would meld into a shapeless mass.

At the same time, however, and in the same place, made up of the same deputies, was an entirely different Estates General. This was a body half of which was composed of the people's deputies, and half of which was composed of deputies sent by the privileged orders. If this Estates General was even to approach an approximation of the proportional breakdown of French society, it was imperative that the three orders meet in common. For if the three orders were to meet separately, then the numerical preponderance of the third estate would be meaningless, and 4 percent of the nation would outvote 96 percent of the nation by a margin of two to one.

That the Estates General was paralyzed for more than a month is not at all surprising, given these differing sets of expectations on the part of the deputies who composed it, not to mention of the constituents whom they represented. The third estate refused to do anything at all until it was joined in a common assembly by the other deputies. It would not even take the first step of constituting itself as an official body—the traditional verification of powers which ensured that each deputy's papers were in order and that each deputy had been duly mandated by his constituents to carry their cahier. The deputies of the privileged orders, however, voted to constitute themselves as separate assemblies of their respective orders and proceeded separately to verify their own powers.

Commissions were established to attempt to work out some form of compromise between the privileged orders and the third estate. But a compromise between two such incommensurable worldviews could never have been achieved. Although nearly half of the clergy and perhaps a quarter of the nobility were sympathetic to the demands of the third estate for a common assembly and a vote by head, there was an intransigent core among the privileged orders who insisted on the traditional means of assembly, many citing imperative mandates ordering them to avoid deliberation in common. And so the impasse persisted.

Fresh blood was injected into the proceedings in Versailles when, almost a full month late, the deputies of the third estate from Paris arrived on 3 June, having been detained by special voting procedures that had delayed both the elections themselves and the tallying of results. The presence of these deputies from Paris radicalized and reinvigorated the other deputies of the third estate. And among these Parisian deputies, none was more influential than Sieyès, who only a week after taking his seat declared to his colleagues that the time was ripe to "cut the cable." At his urging, the deputies of the third estate took a bold initiative: they informed the other orders that they would shortly begin the communal verification of powers. They invited the deputies of the first two orders to join them, warning them that if they did not present themselves when their name was called, they would forfeit the right to be present within the common assembly of the nation's representatives.

This unequivocal summons by the deputies of the third estate to the privileged orders did indeed cut the cable that still tethered them to the old regime. The very act of setting themselves up as legitimate authorities implied that sovereign authority was vested entirely in them; they were willing to share this authority with the deputies of the other orders, but only on the condition that the latter join the political body as equals. This cutting of the cable effectively liberated the deputies of the third estate to march unfettered into a new era of politics, while at the same time sending the privileged deputies into a free fall toward redundancy. As long as they had remained the two privileged orders within the bodily constitution of the nation, their importance was assured. Cut loose from the whole, however, they almost immediately verged on irrelevance. As the revolutionary pamphleteers had been telling them all along, the third estate minus the first two was still the nation; but the first two orders minus the third estate were merely the representatives of a few hundred thousand people, who suddenly began to seem a ridiculous vestige of the past, in their plumed hats and crimson vests.

On 13 and 14 June, as the deputies of the third estate proceeded with the roll call of all deputies to present their powers for verification, several members of the clergy took the bold step of defecting to the assembly of the third estate, marking the beginning of the transformation of that body into a common assembly. By 15 June the verification of powers was complete, and Sieyès rose to speak to his fellow deputies. The verification of their powers having been completed, Sieyès told them, they were now ready to constitute themselves as a political body. But what would they call themselves? After all, now that their body was not composed exclusively of members of the third estate, the name "assembly of the third estate" was no longer appropriate. But instead of a name that reflected the social composition of their assembly, Sieyès urged his fellow deputies to choose a name that reflected their inherent legitimacy. Because theirs was the only assembly whose powers had been properly verified, Sieyès argued, they alone could lay claim to the right to articulate the general will of the nation:

> The verification of powers having been accomplished, it is indispensable that we should occupy ourselves with the constitution of the assembly. It is an established fact that as a result of the verification of powers, this assembly is already composed of representatives sent directly by at least 96 percent of the nation. . . . [S]ince [the right] to concur in the formation of the national will belongs exclusively to verified representatives, and [since] all the verified representatives are in this assembly, it is even more indispensable that we conclude that [the right] to interpret and to present the general will of the nation belongs to [this assembly] and that it belongs only to [this assembly]; no other chamber of supposed [*simplement présumés*] deputies can take away anything from the force of the deliberation [of this assembly]. . . . The name of "Assembly of the Known and Verified Representatives of the French Nation" is the only name that suits this assembly in the present state of affairs.[13]

Because the third estate had verified itself, Sieyès seemed to be saying, and because the right to represent the nation belonged to verified representatives, the representatives of their assembly were the representatives of the nation, in contradistinction to other "supposed" representatives of the nation.

But what, precisely, was the difference between a supposed representative and a legitimate representative? And how could one be distinguished from the other? As Sieyès's colleagues pointed out to him, his proposed name, rather than helping to establish the legitimacy of the new assembly, would instead undermine it. By basing legitimacy on the act of self-verification, Sieyès's proposal actually facilitated rival claims to that same legitimacy. As Jean-Joseph Mounier, one of the more prominent members of the as yet un-named rump assembly, observed, "[Y]ou will be forced to abandon the name [Sieyès] suggests to you, because it does not belong to you alone, be-cause the other chambers call themselves verified, and you leave them the right to say it" (123). And Mirabeau concurred, arguing that Sieyès's pro-posal would base the political legitimacy of the assembly on "a simple for-mal dispute, in which our right [to govern] is based only upon very subtle argumentation" (125).

Mirabeau, Mounier, and several other representatives insisted that the as-sembly instead choose a name that might better convey the sense of unique legitimacy the situation demanded. But Mirabeau seemed concerned with something else: the most dynamic speaker among them, and arguably the most politically astute, Mirabeau seemed to grasp the subtleties of the dawn-ing political order. Referring to Sieyès's somewhat awkward, if accurate, proposed name, Mirabeau asked his colleagues, "[T]his name of 'known and verified representatives,' is it really intelligible? Will it jolt your con-stituents who are used to [the name] 'Estates General'?" Instead, Mirabeau urged his colleagues to worry less about accuracy and to choose a name that might prove more—well—*vraisemblable* to the French people: "Do not take a name that is jarring. Find one that no one can challenge, that [is] more smooth *[doux]*" (111).

Mirabeau suggested that they adopt the name "Assembly of the Repre-sentatives of the People of France," assuring his colleagues that the name was "simple, pleasant, incontestable," and revealing, once again, the extent to which he prized palatability over accuracy. Mirabeau's colleagues, how-ever, could not bring themselves to accept a name that seemed to signify nothing, a name that was "smooth" to the point of obscurity: "Does it sig-nify the commons [i.e., the third estate]? If so, it would not say enough. Does it signify the nation in its entirety? That would be saying too much" (114).[14]

This last point, made by Target, perfectly expresses the reluctance of the deputies to acknowledge the fact that they had stepped across the threshold into a new world, that they had in fact already "cut the cable." They had constituted themselves as a political body that laid claim to a monopoly on the interpretation of sovereign will. They knew, therefore, that they were something *more* than the third estate. But were they the sole representatives of the entire nation? For Target, as for many others, this would be "saying too much."

Over a period of three days, from 15 to 17 June, the assembly struggled to name itself. Mounier, like Target, wanted to find a name that expressed the legitimacy of the new body while still acknowledging that it was not the nation in its entirety. Such a convoluted concept required a convoluted name: "Legitimate Assembly of the Representatives of the Major Portion of the Nation, Acting in the Absence of the Minor Portion" (113). It certainly was not ambiguous, but there was something a bit desperate about a political body that would have to remind people that it was indeed the "*Legitimate* Assembly*." Little better was Rabaut Saint-Etienne's proposal: "Assembly of the Representatives of the People of France, Verified by [Their] Co-deputies, Authorized by Their Constituents to Look After Their Interests, and Capable of Executing the Mandates That Have Been Entrusted to Them" (113).[15] Arguably, this proposed name had a certain advantage over Mounier's suggestion in that it explained its legitimacy rather than insisting on it. But as a name, it did not exactly roll off the tongue. In addition to the above, there were three other proposed names, each in turn rejected by the assembly.[16]

On 17 June 1789, despite the complexity and originality of many of the proposed names, the assembly officially constituted itself as "The National Assembly." It was a name that was neither ambiguous nor heavily descriptive. Above all, it was a name that *seemed* legitimate, without overtly insisting on the fact. But it was also a name that laid claim to quite a bit more than many of the deputies had, only days if not hours before, seemed to think themselves worthy of claiming. Were they indeed the representatives of the nation in its entirety, or were they rather, as they confessed in a wordy proclamation that announced their new name, the representatives of "the near totality of the nation *[la presque totalité de la nation]*" (127)?

Even more important, however, is the word that the deputies chose to leave out of their new name. The word *representatives* had been a fundamental part of almost all of the other suggested names. And yet, in the last instance, they chose a name that referred to the object that they represented rather than to themselves. Like all good actors, they knew better than to call attention to the fact that they were acting, that they were not in truth that which they represented.

And so a new political body was born. But a nagging question would, from that moment onward, surround the circumstances of the National Assembly's birth: was it legitimate or illegitimate? Traditionally the legitimacy of the deputies to the Estates General had rested upon the cahiers to whose will they were bound by their mandates. But had the deputies consulted their cahiers before severing themselves from France's traditional political body? They had not. For no one's cahier would have empowered him to make such a move. The deputies had constituted a new political body solely on their own authority, consulting no one's will but their own. In many quarters it was no doubt a popular move. But it was also a move that effectively severed the representatives from the foundation of their legitimacy. As one of

5. The constitution of the National Assembly and the oath of the deputies who compose it on 17 June 1789. Photo: Bibliothèque nationale de France, Paris.

the National Assembly's most impassioned critics would later write, "The assembly . . . is illegal, from the very moment that it arbitrarily changed the form the French constitution prescribed to it; [the assembly] is guilty before its constituents, from the moment that it scorned the commands they gave to it in their cahiers."[17]

But the rules had changed. In the new political order, one no longer needed the sort of tangible, material artifacts of legitimacy that had been so important to the old regime. The National Assembly's legitimacy would come not from its cahiers or from its mandates but from the willingness of the people to regard it as legitimate. Exactly as if the deputies had been modern actors on the theatrical stage, it mattered little whether their performance was *real;* but it mattered very much whether the public regarded their performance as vraisemblable.

So in the very act of constituting themselves as the National Assembly, the deputies had implicitly violated their mandate and turned their back on the cahiers that had been entrusted to them. No doubt they had done so because they felt that they had the nation's best interest at heart. Events had proceeded too quickly for them to think of returning to their home districts to seek permission for their actions. They had done what had to be done on behalf of the nation and for the nation's benefit. But in doing so, they had set themselves up as the arbiters of the national will. Just as Sieyes's writings had assumed the existence of a theoretical national mandate that superseded the local imperative mandate, so the deputies now violated the expressly stated wishes of their local constituencies in the best interest of the nation as a whole.[18]

Because their mandates could not possibly have spelled out precise instructions for such unanticipated events as the formation of the National Assembly, none of the deputies of the third estate had explicitly violated the letter of their powers, although a case could certainly be made that they were bound to appeal to their constituents for approval of their actions. The case of the privileged orders was different, however. Although several members of the clergy had already gone over to the National Assembly, and the nobility had begun to trickle in as well, several of the representatives of the first two estates were, regardless of their personal inclinations, expressly forbidden by their cahiers from entering into any assembly in which the votes were counted by head rather than by order. And so, although no one predicted the birth of the National Assembly, several representatives were nevertheless forbidden by their mandates from joining it.

On 23 June, the king attempted to resolve the crisis presented by the coexistence of the Estates General (or what was left of it) and the National Assembly. In a royal session, he declared the actions of the National Assembly to be null and void and commanded all its members to return to the traditional form of assembly by order. He nevertheless offered as a consolation the possibility that the three orders might be able to deliberate in common on certain issues of mutual concern in the future with his consent, if indeed they chose to do so. In an effort to facilitate such common deliberations, the king urged those deputies with imperative mandates that prevented them from joining in common deliberation to ask their constituents for new powers. More significant, he declared that "in future sessions of the Estates General, [His Majesty] will not permit cahiers or mandates ever to be considered as imperative; they must be only simple instructions confided to the conscience and the free opinion of the deputies who have been chosen."[19]

At first glance, it might seem somewhat surprising that the king, like many of the representatives, regarded the imperative mandate as an impediment to the nation's effective representation rather than as a guarantee of it. But for the king to take this position is not quite as innovative as it might seem. Monarchs had traditionally frowned upon exceedingly strict mandates, as they tended to limit the extent to which the king could influence the proceedings of the Estates General.[20] Ran Halévi is very perceptive in pointing out the "supreme irony" of the fact that "the king ends by achieving what his ancestors never dared to decree or dreamed of obtaining—the neutralization of the mandat impératif—at the very moment that he could no longer profit from it."[21]

Although the royal session effectively decreed the death of the political body of the National Assembly, the king no doubt thought that the promise of future common assemblies might assuage the anger of the third estate's deputies. In this assumption, he was sorely mistaken, and the royal session gave rise to one of the most dramatic moments of the Revolution: despite the fact that the king had expressly ordered the deputies to return to their separate chambers, the deputies of the third estate remained in their seats. The marquis de Brézé, the young master of ceremonies, came into the hall and reiterated the king's orders: "Gentlemen, you have heard the intentions of the king." To which Mirabeau—always one to sense the potential for a great moment of theater—was reported to have replied, "[I]f someone gave you orders to have us leave here, you should ask for orders to use force, as we shall not leave our places except by the force of bayonets."[22]

The king, fearing no doubt that a show of force might spark a general rebellion in the streets of Paris, chose to do nothing. And the longer the deputies were allowed to remain in defiance of the king, the more they seemed to garner for themselves the undisputed mantle of sovereign authority. On the next day, 24 June, most of the clergy went over to the National Assembly, followed on the twenty-fifth by a large group of the nobility. And it was at this moment that the issue of binding mandates presented itself in a manner that could not be ignored (as the third estate had done) or resolved in the future (as the king had suggested). For now, many claimed, it was only the obstacle of binding mandates, those illogical vestiges of an earlier age, that was preventing the vast majority of the privileged orders from joining the nation's true representative assembly. The comte de Clermont-Tonnerre, a representative of the nobility of Paris, who had joined the Assembly, informed his new colleagues of the situation:

> Gentlemen, the members of the nobility who have this moment just joined the Assembly of the Estates General are ceding to the dictates of their conscience and fulfilling an obligation. But bound together with this act of patriotism is a painful sentiment. This conscience that brings us [here] has detained a large number of our brothers. Stopped by more or less imperative mandates, they cede to an impulse as respectable as ours. (153)

What was to be done, then, to resolve this issue? Several representatives of the nobility seemed torn between their sworn obligations to their constituencies and their heartfelt obligations to the nation as a whole; they were, in other words, torn between the mandat impératif by which they were be-

6. Mirabeau delivers his famous line. Photo: Bibliothèque nationale de France, Paris.

holden to the constituents of their locality, and the theoretical mandate by which they were beholden to the nation in its entirety.[23]

On the very next day, the marquis de Lally-Tollendal, another deputy representing the nobles of Paris, who had also just defected to the National Assembly, presented himself as an example of someone caught in the dilemma mentioned by his colleague Clermont-Tonnerre. In a statement presented to the Assembly, Lally-Tollendal declared himself to be torn between his allegiance to his cahier and his allegiance to the nation as a whole. But if we listen closely to his words, we can almost hear a new tone creeping into the discussion of the binding mandate. For rather than presenting it as an equal claimant to his allegiance, Lally-Tollendal seems to characterize the mandat impératif as something that constrained him from doing what he *ought* to do: "Gentlemen, I present myself to this august assembly, a supporter both in heart and mind of its [inclinations], but being in no way the master of my will on all matters." Although his powers had allowed him to take part in communal verification, Lally-Tollendal complained that he was "indomitably chained to [the voting of] opinion by order." Explaining to the Assembly that the very conscience that had compelled him to join the Assembly also compelled him "to return to my constituents and ask them for new powers," he declared that he would return to the assembly only if his constituents granted him free powers. But if they refused, he would have no choice but to resign: "If my liberty is not granted to me, then, gentlemen, I will with resignation give back to my constituents a mission that I would no longer believe myself capable of fulfilling in a productive fashion, and my wishes, my respects will follow you from afar in your noble endeavors" (158). Lally-Tollendal was a man of conscience. And if his constituents refused to allow him to act upon that conscience and insisted on fettering him with their mandated wishes, he would have to resign. Ostensibly, he was speaking specifically of his constituents' orders never to join a common assembly of the three orders. But his tone and subsequent events would seem to indicate that we are not very far here from a repudiation of the very concept of the binding mandate.

No sooner had Lally-Tollendal's statement been delivered to the Assembly than two deputies rushed to proclaim that the Assembly should not allow such an unfortunate set of circumstances to take place. They therefore urged the Assembly to come to a determination as soon as possible on the status of binding mandates. The Assembly, apparently of the opinion that it did not yet have the authority to take this step, decided that the communal verification of powers of all remaining deputies must be completed before the Assembly could legitimately determine the fate of the mandat impératif.

On the following day, the king, having failed in his attempts to destroy the National Assembly, now bowed to what seemed an inevitability. He formally requested those members of the privileged orders who had not yet defected to the Assembly to join it. Although they heeded the king's request, several members of the nobility did so under protest. On 30 June, along with the powers that they reluctantly submitted for communal verification, delegations of the nobility from approximately thirty bailliages handed in *protestations* declaring that, although they were physically joining the Assembly, they would not take part in any deliberations, as their mandates expressly forbade them to deliberate in common with the other orders. The following letter of protest written by the baron de Montagu is a typical example:

> My constituents have sent me to you in order to submit to the bearing of an equal [financial] burden, and to renounce their financial privileges; but they have compelled me, they have bound me to [the principle] of deliberation by order; they even revoke all of my powers in the case that I do not uphold with all my force this article of my cahiers. One must be in accord with one's conscience. (172)

Here, it would seem, was a form of conscience different from (and competing with) the one invoked by Lally-Tollendal, one which demanded adherence to the will of constituents rather than one's own sense of right or wrong.

The National Assembly, rather than addressing the issues raised by the recalcitrant deputies from these thirty bailliages, reiterated that such issues could not be addressed until such time as the powers of all the representatives had been verified. That same day, however, a royal notice was posted that attempted to resolve the problem presented by binding mandates. The king declared that all deputies who felt themselves constrained by binding mandates should instruct the presiding officer in their respective bailliages to reconvene the assembly of their order in their bailliage for the purpose of issuing "new powers [that are] general and sufficient . . . and without any limitations."[24] Once again, the monarch weighed in on the side of unfettered national representation at the expense of local control over representatives.

Who were these various deputies who were claiming that they were prevented by their mandates from participating in the National Assembly? In part, this group included deputies like Lally-Tollendal, who was, as he put it, "a supporter in both heart and mind" of the National Assembly, but who was nevertheless "indomitably chained" by the orders given to him by his constituents. But there was another group of loyal mandataires who appear to have had a much less favorable view of the National Assembly. Although they had heeded the king's request to join the Assembly, they had no intention of taking part in deliberations. In fact, they had not entirely given up on the idea of the Estates General: the majority of the nobility continued to meet as a separate order *in addition to* the sessions of the National Assembly. And it was this group that issued a proclamation on 5 July, reiterating the fact that they still stood firmly behind the traditional forms of the nation's constitution. They declared that the nobility "has never ceased to regard as inviolable and constitutional [the following] maxims: the distinction between the orders; the independence of the orders; the form of voting by order; and the necessity of royal sanction for the establishment of laws."[25]

Every last one of these maxims directly contradicted the sovereign authority of the National Assembly—the very body on which they now sat. And they did not bother to disguise the fact that they held the Assembly in contempt, referring to the "error of an integral part of the Estates General, which has attributed to itself a name and powers that can only belong to the union of all three orders." And so, we might well ask, what were they doing in the National Assembly? They claimed that they had joined the Assembly in "respectful deference" to the king's request on 27 June, but they stressed that they were "acceding to partial and momentary departures *[dérogations]* from the constitutive principles."[26] The "momentary" nature of this departure from the norm might seem wishful thinking, were it not for the fact that, as everyone was very much aware, the king had begun to amass troops in and around the capital. They no doubt hoped that their visit to the National Assembly would be brief; as soon as the king had gathered sufficient strength, he would have the power to restore the Estates General in its traditional form.

In the meantime, however, this group of nobles held up their allegiance to their constituents as the grounds for their refusal to participate in any active sense in the proceedings of the National Assembly. These deputies were, therefore, claiming the rhetorical high ground: they had joined the National Assembly out of respect for their king, but the oath that they had sworn to be faithful to the views of their constituents prevented their taking part in deliberations. As several of the letters of protest on the thirtieth had insisted, this was not a matter of clinging to the privileges of the nobility; rather, it was a question of conscience and of religion. Although not all of the letters of the thirtieth were critical of the National Assembly, several of them contained pointed reminders to the assembled representatives of the sanctity of the oaths that they had all sworn to their constituents. A deputy from Nivernais observed, "One does not negotiate with *[transige]* one's conscience or with an oath." Or, as a deputy from the Limousin declared: "One does not haggle *[marchandise]* with honor; I speak to the representatives of the French nation; who better than they to judge a point of honor" (172). Such mercantile metaphors are simply too pointed to be accidental. The implication, of course, was that the largely bourgeois representatives of the third estate had no understanding of honor and seemed to think that their mandate was like any other commodity: it could be traded in when no longer of any practical use.

These champions of the binding mandate were no doubt something of an embarrassment to the majority of assembled deputies, who were consulting their cahiers less and less as the days went by and as current events seemed to outstrip whatever relevance their constituents' directions may have had.[27] More fundamentally, however, the championing of the binding mandate constituted a threat to the National Assembly's claim to represent the nation, in that it implicitly privileged each deputy's representation of his bailliage over the National Assembly's obligation to the nation as a whole. In short, the principle of the mandat impératif seemed to be an obstacle to the sovereign authority that the National Assembly was claiming for itself, that of voicing the general will of the nation.

On 7 July, these issues were formally addressed when the National Assembly finally took up the question of the mandat impératif.[28] Charles-Maurice de Talleyrand-Périgord, the bishop of Autun, was the one who introduced the subject, noting that the issue of binding mandates had "greatly disturbed people" (200). And Talleyrand jumped right to the fundamental questions at stake:

> What is a bailliage, or a portion of a bailliage? It is . . . a portion of a whole, a portion of a single state, essentially subject to the general will, whether it participates in the formation of it [concourir] or not, but having essentially the right to participate in it.
>
> What is the deputy of a bailliage? It is the man whom the bailliage has entrusted with [the act of] willing in its name, but willing as it would itself will, if it could transport itself to the general meeting place, which is to say after it had carefully deliberated and compared all the positions of the various bailliages.
>
> What is the mandate of a deputy? It is the act that transfers to him the powers of the bailliage, which constitutes him as the representative of his bailliage, and consequently the representative of the entire nation. (201)

Here, unequivocally, the rights of the bailliage are declared to be subordinate to the dictates of the nation. The whole being much more than the sum of its parts, the general will takes clear precedence over the will of any of the bailliages that form a constituent part of it. Who is the deputy of a bailliage, then? Talleyrand, in very subtle ways, claims for the representative a status rather different from that of the traditional mandataire, whose only function was to re-present the original will of his constituents. Talleyrand argues that the representative must will as his constituents *would have willed* if they could have been at the Assembly. The implication, of course, is that the original will of the constituents would have been altered by the act of deliberating with other bailliages; the constituents would have had to listen to the opinions of citizens from other bailliages before arriving at an opinion of their own. In short, there is no such thing as an original will that can be re-presented in perfect transparency. Rather, the will of the constituents of any particular bailliage is not entirely formed until such time as they have deliberated with other bailliages. And, since this process cannot take place without representatives, the will of constituents can be formed only through their representatives in an assembly made up of representatives from all the bailliages. Constituents, in contradistinction to earlier conceptions of re-presentation, must delegate not only the *exercise* of their sovereign will but the act of willing itself.

The representative, then, according to Talleyrand, *wills* on behalf of his constituents. And representatives deliberate together in a political body so that their particular wills might form the general will of the nation as a whole. In a sense, then, each deputy arrives at the Assembly as a representative of his particular constituency and ends up, through the act of consolidating his will with others', as—in the words of Talleyrand—"the representative of the entire nation." This process is not unlike the theoretical consolidation of cahiers in the Estates General, with the crucial difference that it is the wills of the representatives rather than the wills of the constituents that are being consolidated.

In view of the fact that the binding mandate prevented representatives from performing the necessary function of willing, and therefore impeded the formation of the general will, Talleyrand concluded his address with a proposed decree declaring all mandats impératifs to be "completely null [*radicalement nuls]*" (203). He added, however, almost as an afterthought, the following qualification: imperative mandates ought to be considered "completely null with respect to the Assembly, because this nullity is really only relative," in the sense that mandates still obligated the individual deputy even if the Assembly as a whole no longer respected them. And so we have the odd case of a nullity that is both "completely" null and "relatively" null. Talleyrand, not unlike Sieyès in his writings of a few months earlier, is here still clinging to the notion that a deputy can be both a representative of his constituency and a representative of the nation; in the former capacity he can be somewhat limited, and in the latter capacity he cannot be.

Talleyrand was followed shortly afterward by a representative who saw no reason to maintain *any* aspect of the mandate, even in the form of "relative nullity" suggested by Talleyrand. Biauzat proposed that the mandate be declared null both for the Assembly and for the mandataire himself, suggesting the following amendment to the proposed decree: "Without there being a need for deputies to return to their constituents [for instructions], the National Assembly authorizes all of its members and calls upon them to give their opinions according to their heart and their conscience, except in such particular cases that concern their [particular] province" (203). Here, even the modest injunction to begin deliberations by willing as their constituents might will is thrown by the wayside. Link by link, the representatives to the National Assembly were proposing to unchain themselves from their constituents.

Then Lally-Tollendal stood up. He began by reminding the deputies of the unfortunate circumstances that prevented his active participation in the Assembly. He was a living example of the manner in which the mandat impératif was actively interfering with national representation: "I who have so painfully condemned myself [to my current status] and have renounced the honorable right to vote *[décider]* in this august Assembly." And this self-proclaimed victim of his own mandate proposed, in the clearest language to date, the relegation of constituents to a meaningless abstraction of the whole:

> Each portion of society is a subject; sovereignty resides only in the whole assembled *[réuni]*; I say "the whole" because legislative power does not belong to a portion of the whole; I say "assembled" because the nation cannot exercise legislative power when it is divided. [But the nation] cannot deliberate as a whole *[en commun]*. This deliberation of the whole can take place only through representatives; where I see the representatives of twenty-five million men is where I see the whole in which resides the plenitude of sovereignty; and if [this whole] should encounter a portion of the whole that wishes to oppose the nation, I see only a subject who would claim to be more important than the whole. (204)

If the nation was incapable of deliberating as a whole except through its representatives, and if the general will could be expressed only by the totality of the nation after deliberation, then it stood to reason that the general will could be expressed only by the nation's representatives. The nation, therefore, did not exist in any meaningful sense outside of its political body. In this profound inversion of previous conceptions of the relationship between the body of the nation and its political body, the former was declared to be a meaningless abstraction, and the latter was proclaimed to be a reality. The *corpus mysticum* had become a figment of the imagination. The nation, if it existed in any corporate sense, existed in the National Assembly.

How had individual bailliages, these insignificant particularizations of the whole, dared to stand in the way of the nation itself? Lally-Tollendal explained it all away as one big mistake: "The national assemblies had been suspended for such a long time; the latest ones were so unnatural; it was necessary to go back so far to discover political truths, that everyone was mistaken and each individual believed himself capable of arrogating the right to command" (204). Now, presumably, that political truths had been clarified and the locus of sovereign authority had been properly identified, Lally-Tollendal suggested that the National Assembly might take "a short break" so that those who were bound by imperative mandates might explain how things stood to their constituents and seek new, unrestricted powers from them. At the very least, he suggested, such a move would "fend off unjust complaints" by particular constituencies.

But such a position seemed too meek for a political body that was finally laying claim to an unfettered monopoly on sovereign will. As Bertrand Barère, who spoke next, pointed out: "As soon as one declares null the imperative clauses of mandates, what need does one have to go back to constituents [for approval]? It was not we who, nullifying the imperative clauses, exceeded our powers; it is they [the constituents] who exceeded theirs." One did not, in short, rectify a misdemeanor by appealing to the guilty party. It was for the National Assembly, and it alone, to "remedy the abuses of constituent power" (205).

Although Barère's position certainly seems to pay little regard to the status of constituents, he was trumped in this respect by Sieyès, who always seemed to be present at crucial moments in the transformation of representative theory and practice. At the end of the day's session, Sieyès took the podium and made the seemingly simple remark that there were no grounds at all to deliberate upon the question. As he would elaborate the following day, the question itself was moot: it had already been decided on 17 June when the National Assembly had constituted itself as the sovereign authority.[29] Sieyès no doubt believed that the very act of legislating against the binding mandate might give rise to the perception that the National Assembly was not secure in the authority it had already claimed for itself. But the Assembly might, Sieyès suggested, allow itself "a simple declaration" to clarify matters for those parties who had not yet come to understand the new status quo. Sieyès's simple declaration refers to the fact that several bailliages had greatly impaired the effectiveness of their deputies by "indiscreet mandates" and that "by this error" they had harmed their own interests because they had "in such a manner deprived themselves of their direct representatives to the Assembly"—*direct* representation being interestingly redefined here by Sieyès as representation through one's designated representative. The declaration also informed all concerned that "the French nation being always in its entirety legitimately represented by the plurality of its deputies, neither mandats impératifs, nor voluntary absence of some of its members, nor protestations of the minority can ever interfere with its activity" (207).

After a short time, a vote was called. And by a margin of 700 to 28 the National Assembly accepted Sieyès's basic proposal that the proceedings of the Assembly could never be interrupted by "protestations or by the absence of some deputies" and that, therefore, "there are no grounds for deliberation" on the issue of the mandat impératif. The vote may seem more lopsided than it really was, however, given the fact that of the thousand or so deputies, the vast majority of those who supported the mandat impératif would have paradoxically been prevented *by* their mandates from voting against Sieyès's proposal because they had been forbidden by their constituents to vote in a common assembly of the three orders.

On 8 July, therefore, the mandat impératif was declared to have *already* been rendered obsolete some three weeks earlier, when the National Assembly had constituted itself as the sovereign authority. The representatives to the Assembly had spared themselves the potential awkwardness of explicitly proclaiming that they would henceforth allow themselves to ignore the will of their constituents and that any attempt by constituents to control their representatives would be illegal. But perhaps even a greater coup was the fact that the Assembly managed to put something of a positive spin on the eradication of the mandate: because a large number of the mandate's supporters were clearly members of the nobility whose aristocratic constituencies had given them instructions to prevent the formation of a common assembly and to take no part in such an assembly should one be formed, the Assembly was able to abolish the mandate while claiming that it was protecting the national interest. The representatives had conferred an almost absolute power on themselves, and yet because they had cast the mandate as a tool of the aristocracy, they could portray themselves as defenders of the people.

The National Assembly was not, of course, the sole political body in the nation. If constituents had been cleared from the political stage, there still remained the not exactly inconsiderable body of the monarch to contend with. As far as the king's role in the formation of the national will was concerned, many of the aristocratic representatives who had defended the mandat impératif saw the royal veto as a potential bulwark against the monopoly on sovereign authority that the National Assembly seemed to have arrogated to itself. In supporting the veto, these aristocratic supporters of the mandat were joined by several representatives who had actually spoken out against the mandat but who nevertheless believed that the sovereign authority of the representative body might prove dangerous if not counterbalanced by some other authority. Several individuals who had been instrumental in the formation of the National Assembly, including Mounier and to a lesser extent Mirabeau, now advocated some sort of means of balancing the authority of the National Assembly, ranging from a bicameral legislature, with something akin to the British House of Lords, to a royal veto on all legislation. As Mounier would later warn, speaking on behalf of the constitutional committee, "All bodies, no matter what their composition might be, seek to augment their prerogatives: all authority seeks to grow, if one does not erect a barrier against its ambition. The representatives of the people could become the absolute masters of the kingdom if their resolutions were to encounter no obstacle" (585).

The last defense of the constituent mandate within the National Assembly was mounted within the context of this discussion of the royal veto and other possible balances to the authority of the National Assembly. But unlike earlier defenses of the rights of constituents, which had been put forward largely by representatives of the aristocracy who were resisting their incorporation into a common assembly, the criticism of representative authority and the defense of the rights of constituents articulated on 5 September came from a very different quarter and presented a potentially greater threat to the authority of the Assembly. Jérôme Pétion de Villeneuve, a representative of the third estate from Orléans, raised the issue of the constituent's role in the representative process on behalf of ordinary, nonprivileged constituents, posing the question that was to form a staple of the political discourse of the radical left in the Revolutionary period: If representatives were free to do as they pleased without ever having to consult the constituents who had initially elected them, what was to prevent the representatives from behaving like tyrants?

Pétion, unlike the aristocratic defenders of the mandat impératif, was concerned less with the specific principle of the binding mandate than with the general manner in which constituents were being left behind by a Revolution that had supposedly been enacted for their benefit. He professed to be an opponent of the mandat impératif in particular, arguing that "in all ordinary circumstances, nonlimited *[illimités]* powers ought to be vested in representatives." And bearing in mind the overwhelming obligations of the Revolutionary government, Pétion agreed with the majority of representatives that, under the circumstances, the mandat impératif would have been counterproductive:

> Never have the disadvantages of mandats impératifs been more obvious than in this Assembly; when it is a question of uprooting a host of abuses and prejudices; when it is a matter of introducing a new order of things. . . . [A]fter a century and a half of isolation and oppression, how was it possible to dictate to each representative particular orders? (582)

But, Pétion argued, the fact that constituents could not by themselves undertake the vast Revolutionary project did not mean that it was permissible to ignore them entirely from that point onward. The premise of representative government, he reminded them, was "the very impossibility, the most absolute impossibility" of a populous nation's assembling to decide upon matters for itself. Practical considerations demanded that complex issues could be hammered out only through the deliberation of the nation's representatives. But—and it was a point that the vast majority of his colleagues had seemed content to gloss over—the fact that it was impossible for the nation to assemble in order to deliberate as a whole did not mean that it was impossible for the nation to voice its opinion on defined issues. Why was it impossible for citizens to voice their opinions in the form of a simple "yes" or "no" on various issues? After all, Pétion seemed to suggest without making the point explicitly, the people had seemed perfectly capable of coming to a rational decision when it was a matter of selecting their representatives. And he saw fit to remind his fellow representatives of their humble origins as servants of the people's will—origins that they had apparently forgotten: "The members of the legislative body are mandataires; the citizens who chose them are constituents; therefore, these representatives are subject to the will of those from whom they received their mission and their powers.

We see no difference between these mandataires and ordinary mandataires [i.e., proxies in other fields besides politics]" (582). By reminding the representatives of the fact of their election by primary assemblies, Pétion clearly intended to confront his colleagues with the contradictions inherent in their argument: the representatives were denying to particularizations of the whole the right to participate in the formation of the national will; and yet, it was these same particularizations of the whole, in the form of primary assemblies, to whom the deputies owed their election.

Pétion rather boldly declared that the real reason behind the move to deprive constituents of their fundamental right to participate in the formation of the national will was not, in truth, the impossibility of their assembly but rather the low opinion in which constituents were held by the very people whom they had elected to do their bidding: "Many doubts are raised concerning the wisdom of deliberations [in primary assemblies], and these doubts rest upon [the presumed] ignorance of the people." This disparagement of the people, and this willful amnesia on the part of representatives as to their own origin, seemed to Pétion to be tending toward a new oppression of the people by the very individuals who had been entrusted with the task of liberating them:

> In the system that I am attacking, it is the mandataire who is the master and the constituent [who is] the subordinate; the nation finds itself at the mercy of those who ought to obey it; [the nation] is obliged to submit itself blindly to their orders: it is thus that all the people have fallen into slavery; the powers they have been relieved of have been turned against them, and they have been subjugated with the arms they had designated for their own defense.

Disputing the notion that had gained currency within the Assembly that the task of the representative was not only to voice the general will of the nation but to *formulate* it, Pétion lectured his colleagues on the basic principles of the general will: "All individuals who compose the association have the inalienable and sacred right to participate in the formation of the law. No one can be deprived of this right under any pretext and in any government." And, in this respect, Pétion pointedly observed, "a democratic state should be no different from a monarchical state, and it is not without some surprise that I have heard the contrary [position] put forward" (582–83).

Who else but Sieyès could refute such potentially damaging arguments against the National Assembly's monopoly on sovereign authority? As far as the concept of a royal veto was concerned, Sieyès objected to it on much the same grounds that he had objected to disproportional voting in an assembly of three orders. A system that gave any individual—even the king—more votes than other citizens was a system founded upon injustice: "If one will can be numerically worth two wills in the formation of the law, it could be worth twenty-five million [wills]. Then the law could be the expression of one sole will; then the king could call himself the *only* representative of the nation" (593). A royal veto was, therefore, in Sieyès's eyes, an arbitrary act by one individual citizen: "[T]he suspensive or absolute veto, it makes little difference which one, seems to me no more than an arbitrary order; I can see it only as a kind of *lettre de cachet* directed against the national will, against the entire nation" (593).

But Pétion's challenge proved of a different nature and forced Sieyès into theoretical territory that, up until that point, he had not been quite comfortable treading. Only a few months before, in *Qu'est-ce que le tiers état?* Sieyès had seemed to be on the fence concerning the issue now raised by Pétion. Deputies, he had declared back in January of 1789, in what had seemed a radical statement at the time, were "not only the representatives of the bailliage that appointed them, they are also called to represent the generality of citizens."[30] But now Sieyès was being forced to come down on one side of the fence or the other. Was a deputy in any sense beholden to his constituency? Or was a deputy completely independent from his constituents and capable of forming, together with other deputies, the entirety of the national will?

Pétion's challenge compelled Sieyès to clarify certain aspects of the new representative regime that up until this point Sieyès and his fellow representatives to the Assembly had been somewhat reticent to mention. The National Assembly had managed to claim that it was for all practical purposes the nation itself. The very name that the representatives had chosen for their political body reflected their desire to elide the fact of representation itself. But Pétion had called into question the equation of the Assembly's will with the nation's will, insisting that any representative body that attempted to ignore the fact of representation, that turned its collective back on the very people that it purported to represent, was in truth not representative in any meaningful sense of the word, but rather tyrannical. Sieyès's only defense was to criticize the alternative, the direct democracy that Pétion, at least in part, seemed to be advocating. And in attacking direct democracy, Sieyès was forced to call attention to the essentially *representative* nature of the new regime, to the fact of mediation that the Assembly had seemed so intent on glossing over in its assurances that the representative body was tantamount to the nation itself. In the following statement, which very clearly contrasts democracy with representative government, Sieyès, in explaining the advantages of the latter, is not at all reluctant to admit to the elitism that Pétion accused him of and that he already hinted at in his earlier writing:

> [T]he great majority of men [are] only machines of labor. However, you cannot refuse the quality of citizenship and civic rights to this multitude without instruction, that hard labor absorbs entirely. Because they must obey the law just like you, they too must, also like you, participate in its formation. This participation must be equal.

It can exert itself in two manners. Citizens can give their confidence to a few among them. Without alienating their rights, they transfer the exercise [of their rights]. It is for the common utility that they name representatives for themselves [who are] much more capable than they themselves of knowing the general interest and of interpreting their own will in regard to [that general interest].

The other manner of exercising their right [to participate] in the formation of the law is to participate themselves without mediation in making it. This unmediated participation is what characterizes true *democracy*. Mediated participation characterizes *representative government*. The difference between these two political systems is enormous.

The choice between these two methods of forming the law is not in doubt among us. First of all, the very great majority of our fellow citizens have neither enough instruction nor enough leisure in order to occupy themselves directly with the laws that must govern France; they have decided therefore to name representatives; and since it is the opinion of the greatest number, enlightened men must submit themselves to it just like everyone else. (594)

The decision in favor of representative government had, Sieyès declared, already been made by the "very great majority" of citizens who, recognizing their own limitations, willingly acceded to the delegation of the exercise of their sovereignty to individuals better suited than they to perform the task. Such a statement certainly lends credence to the notion, as Pétion had suggested, that a low opinion of "the multitude" was what lay behind the decision to opt for representative over democratic government.

It would be pointless to deny that a strong current of elitism runs through Sieyès's thought. But we would, I think, be mistaken in assuming that the zealousness with which he and others embraced representative government is solely attributable to their low opinion of the great majority of the people. Something else clearly lay behind the impulse toward representation. Sieyès, even more than he embraced the representative system, feared its alternative—not simply because the majority was incapable of running affairs for themselves, but much more importantly because any attempt to incorporate the will of constituents in the formation of the national will invariably threatened the unity of the whole. Sieyès, to put it simply, was the Jean Bodin of his time, prizing the unity of the political body above all else. In the following statement, Sieyès seemed to take direct aim at Pétion, arguing that the very suggestion that the voice of the nation might exist outside the sole political body of the National Assembly was tantamount to advocating a butchery of the nation into small pieces:

I know that by means of distinctions on the one hand, and confusion on the other, some individuals have contrived to consider the national will as if it could be something other than the will of the representatives of the nation; as if the nation could speak in some way other than through its representatives. Here false principles become extremely dangerous. They tend toward nothing less than the cutting, the dividing into small pieces, and the tearing apart of France into an infinity of little democracies, that would then be united only by ties of a general confederation, a bit like how the thirteen or fourteen United States of America have confederated themselves in a general convention.

This subject merits the most serious attention on our part. France must not be an assemblage of little nations, which would govern themselves separately as democracies; it is not a collection of states; it is a unique *whole,* composed of integral parts. (593)

Sieyes, like Bodin two centuries earlier, believed that the state could be saved from disintegration only if the political body possessed sovereignty absolutely and indivisibly. Bodin, of course, had maintained that such indivisibility was much more likely in a political body composed of one individual than in a political body composed of many.[31] But on this point, Sieyes's absolute adherence to the abstract notion of the equality of rights precluded privileging one individual above the whole; he was convinced that, as he put it, "the inequality of political rights [brings] us back to aristocracy" (593). But, we would do well to ask, did not the very nature of representation destroy this perfect theoretical equality? Would not each representative, in other words, have vastly more power than each individual citizen? In his answer to this question Sieyès reveals something very important:

We must therefore recognize and assert that all individual wills are reduced to their numerical unit; and we do not believe that the opinion that we have formed for ourselves of a representative, elected by a great number of citizens, destroys this principle. The deputy of a bailliage is chosen in an unmediated fashion by his bailliage; but in a mediated sense, he is elected by the totality of bailliages. This is why all deputies are representatives of the entire nation. Otherwise, there would be among deputies a political inequality that nothing could justify, and the minority could make law for the majority. (593)

A perfect equality of rights was maintained (among active citizens, at any rate) because each individual participated in an equal fashion in the process of selecting a representative for his locality. Once a representative was selected, however, he no longer formed a part of the mundane world from which he came but became instead a citizen of a parallel universe made up uniquely of representatives who existed, with respect to one another, in perfect equality. If any ties were maintained between a representative and his constituency, inequalities would exist between them; only cut off from their constituencies could a body of representatives function as a kind of egalitarian nation in microcosm, with each deputy playing his role not on behalf of any particular constituency but rather on behalf of the nation as a whole.

The National Assembly, as far as Sieyès was concerned, was a body that was representative in form but not in content: as a body, its purpose was to represent the active citizenry of the nation in a manageable and practical *form*. And constituencies retained all power insofar as determining who performed this role for them was concerned. But in order to play this part of the nation in absentia, in order to deliberate as if they were the entirety of the nation assembled, representatives had to be entitled to form their own will, completely free from interference by their constituencies. Election, in other words, concerned only the choice of the person of the representative and nothing else—the right to choose the specific form of the representation without any means to convey the content of a constituency's will:

> Because it is evident that five or six million active citizens, spread out across more than twenty-five thousand square leagues, cannot assemble in any manner, it is certain that they can aspire only to a legislature by *representation*. Therefore citizens who name representatives for themselves renounce and must renounce [the right] to make the law in an unmediated fashion themselves: therefore they have no particular will to impose. All influence, all power appertains to [the citizens] over the person of their mandataires; but that is all. If they were to dictate wills, it would no longer be a representative state; it would be a democratic state. (594)

Political theorists had for centuries defended the rights of the nation by declaring that in giving itself representatives, the nation had chosen to delegate merely the *exercise* of its will and not sovereign will itself. Sieyès too seemed to imply that constituencies had not delegated sovereign will, but he meant it in a profoundly new and different sense. He did not mean, as had the defenders of the people's sovereignty, that the content of the people's will was transmitted intact and only the act of voicing it or exercising it had been delegated. He meant, rather, that the nation had not delegated sovereign will for the simple reason that the nation was incapable of forming a sovereign will in the first place. The nation, in short, had no will to transmit because the nation did not exist as a corporate entity outside of its representative body. He made this point explicitly in an unpublished note: "The people cannot *will in common* . . . ; it can do nothing in common because it does not exist in this form."[32] The only legitimate function of the people, as individual citizens, as particularizations of the nation, was to select political actors to play the role of free-willed citizens within a national representative political body.

The National Assembly, then, as a representative microcosm of the nation as a whole, was entrusted with the task of formulating the general will exactly as the nation (or the active part of it) would form it if it could assemble in one place. Each representative within the political body would participate in the formation of the national will exactly as if he were a citizen in the national body, gathering in the public square. Representative government, to put it rather bluntly, was to be a pretend democracy, with each representative acting as if he were a citizen on the Champ-de-Mars. Sieyès had broached this subject a few months earlier in *Qu'est-ce que le tiers état?* with respect to *extraordinary* representatives entrusted with the special task of formulating a new constitution, arguing that a body of such representatives would be "put in the place of the nation itself" and that they ought to "will as individuals will in the state of nature."[33] Now he was claiming this prerogative for the National Assembly.

And finally we come to the essence of the logic according to which representatives, acting as if they were on the Champ-de-Mars, must entirely ignore their constituencies. It is because, in Sieyès's view of things, individual citizens formulating the national will in a democratic state do not do so by forcing their preformed, particular wills upon one another; they do so by the process of open-minded deliberation on the public square—a process that necessarily precludes interference by outside parties:

> [E]ven in the strictest democracy, this method [of concerted deliberation] is the only means of forming a common will. It is not the day before, and with everyone in his own home, that democrats most concerned with liberty form and fix their particular opinion, so that it might then be brought to the public square, only [for them] to return home to start all over, once again by themselves, in the event that they were not able to extract from all of these isolated opinions a communal will of the majority. Let us say it outright: this manner of forming a will in common would be absurd. When we gather together, it is in order to deliberate, it is in order to know the opinion of other people, to take advantage of reciprocal enlightenment, to confront particular wills, to modify them, to reconcile them, so as to obtain in the end a common conclusion of the plurality. (595)

One cannot fail to notice the remarkable resemblance between this process of democratic deliberation and the process by which the multiplicity of cahiers had been traditionally distilled into one. With respect to the National Assembly, however, there would no longer be any question of consulting cahiers; the opinions to be distilled would be those of the representatives themselves:

> This [national will], where can it be, where can one recognize it, if not in the National Assembly itself? It is not in consulting particular cahiers, if there are any, that [a representative] will discover the will of his constituents. It is not a matter here of counting democratic ballots, but of proposing, listening, consulting one another, modifying one's opinion, and finally forming in common a common will. (595)

Constituents must be silent because the national will is formed through the deliberation of representatives. And the representatives, in the act of deliberating on the political stage of their imagined public square, must pay no attention to their constituents, who are consequently relegated to the role of political spectators. The representatives, in short, must act as if they were alone on the political stage. They must act as if they were on the Champ-de-Mars, with nothing to contribute to the common deliberation but their own *personal* opinion:

> It is therefore incontestable that the deputies are in the National Assembly not in order to pronounce the will already formed by their direct constituents, but in order to deliberate and to vote freely there according to their opinion *of the moment,* elucidated by all the enlightenment that the assembly can furnish to each one of them. . . .
>
> The people or the nation can have but one voice, that of the national legislature. . . . The people, I repeat, in a country that is not a democracy (and France would not know how to be one), the people *cannot speak, cannot act* except through their representatives. (595)[34]

Exactly as on Diderot's theatrical stage, the actors in this pretend Champ-de-Mars must pretend that their audience does not exist. The real citizens, for their part, "cannot speak, cannot act," but must sit in silence, exiled from the representative space and reduced the role of spectator. Within two decades of its initial elaboration in theatrical discourse, the revolution in the theory and practice of representation had been brought to the political stage.

Conclusion

Over the course of the summer of 1789, as the new National Assembly progressively whittled away at the vestiges of an older form of re-presentation and replaced it with an entirely new system, the dreams of a generation of political theorists were becoming a reality. The National Assembly had succeeded in claiming for itself a monopoly on the right to formulate and articulate the general will, and as a consequence the nation had ceased to exist as a corporate, willing entity. Outside of the one corporate body that was invested with the right to will on behalf of the whole, the wills of the millions of individual citizens could be nothing other than meaningless abstractions of the whole.

The Declaration of the Rights of Man, ratified by the deputies in late August of 1789, was with respect to the issue of representation a bit behind the times. At the very moment that the representatives to the National Assembly were engaged in a debate whose end result would be the elimination of the role of constituents in the representative process, the Declaration still held out the promise that aspects of democracy might coexist with aspects of representative government. Article VI of the Declaration states, "The law is the expression of the general will. All citizens have the right to take part [*concourir*] personally, or through their representatives, in its formation."[35]

But just as Sieyès himself had gone from a position, in January of 1789, that seemed to allow certain aspects of democratic and representative government to coexist to a position several months later that declared the two political systems fundamentally incompatible, so too would French legislation eventually repudiate the sentiments of the Declaration of the Rights of Man concerning representation. The Constitution, when it was finally adopted in 1791, put an end to what must have seemed by then to be the naive illusions of France's legislators in the early days of the Revolution. Unequivocally adopting the principles of representative government, and repudiating the notion that democratic initiative had a place in the new regime, the Constitution declared that "[s]overeignty is one, indivisible, inalienable, and imprescriptible. It belongs to the nation; no section of the of people, nor any individual, can claim to exercise it."[36] With the nation here implicitly defined as the Assembly itself, the people were decisively excluded from the exercise of sovereignty. As the very next article of the Constitution declared, "The nation, from which alone all powers emanate, can exercise [such powers] only by delegation.—The French Constitution is representative."[37] And such delegation of powers was to be undertaken without any strings attached by constituents: "The representatives chosen in the departments will be representatives not of a particular department but of the entire nation, and no mandate may be given to them."[38] What had been the tenuous arguments of political theorists were now the self-confident principles of the Constitution.

Critics of the National Assembly did not, however, wait until 1791 to see on paper what had already been accomplished de facto. Virtually from the moment of the National Assembly's creation, enemies of the new regime would refer time and again to the rejection of the mandat impératif as the moment when the foundation for a new tyranny had been laid. For those who had envisioned a political body composed of bound representatives who transparently reflected the will of their constituents, the actions of the National Assembly were an assault upon the newly reclaimed sovereignty of the French people. As an epigraph to an anonymous pamphlet declared, there simply was no middle ground between an assembly of bound mandataires and an assembly of tyrants: "Either the deputies who sit in the riding hall [of the Tuileries] are the mandataires of the capital and of the provinces, or they are the usurpers and the tyrants of the nation."[39]

Allegations of tyranny, despotism, and usurpation would be frequently leveled against the National Assembly during the years 1790–93. Critics of the Assembly often implied that the Revolution had been co-opted by its politicians and that the true beneficiaries of the new regime were not the

French people but rather the people's *prétendus* representatives.[40] Counter-revolutionary pamphlets in particular spoke of despotism and tyranny under the guise of representative democracy, of political actors free to do as they pleased on a stage from which the French people had been excluded. As comte Murat de Montferrand put it: "[T]o the [National Assembly] and to it alone belongs the [right] to interpret and to present the general will of the nation. . . . [T]he nation itself has ended up deprived of [the right] to express its wishes, its will, since its representatives have arrogated that exclusive right unto themselves."[41]

Although most allegations accusing the representatives of having usurped the sovereign will of the nation were leveled by enemies of the Revolution, it is interesting to note that the radical left occasionally attacked the National Assembly in remarkably similar terms.[42] Just as deputies of the aristocracy had been joined by members of the radical left in the defense of the binding mandate during the summer of 1789, so too would the enemies of the Revolution be joined by pro-Revolutionary radical commentators in their claims that the nation's representatives had arrogated the sovereign will of the people. As the anonymous author of the radical pamphlet *La corruption de l'Assemblée nationale* declared to his compatriots in 1790, if they had any hope of liberty the French people had no choice but to kill all of their so-called representatives, who had turned their backs on the cahiers that had been entrusted to them:

> You have no other choice, you Frenchmen who wish to be free, than to lop the heads of all these perjuring usurpers; afterward, assemble yourselves, not to name representatives who will be your masters & who will decree that the cahiers that contain your sovereign will shall be regarded as irrelevant, but [to name] deputies [who will be] loyal to their mandates, who will have no will other than that which these mandates will manifest, who will never violate them, & who will remain faithful to all the affairs of the people.[43]

If critics of the National Assembly never tired of accusing the representatives of violating their imperative mandates and of effectively removing constituents from the political stage, perhaps no single act better epitomized this general process than the representatives' declaration of their personal inviolability on 23 June 1789:

> The National Assembly declares that the person of each deputy is inviolable; that all individuals, corporations, tribunals, courts, or commissions that would dare to . . . prosecute, pursue, arrest or have arrested, detain or have detained a deputy on the basis of any proposals, decision, opinion, or speech made by him within the Estates General . . . are [guilty of] infamy and treason toward the nation and guilty of a capital crime.[44]

Although ostensibly the principle of inviolability was intended to protect the fledgling National Assembly from the forces of the monarchy in the wake of the royal session that had threatened its very existence, critics of the Assembly were quick to assert that the principle of inviolability was less a defense against royal troops than a bulwark against the French people themselves. Much like Diderot's fourth wall, behind which actors talked amongst themselves, ignoring the very existence of the spectators in the audience, the principle of inviolability entitled representatives, newly freed from their mandates, to act as if their constituents did not exist. As one counterrevolutionary author complained, "They have foreseen everything; their persons and their possessions are inviolable. What does anything else matter to them; it is in vain that you might scream to them that they have made out of society an assemblage of lunatics . . . ; they are deaf to such complaints; they listen only to their own ambition."[45] And here, once again, the counterrevolutionaries and the radical left would find common ground. As the citizens of the Tuileries section would declare in 1793, "[Inviolability is] an odious privilege, a perfidious cloak with which a corrupt representative could cover himself in order to betray with impunity the interests of the people."[46]

Such allegations, whether leveled by the left or the right, went right to the heart of challenging the believability, the vraisemblance of the Assembly's representation. Whereas traditional deputies to the Estates General merely had to show their cahiers to prove their legitimacy and their right to sit in the assembly, these new representatives had no tangible proof of their legitimacy; they were entirely dependent upon the willingness of the political audience to suspend its collective disbelief—to believe, in short, that the people who composed the National Assembly were not simply a bunch of political actors speaking nothing but their own opinions, but rather the legitimate representatives of the nation, accurately reflecting the will of the nation itself. The legitimacy of the National Assembly ultimately depended upon the people's willingness to equate representative democracy with democracy, to take representation for reality.

Recognizing this essential fact that the success of representative democracy depended upon the political audience's willingness to accept the representation as real, critics of the new regime did what anyone who wished to ruin the effect of a theatrical performance might do: they incessantly called attention to the *fact* of representation itself. They tirelessly reminded their compatriots that the National Assembly was composed not of real deputies of the nation but rather of *political actors,* who were merely pretending to represent the nation; and time and again they called upon the people of France to wake up, come to their senses, and realize that they had placed their trust in a mirage. They told the French people that politics had become theater.

The chapters in the second half of this book explore the interplay between theater and politics during the Revolutionary years. The common theoretical foundation of the new theater and the new politics created an environment in which theatrical and political forms merged with one another to such an extent that they became virtually indistinguishable. At times, the Revolutionaries gloried in their theatricality. At times they were profoundly disturbed by it. But the critics of the Revolution were unswerving in their attempts to make France realize that it had put its destiny in the hands of actors.

II
REPRESENTATION IN THE REVOLUTION

5   Métissage

The Merging of Theater and Politics in Revolutionary France

In 1789, the status of dramatic actors in France remained much as it had been for centuries. Officially, they possessed no civil status, and along with Jews, Protestants, and executioners, they were excluded from all forms of political life. As far as the Catholic Church was concerned, actors were in a state of excommunication; Catholics were forbidden to have anything to do with actors, and unless they had renounced their profession before dying, actors were denied a resting place on holy ground. Unofficially, although the incessant vilification of actors by the Catholic Church had abated somewhat by the middle of the eighteenth century, the social stigma had endured. In the public mind, actors—*comédiens*[1]—remained immoral, incontinent vagabonds, who roamed provincial villages, presenting scandalous spectacles both on and off the stage. Even the more "respectable" actors who performed in the larger cities, often as part of established theater companies, were often not spared the general opprobrium attached to their profession. As a young actor who was performing at the theater of Bordeaux wrote to his friend in 1772, "Actors are reviled here [in Bordeaux]. If an honest man . . . sees in you qualities worthy of esteem, he would never say so aloud; he would only dare call himself your friend when there are no witnesses."[2] Twenty years after writing these lines, the (former) actor Jean-Marie Collot d'Herbois had become one of the most important political figures in all of France. As one of the twelve members of the all-powerful Committee of Public Safety that ruled France during the Terror, the former social outcast had moved to the very center of power.

Collot d'Herbois's journey from the theatrical to the political stage is certainly remarkable, particularly given the stigma attached to actors even in the late eighteenth century. Even more extraordinary, however, is the fact that he was not alone: almost at the very moment of the Revolution's birth, actors rushed to fill positions of prominence in the Revolutionary government, administration, and military. The reaction of nontheatrical contemporaries to actors' involvement in the Revolution ranged from horror and confusion to acceptance of the actors' new role as the necessary and positive outcome of the Revolutionary agenda on natural rights.

Individuals who were suspicious of the Revolution recoiled in horror at what they perceived to be a veritable swarm of actors making their way onto the political stage; here, they thought, was tangible proof of the general theatricalization of French politics and society for which the Revolution was to blame. Almost as if they were witnessing the crumbling of a barrier that had previously separated raw sewage from fresh water, these individuals reacted as if their world was being contaminated by profane beings who only months before had been kept at bay by an officially sanctioned cordon sanitaire. Even for many individuals who were sympathetic to the Revolution, this swirling together of previously discrete forms was a source of great worry and confusion: the Revolution had given birth to a world in which actors mixed familiarly with politicians and in which the political and the theatrical intermingled to such a great extent that neither was properly distinguishable from the other.

In this chapter, I am primarily concerned with establishing the very *fact* of this intermingling. From theatrical actors who embraced political careers, to the pronounced theatricality of Revolutionary politics, to the overwhelming importance of spectacles for the Revolutionary government(s), I am here concerned with assembling in one place the various personages and entities that occupied this new theatrico-political "site" brought into existence by the Revolution.[3]

Political Actors

On the eve of the storming of the Bastille, when the inhabitants of Paris took up arms between 12 and 14 July 1789, with the intention both of fighting the royal troops and of imposing order on the increasingly chaotic situation, a municipal guard militia (soon to be called the National Guard) was spontaneously created.[4] Each district formed its own detachment made up of volunteers from the neighborhood. And theatrical actors, like the other inhabitants of Paris who were comfortable enough financially to be able to properly equip themselves, joined in the formation of these detachments. Actors joined detachments primarily in the Cordeliers district and in the St.-André-des-Arts district, the two districts that not coincidentally housed the more prominent theaters of Paris. Of the actors who volunteered, several were elected to high-ranking positions in the guard. In the following statement, Jean-Baptiste Naudet, an actor at the Théâtre-Français, modestly describes how he came to assume command of the guard in his district:

During the time of the revolution, on 13 July, disturbed by the rumors that were spreading around Paris, & sharing the alarm of my fellow citizens, I reported to my district, in order to share in their danger and their duties: I was entrusted with the command of a post, which I eagerly accepted. My post was at the Théâtre-Français.

I found myself at the head of forty-three individuals, among whom numbered comédiens. We entrenched ourselves in a location that we believed would be one of those by which the [royal] troops would enter. I was in charge of this fortification. Saint-Prix [also an actor at the Théâtre-Français] brought over some lead, out of which I made two thousand bullets. M. Dugazon [another actor at the Théâtre-Français] furnished a barrel of gunpowder; I prepared cartridges. The Parisians showed a great deal of courage, which I augmented, if at all possible, by raising their level of confidence; & I can say that the post we manned would have been well defended [had it been attacked]. I ask no thanks for what occurred; I intend only to praise the courage of my fellow citizens.[5]

Naudet is careful here to downplay any ambitions on his part. His assumption of command seems natural enough: he "found" himself at the head of a small detachment, and he did his best to encourage those under his command. Nowhere in the above statement does Naudet betray any sense that his assumption of military command was at all incongruous with his profession, and indeed he mentions casually enough that several other actors participated in the fortification of the area around the Théâtre-Français.

Those whom Naudet commanded apparently had few qualms about being led by an actor. Five days after the events described above, Naudet was formally elected by his troops as the colonel of the regiment. In those same elections, another actor at the Théâtre-Français, J. B. Jacques Nourry, who was known to everyone by his stage name, Grammont, was named lieutenant colonel. Their colleague J. B. Henri Gourgaud, known to all as Dugazon, was named captain.[6] And in addition to these three individuals, the actors Saint-Prix, Marcy, Champville, and Talma, all of whom performed at the Théâtre-Français, were elected as officers of varying rank.[7] The Théâtre-Français itself was closed from 12 July until 20 July,[8] and we can only speculate whether the closing was due to the understanding on the part of the directors that prospective spectators might be preoccupied with political events or to the simple fact that so many of the theater's actors were busy commanding the troops of the district guard.

If, in the heady days surrounding 14 July, Naudet and his troops imagined that for a bunch of actors to assume control of a detachment of the National Guard would not provoke controversy, they were soon brought back to reality. No sooner had the dust cleared than several accounts, ranging from amused satire to vitriolic indignation, were published about these "comédiens commandants."[9] In fact, Naudet's modest account of his assumption of command was written in direct response to his many detractors and is contained in a pamphlet aptly entitled *Réponse de M. Naudet, comédien du roi, aux injures répandues contre lui dans différens journaux* (Response by Mr. Naudet, *comédien du roi,* to the insults that have been spread against him in several newspapers).

Indeed, in almost every instance in which actors crossed over onto the political stage, they were lambasted by journalists and pamphleteers who were quick to unmask these migrations as evidence of both the insatiable political ambitions of dangerous clowns and the inherent theatricality of the Revolution itself. Many of these authors seemed convinced that the actors' election was either a mistake or a provisional measure to meet the needs of a temporary emergency: "These individuals were probably only provisionally called to these positions, & one can only assume that they will either step down and thank the citizens for the remarkable honor that has been bestowed upon them; or that these same citizens will take them out of office once [formal] appointments are made in each district."[10] But this was not to be the case. Naudet would remain active in the National Guard well into the Revolutionary period and would even be accused (most probably unjustly) of using his troops to force helpless theater spectators into submission.[11] Dugazon went on to become the aide-de-camp of the sectional commander of the National Guard, Antoine-Joseph Santerre. And, according to Louis-Sébastien Mercier, Dugazon would, in his capacity as a military officer, order the drumroll that preceded Louis XVI's execution.[12]

The military service of Naudet and Dugazon, however distinguished, was eclipsed by the illustrious military career of their colleague Grammont, who was among the most politically involved actors of his day.[13] He associated with the likes of Georges-Jacques Danton, Camille Desmoulins, and Marie-Jean Hérault de Séchelles, and his star rose (and fell) along with theirs. For the first two years of the Revolution, Grammont continued to serve in the National Guard while at the same time performing at the Théâtre-Français. Toward the end of 1791, Grammont moved to the politically left-wing Théâtre de Montansier. In 1793, he was hired to serve as adjutant general on the staff of Charles-Philippe Ronsin, the recently appointed brigadier general. The fact that Grammont was plucked from relative military obscurity to serve on Ronsin's general staff was no doubt related to the fact that Ronsin was not only a brigadier general; he was also a prolific playwright. After being hired by Ronsin, Grammont engaged in a little theatrical cronyism of his own, bringing several of his fellow actors on board with him onto the general staff.[14]

Oddly enough, just as Dugazon was rumored to have been involved in the execution of Louis XVI, so Grammont was reported to have headed the cortège that accompanied Marie-Antoinette to the guillotine.[15] Grammont himself would later meet the same fate, however, when he and several other defendants (including prominent dechristianizing politicians Pierre-Gaspard Chaumette and Jean-Baptiste Gobel, as well as the widows of Desmoulins and Jacques-René Hébert) were tried, convicted, and executed en masse for the crimes of "debauchery" and "atheism" after one of the Terror's show trials.

Naudet, Dugazon, and Grammont were all actors at the Théâtre-Français in 1789, and indeed most of the actors who participated in the National Guard in the earliest days of the Revolution were from the same theater, a circumstance that was no doubt related to the fact that the Théâtre-Français, otherwise known as the Comédie-Française, was the most prestigious theater in France at the time, and its actors, who had the right to refer to themselves as the Comédiens du roi, were accorded a greater degree of respect than their colleagues from other theaters.[16]

As the Revolution progressed, however, and as the stigma attached to actors was increasingly dismissed as an irrational prejudice of the old regime, actors from the less prestigious theaters began to enlist in various military units, and many of them eventually rose to positions of command as well. For example, the actor Fusil, who performed at the Spectacle des Variétés amusantes, served in 1793 as the aide-de-camp of General Tureau in the Vendée and went on to play an important role in the suppression of the Lyon rebellion.[17] Another actor, by the name of Dufresse, quit his job at the Théâtre Montansier to become a captain in the army; the following year he was promoted to the rank of adjutant general of the Armée révolutionnaire in the northern region.[18] He was, however, arrested for his excesses in July of 1793 (it had been his idea to have a guillotine-on-wheels as the image for the wax seal of the Armée révolutionnaire of the North). Dufresse was eventually acquitted and reinstated and went on to become a general-baron of the Empire, serving in numerous campaigns and later as governor of the Deux-Sèvres.[19] Yet another actor, by the name of Saint-Preux, who performed at the Théâtre de la Cité, joined the National Guard in August of 1789; in 1792, when many of the theatrical troupes of Paris formed individual detachments to defend the nation against foreign invaders, Saint-Preux was named a second lieutenant of his theater's troop.[20] He must have distinguished himself in this capacity, for in 1793 Saint-Preux was asked by the minister of war to serve as the *commissaire* of the Conseil exécutif to watch over the French armies in Italy. He went on to serve *en mission* several times at the special request of the minister of war and at one point found himself in command of ten thousand soldiers. After performing his duties with distinction, Saint-Preux returned to his job as an actor at the Théâtre de la Cité.[21]

The actors I have mentioned are for the most part those who distinguished themselves in their military service. Countless others served in the rank and file. And there were those as well who cannot exactly be said to have served with distinction: one Parisian actor by the name of Fouchez, known by the stage name of Clairval, a performer in a traveling theater company, rose to the rank of lieutenant in the Armée révolutionnaire of the North. Clairval crossed over into enemy territory, where he defected along with General Dumouriez, and shortly thereafter took advantage of the opportunity to perform as an actor in the Belgian theater. He was later court-marshaled for this act of military (and theatrical) treason.[22]

As surprising as the impressive careers of these actor-soldiers might be, particularly in light of the stigma still attached to their profession, more surprising—and for the purposes of this study, more significant—were the actors who embarked upon careers as political representatives. After the long-standing injunction against their eligibility for public office was lifted in December of 1789,[23] several actors brought their oratorical skills to the political stage, achieving a success that would have been unthinkable only months before. And indeed, to many disaffected members of the French population, the thought of actors playing a role in politics remained unthinkable, or at the very least unacceptable.

Here, it seems appropriate to return to the story of Collot d'Herbois, no doubt the most infamous example of an actor turned politician. After his experiences in Bordeaux, where he had written of his ill-treatment at the hands of the provincial bourgeoisie, Collot d'Herbois moved to the city of Lyon, where he worked as an actor at the Théâtre de Lyon, eventually becoming its director in 1787. He had begun writing plays as well, and in 1789 he moved to Paris to continue his career as a dramatist. In December of 1789, Collot was fortunate enough to see one of his plays performed at the Théâtre-Français.[24] Over the next year or two Collot went on to achieve both critical and popular success as a Parisian playwright.[25]

Even while Collot was busy writing plays for the theatrical stage, he was becoming increasingly involved in political activities. He joined the Jacobin Club early in the Revolution and quickly became a prominent member.[26] In 1792, Collot was elected to the National Convention as a deputy of Paris. By March of 1793, Collot was named to the alternating honorary post of president of the Jacobin Club. And in September of 1793, Collot reached the pinnacle of his political career (and indeed the pinnacle of Revolutionary politics as a whole) when he was named to the all-powerful Committee of Public Safety. Collot remained on the twelve-member committee until, fearing a purge, he was instrumental in the overthrow of Robespierre on 9 Thermidor.

Not unlike the *comédiens commandants*, who were subjected to the heckling of those disbelievers who could not forget that these supposed officers were in truth actors, Collot could never quite escape the taint of theatricality no matter how high he climbed in his political career. For some individuals, Collot would never be anything but an actor pretending to be a politician, although it may not have been very prudent to mention this conviction out loud. When Hébert's widow was put on trial (coincidentally, alongside the actor Grammont), a witness by the name of Marie Jolly (herself an ac-

7. Portrait of Collot d'Herbois. Collection of the author.

tress at the Théâtre-Français) testified that Mme Hébert had once heckled Collot from the audience at the Cordeliers Club:

> [I]n the meeting of the Cordeliers in which the deputation from the Jacobins arrived . . . [the witness Marie Jolly] found herself seated next to the wife of Hébert, and the moment when Collot d'Herbois, deputy, stood up on the speakers' platform, [another] citizeness asked Mme Hébert whether this citizen [on the platform] was a patriot. [Mme Hébert] responded that it was Collot d'Herbois, an actor and a schemer; [the witness further stated] that the entire time that Collot d'Herbois was speaking, Mme Hébert kept saying with irony, "It's a coup de théâtre; doesn't it seem like he's acting in a play *[ne semble t'il* [sic] *pas qu'il joue la Comédie]*?"[27]

If references to Collot's stage career could be dangerous at the height of his power, when Collot himself was put on trial after Thermidor for having masterminded the brutal suppression of the federalist rebellion in Lyon, references to his theatrical background were almost obligatory. Numerous pamphlets, not to mention official evidence presented at Collot's trial, all claimed that the true motive for Collot's savage treatment of the Lyonnais had been his personal revenge for having been booed off the stage some six or seven years earlier, when he had been an actor at the Théâtre de Lyon. In fact, Collot was actually accused of taking the time, amidst the horrors of the "rape" of Lyon, to search out citizens of the city who had been in the parterre on that fateful day when he had been forced to endure the audience's whistles of disapproval; having found them, he lined them up before a cannon and exacted his revenge.[28]

Worth mentioning also, in connection to the repression of the Lyon rebellion, is the curious coalition of people with a theatrical background who, in a variety of different capacities, seem to have descended on this city at the same time. According to the historian Richard Cobb, the troops Collot accompanied to Lyon were "the strongest detachment of the Parisian *armée* ever brought together, with one clear aim: to accelerate the measures of repression."[29] And the general in command of these troops was none other than the playwright turned brigadier general Ronsin. On Ronsin's general staff was the actor Fusil, who not only took part in the military repression of the city but also performed as a member of the *commission temporaire*, responsible for the subsequent judicial repression of Lyon and its environs.[30] And, last but not least, Antoine Dorfeuille, an itinerant actor before the Revolution, was appointed president of the Commission de justice, in which capacity he sent hundreds, and by some accounts thousands, of Lyonnais to their death. Dorfeuille seems to have embraced his new position with relish, characterizing his judicial repression of the Lyonnais, in a letter to the president of the National Convention, as a "festival" of justice: "May this festival forever impress terror upon the souls of rascals and confidence upon the hearts of republicans! I say festival, citizen president; yes, festival is the word. When crime descends to the grave, humanity breathes again, and it is the festival of virtue."[31]

Inevitably, the extraordinary confluence of actors appearing on the Revolutionary stage, and involved in the repression of Lyon in particular, proved fodder for claims of a revolutionary/theatrical conspiracy. At the close of the century, Louis-Abel Beffroy de Reigny, a consistent critic of the theatricality of Revolutionary politics, began compiling a dictionary of all the new words, concepts, and people that the Revolution had brought to light. Under the heading "Collot d'Herbois," we find not only the accusation that the repression of Lyon was the result of Collot's personal vendetta as an actor, but also the accusation that the large number of actors who played a role in Revolutionary politics was no mere coincidence; the *"Comédien-Législateur"* Collot d'Herbois himself was responsible for masterminding the theatrical infiltration of the Revolutionary stage:

> Collot d'Herbois, no sooner invested with the so-called *[prétendu]* power of representative, delegated a portion [of that power] to a bunch of his *comédien* and *histrion* friends; and it is to [Collot] that we owe the strange spectacle of a band of generals, *commissaires,* aides-de-camp, etc., entering from the [stage] wings and placing, in their turn, their old comrades [in positions of power].[32]

Conspiracy or not, there is no question that the various theatrical and political threads are at times difficult to untangle; in this respect, the career of another actor-politician, Fabre d'Eglantine, serves as a case in point. Philippe-François-Nazaire Fabre, who later added the stage name d'Eglantine to his other names, began his theatrical career in 1772 as an actor in a traveling theater company.[33] After performing on the stages of half a dozen French cities, Fabre eventually found his way to Lyon, where he performed at the Théâtre de Lyon for the 1784–85 season and where he made the acquaintance of Collot d'Herbois. Fabre moved to Paris in 1787, where despite some initial difficulties, he began to achieve a certain degree of success as a playwright and even had several of his plays performed at the Théâtre-Français.

At the very beginning of the Revolution, Fabre became active in politics. He allied himself with Danton and became one of the more important members of the Cordeliers Club. Fabre was named secretary of that society in 1790 and later that same year assumed the position of president of the Cordeliers district; in this latter capacity, incidentally, Fabre drafted a decree declaring that all theaters within his district were under the exclusive control of the district government and were off-limits to the National Assembly.[34] In 1792, Fabre was elected as a deputy of Paris to the National Convention, where he is perhaps best remembered for his role in the creation of the Revolutionary calendar.

While a representative to the National Convention, Fabre continued to enjoy success as a playwright,[35] although the theatrical almanac of 1792 does claim that one of his plays was booed by spectators—a theatrical reaction that Fabre apparently interpreted as a political insult, for he proceeded to denounce the audience at the subsequent meeting of the Jacobin Club.[36] To make matters more confusing, Fabre was at this time involved in a relationship with Marie Jolly, the very same actress who was in attendance at the Cordeliers Club when Collot d'Herbois came to speak, and who would later bear witness against Hébert's wife for calling Collot an actor.[37]

Fabre's political and theatrical careers came to an end in January of 1794, when he was arrested for having "trafficked his opinion as representative of the people."[38] And a month later, Robespierre would denounce Fabre as the "principal author" of a "whole system of imposture and intrigue."[39] In a sequence of events not unlike the retrospective unmasking of Collot, when Fabre had fallen from grace and the veil of power had been lifted, critics invariably saw only a duplicitous actor with his own personal agenda posing as a legitimate representative of the people.[40]

Another theatrical figure who played a comparatively minor role in Revolutionary politics, but whose name was nonetheless linked to many of the key political players of the day, was Jean-François Boursault-Malherbe. In 1789, Boursault was an actor as well as director of the main theater of Marseille. After the storming of the Bastille, Boursault, by his own account, helped to lead the assault on royal positions in Marseille and went on to help found Marseille's Assemblée patriotique.[41] Shortly thereafter, Boursault moved to Paris, where he became active in political clubs and where he allied himself with the likes of Collot d'Herbois and Jacques Nicolas Billaud-Varennes.[42]

In 1791, when theatrical enterprises underwent deregulation and it became permissible for any citizen to open a theater, Boursault founded the most radical political theater of his day, which went by the somewhat misleading name of Théâtre Molière. Among the first plays to be produced at this theater was the virulent antiroyalist, anti-aristocratic, and anticlerical tragedy *La ligue des fanatiques et des tyrans,* whose author was none other than the future Brigadier General Ronsin.

During the 1791–92 theatrical season, Boursault directed as well as acted in several plays, many of which were rather heavily laden with radical political content. The revenues of the Théâtre Molière were apparently somewhat disappointing, however, and with the severe decline in spectatorship associated with the political upheaval of 10 August 1792, Boursault's theater came perilously close to bankruptcy. In early September of 1792, Boursault took it upon himself to send a letter to Danton, who as a result of the events of 10 August now headed the Provisional Executive Council. Boursault's letter to Danton and his fellow ministers requested government subsidies for the Théâtre Molière; accompanying the letter was a personal note of support from Chaumette, a prominent member of the insurrectional Commune.[43]

The letter was well received by Danton, who forwarded it to the minister of the interior with the following note of support:

> I have the honor of sending to you, sir, a report by Mr Boursault, the director of the Théâtre Molière, which requests [government] aid to avoid both his bankruptcy as well as that of his theater.
>
> It is for you to appreciate, sir, in your wisdom, to what extent the generosity of the nation can be extended to a theater, in its moment of need, which has presented to the public only those plays which are appropriate to the acceleration of the progress of the Revolution. [signed: The Minister of Justice, Danton].[44]

Such important political connections were no doubt responsible for the fact that shortly after the above exchange of letters, Boursault crossed over from political theater to the theater of politics. He was named an elector of the city of Paris and immediately handed over the leadership of the Théâtre Molière to one of his associates: one can only speculate as to whether this decision was merely the result of a busy schedule, or whether Boursault suspected that a role played simultaneously on the political and theatrical stages would elicit unwelcome comments from a wary political audience.

After several months, Boursault attained the post of "supplementary" deputy to the National Convention, in which capacity he served on several government missions in the provinces. After Thermidor, Boursault returned to the world of the theater, where he resumed his position as director of the Théâtre Molière. Changing with the times, and no doubt sensitive to the backlash against Jacobin radicalism, Boursault rechristened his theater the Théâtre des Variétés étrangères; instead of Jacobin political plays, Boursault now presented such politically neutral fare as German Sturm und Drang in translation.[45]

Despite the fact that Boursault's political star did not rise nearly as high as Collot d'Herbois's or Fabre d'Eglantine's, he was nevertheless subject to the same antitheatrical attacks. Indeed, perhaps because Boursault was not as powerful, his critics did not have to wait until his downfall in order to express themselves. In a pamphlet written by Boursault's creditors (of which he apparently had many), he was accused, much as was Fabre, of acting the role of a politician for motives of personal gain:

> We will prove to Boursault that no matter how talented he has been at fooling his fellow citizens as if he were [acting] at the theater *[jouer ses concitoyens comme à la comédie]*; no matter how much skill went into creating the particular roles he put on for each one of us (and he came up with quite a few of them)—we will prove to him, we say, that all that glitters is not gold.

And his creditors went on to contrast their own heartfelt patriotism to Boursault's actorly insinuation onto the political stage: "[Unlike Boursault] . . . we have not presented ourselves as actors on the patriotic arena of our sections. With republicanism in our hearts, we have allowed our morals [and] our actions to speak [for themselves]."[46]

Such attacks on actors who entered politics should remind us that they had to overcome a significant degree of hostility and suspicion on the part of the general public in order to make the transition from actor to politician—a fact that makes their presence on the Revolutionary stage all the more surprising. And indeed, I have mentioned only the more prominent of the actor-politicians; other actors took part in the political life of Revolutionary France at a less visible level. Antoine Trial, for example, an actor at the Opéra-Comique, became a friend of Robespierre and assumed the civil post of *commissaire municipal,* in which capacity he was eventually to sign Robespierre's death certificate.[47] Countless others took part in the less official aspects of Revolutionary politics. Actors were present at the storming of the Bastille,[48] and they also played a part in several provincial uprisings in the summer of 1789.[49] In fact, the role of an actor by the name of Bordier in a political uprising in Rouen in the summer of 1789 was the impetus for a veritable textual explosion of antitheatricality and became one of the most controversial episodes of that summer.[50]

For those actors who chose not to—or were not able to—break into official politics, clubs often provided an outlet for political expression. Actresses in particular, who were forbidden to assume political office because of their sex, were active in political clubs and in one case even founded one. Mme Vestris, for example, the sister of the soldier-actor Dugazon mentioned above, achieved a great deal of success both on the stage of the Théâtre-Français and in the political clubs of Paris. As a theatrical almanac declared in 1792, "If women could be appointed deputies to the National Assembly, [Mme Vestris] would have had all of the votes of her section a long time ago. She attends [political] clubs, rushes around the sections, drafts motions, and often goes to see the municipal authorities; she is, in short, a woman citizen like no other."[51]

But the actress who left the most indelible mark on Revolutionary politics was undoubtedly Claire Lacombe, who, despite her late arrival on the political scene, became the co-founder of the most important political organization for women in Revolutionary France: La Société des citoyennes républicaines révolutionnaires. In 1791, Lacombe was an actress in the theater of Marseille, and even at the beginning of 1792 she was still working as an actress, although she had moved to the theater of Toulon.[52] At some point before the summer of 1792, however, Lacombe moved to Paris, where she made her political debut in a rather remarkable fashion: she managed to make her way to the platform of the Legislative Assembly, where, after declaring herself to be "a Frenchwoman, an artist without a position," she not only called for the replacement of Lafayette but offered her services to the nation in "combating the enemies of the Fatherland."[53] The deputies were so impressed by her speech that they ordered its immediate publication.

Lacombe's political career reached new heights when, some two weeks after her speech at the Legislative Assembly, she took part in the storming of the Tuileries and was wounded in the assault. She was awarded a tricolor sash for her heroism, which she in turn presented to the Legislative Assembly. Shortly afterwards, she took to delivering speeches in many of the political clubs, most notably the Jacobin Club, and read several petitions before the National Convention.[54] And it was also at this time that Lacombe co-founded with Pauline Léon the Société des citoyennes républicaines révolutionnaires.

Lacombe's Société aided in the downfall of the Girondins during the summer of 1793. But no sooner did the Jacobins consolidate their power than they began to move against the Société des citoyennes républicaines révolutionnaires, as they did against many of the other clubs that had helped to bring them to power. On 16 September, Lacombe was denounced in the Jacobin Club, and we should note her attacker's emphasis on Lacombe's talent for speaking: "The woman who is denounced before you is very dangerous in that she is very eloquent; she speaks well at first and then attacks the constituted authorities. In a speech I heard she fired a red-hot broadside into the Jacobins and the Convention."[55] Lacombe managed to avoid imprisonment until her arrest on 2 April 1794. Despite petitions submitted on her behalf by Collot d'Herbois and others, Lacombe remained in prison until August of 1795, after which she resumed her theatrical career at the theater in Nantes.

Given the number of actors who played a role in Revolutionary politics, one is tempted to ask whether the reverse phenomenon took place: Were there any Revolutionary political figures who embarked on a theatrical career? According to Paul d'Estrée, an early-twentieth-century historian of the theater during the Terror, several prominent political figures secretly tried their hand at playwriting, but they often preferred romantic dramas and farces to the political plays that we might have expected of them:

Camille Desmoulins read his play *Emilie ou l'Innocence vengée* to his friends; Saint-Just wrote the farce *Arlequin-Diogène;* Vergniaud [the prominent Girondin and renowned orator] co-authored *La belle fermière;* and [member of the Committee of Public Safety] Billaud-Varenne wrote several comedies and operas, which alas never left his desk to confront the stage lights.[56]

But if several actors made their way into the world of politics, and a few politicians harbored secret theatrical ambitions, we should be careful not to conclude that the theatricality of the Revolution resides simply in these individuals who performed (or wanted to perform) on both stages. In fact, the very possibility of their crossing over is itself no doubt a consequence of a general convergence of theater and politics at a more fundamental level: the merging of the theatrical and political *forms* themselves. Revolutionary politics borrowed, at its very inception, from the theatrical mise-en-scène. And Revolutionary theater increasingly came to be regarded as an affair of state. Politics, in short, became entertaining. And theater suddenly became important.

Theatrical Politics

The most striking example of the theatricalization of politics in Revolutionary France is undoubtedly the manner in which the debates in the National Assembly were conducted, and in particular the innovation of large, theatrical-style audiences that attended the sessions of the nation's representatives. Even before the National Assembly had officially come into existence, the deputies of the third estate had distinguished themselves from the deputies of the first two estates by breaking with tradition and allowing an audience to witness their debates. As a British Embassy official observed in his dispatch to London in May of 1789,

> The Tiers-Etat meet regularly every day in the grand Assembly Hall and admit strangers to hear the Debates, from which much inconvenience has arisen and their deliberations much prolonged. I am told that the most extravagant and disrespectful language against Government has been held, and that upon all such occasions the greatest approbation is expressed by the Audience by clapping of hands and other demonstrations of satisfaction; in short the encouragement is such as to have led some of the Speakers to say things little short of treason.[57]

English observers in particular seemed struck by the "disorderly" nature of debate among the deputies. Upon observing a session of the assembly of the third estate in June of 1789, Arthur Young complained of a "want of order among [the deputies]; more than once to-day there were an hundred members on their legs at a time, and Mons. Bailly absolutely without power to keep order."[58] But it was not the deputies alone who were to blame for the tumult; the spectators were equally responsible for the chaos: "[T]he spectators in the galleries are allowed to interfere in the debates by clapping their hands, and other noisy expressions of approbation: this is grossly indecent; it is also dangerous."[59]

If English observers seemed struck by the "disorderly" character of the debates in the National Assembly, no doubt implicitly comparing the Assembly with their own House of Commons, French observers seemed inclined to perceive the proceedings of the Assembly less as disorderly than as ordered by a set of rules that—at least for some individuals—seemed entirely inappropriate to political discourse: those of the still boisterous theatrical parterre. In January of 1790, for example, the *Mercure de France* reported an incident in which a speech by Mirabeau was interrupted by whistles, the most common form of expressing displeasure among theatrical audiences; the *Mercure* lamented, "[A]nd thus it is true that a certain segment of the public gives itself the right to treat and regard the deputies of France as if they were actors *[comédiens]*."[60]

Even apart from the behavior of spectators, one need only look at the architecture of the halls in which the various incarnations of the National Assembly gathered in order to understand that the phrase *political stage* was no mere metaphor during the Revolutionary period. And in fact, a brief history of the various locales in which the Assembly met reveals not only that each of the *salles*—a term, incidentally, that has both theatrical and political connotations—was constructed and perceived as a kind of theater, but also that each successive salle was decidedly more theatrical than the previous one. If we were to go back as far as the convocation of the Assembly of Notables in 1787, we would find that the salle constructed especially for this assembly was built inside a large hangar, which had been recently built to house props and scenery for the Opéra of Versailles, on the grounds of the Hôtel des Menus-Plaisirs, the administrative office in charge of arranging all royal spectacles and festivities. When the king came to inspect the new salle, two days before the official opening, he was shocked by the "theatrical" quality of the building and in particular by the lavish spectator boxes that had been built at the top of the hall, along the sides. The king felt that these spectator boxes were inappropriate to a political assembly that was meant to conduct its deliberations behind closed doors, and he ordered the spectator boxes removed, thereby delaying the opening of the Assembly of Notables an entire month.[61]

Two years later, the Estates General met in a newly constructed salle built on the grounds of the Hôtel des Menus-Plaisirs (as a matter of fact, on the same spot as the now-demolished Assembly of Notables and designed by the same architect). This time, spectator boxes were left intact; in fact, the walls on three sides of the salle supported "amphitheaters" that provided an impressive amount of spectator seating for the invited audience (see fig. 5).[62]

When the newly formed National Assembly followed the king to Paris in 1789 in the wake of the October Days, after a brief stint in the archbishop's palace the Assembly moved on 9 November to the *salle du manège,* the riding hall of the Tuileries Palace that had been the site of horse shows in the old regime and was therefore well equipped to handle spectators. Arthur Young found the atmosphere of this venue as boisterous (and as troubling) as that of the one in Versailles:

> [T]here is a gallery at each end of the saloon [i.e., hall] which is open to all the world; and side ones for admission of the friends of the members by tickets: the

audience in these galleries are very noisy: they clap, when anything pleases them, and they have been known to hiss; an indecorum which is utterly destructive of the freedom of debate.[63]

It was in this same *salle du manège* that such dramatic events as the trial of the king unfolded, an event whose historical import did not prevent audiences from behaving as if they were watching a show. As Mercier described the scene to his readers, "No doubt you imagine a state of composure, a kind of awe-inspired silence in that auditorium. Not at all. The back of the hall was converted into loges in which ladies dressed with the most charming carelessness ate oranges or ices and drank liqueurs."[64]

The next locale for the Assembly (at this point the National Convention) was not only theatrical, it *was* a theater. On 10 May 1793, the Convention moved into the Salle de Spectacle in the Tuileries Palace, a theater that had previously housed the actors of the Comédie-Française and the Théâtre de Monsieur. According to the historian Joseph Butwin, although the theater was refurbished and redecorated, it "never lost its theatrical character."[65] On the occasion of the Convention's transference to the Salle de Spectacle, Robespierre implicitly compared this new political arena to dramatic theaters by contrasting the architectural sluggishness of the new regime with the theater-building mania of the old: "The kings or the officials of the old government had a magnificent opera house built in a few days, and, to the shame of human reason, four years have gone by before we have prepared a new place for the national representation!"[66]

Although the behavior of spectators and the very character of the buildings in which the assemblies met were very much within the theatrical realm, it was undoubtedly the performances of what can only be described as "political actors" that most clearly impressed upon contemporaries the extent to which theatrical forms had invaded the political arena. If some faulted the spectators for their behavior, others, such as Edmund Burke, seemed to think that the blame might be shared equally between the spectators and the political actors themselves: "They [the representatives to the National Assembly] act like the comedians of a fair before a riotous audience; they act amidst the tumultuous cries of a mixed mob of ferocious men, and of women lost to shame, who, according to their insolent fancies, direct, control, applaud, explode [boo] them; and sometimes mix and take their seats amongst them."[67] Indeed, there were reports that deputies had taken acting lessons or were planting claqueurs in the audience to applaud their speeches.[68] And the oratorical skills of several of the deputies garnered them the applause of both political and theatrical critics. In this respect, Mirabeau, arguably the greatest orator of the Assembly, seems to have occupied a place in the public mind that stood on the very threshold of the political and the theatrical.

Certainly, if we look at Mirabeau's critics, counterrevolutionaries and Jacobins alike never tired of calling him a comédien, thereby hoping to cast aspersions not only on his political legitimacy but also—at least for the counterrevolutionaries—on the legitimacy of the Revolution itself.[69] But observations on Mirabeau's dramatic style were not always intended as criticisms. Actors themselves were apparently impressed by Mirabeau's theatrical talents. According to the memoirs of the actor Fleury, Mirabeau had just completed a particularly rousing speech when the great actor Molé rushed up to him and reflected on the career he might have had in the theater: "Oh! monsieur le Comte . . . what a speech! what a voice! what gestures! my God! my God! how you have missed your calling!"[70]

Indeed Mirabeau was so renowned for his skills as a politician and an orator that his contemporaries seemed somewhat confused as to how to perceive him: Was he a great representative of the nation, or a great orator? Did one admire his speeches for their content or for their delivery? When, for example, spectators had gathered to attend a performance of the controversial political drama *Brutus*, the opening act of the play had to be postponed when audience members spotted Mirabeau and another deputy from the Assembly in the audience: "[Spectators] showered them with applause, . . . [and sent] a deputation from the parterre to invite [Mirabeau] to descend to the galleries so that everyone could see him with ease."[71]

Perhaps the most tangible evidence of contemporaries' inability to categorize Mirabeau as either a political or a theatrical figure is provided by a text that was originally published in 1786 with the title *Le poëte au foyer, ou L'éloge des grands hommes du Théâtre François, scène lyrique nouvelle en prose* and republished in 1791 with a few slight modifications as *Le poëte au foyer, ou L'éloge des grands hommes du Théâtre de la Nation; y compris celui de Mirabeau. Scène lyrique nouvelle.* Although the change from "Théâtre-Français" to "Théâtre de la Nation" merely reflects that theater's name change, the addition of Mirabeau to the great men of the theater defies comprehension unless we recognize the existence of that liminal area between politics and theater that admitted such possibilities of *métissage.*[72] The earlier version of *Le poëte au foyer* contains a series of reflections by a narrator as he passes before the busts of the great men of the French stage (Molière, Corneille, Racine, Regnard, Destouches, Crébillon, Voltaire). Apart from a few minor changes,[73] the 1791 version of this play contains the identical series of reflections with one major change: after the reflection on Voltaire is the following heartfelt paean delivered to the bust of the recently departed Mirabeau:

(To [the bust of] Mirabeau, with resolve:) Active citizen, upholder of France, the greatest of heroes, brave soldier, well-known merchant, good patriot, rare and sublime genius, man above the prejudices of the nobility, [above] pride, insolence, and impertinence; friend of humanity, equality, democracy in the midst of aristocracy. . . . How many tears do we shed upon your tomb![74]

Finally, when the editors of the almanac of theatrical productions of the year 1792 struggled to differentiate between good and bad forms of notoriety (*célèbre* [celebrated] and *fameux* [famous] respectively), they felt no qualms about applying these terms to actors on both the political and theatrical stages, and the example of Mirabeau came immediately to mind:

> Several journals, in giving an account of a [theatrical] debut made reference to the FAMOUS Préville. This expression does not do justice to a man of whom one can only say and think good things; and Famous does not suit him. We used to say the famous Mandarin and the celebrated Baron; just as today we say the FAMOUS Brissot and the CELEBRATED Mirabeau.[75]

If Mirabeau, as an individual, seems to have occupied a kind of liminal space between the political and the theatrical, the same can be said for a variety of spectacles that were neither properly theatrical nor political, but rather both at the same time. One such political spectacle was the Spectacle militaire, the brainchild of a man by the name of Texier, who called it "a little spectacle, different from all those that are established in this city."[76] Indeed it was: Texier proposed to reenact several Revolutionary "battles and sieges," presumably replete with all the military accouterments, in the circus pavilion that stood in the center of the Palais-Royal and that was known as the Cirque national. That the Spectacle militaire was not easily categorized is evidenced by the fact that Texier first applied for permission to the major general of the National Guard of the city of Paris, who issued the following reply: "The general permits [the proposed spectacle] and refers [Texier] to the mayor and to the Bureau of Police, both for the permission to open a spectacle and for the [censorship] approval of his plays and pantomimes."[77]

A somewhat different take on political spectacle, which was also to be found at the Palais-Royal, was the exhibit established by Peter Curtius, a naturalized French citizen of German origin. Part house of horrors, part wax museum, Curtius's show was changed periodically to suit the taste of Parisian crowds. In 1791, one would have found the shirt worn by Henri IV at the time of his assassination, in which one could still see the hole made by Ravaillac's knife (for the benefit of skeptics, the shirt was "accompanied by all of the authentic and historical certificates"). Close by, there was what Curtius claimed to be the mummified corpse of an Egyptian princess who had died three hundred years earlier. And alongside the shirt and the mummy, there were the wax figures of the king, Paris mayor Jean-Sylvain Bailly, Lafayette, and "several of the illustrious deputies of the National Assembly."[78]

Undoubtedly the most popular example of political spectacle, however, was the Assemblée fédérative des Amis de la Vérité, which as coincidence would have it also took place in the Palais-Royal in the same circus pavilion that Texier had chosen for the site of his military spectacle. The Assemblée fédérative was a kind of "pretend" National Assembly, open to club members of the Amis de la Vérité who, for the price of nine livres every three months, were entitled to gather on Fridays (and later Mondays as well) to pretend that they were legislators and harangue one another.

At first glance there are several factors that might lead us to categorize the Assemblée fédérative as more spectacle than politics. The Assemblée did, after all, meet in a circus pavilion, which on other days of the week was used for dances, concerts, and galas.[79] And there was also the fact that these representatives for a day were charged an entrance fee by the club president–theatrical entrepreneur abbé Fauchet. The same almanac of spectacles that reported on Curtius's wax museum also included the Assemblée fédérative in its list of spectacles and observed somewhat sardonically:

> M. l'abbé Fauchet . . . has installed [in the Cirque national] a miniature [version] of the National Assembly under the name of Amis de la Vérité, with the following difference: that our real legislators are paid to make laws, whereas the Amis de la Vérité pay and take up a collection amongst themselves in order to make laws for us.[80]

Critics of the Assemblée fédérative were quick to point out the theatricality of its proceedings. The radical journal *L'orateur du peuple* reported, "No one can hear anything, but they applaud and boo to excess. . . . [And it is] with these acrobatics *[batelage]*, these grand words, [and] these staged scenes *[scènes de tréteaux]* that our enemies attempt to lead the people on a false path."[81] This remark, which seems virtually identical to contemporary criticisms of the National Assembly, serves perhaps to show that the Assemblée fédérative had been all too successful in its imitation of the National Assembly, theatricality and all. And it is important to point out that, if the meetings of the Assemblée fédérative had been purely and unselfconsciously theater, no one would have taken the trouble to paint them in theatrical terms. But it was precisely the fact that members of the Amis de la Vérité insisted on their political relevance that drew the fire of critics. And as the following account of the opening session of the Assemblée fédérative indicates, the Amis de la Vérité had good reason to think of themselves as a legitimate political organization:

> The inauguration of the Assemblée fédérative des Amis de la Vérité took place at the Cirque national on Wednesday the thirteenth of this month [October 1790]. . . . A large number of deputies of the National Assembly, MM. the Electors of 1789, former provisional representatives of the Commune [of Paris], many members of the new municipality, and [many members] of all the patriotic societies of the capital . . . formed an assembly of four to five thousand people, not counting the attentive female spectators with which the galleries of the Cirque were filled.[82]

M.ʳ Lucas se disant Député, et faisant sa motion au Palais Royal.

8. Mr. Lucas believing himself to be a deputy and making his motion at the Palais-Royal. Note the circus pavilion in the background. © Photothèque des Musées de la Ville de Paris/negative: Andreani.

Such an impressive premiere is testimony to the political importance of the society as well as of its leader, the abbé Fauchet. Although the almanac of spectacles may have portrayed Fauchet as a theatrical entrepreneur and a showman, he himself preferred the title *"procureur-général"* (attorney general) of the assembly. Before we write off Fauchet's title as hubris, however, we should consider the fact that he probably had good reasons to think of himself as something more than an entrepreneur of spectacles. He was the co-founder of the journal *La bouche de fer,* a liberal political journal whose contributors included Anacharsis Cloots, Condorcet, Thomas Paine, and Etta Palm. And, even as early as 1790, he could claim significant experience in the world of politics. In addition to being *procureur-général* of the Assemblée fédérative, he had been an original elector of 1789, a member of the Comité permanent, the body that eventually became the Paris Commune, and a four-time president of the Commune itself.[83]

Indeed, Fauchet's political connections were such that he had some very influential friends. When his Assemblée fédérative was derided as an admission-charging spectacle, none other than Camille Desmoulins stood up in his defense: "I certify that [Fauchet] professes the same doctrine as the Jacobins . . . ; I certify that I have never noticed any other difference between the two [political] clubs other than that in the former one pays nine livres, and in the latter, twelve livres."[84]

Others were less credulous of his sincerity. We have already seen how the *Orateur du peuple* characterized Fauchet's Assembly as a theatrical event with dangerous political implications. When Fauchet was later elected to the Legislative Assembly and to the National Convention, the *Mercure* found his political performance disturbingly theatrical: "Almost with each sentence, M. Fauchet was interrupted by the applause of the galleries and by outbursts of laughter from the Assembly that seemed as if it were enjoying the performance of a fairground entertainer *[le spectacle d'un saltimbanque]*."[85]

Depending upon the observer, therefore, the Assemblée fédérative was either a theatrical performance with political aspirations or a festive political assembly of the people, which just happened to meet in a circus pavilion. Abbé Fauchet was similarly characterized as either a showman with political pretensions or a farcical politician. The various spectacles and individuals that I have mentioned here, and indeed the National Assembly itself and its deputies, seemed to have occupied a conceptual position that was neither political nor theatrical, neither serious nor laughable, neither sacred nor profane, but all at the same time.

In this swirling mass of representative forms that defy categorization, one must include not only the theatricality of politics but the politics of theater as well. Just as the antics of the National Assembly were often compared to the behavior of theatrical actors and audiences, so the political battles in the theaters were often compared to the scene at the National Assembly. Take, for example, the political uproar that arose when the actors of the Théâtre-Français announced their decision to expel one of their own for having attempted to recruit the parterre in his efforts to force the Comédiens-Français to perform the controversial Revolutionary drama *Charles IX*. The following account of this announcement of expulsion and the audience's reactions to it details not only the various denunciations with decidedly political overtones, but also an invocation of the image of the National Assembly that seems strangely appropriate to this theatrical-political squabble:

[The Actor Fleury announced:] "My troupe, persuaded that M. Talma has betrayed its interests and compromised the public tranquillity, has unanimously decided that they will have nothing further to do with him, until such time as the [authorities] have come to a decision [on this matter]."

This short harangue was applauded by some and booed by the majority. The tumult had reached its apex when [the actor] Dugazon burst forth from the wings onto the stage: "Gentlemen," he cried, "the Comédie [-Française] will take the same actions against me as [they have taken] against Talma. I denounce the entire Comédie: it is false that Talma has betrayed this society and compromised public safety; his only crime is in having told you that we could perform *Charles IX*, and that's it."

At these words, disorder and tumult erupted once again in every corner of the salle; motions were made from every corner, orators from [political] clubs vied for the right to speak. . . .

Sulleau, the editor of a morning newspaper, tried to restore order and, parodying in a very buffoonish manner the president of the National Assembly, he
called on people to speak, cried out "Order! Order! Order!" shaking an enormous bell with all the force of his arms, and in the end, put on his hat, when he
realized that all his efforts were in vain. . . . [Eventually] the agitation had
reached so violent an intensity that it was necessary to call in the military and
to go and warn the mayor of Paris.[86]

Theatrical actors and audiences were not the only ones to recognize the
political importance of theater. Revolutionary legislators, keenly aware of
the need to propagate the ideals of the Revolution to a largely illiterate populace, repeatedly took advantage of the theater's potential as a school of
public education. Particularly as the Revolution moved to the left, in the
years 1792–94, government officials played a greater and greater role in encouraging theatrical productions with overt political messages. We have already seen Danton's interest in Boursault's political theater, and this was but
one of the many governmental forays into the world of the theater. Government involvement in theatrical productions would reach its apex in the carefully choreographed festivals and state-subsidized political dramas of the
Terror (not to mention the strange spectacle of political executions). But the
subject of theatricality and the Terror is a complex one that must be addressed on its own terms.[87] I would like to conclude this chapter, therefore,
with a narrative of certain events that took place immediately before the Terror, in the winter of 1792–93; it is a narrative derived from a series of letters
between a theatrical entrepreneur and the minister of foreign affairs—a
story that, perhaps more than any other, gives an indication of the extent to
which politics and theater had become intertwined by the eve of the Terror.

In the autumn of 1792, the armies of France prepared for an invasion of
neighboring territories, having only just repulsed the forces of the anti-Revolutionary coalition from French soil. To many, it seemed only natural to
hope that the people of Europe might embrace the French armies as enlightened liberators rather than foreign invaders. For the first time in the history
of Europe the conquest of neighboring territories would not simply be an exercise in military might but also, the Revolutionaries hoped, a philosophical
victory—a victory of the new ideals of justice, liberty, and equality over prejudice, injustice, and tyranny. Perhaps it was natural, under such circumstances, for those in command to think of calling upon the theater as an indispensable tool in the conquest of foreign minds. In France itself, the
government had already taken such steps as sponsoring free "educational"
performances of Revolutionary dramas for those who could not afford to
pay for their own tickets. What could be more simple than to sponsor similar performances for the benefit of the soon to be "liberated" Belgians and

thereby take advantage of their shared language to spread the principles of the Revolution?

But even if we might find it perfectly understandable that the French should think of exporting the Revolution by theatrical propaganda, there remains something remarkable about the story I am about to tell. There was a curious urgency to the desire to export French actors to Belgium, an urgency that was perhaps more about the *form* of the political messengers than about the *content* of the message. It was almost as if one could not export the Revolution without simultaneously exporting its theatricality. In the following account of what is arguably the first theatrical propaganda troupe in modern times, one glimpses not only the easy familiarity with which government and military officials mingled and exchanged ideas with theatrical entrepreneurs and actors but also the shared, almost unexamined assumption that the one thing the Belgians truly needed, almost at the moment of their "liberation," was a horde of actors shipped in from Paris.

The story begins in October of 1792, when General Dumouriez, fresh from his rout of enemy forces at Valmy, had arrived in Paris to acknowledge the appreciation of a grateful people. Everyone knew that the general would shortly be departing for the imminent invasion of Belgium, and he was flooded with a variety of invitations during his brief visit to the capital. One of these invitations was from Mlle de la Montansier, a sixty-two-year-old theatrical entrepreneur known to everyone as La Montansier and a fixture in the Parisian theatrical world.[88] Dumouriez graciously accepted her invitation to attend a performance of *Le départ des volontaires* on the evening of 11 October at the Théâtre de la Montansier. During the intermission, La Montansier took the opportunity of the general's visit to propose a very interesting idea. As she would report her conversation with Dumouriez in a letter to government authorities the following month, "I asked for his approval to bring to Brussels—as soon as he entered [that city]—a propaganda troupe [of actors]." In response, the general "smiled, agreed, and gave me a rendezvous for Christmas [in Brussels]."[89]

Dumouriez seems to have erred on the side of caution: his troops arrived in Brussels more than a month ahead of schedule, on 14 November. No sooner did La Montansier hear the news of the conquest of Brussels than she set about putting her plans into action. She immediately dispatched her lover and business partner, the actor Neuville, to Brussels, where he met with Dumouriez to discuss the arrival of the propaganda troupe. Dumouriez was still enthusiastic about the idea, although he apparently did not think it would be proper simply to oust one of the Belgian theater companies so that La Montansier and her troupe could move in; he therefore delegated General Moreton on his staff to look into the matter.

Fortunately for La Montansier and her project, one of her very own actors, a man by the name of Dufresse, who like so many other actors had pursued a military career on the side, had recently been appointed to General Moreton's staff.[90] Neuville and General Moreton, presumably with the intercession of Dufresse, began discussing the possibility of combining Montansier's troupe with a local Belgian troupe, thereby resolving the problem of how to occupy an existing theater without dispossessing its resident troupe. As La Montansier reported in detail to the minister of foreign affairs, Lebrun, she was very excited about the possibilities offered by such a combined Franco-Belgian acting troupe:

> The Belgian troupe possesses a superb opera [company] and superior voices, both male and female—and especially [an actor] by the name of Mick who performs the roles of Lazir and Cheron. My [company] possesses Saint Val, Dufresse, the aide-de-camp of General Moreton, Grammont [the actor-soldier],[91] and other talented individuals: with this variety of talent of both genres, we will be able to provide for Brussels everything that has come out to date in terms of patriotic plays and items that could even be pantomimed, such as the *Marseillaise* for which I have a superb score that I have not been able to bring off in Paris because of the pomp that it requires.[92]

We ought to step back for a moment and ponder the context of this letter: in the midst of international war and political radicalism, a Parisian theatrical entrepreneur was corresponding with the minister of foreign affairs on the specifics of a Franco-Belgian theater company. And we should also note that Montansier's letter to Minister Lebrun was written exactly twelve days after the capture of Brussels, by which time her associate Neuville had not only arrived and negotiated with Dumouriez and Moreton but managed to relate the details back to Montansier in Paris. All of this would seem to indicate that Neuville had been dispatched to Paris virtually on the day of Brussels's capture: such was the urgency of this mission.

Montansier's purpose in contacting Minister Lebrun was to garner the support of government officials so that her troupe would officially be under the protection of French forces. Like any good entrepreneur, as future correspondence would bear out, she hoped to plant the seed for more tangible support in the form of direct government subsidies; for the moment, however, she asked simply for the government's endorsement:

> [A]ll my preparations are under way for the departure of the members [of our troupe] and of the baggage necessary for my enterprise. And so that neither one nor the other encounters any difficulties on the road, nor any delay, and so that they receive security and protection in Brussels or in the other towns of Brabant, I dare to ask you for some sort of public writ *[acte ostensible]* that would manifest some sort of goodwill on the part of the government for this enterprise and for the members who are participating in it.

And then, to press her point, Montansier stressed the strategic importance of this mission to "propagate" the ideals of the Revolution and expressed the hope to Minister Lebrun that the Executive Council would agree with her:

> The Belgian *[Brabançonnes]* heads are still filled with prejudices. What I am doing as an individual should perhaps be seen by the ministers, as wise as [they are] patriotic, as a very essential measure in order to propagate the great principles of our Revolution: I will go so far as to think that, if it succeeds, it will have earned the right to the goodwill of the Fatherland, and if it does not succeed it will have still [earned the right] to its encouragement. But it is for the wisdom of the [Executive] Council to consider what circumstances might require or merit. My only objective at this moment is to beg you to accord me this ostensible sign of goodwill that I solicit with confidence of a minister who is equally estimable for his enlightenment as for his talents and his personal qualities.[93]

To this letter, Montansier appended a list of proposed theatrical productions to be performed in Brussels, including such well-known dramas as Voltaire's *Brutus* and *La mort de César* and Chénier's *Charles IX*, all of which had caused a sensation among Parisian audiences. Also worth noting in the context of our discussion here is that of the four comedies in the suggested repertory, three were by the actor-playwright-politicians Fabre d'Eglantine and Collot d'Herbois.[94]

The letter could not have arrived on the minister's desk at a more opportune moment. Only days earlier, Minister Lebrun had received a report from a man by the name of Chépy, one of the ministry's agents *en mission*, who had suggested that the Belgians were badly in need of a little enlightenment:

> I arrived in Brussels the day before yesterday. . . . Here are the results of my first impressions: Mons seemed cold to me: it had more the air of a conquered city than a liberated one. In the intervening countryside on the way to Brussels, I was aware of stupor more than any other sentiment. In Brussels: a frightening carelessness, no political ideas whatsoever, a fear of ghosts (of the Austrians)— the nobility and the clergy moving about, intriguing, the third estate divided, without principles, without any position, without enlightenment: in truth we will have many obstacles to overcome, and it will be necessary to deploy a bit of force and moreover to rely on our energy and our indefatigable activity.[95]

What better method of counteracting the Belgian "stupor" than a troupe of Parisian actors? A few rousing dramas, a few politically appropriate comedies, and some inspirational songs and marches might be just what the Belgians needed to see that they had not been conquered but liberated—liberated by a people who, at the very least, knew how to put on a good show. No doubt with Chépy's observations in mind, Minister Lebrun wrote back to Montansier immediately upon receipt of her letter:

I cannot but applaud the laudable desire to propagate, with all of the powerful means at your disposal, the principles and love of liberty and of equality in Belgium, while the success of our armies are liberating the Belgian inhabitants from the servitude and the slavery into which they have been plunged for so long. Your enterprise is so beautiful that I must rush, on my part, to obtain for you all the encouragements of which it is worthy.

These were not empty words of praise. Lebrun promised to bring Montansier's project to the attention of the Executive Council that same night, assuring her that the council would be equally enthusiastic about her proposal. And then, in a remark that no doubt riled La Montansier, Lebrun informed her that she was not actually the first theatrical entrepreneur to have thought up the idea of flooding Belgium with French actors: "You will find yourself in good company in Brussels, as I am informed that our best artists of the Opéra and from other theaters of the capital have proposed to make an appearance there and to unite with us in instructing the Belgians in the great art of liberty by the charm and the gaiety of their talents."[96]

True to his word, Lebrun presented Montansier's project to the Executive Council. And, as he had suspected, their reaction was equally enthusiastic. They immediately issued a decree along the lines that Montansier had suggested and made a promise of future "encouragements." Lebrun took the opportunity to address the issue of expenses: "I am proud to be at this moment the agent of the [Executive] Council in informing you of its satisfaction, and I invite you to come and see me in order to determine together what can be done to compensate you for the expenses that will necessarily be entailed in the execution of your project."[97]

La Montansier's reply was as immediate as it was effusive:

> Worthy Citizen Minister,
>   I am in receipt of your second letter, and I am rereading it in order to convince myself that it is no illusion. How kind are your expressions and your conduct! How touched I am! How shall I describe my gratitude to you: oh! when the interests of *la chose publique* inspire in us such goodwill toward brothers, it is beautiful to find oneself a Republican, and to have in one's ministers veritable fathers![98]

With La Montansier's troupe committed to Brussels, foreign minister Lebrun was free to deploy the remaining troupes elsewhere in Belgium. Two days after his note to La Montansier informing her of the Executive Council's response, Lebrun dashed off a note to the administrators of the Opéra. Liège had just fallen to Dumouriez's troops, and it was to this freshly liberated city that Lebrun planned to dispatch his next theatrical battalion waiting in the wings:

I have this moment received the good news of the entry of Dumouriez into Liège, after a stubborn battle of ten hours, and it is with this first city that your artists should begin their patriotic mission. I owe you thanks for the alacrity with which you have undertaken this enterprise. It is an act of patriotism of which the [Executive] Council was appreciative. [The council] thought that nothing should be lacking to the performance troupe, and they invite you to submit the costs of costumes that may be necessary, persuaded that at the same time that one speaks to the heart, it is also necessary to speak to the eyes.[99]

As with Montansier's troupe, the urgency with which the troupe from the Opéra was dispatched to the front is telling. A cultural invasion was needed to consolidate the gains made by the military. As Lebrun put it, the performers will "propagate (by the charms of gaiety and the graces that are part and parcel of their talents) the principles of liberty and equality that the force of our arms have established in Belgium."[100]

Although I did not discover the fate of the Opéra troupe in Liège, the fate of La Montansier's troupe in Brussels is well documented by her continued correspondence with Lebrun. La Montansier arrived in Brussels, along with her troupe, at nine o'clock in the morning on 2 January 1793 and reported immediately to General Moreton, whom Dumouriez had delegated to handle the establishment of her troupe. Moreton greeted her very warmly but proceeded to apologize profusely: as much as he had hoped to do the bidding of the Executive Council, the theater owners of Brussels had let it be known in no uncertain terms that they had no intention of cooperating with La Montansier. Far from considering the combined Franco-Belgium troupe that La Montansier had hoped to create, the theater owners would not even allow French actors inside their theaters "at any price whatsoever." It would seem that if the Belgians had not been successful in repulsing French military might, they were doing their best to resist the theatrical invasion. Nevertheless, Moreton promised La Montansier that he would "make use of all the authority that was at his disposal" in order to persuade the Belgians to come to an arrangement, "while observing, however, the respect that is due to property."[101]

A meeting was arranged in Moreton's headquarters between Montansier and the Belgians. They suggested that they would be willing to rent out a theater, but for a sum La Montansier found exorbitant. As she wrote in her letter to Minister Lebrun, however, the importance of the mission left her no choice but to accept: "I confess to you, I see no other means by which to fulfill the desires of the Executive Council than to come to an agreement with the [Belgian theater] directors, convinced that if the revenues do not meet my expenses and there is a deficit, [the council] will come to my aid." La Montansier assured Lebrun, however, that if the French government was going to have to subsidize her mission—as was appearing increasingly likely—the government's money would be well spent, no matter what the cost might be:

I assure you, Minister citizen [*sic*—the appellation was relatively new], that never has an expense been more well spent. After the small amount of time that I have been here, and from everything I hear, I think I can tell you that this country is far from the public spirit that ought to animate it. The aristocracy still reigns. The nobles still have a lot of clout; priests have a great deal of influence: religious prejudices reign here in all their force. The inhabitants are very wary; it is difficult to get through to them, and I think that it is necessary to employ all the means that the politics of a free people can sanction in order to strip off the blindfold that covers the eyes of the inhabitants of this country.[102]

Before La Montansier had given her final acceptance of the Belgian proposal, no doubt awaiting word from Paris that the government would cover her losses, the Belgians apparently had the audacity to launch a surprise theatrical counterattack: "Would you believe it? During this interval [while thinking over their proposal] they performed *Pierre le cruel,* an anti-Revolutionary tragedy by De Belloy." For Lebrun's benefit, La Montansier cited a few of the "aristocratic verses with which the work is riddled," including such lines as "[E]ven a guilty king is a sacred object."[103] What La Montansier neglected to mention, understandably enough, was that her intimate acquaintance with the play stemmed from her having produced it at her theater in Paris little more than a year before—testimony to the swiftness with which the political climate changed in those crucial years 1791–93.[104]

January 1793 was a different world from the fall of 1791, and Citizeness Montansier, as an agent of the minister of foreign affairs of Revolutionary France, was very clear in her abhorrence of what, under existing conditions, could only be construed as royalist propaganda. She and General Moreton "invited" the Belgians to a meeting at the general's headquarters. During this meeting, which lasted from eleven in the morning until nine at night, General Moreton played a heavier hand. He informed the Belgian theater directors of his extreme displeasure and let them know that if they ever again attempted to perform any such play, he would

> make use of all his power to punish them severely, and that, furthermore, the best method of removing from them the means [of doing so in the future] would be to come to an arrangement with [Montansier], because the Executive Council of France believed, in its wisdom, that it was necessary to send a patriotic troupe to put on plays suitable for the enlightenment of the public spirit and to propagate the principles of liberty and equality.

According to La Montansier, "This dressing-down by the general rendered them better disposed to enter into an agreement." And after ten hours of negotiations, Moreton, La Montansier, and the Belgian theater owners came to an understanding: the French troupe procured a lease through Easter, although at terms that to La Montansier seemed "very onerous."[105]

If La Montansier (and France) had to some extent been taken advantage of by the crafty Belgians who had "consulted their [own] interests rather than their patriotism," she nevertheless prided herself on having stipulated that the lease should run through Easter, "regarding it as very important to perform during the holy week and to strike the first blow against the religious abuses with which this country is infected." In addition to going head-to-head with religious spectacles, Montansier hoped to offer several free performances for the city's poor, reminding Lebrun that "it is important to enlighten this class!"

At the conclusion of this last letter to Lebrun, La Montansier did not neglect to mention the unpleasant necessity of government subsidies for her enterprise: "I have no doubt that because of my good and useful intentions, the executive power will come to my aid, in the event that the [theater's] receipts do not equal the expenses. . . . I am far from imagining any kind of profit; the happiness of being useful to my country will be the sweetest recompense, but at the same time I cannot hide from you that I will not [personally] be able to bear any kind of deficit." And here, La Montansier took it upon herself to suggest a political solution to the anticipated shortfall: "I believe . . . that the provisional representatives of the Belgian people would be able to subvent any losses that I might have if the Executive Council of France should judge it proper to invite them to do so."[106]

We know that La Montansier's propaganda theater was not exactly an unqualified success. The bill that she would eventually present to the Executive Council contained a rather hefty deficit.[107] And as for the free performances intended to enlighten the poor, an agent of the French government reported back to the Ministry of Foreign Affairs that "[t]he three or four times that free performances were given, the hall was filled only with French soldiers; not one native inhabitant showed up."[108] What the minister of foreign affairs and La Montansier had hoped would lead to a cultural awakening of the Belgian people in the end proved to be little more than a morale boost for French troops garrisoned in Brussels or passing through. If the Belgians themselves were unmoved by La Montansier's productions (or unwilling to attend in the first place), then at least French troops knew a good show when they saw one. As the government agent reported back to Paris: "A great number [of soldiers] pass through here; they go to the show [spectacle]; the patriotic plays electrify them. . . . After the play, they get up on stage and dance the carmagnole and sing the Marseillaise."[109]

On 24 March 1793, Austrian forces reclaimed Brussels, forcing French troops (and troupes) into a hasty retreat. In the confusion, La Montansier was forced to abandon ten trunks filled with expensive costumes. When, upon her return to Paris, she presented her final bill to the National Convention, she offered to swallow the expense of the abandoned trunks, but hoped that "the council, in according some sort of compensation to the artists who compose the troupe, will render justice to their zeal and patriotism."[110] Such, then, was the ignominious end of a project that had engendered such enthusiasm at the highest levels of the French government. Although it had spent some 53,000 assignats of the government's money, it was not clear that the first propaganda troupe of the modern world had enlightened anyone at all.

The success or failure of Montansier's troupe is immaterial for our concerns here, except insofar as it indicates that Revolutionary principles and the Revolutionary zeal for theater may have had difficulty crossing national-cultural boundaries. Much more important, for the purposes of this study, is what Montansier's mission tells us about the interconnections between theater and politics in Revolutionary France on the eve of the Terror. Virtually simultaneously with Belgium's fall into French hands, officials at the highest levels of government were conferring with French theater entrepreneurs about the logistics of dispatching French actors in order to complete their conquest of neighboring territories. One might argue that these French theater troupes were nothing more than the means toward the specific end of educating the Belgians in Revolutionary principles and that French actors were in some sense no different from propaganda pamphlets. If this were the case, then why not simply flood Belgium with Revolutionary literature? The answer, of course, is that the fall of Belgium offered the Revolutionary government the unique opportunity to export something that could not be conveyed by the written word: the exciting theatricality of the Revolution. They hoped that the same spirit that "electrified" the French military troops who attended Montansier's performances might animate the Belgian populace with enthusiasm for the Revolution. Belgian "stupor" could be eradicated by armies of Revolutionary actors, just as Belgian territory had been captured by the Revolution's soldiers. And to this end, the French government was willing to devote not only large sums of money but the time and efforts of France's generals who, in the middle of the most important military conquest to date, reserved entire days in order to bring about Revolutionary theater on Belgian soil.

Actors storming the political stage, politicians in the National Assembly behaving like actors, and both of them suddenly discovering the profound importance of political theater—all of these phenomena testify to the convergence of politics and theater in Revolutionary France. Within a remarkably short span of time, France had been transformed from a nation in which actors were virtually ostracized from every aspect of social and civic life into a nation in which actors and politicians—and theater and politics in general—mixed so familiarly that they had become virtually indistinguishable.

6 Theater Critics
Reactions to Actors on the Political Stage

At the dawn of the Revolution, actors made up the largest group of the politically disenfranchised in France after women and Protestants.[1] Of uncertain civil status, excommunicated by the Catholic Church, and socially ostracized, they had tended to marry amongst themselves. In short, their profession, often inherited rather than embraced by choice, had set them apart as an outcast people.

As the previous chapter detailed, however, in the earliest of the Revolutionary *journées* quite a few actors seemingly overcame the deeply rooted prejudices against them to join the vanguard of the Revolution. Even if the National Assembly would not declare actors full citizens of the French nation until late December of 1789, many actors did not hesitate to take part in the Revolutionary enterprise. Quite a few actors sought and attained positions of importance in the military, and others began to involve themselves in political affairs. It was almost as if the old regime and the old way of thinking had melted away in an instant. Or had it?

In truth, the actors' debut on the political stage was by no means greeted with universal applause. The logic of the old regime that had kept actors in a world apart did not disappear overnight. Although for quite some time "enlightened" circles had been branding the exclusion of actors an "irrational prejudice" and it had become somewhat fashionable to treat actors as one's equal, many people nevertheless persisted in regarding actors as somehow tainted. If in theory many people were willing, in the spirit of the new Revolution, to accord actors certain civil liberties that had hitherto been denied to them, such individuals were often wholly unprepared to accept the logical consequences of this liberty. One might speak vaguely of actors as citizens, and even condemn the Catholic Church for its centuries of hostility toward actors, and yet at the same time balk at the prospect of an actor playing any active, visible role in the Revolution. As long as they kept to their theaters, amusing the public in the evenings, one was prepared to accept them as French men and women. But as soon as they crossed the threshold into the light of day, they were actors—*comédiens*—who had stepped out of their element. It would be some time before actors and their fellow pariahs of the old regime—executioners and Jews—were considered by others and indeed felt themselves to be fully equal citizens of the nation.

The curious thing about the general anxiety concerning actors' involvement in public life is that it was not limited to any particular political grouping. Enemies of the Revolution were quick to seize upon the actors' assumption of positions of command as the epitome of the general absurdity of the Revolution itself. But loyal supporters of the Revolution were just as likely to be troubled by the actors' forays onto the public stage. In a political world fraught with anxiety and uncertainty and already rife with charges of imposture and theatricality, the prospect of having theatrical actors perform political and military roles was simply too problematic; the new government had enough trouble convincing people of its legitimacy without worrying about how to incorporate erstwhile outcasts who told lies for a living.

No sooner did actors attempt to assume roles in the new Revolution, then, than a flood of pamphlets poured forth from both the right and the left condemning their involvement in political and military affairs. Actors were variously characterized as histrionic agents of dangerous political radicalism, or conversely, as pawns of the counterrevolutionary aristocracy. For individuals across the political spectrum, actors posed the risk of contaminating the political order with an aura of illegitimate and dangerous theatricality.

The hostility that greeted the actors' presence on the public stage was a manifestation of a general anxiety that lay just beneath the surface and that actors seemed uniquely capable of inciting. In the following pages, I focus on particular episodes in which the presence of actors where—in the eyes of many—they should not have been provoked a torrent of hostile recriminations. By reading these accounts carefully, we gain insight not only into antitheatricality itself, but also into a more general hostility toward representation that flared up on both the extreme right and the extreme left and that lay at the very heart of both the counterrevolutionary and the Jacobin mindset.

Les comédiens commandants

In July of 1789, as the people of Paris took to the streets, the excitement of the moment seemed to spell a kind of holiday from conventional mores. Despite the lingering stigma still attached to their profession, several actors of the Théâtre-Français not only joined the bourgeois municipal guard (soon to be the National Guard) in the districts closest to their theater but found themselves cresting the wave of patriotic fervor and were actually elected by their fellow guardsmen to positions of command. As we saw in the preceding chapter, the actor—now colonel—Naudet had been careful to assert that he had not sought a leadership position, but had rather "found myself at the head of forty-three individuals."[2]

Naudet's version of the story—that the actors had been thrust almost without their realizing it into the limelight—did not prove palatable to everyone. As one pamphleteer saw the situation, far from having grudgingly accepted leadership positions from their troops, the actors had skillfully intrigued and manipulated their way into positions of command:

> Several individuals accustomed to showing themselves in public have gotten the idea that they would be able to do so to greater advantage if they had themselves elected officers of the Parisian National Guard. (In the district of the Cordeliers, of St.-André-des-Arts & others, these individuals have solicited and obtained the positions of colonel, of lieutenant colonel, captain, lieutenant, and second lieutenant; none of them seems to have sought the rank of soldier. . . .) In order to accomplish this, they had only to indicate their wishes to their young admirers.[3]

This conspiracy of actors was, the pamphleteer claimed, part of a larger conspiracy of "aristocratic corrupters," whose agents are "filthy chameleons" and can be recognized by the following attributes: "[They are] indiscreetly zealous, . . . [they] show themselves everywhere, speaking endlessly."[4] This author, soon to be followed by countless others, was among the first to raise the specter of a France that had unwittingly fallen prey to a conspiracy of strange individuals who, whether they were actual theatrical actors or not, seemed to exhibit an irrepressible desire to be seen and heard and an uncanny "chameleon-like" ability to change themselves to suit the exigencies of the moment.

One of the most interesting antitheatrical texts to appear in the early months of the Revolution was an anonymous pamphlet entitled *Les comédiens commandans* (Comédiens in command), written in the form of an open letter to the citizens of Paris, denouncing the recent election of actors to command positions in the National Guard. Ostensibly authored by a naive "provincial" freshly arrived from the provinces, the pamphlet is in fact a rather sophisticated attempt (no doubt by a Parisian) to expose the inherent absurdity of comédiens in command—an absurdity so glaring that even a know-nothing provincial could not fail to notice and be revolted by it.

The pamphlet begins with the provincial's arrival in Paris within a month of the fall of the Bastille. He is so fervently patriotic that he can barely contain his enthusiasm: "The [eagerness] to hear, to question, to see, to admire, brings me to the point that I think I could stay awake for six months, and I am far from complaining about it. Each day, each night, each instant offer new scenes that I gather together with careful precision, in order to instruct my good fellow citizens of the provinces."[5] Explaining his motivations for drafting an open letter to the citizens of Paris, however, the provincial lets it be known at the outset that something is rotten at the very core of this most Revolutionary city: "All of this is beautiful, without a doubt, admirable. But sirs, within this whole, something took me by surprise & I will attempt to make it known to you" (4). In the eyes of the provincial, then, something absurd, something fetid has surreptitiously passed into the new Revolutionary society. And somehow, many Parisians seem too caught up in the moment to perceive it; even if some of the characters in the narrative will betray an awareness of the absurdity, they are somehow content to simply laugh and move on. It is only through the commonsense eyes of the provincial that the reader will begin to understand something that the wily Parisians seem unable to recognize: the very presence of actors on the Revolutionary stage threatened to turn the sacred drama of the Revolution into a cheap farce.

On the day after his arrival in Paris, the provincial learns of a flag benediction ceremony that is about to take place in the Cordeliers district. After inquiring as to whether all are welcome at "this august and imposing ceremony," the provincial is informed that attendance requires a "ticket." The provincial expresses both surprise and despair at the need for a ticket but nevertheless resolves to get hold of one. After asking all the people he encounters whether they have a spare ticket, he is eventually told by several citizen-soldiers that the only means of procuring a ticket is to approach one of the commanding officers of the district: M. Naudet, Colonel; M. Grammont, Lieutenant Colonel; M. de Saint-Pry and M. de Marci, both officers. The provincial, however, hesitates to approach these officers because "their very names inspir[ed] in me such a feeling of respect, I did not yet dare to make a nuisance of myself by approaching their lordships" (5). And, despondent, he gives up all hope of seeing the ceremony.

On his way back to his lodgings, however, our hapless provincial passes in front of the church where the ceremony will take place and decides to linger outside, hoping at the very least to catch a glimpse of the passing troops. At first, the provincial seems in awe of the spectacle: "At three o'-clock, the roll of the drums announced the arrival [of the troops]. Each company advanced in order, colors unfurled, preceded by its commanders and its officers." In the midst of this imposing splendor, the provincial is somewhat taken aback by the rather loose demeanor of an officer by the name of Dugazon. And yet, precisely because this officer seems so much less intimidating than the others, the provincial musters the courage to approach him for a ticket: "The offhand, rather careless way in which he led his company convinced me that he was easily approachable" (6). As the provincial approaches the officer, hat in hand, he is stopped by an individual who suggests, in a laughing tone, that it is not appropriate to interrupt an officer in the course of his duties. When the provincial seems befuddled as to why this seemingly serious statement merits laughter, the Parisian responds, " 'Oh! oh! what a dope! Oh! the pro[vincial]! . . . Oh! Oh! the provincial! Oh! what a good one! Oh! if only he knew! . . . But! Oh! But! boy will he laugh! Oh! will he laugh! when! . . . Then again . . . but . . . no . . . no, sh! . . . sh! oh! he'll find out soon enough what they are!' " (7).

With this response, the reader is none too subtly being set up for a clear contrast between the reverence and respect in which the provincial holds the officers and their ridiculous unworthiness of that respect. In the following scene, the jarring contrast becomes evident when our provincial, having managed finally to gain admittance to the ceremony, describes his soon to be interrupted awe at the beauty of the solemn Revolutionary spectacle:

> Filled with sweet, delicious impressions, savoring for quite a while the inexpressible charm of this ceremony that was so new to me; I was completely absorbed, when a raucous and annoying voice scream[ed] "Hey! Naudet! Naudet! Hey you! Hey you! Naudet! Listen up!" [and] pulled me out of my trance. I raised my eyes and realized that the person shouting was M. Grammont, who was, in such a manner, trying to get the attention of M. Naudet, his colonel. I was struck by how inappropriate *[peu décent]* his tone was and could not imagine how someone whom I would have expected to have the manners appropriate to his rank could be so ill-mannered. (9)

At this point in the narrative, the Parisian who earlier stopped the provincial from approaching Dugazon in such a strange mock-serious tone now reappears and asks the provincial for his opinion of the tone in which the lieutenant colonel addressed his colonel. The provincial confesses that he is "revolted." The Parisian then asks in disbelief: "Have you then never heard of *les* Naudet, *les* Grammont, *les* Saint Pry, *les* Marci, or *les* Dugazon?"— prefixing the names of these actors with the definite article that was appropriate to their true station.[6] The provincial confesses that the names sound familiar, and it is only then that the Parisian lets him in on the joke: "[T]hese men are comédiens dressed up as military men *[ces Messieurs sont des comédiens revêtus de titres militaires]*." The provincial exclaims, dumbfounded: "What! . . . Comédiens?" And the Parisian replies, "In the fullest meaning of the term" (9–10).

Although the image of actors as military commanders might be somewhat amusing to the modern reader—it would seem to have the makings of a relatively formulaic comedy—it is difficult for us to grasp, at a distance of more than two centuries, the extent to which the hybrid of the actor-soldier was not simply amusing but also profoundly troubling to the inhabitant of the late eighteenth century. As the author of this pamphlet makes clear, speaking through the mouthpiece of the no longer naive provincial, the problem revolves around the breaking down of familiar categories, the crossing over of previously impenetrable boundaries. These Parisian actors were doing what no other actors in the world had ever had the audacity to do:

> In truth I remain astounded when [I think that] these individuals are enjoying in Paris the prerogative of marching at the head of a district, while Roscius in Rome, [and] Garrick in London, in due consideration of their nations, never had the idiotic and vain ambition to aspire *[prétendre]* to [a position] of command! Their good sense, their judgment enabled them to know their status *[les mettaient à même de se classer]*, & they knew very well that although renowned as precious in the theatrical arts, they would have been deemed ridiculous in the military arts. (10–11)

Actors were not and could never be military officers because actors were fundamentally different. They belonged to a different "class" of men, and only the unbridled arrogance of these *comédiens commandants* prevented them from knowing, as all other actors in history had known, their true status—or, literally, how to "class themselves." All that they could ever be—as the Parisian had described them in revealing the joke to the provincial—were "comédiens dressed up as military men." And no matter how they dressed, they were incapable of behaving in any other fashion than as the actors they truly were; whether inside or outside the theater, they would always act as if they were onstage. As the provincial soon discovers, for example, the actors cannot resist the temptation to post meaningless military notices, signed by them, simply as an excuse for getting their names posted throughout the district; they are, in short, apparently incapable of distinguishing between an important military announcement and a theatrical *affiche*.

If actors, then, had difficulty distinguishing between the theatrical world and the *theatrum mundi*, the fact nevertheless remained that everyone else could not help being painfully aware of precisely this difference. At issue was the fundamental impossibility of structuring a force of order around individuals who inherently could not be taken seriously. Referring to a funeral procession in which a citizen-soldier was accompanied to the cemetery by a detachment of the guard headed by the actor Grammont, the provincial asks: "Was [Grammont] in his [rightful] place? It was evening. *Risum teneatis amici!* [You're not supposed to laugh, friends!]" (12). Evenings, in other words, were when Lieutenant Colonel Grammont was supposed to be amusing spectators at the theater. But he was not where one expected to find him, and he was not doing what he was supposed to be doing. The end result was that the solemnity of this spectacle risked being reduced to farce, and one was forced to resist the impulse to snicker.

The actors, by not being where one expected to find them (and being where one did not expect to find them), were powerful agents of disorder in a society that was already reeling from political and cultural disruption. Day and night, the solemn and the silly, the sacred and the profane were becoming hopelessly indistinguishable:

> And so, gentlemen, we encounter, whether in the morning or the night, our comédiens in uniform, going through their paces. Even Chamville, [who plays] that amiable [stock character] Crispino, is *getting mixed up in it;* if you don't suppress this military frenzy in them, soon we will have neither tragedies nor comedies performed. (12, emphasis added)

The solution to the problem was a matter of simple common sense: it was time to reestablish the boundaries between two things that should never have been mixed in the first place; everyone should go back to doing what they were meant to do:

> [The task of the actor is] to amuse us—I will soften the term—to instruct us. . . . Devoted by profession to pleasure, to the amusement of the public, [the comédien's] duty is to make himself agreeable to that public, and not to command it. I would tell him that the National Guard, not being in the business of comedy, should not have comédiens for leaders. (13)

These *comédiens commandants* were, then, monstrosities. They were part soldier, part clown. In the words of another pamphleteer, they were *marchandise mêlée* (mixed goods, i.e., apples and oranges).[7] There could be only one solution to the problem. As the provincial warns Parisians at the conclusion of his letter, chaos will result if they do not restore the traditional "order" of things: "[S]oon we will see . . . [all of our *farceurs*] passing themselves off as Caesar, Pompey, and Alexander. This will be a truly pitiable situation, gentlemen, but it could happen if you do not put things in order *[si vous n'y mettez ordre]*" (14).

But there is something more. We would miss a crucial aspect of Revolutionary antitheatricality if we stopped at this relatively straightforward desire to return to a time in which the differences between life and theater, citizens and clowns were much more plainly drawn. The stigma attached to actors, the disdain in which they were so commonly held, was not simply a reflex prejudice whose logic had been lost somewhere in the distant past. Many of those who expressed antitheatrical sentiments knew—or at least thought they knew—why actors were different from other people. There was a widespread perception that the act of performing before an audience was inherently debasing; acting, in other words, was a form of prostitution in which individuals allowed themselves to be used by paying spectators. What seemed to bother people most was the fact that actors allowed themselves to be *sifflé*—literally whistled at, the French equivalent of booing, but referring in general to the host of indignities to which actors were subjected by spectators. This public humiliation in return for money made the actor unsuitable for public functions. As the author of *Les comédiens comman-dans* asked in the epigraph to the pamphlet: "Exposed to sifflets, ought they to be commanding?" The answer to this question, as the author spelled out toward the end of the pamphlet, was a resounding no: "[I]t is the ultimate in ridiculousness that a Parisian bourgeois should be militarily at the command of an officer whom he can daily, for the sum total of forty-eight sous, applaud or siffler at his whim. This contrast undoubtedly defies *[révolte]* common sense" (13).

These commanding officers, far from being the authority figures that a force of order would seem to require, could be bought for a nominal sum. For the price of a theater ticket, one could, in a sense, have one's way with them, using them however one wished. Paying spectators could whistle them off the stage, force them to come back on the stage, heckle them, or force them to perform an entirely different play. And the citizens of the Cordeliers district could do nothing but watch helplessly as their commanding officers became the playthings of the audience.[8] According to Camille Desmoulins, it was precisely this concern that prompted what he calls "an amusing discussion" in the sectional assembly of the Cordeliers district:

> The Cordeliers district has already shown that it looks upon this profession [of acting] as did the Greeks, and it has named M. Grammont captain; this fact gave rise to an amusing discussion. Sirs, said one individual, I am very proud to have as my commanding officer Orosmane or Tancrède [military characters in plays]; but for the honor of the district, I motion that it be forbidden to the fifty-nine other [districts] to siffler our captain from the parterre.[9]

In the above account, it seems clear that Desmoulins harbors no ill feelings toward actors. Moreover, he seems to be making light of the concerns of the citizens of the district who, he says, although they are quick to affirm their support of the actors that they have elected to leadership roles, nevertheless express a certain anxiety as to how their commanding officers will be treated by those outside the district. The fear, of course, is that they will be treated like actors. And the solution, as least as far as Desmoulins relates the discussion, would seem to lie in forcing spectators to treat Grammont, Naudet, and the others like officers of the guard rather than like actors.

Desmoulins's story, regardless of how truthful an account it may be, suggests that although certain segments of the population had managed to overcome their prejudices to the point that they could elect actors as commanding officers, they were not entirely free from the anxiety brought about by the tangible results of their spontaneous decision. Although in Desmoulins's account the citizens of the Cordeliers district could clearly accept that an actor could become a commanding officer, they just as clearly had problems with the notion that a commanding officer could, each evening, become an actor. A *comédien commandant* could be one or the other; but it was difficult to accept that he could be both.

Bordier

It seems clear that the source of much of this anxiety about the mixing of categories that was common to both the supporters and the detractors of the actors in question lay in the fear that something that was supposed to be taken very seriously might become the object of ridicule. A roughly contemporaneous event that took place in the provincial city of Rouen would show, however, that the mixing of actors and Revolutionary politics was not always a laughing matter. The controversy that swirled around the actor Bordier and his escapades in the region of Rouen had a decidedly more violent tone than the debate that embroiled Naudet, Grammont, and their colleagues in Paris. In the pamphlets that discuss the Bordier affair, the image of the actor let loose on the Revolutionary stage is much more insidious than the image of the *comédiens commandants*. This is not to say that the portraits of Bordier are drawn without humor, but it is a strange amalgam of both humor and horror. And Bordier himself seems to provoke a peculiar mix of scorn and desire for violent retribution on the part of his critics.

The wildly diverging narratives of Bordier's actions in August of 1789 make an objective account extremely difficult to piece together. The various pamphlets agree on two basic facts, however: (1) on the night of 3 August 1789, Bordier, who enjoyed a certain notoriety in Paris for his performances at the Théâtre des Variétés, and an accomplice named Jourdain were at the head of a group of individuals who pillaged the Hôtel de l'Intendance of Rouen, the official residence of the local representative of monarchical authority; (2) both Bordier and Jourdain were hanged on 21 August by the official executioner of Rouen.

Neither the actions of Bordier and Jourdain, nor those of the "mob" that was supposedly under Bordier's control, nor even the harsh response of the Rouen authorities was particularly unusual, considering the climate in which they occurred. In the weeks that followed the popular uprisings in Paris on 13–14 July, provincial France was shaken by hundreds of disturbances not unlike the one in which Bordier and Jourdain were involved. Their attack on the Hôtel de l'Intendance of Rouen and their consequent execution must therefore be seen in the larger context of the Great Fear and the concurrent fear of brigands that gripped France in the summer of 1789.[10]

What sets the Bordier affair apart from the other disturbances of that summer, however, are the number and tone of the pamphlets that rushed into print to comment on the events in question. Particularly interesting, for our purposes, is the fact that Jourdain, found equally culpable by the authorities, was virtually ignored by the pamphleteers, who reserved the full extent of their anger and indignation for Bordier. Bordier was not some run-of-the-mill "brigand," yet another nameless stooge of the aristocracy sent forth to disturb the peace. Bordier was an actor. And that was a fact that demanded commentary.

Whatever the truth may have been involving the events of 3 August, and whatever Bordier's intentions may have been, his involvement in the uprising in Rouen clearly struck a nerve. At issue was not simply that the Hôtel de l'Intendance had been sacked but that it had been sacked by an actor. And the vilifications heaped upon Bordier came, interestingly enough, from a variety of different political quarters that were nevertheless united in their common disbelief, amusement, horror, and indignation that a Parisian actor, a comédien, would presume to play a role in the real-life drama that was unfolding in France during the summer of 1789.

A pamphlet entitled *La mort subite du sieur Bordier* (The sudden death of Mr. Bordier), which was published shortly after Bordier's execution, begins its narrative not with the events of the night of 3 August but rather with the essential fact of Bordier's true identity:

> There used to be, for quite a while, in Paris, a man named Bordier, an insignificant itinerant actor *[petit acteur forain]*, tolerably playing the role of valet in the farces of the [Théâtre des] Variétés. Well, this actor has just finished his career in a manner that cannot exactly be described as honorable.[11]

The pamphlet then proceeds to tell the story of how Bordier the relatively harmless and amusing comédien was transformed into Bordier the agent of the aristocracy, whose ability to play a role "tolerably" was put to a new and insidious purpose:

> [Bordier] had received in Paris a rather large sum of money to further the plans of the aristocracy. . . . [H]e fired up the spirits [of others], knew how to win them over, indoctrinated them, and ended up making creatures of the aristocracy out of them. (2)

Bordier's powers of persuasion eventually found unsuspecting victims in the form of a band of brigands who unwittingly attacked the coach in which Bordier was traveling on the outskirts of Rouen. Needless to say, Bordier had no difficulty in turning the brigands from their original designs, and, "because he was a naturally gifted speaker, he was named their leader" (2).

With the band of brigands now under his command, Bordier fulfilled the designs of the aristocracy and embarked upon the rampage that made him notorious: "There was no excess that they would not commit; they pillaged homes, châteaux, they ravaged fields and harvests; in short, nothing was sacred to them" (2). When, finally, he was apprehended by the authorities, the cunning Bordier attempted once again to make use of his uncanny powers of persuasion:

> Le sieur Bordier readily [attempted to] exonerate himself; . . . [he claimed that] after having been taken prisoner by the brigands, they had forced him to become their leader, and that he had preferred taking this course of action to exposing himself to the inevitable death that would have been the result of his refusal. As for the rest, he never aspired to anything more than to see himself relieved of a command that had always been a burden to him and that he exercised only with the greatest repugnance. (6)

Here, it would seem, Bordier is attempting to use the strategy of his actor-soldier colleagues in Paris; rather than assume responsibility for his actions, he instead hopes to pretend that, like Naudet and the others, he simply "found himself" in command.

The author of *La mort subite du sieur Bordier* does not, of course, fall for this story; instead, he paints a picture of the actor Bordier as a man who, despite the fact that he was only a "tolerable" actor, possessed an extraordinary ability to bend the will of others. He "fired up the spirits" of the Parisians. He managed to transform himself from unsuspecting victim of brigands to brigand leader almost instantaneously, leading them on a rampage. And all of this was done not out of Bordier's convictions but rather because nameless aristocrats had given him a large sum of money. Bordier, only a mediocre actor in a second-rate theater in Paris, was nevertheless a powerful weapon in the hands of the counterrevolution.

A similar portrait of Bordier is contained in a play entitled *Bordier aux enfers* (Bordier in Hades). As in the previous text, Bordier is implicated in a nationwide conspiracy, but instead of being the agent of aristocrats, he is here portrayed as an accomplice of those who frequented the Palais-Royal, the unofficial meeting place of such radicals as Danton and Desmoulins. Significantly, the author of *Bordier aux enfers* not only characterizes Bordier, the comédien, as a political firebrand, but conversely attributes an air of shabby theatricality to the more radical and popular politics of the Revolutionary *journées*. Thus, when Bordier, at the beginning of the play, finds himself in Hades, he encounters one of his co-conspirators who informs him in the following language that she was killed during the march on Versailles: "I'd gone and joined the comic troupe from la Halle, but when I got there [Versailles] some moron . . . put a little too much lead in my head." [12]

At this point in the play, Bordier is approached by the king's guards who were murdered by the crowds and are now, conveniently enough, employed as guards in the underworld. One of the guards asks whether he is not Bordier, "that comédien from the [Théâtre des] Variétés?" Bordier replies as follows, confessing his ties to radical politics and not incidentally making explicit the connections between the true-seeming lines delivered by actors and the inspiring if empty rhetoric of the Parisian radicals:

> Yeah, that's right, Bordier, comédien, but Bordier the most excellent, the most applauded of all actors, Bordier capable of playing more than the role they would have had him play outside the theater, or on the stage; you probably don't realize that I was one of the pillars of liberty, one of the agents of the political body whose august senate is headquartered in the Palais-Royal, where I shone more than once among the most vehement orators, & my ideas were considered to be so interesting that I was appointed to go to the capital of another province, and bring the sacred fire. . . . [But they] didn't want to hear the truth no matter what color I painted it; imprisoned as a true victim of despotism, interrogated on various details, which I answered in that comic manner that has won me so many converts, they cruelly sentenced me to a death . . . that I shall never get over; & they hanged me from a rope; and that's how they fooled me— me who fooled everybody else. (14)

Bordier is here portrayed as someone who is much more concerned with the form in which his political addresses have been delivered and with the effect that he has had on spectators than with the content of the ideas themselves. Once again, as in the previous pamphlet, the portrait of Bordier is of a man without stable and heartfelt convictions, a man willing to paint the truth in whatever "color" serves his purposes.

Unable to bear the endless patter emanating from Bordier's mouth, the guard finally silences him, lamenting the fact that the French people seem to be unable to distinguish between those who truly have their best interest at heart and those who merely appear to do so: "Shut up, you wretch. . . . [H]eaven hope that all those who've followed in your footsteps meet the same end, & that the people, good, but too credulous, may distinguish between those who desire only their happiness and the sycophants who are their enemies" (15). And isn't that what makes Bordier so dangerous? In a world in which tangible legitimacy had evaporated almost overnight, in which the embodiment of the nation had been replaced by innumerable political factions, all of which claimed to speak on behalf of the nation, how was one to distinguish between true patriots and those who merely appeared to be true patriots? Actors, skilled in the art of vraisemblance, could wreak havoc in a new political culture in which all claims to legitimacy were discursive and abstract rather than embodied and concrete. Bordier's crime was not only his pillaging of the region; it was also his having taken his talent of make-believe beyond the threshold of the Théâtre des Variétés and into the theater of politics. Brought before the judges of Hades, Bordier is admonished in terms that recall the pamphlets that condemned the *comédiens commandants* for getting "mixed up" in affairs outside the theater: "To what ends did you put your talent for expressing yourself? Why did you get mixed up *[te mêlais-tu]* in public controversies? Was that the place of a man to whom God had given the lucrative talent of amusing the public?" (25).

Bordier's powers of persuasion are contained by the judges in Hades in precisely the same manner as they were contained by the judges in Rouen— with one crucial difference: given the fact that hanging him once did not seem to prevent him from ranting on even in death, the judges of Hades sentence him to be hanged repeatedly for all eternity.

The extremely effective solution of hanging Bordier is also the subject of a peculiar drawing entitled *Avis aux perturbateurs du bon-ordre par feu Bordier, mort en l'air à Rouen le 21 août 1789* (Advice to the disrupters of order by the late Bordier, dead in the air in Rouen). In this drawing, Bordier, dressed in full Harlequin regalia, replete with blackface, poses before the gallows. Although the particular political agenda of this drawing is difficult to ascertain, it shares with the two preceding texts a characterization of Bordier as both preposterous and deeply disturbing, a dangerous clown about to be silenced permanently.

The various condemnations of Bordier[13] prompted two pamphlets written in the actor's defense, both of which give the impression that their authors were bewildered by the vicious nature of the texts that condemned him. As one of the authors complained, "They accuse him, . . . of having cut off the head of the Intendant from Paris, . . . of having been brutal enough to make [the head] kiss his son, and having half of the heart hung up in his bedroom."[14] Clearly, the author contended, the outlandish picture painted of Bordier was an indication that those who condemned him had ulterior motives: "The portrait is too outrageous, it is too revolting so as to blind us to the designs of the portrait's painter; it only remained for [the pamphleteer], as a final touch to this shameless project, to represent Bordier as a cannibal with revolting lips [the color of] the blood of his treacherous and criminal heart."[15]

Significantly, this pamphlet in defense of Bordier was dedicated to the "destroyers of the aristocrats, by order of the enemies of despotism," with the implication that the detractors of Bordier were part of an aristocratic conspiracy. And Bordier himself is depicted in both pamphlets that are sympathetic to him as a patriot who gave his life for his country, and his execution is portrayed as a virtual crucifixion at the hands of the aristocracy, a sort of patriotic passion play: " 'Citizens,' [Bordier] shouted, 'I die for you, I die an innocent man, I die for my country.' The spectators dissolved into tears."[16]

Clearly, the political affiliation of the various authors had little to do with whether they wrote in condemnation or in defense of Bordier. Rather, a more ambiguous but no less strongly felt sensibility, which cut across political lines, seems to have decided the pamphlets' authors. If one was prepared to accept the presence of actors on the public stage, then Bordier was the innocent victim of a counterrevolutionary conspiracy that used antitheatrical-

Avis aux Perturbateurs du bon-Ordre.
PAR FEU BORDIER
Mort en l'Air a Rouen le 21 Aoust 1789.

Vous verrez que je serai pendu
pour arranger l'affaire.

Nuit aux Aventures Act III
Sc IX rôle de Frontin.

9. Bordier, dressed as Harlequin, about to be hanged. Photo: Bibliothèque nationale de France, Paris.

ity as a pretext for bringing about the downfall of a true patriot. If, however, one was deeply unsettled by the thought of actors mixed up in Revolutionary affairs, then Bordier was undoubtedly the devious agent of nefarious forces. No matter whether he was doing the bidding of the aristocracy or of Parisian radicals, Bordier had the power to sway his audience; he had unusual political talent. And yet he had no convictions; he was form without content, unbridled ambitions, the paid stooge of a larger conspiracy. He had been sent forth, spewing believable but empty phrases, for no other purpose than to destabilize the French nation, just as one might spread counterfeit currency in an enemy land to sow confusion.

Actors on the Defensive

Apart from the protestations of Bordier's friends, actors seem to have been relatively mute concerning the Bordier affair. Particularly the actors who belonged to the more prestigious theater companies, and consequently those with the greatest chance of being eventually included within the ranks of the bourgeoisie, no doubt wished to distance themselves from the wild activities of a *farceur* from a second-rate theater company. But the *comédiens commandants* were a different story: these were distinguished actors from France's foremost company. If ever the virtues of the patriotic citizen could be embodied in an actor, it was in the likes of Naudet, Grammont, and their colleagues who had been elected by the district of the Cordeliers to positions of command. The hopes of all upstanding actors throughout the country for a civil status were therefore dependent upon the public's willingness to accept these patriotic actors, and others who might follow in their footsteps, as equal citizens within the new—and constantly evolving—social order. On 31 August 1789, therefore, upon hearing of the election of another member of their troupe to the position of second lieutenant in the guard of the neighboring district of St.-André-des-Arts, the actors of the Théâtre-Français drafted the following letter as an expression of gratitude on behalf of all actors in France:

> The comédiens of the French nation offer the homage of their respect to the district de St.-André-des-Arts.
> Named to honorable positions at that moment when all Frenchmen battled for liberty, our enthusiasm, sirs, seemed to acquire even greater strength from the honor of marching at your side.
> A legal and more universally decided [*plus combiné*] appointment has established one of us in the rank of second lieutenant.
> The courage and determination the members of this district have shown in the face of the vain efforts of a forever-unjust prejudice ... bond us to you for eternity; united by sacred ties, by the ties of citizens, of brothers; if only you

could read the depths of our hearts, you would see the indelible mark of our love and gratitude.

Accept then this oath from all of us—never have we uttered one more pure and more solemn: "We swear, all of us, to live and die in the defense of liberty, the glory of the nation, and the more perfect prosperity of the district of St.-André-des-Arts."[17]

Although they were certainly aware that a "forever-unjust prejudice" was the root cause of the outcry that had greeted the election of their colleagues to the guard, the actors seemed to think that this prejudice might be combated by their attestations of undying loyalty to the French nation. Unaware or perhaps refusing to see that a certain segment of the population regarded their profession as inherently incompatible with full civil status (which implied eligibility for all forms of public office), the actors persisted in the belief that tangible proofs of their patriotism might convince their critics to reconsider their position. On 24 September 1789, the actors of the Théâtre-Français resolved to send a patriotic gift to the National Assembly, and they drafted the following letter to be read when their gift was presented:

> To the President of the National Assembly:
> The comédiens [of the Théâtre-]Français . . . offer to the august Assembly a feeble token of their respect *[tribut de leur hommage].* . . . [W]e presume *[osons]* to beseech you to accept . . . the sum of twenty-three thousand livres.[18]

As was customary at the time, their gift was presented to the National Assembly as a donation on behalf of the poor.

The resolution to offer the donation was formally presented to the National Assembly by a delegation of four actors from the Théâtre-Français on the morning of 26 September. The president of the Assembly duly thanked them for their patriotism, remarking that "it would not be possible, gentlemen, to put to a more noble use the remuneration earned by talents that contribute to the solace and happiness of humanity." The details of this gift and of the president's thanks and praise were immediately disseminated in print, most probably at the request and expense of the actors.[19]

The desperation with which the actors of the Théâtre-Français sought to impress the National Assembly and indeed all of France with their patriotism is perhaps most clearly revealed by the fact that, unknown to almost anyone, the Théâtre-Français was massively in debt at the time. This gift to the National Assembly on behalf of the poor was but one of many made to various branches of government[20]—so many, in fact that by the time this gift came due, early in 1790, the Théâtre-Français was in debt to the tune of 1,200,000 livres. As an official of the municipal government remarked in February of 1790, after being put in charge of a review of their finances,

The only confession that we have managed to obtain from [the Comédiens-Français], is that at this point in time their expenses absorb their earnings, that for more than a year, [their earnings] have been more or less nil, & that the sums that the Comédiens-Français have given to the poor are partly the cause of this deficit. Thus, honored in the eyes of the public for their patriotism, they come whining to us about its effects.[21]

The culmination of the efforts of the Comédiens-Français to convince their fellow countrymen of their patriotism occurred in November of 1789, when they officially changed the name of their theater to the Théâtre-National (also referred to as the Théâtre de la Nation). Whether in conscious or unconscious mimicry of such institutions as the Assemblée nationale or the Garde nationale, the Comédiens-Français clearly thought this rechristening of their theater would impress upon the French people the depth of their patriotic feelings. As a delegation of Comédiens-Français remarked to Bailly, the mayor of Paris, "[W]e believe that we before all other comédiens have the right to the very glorious title of Comédiens de la Nation."[22] They did not, however, take this title. It is an apt commentary on the political situation at the time that they chose to retain their official title of Les Comédiens français ordinaires du roi, while at the same time changing the name of their theater to the Théâtre-National. By doing so they managed not only to cover their bets against the unexpected vicissitudes of a constantly changing political situation but also to achieve a compromise that took into account the varying political allegiances of the members of their corporation.[23] With Bailly's stamp of approval, therefore, on 3 December 1789 the first playbill was printed that announced the evening's performance as follows: "Théâtre-National. Les Comédiens ordinaires du roi will present. . . ."[24]

The clearest indication that the Comédiens-Français had entirely missed the point of their critics was the fact that by changing the name of their theater they had actually exacerbated fears concerning their political ambitions rather than allayed them. For some, the decision of the Comédiens-Français to adopt the name Théâtre-National was an example of their "ridiculous pretensions."[25] For others, more deeply disturbed by the actors' aspirations, the "ostentatious title of Théâtre-National, which the Comédiens-Français have usurped with the aim of impressing the people," was yet another sign that the actors were "serving as tools for the wild schemes of the aristocracy."[26] Yet another critic claimed that the actors were trying to claim for themselves and for their theater a name that properly belonged to the plays that they performed:

Our dramatic masterpieces constitute the theater of the nation, no matter in what country they are read or performed. To call the theater hall in which they are represented by this name [Théâtre de la Nation] is to mistake the form for the content *[prendre le contenant pour le contenu]* . . . ; and it seems to us that before arrogating it to themselves, they [the Comédiens-Français] ought to have already obtained the consent of the nation, or at least of [the nation's] representatives.[27]

The actors, who were meant to be merely a mouthpiece, were endeavoring to lay claim to the glorious character that was properly associated with the plays that they performed; the representatives, in short, were attempting to pass themselves off as the object of their representation—a criticism often made of political representatives as well.

The new name of Théâtre-National was problematic for yet another reason—a reason that can, at times, be difficult to tease from the textual evidence precisely because to articulate it was to draw attention to the very thing whose existence one was endeavoring to deny. In other words, to say that the actors had drawn a parallel between themselves and the representatives of the nation, between theatrical and political representation, was to acknowledge that such a parallel had crossed one's mind, that such an analogy was conceptually possible. Given the fact that actors were still the object of considerable revulsion, and the representatives of the National Assembly were not entirely themselves on stable ground, few supporters of the new government deemed it prudent to call the actors to task; to do so would be to make explicit a parallel that the actors themselves had made only implicitly. And yet, as the following excerpt from a contemporary play reveals in a somewhat offhand manner, one could hardly ignore the fact that to append the adjective *national* to the word *théâtre* was to blur the distinction between the theatrical and the political:

THE BARONESS.
National Theater. . . . Aren't you a little bit shocked by this new name?
THE VISCOUNTESS.
Well, who wouldn't be? Everything around us is becoming a horrible monotony. National Militia, National Guard, National Cockade! Soon we'll have National Marionettes.[28]

Although supporters of the new Revolutionary government often went to great lengths to avoid drawing any explicit analogy between actors and politicians, a debate was about to erupt in public opinion that would force them to speak of actors and politicians in the same breath. The question of the actor's civil status, which would be debated in public as well as in print and eventually in the National Assembly itself, would essentially force individuals to confront the extraordinarily problematic question of whether actors could ever become political representatives—a question that not only brought the actor into the political spotlight but could not help lifting the curtain on the theatrical underpinnings of political representation.

Naturalizing the Actor: The Case for and against the Civil Status and
Political Eligibility of Actors

During the first few months of the Revolution, until it was finally addressed within the National Assembly in late December 1789, the question
of the actor's civil status was the subject of impassioned debate in the forum
of public opinion. To a great extent, those who opposed granting a civil status to actors put forth the same arguments as those who had asked the question of whether actors, who were "exposed to sifflets," ought to be allowed
to command a detachment of the guard. For the author of a pamphlet entitled *L'homme aux trois révérences, ou Le comédien remis à sa place* (The
man of three bows, or The comédien put back in his place), it was the control that spectators exercised over actors that made the latter unsuitable for
citizenship. As far as the author of this pamphlet was concerned, it was the
actor's own willingness to be subservient to spectators that set him apart
from other men.[29] In the eyes of a venerable old gentleman who serves as the
author's mouthpiece in a fictional debate that takes place in a bookstore in
the Palais-Royal, the curtain call at the end of the play offers the clearest evidence of the actor's debased status:

> If an actor is offstage, & you have the sudden desire to see him again, you call
> him back with loud shouts: can he refuse to appear? No.
>   In presenting himself before you, what does he do?—One bow *[révérence]* to-
> ward the king, one bow toward the queen, & one bow toward the gentlemen
> of the parterre. There, head lowered, two arms hanging feebly, he waits with all
> possible humility for you to deign to dictate your orders to him. He receives
> [these orders] without daring to reply; he promises, in the name of his col-
> leagues, that they will do all in their power to please you; he asks your indul-
> gence; he admits that he needs it, & he believes himself only too happy if he
> manages to earn your praise. Is such a man your equal? No, very certainly not.[30]

The old gentleman goes on to cite a 1779 text, which just happens to be conveniently lying on one of the shelves of the bookstore, in which actors are
characterized as having sold themselves into a kind of debased existence:

> [A] comédien pawns his liberty to such an extent that for some money he be-
> comes a kind of slave of the public. . . . One must agree that a man who sub-
> mits himself to such a total abnegation of his own existence, & who alienates
> such a great portion of that precious liberty, without which man is nothing, has
> no right to demand from his fellow men that degree of esteem which one can-
> not refuse to [practitioners of] more honest professions.[31]

And so the question of the actor's civil status, a question that arises from the
Enlightenment notion that men are born equal in rights, is a flawed question,

for it ignores the fact that some individuals are happy to "pawn" their liberty for a little cash. Actors, in short, by actions undertaken of their own free will, have made themselves into something less than other men: "In vain do they tell us that we are all equal in rights; it isn't true: the comédiens are an exception to the rule."[32]

But something more was at stake than the straightforward question of the actor's civil rights, something that not everyone was prepared to mention outright: if brought to its logical conclusion, a full civil status would imply that actors were free to pursue any path that was open to other men. What many found extraordinarily troubling was the possibility that, as the elderly gentleman in *L'homme aux trois révérences* bluntly put it, "as soon as [the comédiens] are citizens like you and me, they will be electors, eligible [for public office], & consequently deputies [in the National Assembly]."[33]

And if the idea of a *comédien commandant* was laughable, the prospect of an actor-politician seemed to border on the absurd. Once again, the incongruity of authority-figure-by-day, actor-by-night proved too jarring, too ridiculous: "I admit that I would laugh heartily at seeing [the actor] Dazincourt bringing a decree to the king for his sanction by day, & amusing the good Parisians with the insipid pranks of Figaro by night."[34]

Louis-Marie Prudhomme, in his radical journal *Révolutions de Paris*, similarly objected to the "incompatibility" between the actor and the public representative; interestingly enough, however, Prudhomme held out the possibility that actors might be worthy of citizenship, as long as they were precluded from eligibility for public office:

> I do not see why an actor who has paid his share and who has enlisted in order to spill his blood for his country should not be a citizen; but I see very well why he is not eligible [for public office]. His profession is incompatible with public office. Could you imagine [the actor] Frontin as the mayor? Could you imagine him going down into the parterre where some sort of disturbance is taking place in order to reestablish order? especially when the disturbance was a result of [the spectators'] having lost all patience with his overacting and his jibes. Can one imagine that he could study his lines, rehearse, perform, and acquit himself of the duties of a public administration, which under unexpected circumstances would force him in the middle of a play to abandon the caduceus [the wand of Mercury] in favor of the commander's staff?[35]

Prudhomme was somewhat unusual in allowing for the possibility that actors might become citizens, while at the same time steadfastly opposing their eligibility for public office. Most individuals who declared themselves to be in favor of actors' civil rights studiously avoided the question of the actors' eligibility. A veritable public relations campaign was unleashed in the months that preceded the National Assembly's debate on the question, and the actors' friends and supporters put a variety of arguments in print as to why actors should be granted a civil status, but the question of eligibility was almost nowhere to be found. To a great extent, these arguments centered on the actors' potential utility to those who would govern over the morals of the nation, rather than on the inherent equality of the actor as a man. Such texts, in other words, seem to have accepted the essential fact that actors were *different,* and yet they nevertheless argued that this difference could be put to good use. Rebutting the notion that the art of acting was "degrading," one of the actors' most loyal supporters remarked, "The comédiens appear to me to be on the contrary the instruments of which the moralists of a nation make use. They allow us to see in the mirror of human life, our passions, that we may become educated to overcome them; our absurdities, that we may blush at them; and our faults, that we may correct them."[36]

Another pamphlet, entitled *La civilisation des comédiens, ou La demande que personne n'a faite à la nation assemblée* (The naturalization of the comédien, or The demand that no one has made to the nation assembled), similarly attempted to portray the actor as a kind of professor of morality who was dedicated "to improving [others] by satirizing vice and absurdity, to elevating the soul . . . , to turning [others] away from crime by instilling the horror of crime, and to rendering dear the virtue that they reproduce in all its forms."[37]

Such images must have seemed jarring to the French reading public, which was much more used to reading racy and titillating accounts of actors' sexual exploits than heartfelt paeans to actors' moral virtue.[38] And yet the actors themselves must have felt that their supporters had a reasonable chance of remaking their image in the public mind, for in a letter addressed to the National Assembly the actors also tried to present themselves as professors of morality. In an unpublished document written by the actors directly to the representatives of the National Assembly, one finds the clearest and boldest expression of belief in their potential utility. This document, which merits quoting at length, not only paints the talent of the actor as indispensable to government, but gives the impression that the actors were attempting to strike a deal with the National Assembly: in return for civil legitimacy they were promising to put their unique ability to influence people—a talent all the more effective in that it was accomplished surreptitiously, without the spectator's even being aware of what was happening—at the service of the new government:

> Who are we then, gentlemen, that we should suffer an injustice in which our masters the playwrights do not share? We dare to say this with the frankness that is permitted by both the justice and the enlightenment of the august senate that will not turn a deaf ear to our complaints. Yes, gentlemen, we are the speaking printing press *[imprimerie parlante];* we insinuate *[insinuons]* the written lessons of equity, justice, and tolerance into those whose situation or

whose aversion to effort prevents them from reading. It is for them (and it is known that their number encompasses three-quarters of the nation) that we repeat each day the sublime lessons that the tragic authors have concealed *[voilés]* in heroic characters *[noms voués à la grandeur]*, and that the comic [authors] disguise beneath the simple and naive appearance of gaiety.

If the love of tolerance that Voltaire embraced had existed only for his readers, we would have had in truth but a small number of citizens whose love of letters and reading had rendered [them] docile to these precepts; we would have had, in the end, a National Assembly [that was] enlightened, tolerant, and a guardian of tolerance; but the rest of the nation, which cannot read, or which reads passively without thinking about what they read, would still be intolerant, [and] would persecute the followers of foreign religions; and the august assembly would find far fewer citizens eager for its enlightened insight *[lumière]*, and docile before its decrees. Happy [are we] if our humble work, by spreading the instruction and love of peace throughout all classes of French people, has contributed if only from a distance to facilitating the execution of your wise creations.[39]

Here is a bold promise of complicity between the representatives on the theatrical and the political stages: together, the actors suggested, they could remake the social fabric. Actors could provide the representatives access to the vast majority of the nation who lay beyond the reach of their wise, but printed, words.

This promise of complicity between actor and politician, which sought to show that a close relationship between the two could be mutually beneficial, could not help but make the case that actors and politicians were, at least in part, really not that different from one another: if the latter were attempting to remake the nation from the podium of the National Assembly, the former were promising that they could accomplish this even more effectively from the stage. This affinity between the actor and the politician was pointed out much more explicitly, if in a decidedly more negative fashion, by the firebrand playwright Marie-Joseph Chénier, who dared to utter in a pamphlet what no other supporters of the Revolution could bring themselves to say. Refuting the arguments presented by those who opposed the actor's naturalization, Chénier wrote,

But you will mention [as an argument against their civil rights] that the comédiens are exposed to the tumultuous disapproval of the public. If this is the reason for your denying them citizenship, I will tell you once again: be consistent in your injustice. Take away the citizenship of all those who speak in public, even the orators of the National Assembly: they are exposed to the same fate. I do not of course wish to establish any other connection between them and the comédiens; but in the end that rapport exists.[40]

To a great extent, the debates that took place in the National Assembly at the end of December 1789 can be read as an attempt by the representatives—or at least those representatives who supported granting actors a civil status—to accept the actors' potential utility to the new regime while at the same time avoiding anything that might risk connecting the representatives to the actors. It was a very fine line to walk: they had to overcome an extraordinary hostility toward actors by bringing to the attention of the general public (as well as their fellow deputies) the actors' potential usefulness, but they had to do this as quietly as possible, without fanfare, and in such a manner that would not make it seem as if they and the actors were in any sense allied. The purpose was to naturalize the actor—in the sense of both giving him citizenship and making him unprofane—and not to celebrate him.

Almost as if they were dealing with distant relations with a sordid past who if left to their own devices might be a source of great embarrassment, the representatives to the National Assembly were eager to find the actors a niche in the new order where they would stay out of trouble. As far as the vast majority of the representatives were concerned, the actors could play a role in the Revolution, but that role was clearly to be within the theater, not outside it. The actors might be put to good use safely teaching the lessons of patriotism and devotion to democracy in the theaters, rather than out on the streets getting mixed up in public affairs. In short, the actor on the theatrical stage was a far more useful, far less embarrassing prospect than the actor prancing on the edges of the public stage, mouthing political slogans and casting a theatrical shadow on the legitimacy of representative democracy.

The Debates in the National Assembly

On 21 December 1789, the National Assembly took up the question of the actor's civil status. In a debate intended to resolve the civil status of all excluded men in the old regime—a category that comprised an unlikely assortment of social outcasts such as actors, Jews, Protestants, and executioners—several notable individuals spoke on behalf of the actor. Pierre-Louis Roederer, an important political figure who would later be elected *procureur général syndic* of Paris, was the first to speak of actors: "I appeal on behalf of a class of citizens that is rejected from every post in society, [and] that has its significance *[intérêt]* and its importance. I would like to speak of the *comédiens.* I believe that there is no solid reason, either moral or political, to oppose my appeal."[41]

This statement was immediately supported by Clermont-Tonnerre, who had been elected to the Estates General as the representative of the nobility of Paris, and had become one of the more prominent members of the National Assembly. For Clermont-Tonnerre, the actor's case for civil legitimacy was so self-evident that he would "not add one word to something that had no need of elaboration in order to impress you [with its importance]" (694). The session adjourned shortly after this comment, and when the Assembly reconvened, on 23 December, Clermont-Tonnerre added not one word, but several. He began his discussion of the comédiens with an apology for having to discuss them in the same breath with executioners: "I blush at having to associate the children of the arts with the instrument of the penal code; but the objections [leveled against both of them] force me to do so" (754). He then proceeded to enumerate the arguments against the civil rights of actors, including "the frivolity and often the danger of the plays of which they are the instrument." For Clermont-Tonnerre, the problem lay not with the theatrical form in itself but rather with the content of the plays: "None of the vices with which they are reproached is inherent to the profession." In other words, if government were to take a greater interest in the content of the performances, theater might become a useful tool of moral and political education:

> I believe that a wise legislature, and one that wanted to establish the constitution on the reform of public morals [*moeurs*], could make these inconveniences disappear, or at least diminish. I believe that the memory of the virtues of our ancestors, that the representation of the dangers of human passions, and the propagation of useful truths, either of personal morals [*morale privée*] or of political morals, can, in the proper nature of things, be presented to us by honest citizens. . . . [T]here is in this matter but one principle to follow: abolish those plays that are the shame and the downfall of morals and of public decency; and [put] an end to the stigmatizing of men who will exercise their talents in theaters that will have become useful. (755)

Essentially the same ideas were expressed by a man with very different political views. Robespierre took the floor shortly afterward and agreed with Clermont-Tonnerre that theaters and actors had important roles to play in society. Robespierre began his statement, however, by expressing his conviction that no special amendment that explicitly named the comédiens was necessary:

> I do not believe that you need a law that concerns the comédiens. Those who are not excluded are called. It was a good thing when a member [of the Assembly] appealed on behalf of a class that has been too long oppressed. The comédiens will earn greater public esteem when an absurd prejudice no longer opposes their receiving it; thus the virtues of individuals will contribute to the purification of the plays, and the theaters will become the public schools of principles, good morals, and patriotism. (757)

Robespierre's opinion that the comédiens ought to be "called" without being explicitly named betrays, I believe, the desire on the part of many deputies to grant a civil status to actors as discreetly as possible. As the following day's events would reveal, the last thing anyone wanted was for the actors to call attention to themselves as they made their somewhat perilous journey from outcast to citizen.

On 24 December, thinking perhaps that the political representatives might not have sufficiently grasped their potential utility, the comédiens of the Théâtre-Français drafted a letter to the president of the National Assembly. Referring to themselves as the "*organes* and vessels *[dépositaires]* of the dramatic masterpieces," they pretended to inquire as to whether the National Assembly "had decreed anything" relating to their civil legitimacy. They also took it upon themselves to remind the president of a few cogent details:

> The Comédiens-Français, from whom you have deigned to accept homage and a patriotic gift, remind you, sir, as well as the august Assembly, of their most formal desire never to employ their talents in any manner other than one that is worthy of a French citizen, and they would consider themselves happy if legislation, by reforming the abuses that can creep into the theater, would deign to seize hold of them as an instrument of influence on morals *[moeurs]* and on public opinion.[42] (776)

The letter from the Comédiens-Français was not received with a great deal of enthusiasm, either by the actors' supporters or by their opponents. For the latter, however, the actors' letter served the useful purpose of demonstrating the very characteristics that made actors unworthy of citizenship. The abbé Maury, who led the forces opposed to the actors' naturalization, declared that it was of "the utmost indecency that the comédiens should give themselves the license of having a direct correspondence with the Assembly." Abbé Maury, undoubtedly because of the passionate nature of his response, was quickly called to order by the president; nevertheless, he continued to speak, clarifying his previous statement:

> Our meetings are public; tomorrow twenty journalists will perhaps give a distorted account [of what I have said]. And so! I have nothing to retract; but [I wish] to explain what I have said. I did not mean to complain about the fact that the comédiens have written to the president; I merely observed that they did not need to write him in order to find out whether there was a decree for or against them; it is this affected ignorance on their part against which my statement was directed. (776)

There followed a "great tumult" concerning whether the president was indeed within his rights to call the abbé Maury to order.

The abbé was right, of course. The private correspondence of the comédiens reveals not only that they were well aware of the proceedings in the National Assembly, practically keeping a vigil as they awaited the outcome of the debates, but that their supporters were actively lobbying the representatives and keeping the comédiens informed every step of the way.[43] The objections of abbé Maury, combined no doubt with the embarrassment of many of the actors' supporters, who must have cringed at the comédiens' calling attention to themselves in such an obvious manner, resulted in the Assembly's decision that the letter not be transcribed in the *procès-verbal*. Robespierre was not alone in his wish that they be called but not named.

The discussion of civil legitimacy continued after the interlude of the actors' letter, focusing that day primarily on Jews. Antoine Barnave, one of the most influential deputies of the Assembly, who along with Alexandre Lameth and Adrien Duport composed the "Triumvirate" that headed up the more radical deputies, stood up to speak. Although he declared that he did not believe that any citizen should be deprived of his rights because of his religious beliefs or his profession, Barnave nevertheless suggested that perhaps the Assembly ought to permit itself to mention only the Protestants by name in any decree conferring civil status on excluded groups (781). Barnave's suggestion seems a rather clear indication of a somewhat conflicted desire, which he shared with many of his colleagues, to grant a civil status to the old regime's outcasts and yet not draw attention to the fact that they were doing it. Jews, executioners, and actors did not enjoy a very positive public image, but Protestants were an entirely different matter: one could safely champion their cause without risk of political repercussions.

A short while later, Bon-Albert Brois de Beaumez, deputy from Artois, took the floor. Like Clermont-Tonnerre and Robespierre during the previous session, Brois de Beaumez spoke of the potential utility of theater and offered an interesting suggestion as to how this goal might be assured:

> Perhaps one day you should destroy those little theaters, too numerous in Paris, that corrupt the populace by enticing *[éloignant]* them from their workplaces. This destruction and your decree will make French theaters into useful schools, where we will instruct ourselves all the better the more we esteem both authors and actors. (781)

This last comment was followed by a brief, if impassioned, warning by the marquis de Lezay-Marnézia, who urged his colleagues to read Rousseau's *Letter to d'Alembert on the Theater* before "giving [actors] the right to be seated in your administrative assemblies" (781). And here, finally, someone had mentioned the unmentionable; Lezay-Marnézia had uttered what everyone else was trying so hard not to say. Everyone was trying desperately *not* to talk about actors' eligibility for public office, but merely to speak of their civil status as if they would live out the rest of their days within the confines of the theater. The possibility of actors' choosing to play an extratheatrical role in Revolutionary society was a subject that few wanted to broach.

Mirabeau, acting almost as if this unpleasant interlude by Lezay-Marnézia had not taken place, stood up and agreed wholeheartedly with Brois de Beaumez's assessment that the comédiens must become valued citizens. In a statement that closed the debate, and that preceded the vote by which the actors were to gain their civil status, Mirabeau, perhaps the greatest orator in the Assembly, declared that the question of the actors' civil status was moot; the general will had already spoken: "[T]he powers of one of our colleagues, the deputy of Metz, have been signed by two comédiens. It would therefore be absurd—impolitic even—to refuse the comédiens the title of citizen that the nation has bestowed upon them before us" (782). Mirabeau here seems to be suggesting that the National Assembly might spare itself the trouble of granting actors a civil status by simply declaring the subject to have already been decided by the nation.[44]

No doubt, however, the representatives must have realized that resentments against the outcasts were such that some kind of statement was necessary, that they could not be naturalized simply by claiming that they had already been so. But there was another way by which a definite naturalization could be effected without actually naming any specific groups: when the Assembly went to a voice vote, the majority approved a decree that declared all "non-Catholics" legitimate candidates for all public offices, with the exception of the Jews, who would have to wait until the Assembly could examine their situation in greater detail. And so, without naming them directly, the actor and the executioner were implicitly "not excluded": "[O]nly those reasons that result from constitutional decrees can be held against the right of any citizen to stand for office" (782). A decree, therefore, that granted actors and executioners a civil status did so by a double negative. Just as Robespierre had put it, "Those who are not excluded are called." And just as Barnave had suggested, only the Protestants, or at least the "non-Catholics," were named.

Despite the fact that their letter to the National Assembly had not been accorded a place in the *procès-verbal;* despite the fact that they were granted citizenship in the same line that simultaneously conferred that right on the despised executioners of France; and despite the fact that they were neither mentioned in the decree, nor so much granted citizenship as not excluded from it, the comédiens of France were overjoyed. As the actor Dazincourt wrote to his female colleague La Chassaigne that same evening: "I offer up to your perfectly understandable impatience the pleasure, perfectly understandable as well, of informing you of good news: no profession will be a motive for [civil] exclusion."[45]

The supporters of the actors had much to celebrate as well. In a letter written that same night, the abbé Bouyon, the actors' most loyal advocate and author of several pamphlets arguing their cause, expressed his happiness at the outcome of the debates; and he encouraged the Comédiens-Français to express their gratitude (on behalf, no doubt, of all French actors) to the politicians who had helped them:

> I am joyfully content with the favorable decree that has just been pronounced by the National Assembly in favor of MM. les Comédiens. My efforts with a great number of deputies were successful, and here is my reward. I ask of you only that this very evening you elect a deputation among your colleagues to

[visit] M. de Mirabeau, and especially M. Briois de Beaumès *[sic]* the deputy from Artois, who by his eloquence and energy decided, so to speak, even the undecided in favor of your cause. Your visit arranged for tomorrow, Friday, in the morning, will flatter this generous and just deputy, and I myself will be flattered by this indispensable action.[46]

The representatives to the National Assembly had much to be pleased about as well—at least the majority who had supported the actors' civil legitimacy. They had managed to confer a sacred right on those who had only recently been considered the most profane men in France. But more important, they had managed to confer that right without compromising their own legitimacy. Even the one comment, by Lezay-Marnézia, that had spoken of politics and actors in the same breath had been intended not to impugn the politics of the Revolution but rather to protect the political from contamination by actors.

But if the representatives had been able to control the terms of the debate within the Assembly, they were powerless to do so in the realm of public opinion. Whereas the deputies themselves had taken care to avoid drawing any parallels between actors and political representatives, the enemies of the National Assembly were forever on the lookout for the opportunity to bring such parallels to the attention of the public and to expose what they took to be the dangerous comedy of the entire Revolutionary political enterprise. The fact that the National Assembly had bestowed a civil status and political eligibility on actors was an opportunity that was simply too good to pass up. The author of the satirical pamphlet entitled *Evénemens remarquables & intéressans, à l'occasion des décrets de l'auguste Assemblée nationale, concernant l'éligibilité de MM. les comédiens, le bourreau, & les Juifs* essentially took the debates on the civil legitimacy of outcasts and went to town.

The pamphlet begins with an impassioned plea to the National Assembly against the actors' naturalization. Instead of Lezay-Marnézia quoting Rousseau, however, it is Jean-Jacques himself at the podium, presumably risen from the dead in his desperation to warn the French people. Much of the speech is lifted directly from Rousseau's *Letter to d'Alembert on the Theater*, with Rousseau detailing the various reasons why actors are a different class of human being. In the middle of Rousseau's speech, Mirabeau stands up, pushes the old sage aside, and says, "Shut up, Jean-Jacques; I want to speak." And then, in a very clever play on Mirabeau's characterization of the actor's civil status as a moot point that had already been decided upon by the nation, the fictional Mirabeau delivers the following speech to the Assembly:

You are deliberating as to whether you should admit comédiens into your political assemblies? You're thinking about it? Hasn't this question already been decided? & [how] can you debate it any longer? Open your eyes, and take a look at me. . . . And they dare to ask whether comédiens are eligible, when they see that I've been elected! . . . And when they will have decided that comédiens are inadmissible, then perhaps they'll tell me—I know, gentlemen, what you will say; I foresee it, I anticipate it; I will say it myself: Yes. I admit it openly. I have played *la comédie*, in Aix, in Versailles, in Paris; I've played in Berlin, in—well everywhere really. I make no secret of it; I'm proud of it; . . . Well, gentlemen, are you happy? Have I shown myself to be any other than I am? I am undoubtedly a comédien, a tragedian even, & nevertheless a deputy, & nevertheless a legislator! . . . And do I not recognize in this august assembly thirty, forty, fifty of my colleagues [who are] comédiens, tragedians, like myself?[47]

For the author of *Evénemens remarquables & intéressans,* the question of the actor's political eligibility was also moot; but it was moot because the National Assembly was already infested with actors.

In the second section of the pamphlet, the author details the consequences of the National Assembly's decree. In a provincial town, a troupe of actors runs for public office, sweeping the election with their engaging theatricality. The results of the election are then published in the form of a cast list replete with character descriptions, with each of the town's municipal positions going to one of the stock figures in French dramatic comedy: the part of the mayor will be played by M. Crispin; the part of *procureur-syndic* performed by M. Scapin, etc. etc.

This fear that actors, newly legitimized, would invariably come to play a role on the political stage was a recurrent theme among those who stressed the fundamental importance of differentiating between the theater and civil society, between actors and citizens. As Rousseau had warned in his *Letter to d'Alembert on the Theater* in 1758, if the Genevans were to make the mistake of allowing a so-called legitimate theater company into their city,

> I would not even give [the actors] thirty years [before they will] be the arbiters of the state. We will see those aspiring for public office soliciting the support [of actors] in order to obtain votes; elections will be held in the dressing rooms of actresses, and the leaders of a free people will be the lackeys of a band of histrions.[48]

Similarly, within the context of the Revolution itself, a critic of the actors wrote the following words, upon hearing the news of the Assembly's decree: "I have no doubt at all now that the comédiens will one day be mayors of Paris, general commanding officers of the guard, or what would be even more amusing, president of the National Assembly."[49]

In part, this fear that actors, liberated from the constraints of the past, could not help but swarm and ultimately overwhelm the political sphere

Élection des Officiers municipaux de Na......

Maire . . . . M. CRISPIN.

Jeune homme d'environ trente ans , acteur parfait , une pantomime variée , souple , expreſ-ſive , un maſque admirable , geſte animé , gaieté charmante ; ce ſera un merveilleux Maire.

Procureur-Syndic . . . . M. SCAPIN.

On ne vit jamais une telle ſcience de plier & déplier ſa phyſionomie ; un air de quiétude enve-loppé dans ſon manteau , & pendant ce temps ſes mains trottent & ſe fourrent par-tout. Excellent Procureur-Syndic.

Subſtitut du Procureur-Syndic... M. PASQUIN.

Plus leſte , plus léger , mais moins profond dans ſon jeu ; cependant très-bon pour un Subſtitut.

Membres du Bureau de la Municipalité.

M. CASSANDRE. *On l'appelle le bon homme ; il a le ridicule d'être toujours amoureux à ſon âge ; mais cela prouve , dans le fond , une belle*

B

10. A cast list of elected officials. From the pamphlet *Evénemens remarquables & intéressans, à l'occasion des décrets de l'auguste Assemblée nationale, concernant l'éligibilité de MM. les comédiens, le bourreau, & les Juifs* (n.p., 1790). Photograph courtesy of the Department of Special Collections, the University of Chicago Library.

arose from a deep-seated conviction that their talent was dangerous and that the art that they practiced had for centuries been cordoned off from the rest of society for a reason. As we have seen, even those who supported a civil status for actors did so with the hope that actors could prove useful within the confines of their theaters, not outside it. They intended primarily to confer civil status on those who they hoped would become professors of a new morality; political legitimacy was merely a logically necessary component of that status, and few dared mention it within the course of the debates. For the actors' critics, however, it simply was not possible to believe that actors would remain in their theaters. Like some sort of monstrosity that had been chained behind bars for generations, harmlessly amusing the public, actors, with nothing to hold them in their place, would inevitably overwhelm the world from which they had been so completely excluded.

But there was another aspect to this fear of actors and the urgent need of political commentators to expose the connections between theater and politics, actors and politicians. As is clearly evident in the pamphlet *Evénemens remarquarbles & intéressans,* the expression of anxiety about actors was often the flip side of an anxiety about the new political culture. Like the actors whom they had liberated, these representatives to the National Assembly were themselves the object of derision and fear, amusement and horror. For many, the representatives to the Assemblée prétendue nationale (so-called National Assembly) were themselves frauds, charlatans, and actors who were merely pretending to represent the nation but in truth had no legitimacy whatsoever. The fear of actors and the fear of political actors were therefore rather closely related. The following chapter explores these fundamental Revolutionary anxieties within the context of a much broader, long-term eighteenth-century suspicion of abstract concepts in general.

7 The Fear and Ridicule of Revolutionary Representations

From our vantage point, more than two centuries removed, the rhetoric of the counterrevolutionaries seems strange. One is tempted to think that they could not settle on a single plan of attack and therefore covered the Revolution in a barrage of unrelated and almost contradictory epithets: the Revolutionaries were murderers and clowns, tyrants and actors. Almost as if they could not make up their minds, the Revolution's enemies were at one and the same time frightened and amused, horrified by and scornful of what they saw. The reaction to the farcical actor Bordier is a perfect example of this: one need only look at the illustration of Bordier standing before the gallows in full Harlequin regalia to see how a single individual could embody the potential for both farce and wild violence (see fig. 9).

Nowhere is this ambivalence, this incongruous reaction to the Revolution more in evidence than in the writings of that counterrevolutionary extraordinaire, Edmund Burke:

> Everything seems out of nature in this strange chaos of levity and ferocity, and of all sorts of crimes jumbled together with all sorts of follies. In viewing this monstrous tragi-comic scene, the most opposite passions necessarily succeed, and sometimes mix with each other in the mind; alternate contempt and indignation; alternate laughter and tears; alternate scorn and horror.[1]

Burke's strange, mixed reaction to the Revolution is mirrored throughout the literature of the counterrevolution, both in England and on the Continent. The Revolutionaries themselves were quick to write off such outbursts as the irrational blather of unenlightened minds; these criticisms made no sense precisely because they were not rooted in rational thought but were instead based upon the unthinking "prejudices" of those who simply wanted to cling to the past.

In the pages that follow, I attempt to uncover the logic that underlay counterrevolutionary rhetoric. If we are careful to look where the criticisms are directed, we will see that there is, despite appearances to the contrary, a perfectly logical explanation for the fact that the Revolution's enemies did not know whether to laugh or cry—or perhaps, to put it more accurately, knew to do both.

My purpose in digging into the rationale of the counterrevolutionaries is, in part, to understand the logic of antitheatricality that so pervaded their texts. But it is also to shed some light on a vexing question that has aroused surprisingly little discussion among scholars of the period: Why does counterrevolutionary rhetoric sound so similar to Jacobin rhetoric?[2] Why, in other words, when their politics seem so vastly different, were both the extreme right and the extreme left so obsessed with theatricality and fraudulence, with paper money and the corruption of representatives? Why, in short, were they both so frightened of abstract representations?

Right-Wing Anti-abstractionism and Its Historical Context

I would like to begin by taking a close look at a relatively obscure pamphlet that appeared in 1791, entitled *Qu'est-ce que l'Assemblée nationale?* (What is the National Assembly?). Published anonymously, but most probably written by the comte Murat de Montferrand, the pamphlet was very clear in its intent, declaring itself in its subtitle to be a *Grande thèse en présence de l'auteur anonyme de Qu'est-ce que le tiers? Et dédiée au très-honorable Edmund Burke, comme à un véritable ami de la vraie liberté* (Grand argument in opposition to the anonymous author of What is the Third [Estate]? And dedicated to the very honorable Edmund Burke, as a genuine friend of true liberty). And, as if to show that the rebuttal of Sieyès was taken very literally, the pamphlet begins with a twist on Sieyès's famous questions and answers:

What is the National Assembly?—Everything.
What was it before 1789?—Nothing.
What should it have been?—Something.

In the middle of *Qu'est-ce que l'Assemblée nationale?*—sandwiched in between rather straightforward attacks on the National Assembly—are ten or so pages that cannot help striking the modern reader as entirely incongruous with the rest of the text. Their subject is metaphysical abstraction. Abstraction? How, we ask, does a philosophical treatise on the dangers of metaphysical abstraction relate to the evils of the National Assembly? And at first glance, the connection is not altogether clear:

> An abstract idea is nothing other than the result of an operation of the mind by
> which, separating this or that attribute common to many objects, [the mind]
> considers [that attribute] alone by abstracting it, which is to say by leaving to
> the side all objects to which [that attribute] might belong.[3]

This sentence expresses nothing more than the concept that, for example,
such essential qualities as whiteness, cold, and softness might be separated
from, or abstracted from, the reality of a handful of snow, and that each of
these qualities could be considered as a discrete concept in and of itself, entirely divorced from the reality from which it was derived. Although somewhat jarring within the context of this pamphlet, the idea that abstract concepts are *abstracted from* objective reality was a relatively commonplace
observation within the context of eighteenth-century writing. One need only
look under the heading of "Abstraction" in the first volume of the *Encyclopédie*—that most authoritative text of enlightened thought in the mid-
eighteenth century—to find an essentially identical statement published
forty years before the pamphlet in question:

> By thinking, we form for ourselves a singular concept which we detach from
> everything which could have given us cause to form it; we consider it separately
> as if there were some sort of real object which corresponded to that concept in-
> dependent of our way of thinking.[4]

For the author of *Qu'est-ce que l'Assemblée nationale?* abstraction was
an evil. It was not so much the *formation* of abstract concepts that disturbed
him. In some sense, he recognized the inevitability of abstract concepts as an
unavoidable consequence of man's inability to process the multiplicity of
phenomena in the universe; we are forced to formulate associations between
different objects and describe them by certain abstract attributes that they
seem to share in common, for the simple reason that we are unable to remember each individual object in all its uniqueness:

> The method of abstractions is a great relief to the human mind because it gives
> us the means of embracing by one single sign the quality by which a large num-
> ber of objects have something in common with one another *[se conviennent]* &
> [of embracing] a certain rapport that exists among them; but if our faculties
> were less limited, they would have less need of generalization. Individual [ob-
> jects] would be classified individually and not collectively; we would soon per-
> ceive a thousand differences between those objects that seemed to us to be most
> alike. (94–95)

What disturbed the author of the pamphlet was not this simple act of abstraction. Rather, it was what one did with these abstractions, treating them
as if they were real and forgetting that they are merely mental crutches that
enable us to perceive the world around us:

But since no characteristic can exist independent of the object that possesses it, it follows that abstract ideas express nothing more than a construct of the mind, & not any entity that exists in nature. It follows furthermore that all philosophical and political reasonings that are dependent upon abstract ideas are liable to lead us into strange errors, whenever we wish to apply them to any of the objects from which we have abstracted them. (94)

The problem, in short, was twofold: The first mistake was to mistake an abstraction for a tangible reality. And the second mistake was to take this reified abstraction and to apply it back to the physical world from which it was abstracted out of context, for the real world is made up of unique, individual objects rather than general categories: "In effect, we never act in a universal or a general manner, but always in relation to individual [entities] of some sort, from which it follows that, more often than not, we cannot apply to them the theory that we have built upon abstract propositions" (95–96).

But here again, the pamphlet's author is not being particularly original. The dangers inherent in the process of abstraction were a well-known subject of pre-Revolutionary philosophical writing. The very same article in the *Encyclopédie* to which we turned above for a definition of abstraction also warned that "when we do not take care to . . . take [abstractions] for what they are worth, they distance the mind from the reality of things, & become the source of a great deal of errors."[5] And some twenty-five years later, in the supplement to the original *Encyclopédie,* the article "Abstraction" was perhaps even more wary than the earlier entry; while acknowledging that the ability to engage in abstract thought is a fundamental part of what separates man from animals, the article nevertheless warned against the serious repercussions that would result from the "abuse" of abstractions:

Whatever advantage, however, that we derive from the capacity to abstract; whatever superiority we may have in this respect over beasts, let us not forget that on the one hand this faculty is necessary to us only because of the limits of our knowledge; & on the other hand the abuse that it is so easy to make of it is, for us, a disastrous *[funeste]* source of futile disputes & dangerous errors.

And the article went on to list the "various traps which the acceptance [*agré-ment*] of universal ideas holds out for us."[6]

So the anti-abstractionist diatribe in the middle of *Qu'est-ce que l'Assemblée nationale?* is not particularly unusual within the context of mid- to late-eighteenth-century philosophical discourse.[7] What is unusual about this minitreatise on the dangers of metaphysical abstraction, however, is the fact that it exists in the middle of a pamphlet whose ostensible subject is the National Assembly. And we are still left to puzzle, Why? Why dredge up this old ambivalence toward abstractions? What does all of this have to do with the National Assembly? And this is a question with many answers.

On one level, the answer is relatively straightforward: in the eyes of the pamphlet's author, the representatives to the National Assembly were palming off abstract principles as the basis for a new Revolutionary society, as if these principles were a tangible reality rather than an arbitrary human construct. The pamphlet's author could not help finding the claim that governments ought to be "based" on abstract principles nonsensical, or at the very least topsy-turvy. The principles of government were meant to be derived *from* reality rather than pulled out of thin air and imposed *upon* reality:

> It is necessary to study the real and positive details of governments. . . . Nothing equals the absurdity of wanting to establish general abstract propositions in order to deduce from them the details of how to put them into practice. The legislator of this or that state must consider its position, its size, its soil, its fertility, its climate, the morals *[moeurs]* of the inhabitants, their customs, in a word all the relations interior and exterior, and according to these data imagine the laws that he believes would be most appropriate to calling forth and maintaining happiness. (97–98)

To do the opposite, however, to invent abstract principles that one then imposed upon reality, would be to do what so many philosophers had warned against with respect to metaphysical abstractions. It would be to privilege reified abstractions at the expense of the reality from which those abstractions were originally derived. It would be to ask the French nation to forsake the world of tangible reality and to dwell instead in the fantastic world of the philosopher's or the politician's imagination:

> But the legislator who takes the opposite route and who, putting forward general and abstract propositions as principles, wants to deduce positive and effective details as corollaries, *who takes the definition of words for the definitions of things,* such a person resembles, as Locke remarks, those people who, without money and without any knowledge of [real] currency, count enormous sums with tokens that they [nevertheless] call *écus, louis,* etc.; whatever calculations they may make, the results will always be only tokens. (98–99)

These representatives to the National Assembly, who were so intent on foisting their political abstractions on the French people, were building a regime that had no tangible basis in reality. And thus the pamphlet's interlude against abstraction concludes by paraphrasing Burke's criticism of the Revolution: the representatives to the Assembly stand accused of wanting to build "an imposing edifice supported by columns that would be resting on thin air" (99–100).[8]

This ambition of the representatives to build castles in the sky would be laughable of course, were it not for something about these fictions that posed a very *real* danger: they were enormously seductive. It was almost as if people were incapable of resisting the allure of abstractions and if given a choice between real objects and representations would inevitably choose the latter. This was a danger that Rousseau had explicitly called attention to in *Emile* when he warned those entrusted with the education of children to "substitute the sign for the thing [it represents] only when it is impossible for you to show [the thing itself]; because the sign absorbs the attention of the child and makes him forget the thing represented."[9] And now, according to the counterrevolutionaries, there was no one in this postpatriarchal society to play the role of public guardian, no one to protect the naive mass of citizens from an unscrupulous government intent on seducing the people with abstractions.

Nowhere is this obsession with the ability of abstractions to replace the real more in evidence than in the discourse surrounding one of the greatest pet peeves of the Revolution's critics, the assignats. Originally conceived in December of 1789 as a government bond issue backed by the value of nationalized church property, the assignat became legal tender, a form of paper currency, in 1790. Its value depreciated on an almost daily basis, a casualty of a vicious circle of government overprinting and lack of public confidence. But the vituperation to which the assignat was consistently subjected was not a simple function of its constantly eroding value. Rather, as an abstract representation of value that had replaced an embodiment of value (in the sense that the assignat signified value, whereas precious metals inherently contained value), the assignat served as the perfect illustration of how abstractions, when not used with extreme caution, easily overwhelmed the existing order of things. As the author of *Qu'est-ce que l'Assemblée nationale?* declared,

> It is therefore in the essence of paper to make silver *[argent]* disappear, either by forcing it to flee or by chasing it away. . . . [F]orced paper cannot be a sign of worth, because its value is intrinsically nothing, and [its value is also] capricious like the opinion that gives it whatever [worth] it has. Nevertheless, as soon as it is established, it becomes, contrary to nature, the sign of all exchanges and of all momentary values without being [the sign] of permanent values. . . . As soon as forced paper is established, metal goes out of service, that of being the sign of value, and becomes merchandise, since its value is itself determined by another sign. (201–3)

Similar assurances that precious metals were destined to be entirely replaced by the pernicious innovation of paper money can be found in numerous texts of the Revolution's critics.[10] This anxiety that paper would replace specie was not a simple economic gripe but rather a manifestation of a broader suspicion of abstractions in general. The very same people who decried the inundation of paper were afraid that, on virtually every level of social and political life, fictions would replace reality, the vraisemblable would supplant the vrai, the artificial would replace the natural, and representations would inevitably replace the thing they represented.

There is one final aspect of abstractions that bears mentioning, as it should help to complete our understanding of the mixture of horror and scorn that characterized counterrevolutionary critiques of the Revolution: the inherent violence and the monstrosity of abstraction. As the pre-Revolutionary discourse on abstractions had been careful to point out, the etymological roots of the verb *abstraire* bore testimony to the conceptual violence that was inherent in the process of abstraction. Both the original *Encyclopédie* and the supplement prefaced their articles on abstraction by reminding readers that the verb *abstraire* was originally from the Latin verb *abstrahere,* which meant "to separate one thing from another, to take from *[tirer]*, to put aside *[mettre à part]*." Abstraction literally and originally meant to rip apart—the primal action from which all metaphysical abstraction proceeded. Each representation, in short, owed its very existence to an original dismembering of a preexisting whole: "[Abstraction] consists in separating one from the other and independently considering each of the different ideas that the total idea of an individual [whole] presents."[11]

Abstraction, then, within the pre-Revolutionary philosophical discourse, had been understood as both the original *abstraction from* a preexisting whole and the recombination of these abstracted parts into a new, artificial construct. Where the critics of the Revolution differed from pre-Revolutionary philosophers was the context in which they applied their observations: the counterrevolutionaries took what was essentially a metaphysical discourse and transposed it onto a political reality. The National Assembly, then, was not merely guilty of mouthing abstract principles ungrounded in historical reality; the National Assembly was actively engaged in the dismembering and the reconstitution of the geographical, mystical, and political body of France itself. And so, for example, with respect to the first of these dismemberings, the author of *Qu'est-ce que l'Assemblée nationale?* decried the decision to split France into departments as

> that extravagant dissection of the kingdom into eighty-three republics, which . . . form little states absolutely isolated in a big [state] whose dissolution they will very soon bring about [altogether] if there is no center of power with enough energy to subjugate the whole, and will finish by replacing [the state] with a federalist government. (213)

France, then, as a geographical entity would be "dissected" into parts, only to be reconstituted as a federal assemblage of minirepublics.

In addition to this splitting of the geographical body of France into eighty-three different parts, the pamphlet's author decried what he saw as the splitting apart of France's traditional mystical body. By the very act of forming the National Assembly, the representatives had done what Sieyès had exhorted them to do: they had abstracted the third estate from the body of the nation and had reformulated this portion of the nation into a new assemblage of equal citizens. In doing so they had cast aside the privileged orders as so much detritus—an act the author of *Qu'est-ce que l'Assemblée nationale?* characterized, referring in particular to the fate of the aristocratic order, as nothing less than the beheading of the corpus mysticum:

> [T]he order to which the general will, expressed by a legal consensus throughout all antiquity, has accorded a distinguished rank, a privilege that makes of it a kind of magistrature for the common good and utility, & that possesses a legitimate title to a considerable portion of the territory of the society, is an integral, essential part of the people, as a head is [an integral, essential part] of the body; & just as a body that is deprived of [a head] becomes a cadaver, so the third [estate] without the nobility is no longer the people, & the state then suffers a political death. (77)

Here, incidentally, we see something of a twist on the words of the fifteenth-century theorist Jean Gerson, who in declaring that "a head without a body cannot survive" had meant to argue that a people and their king must behave as if they constituted a single body.[12] But in the above quotation, the nobility is cast in the role of the king: it is the nobility that has been "beheaded" from the body of the nation and whose death will ultimately spell the death of the entire body politic. This association of the nobility with the head, although something of a departure from traditional conceptions of the corpus mysticum, may very well shed light on the meaning of the spectacles of severed heads that were associated with the earliest popular rebellions in the streets of Paris as well as with the more formal ceremonies of execution by guillotine that would come later. Each aristocratic head on a pike, or held up by the executioner for the crowd to behold, was a graphic expression of what the Revolution considered expendable; it was a celebration of the redundancy and the powerlessness of the privileged orders.[13]

The National Assembly, then, owed its very existence to the dismembering of France's corpus mysticum. And here we come to a fundamental part of counterrevolutionary anti-abstractionism that goes a long way toward explaining the vituperation to which the Assembly was subject. The National Assembly was not simply the purveyor of abstractions, the unscrupulous disseminator of paper currency and so on. *The National Assembly was itself an abstraction.* These representatives had been wrenched from, *abstracted from* the political body of the nation. And now, as representatives of a part of the nation's body made to stand in for the whole, this representative body threatened—just like the assignats with which they were flooding France—to replace the thing it was meant to represent:

> Once it had seized all forms of power, [the National Assembly] abused them; . . . it said: sovereign power resides in the nation, and it nevertheless arrogated it and forbade its usage to the nation . . . it said: I am really balancing the state deficit, and instead of returning the silver that was loaned to it, it paid with a discredited paper, the execrable symbol of pillage, of sacrilege, of bankruptcy and of tyranny; and in rendering forced currency it has destroyed all confidence between citizens. (266–67)

The National Assembly, then, as both the purveyor of abstractions and the living abstraction of France's mystical and political body, was in the eyes of its critics responsible for a host of crimes on a variety of different levels. Its very existence was predicated on the dismembering of the nation's mystical and political body. And on a daily basis it was, in a sense, remaking France in its own image, dismembering bodies, both physical and metaphysical: "The National Assembly . . . has coldly calculated the number of atrocities that it was necessary for it to commit in order to arrive at its goal, debated the purity of blood shed before its eyes, and one by one severed all the heads, physical and political, necessary to assuage its taste for destruction" (267).

The rhetoric of the counterrevolution now becomes clear: the seemingly irrational and contradictory complaints that the Revolution was both a farce and a horror have a logic after all. The National Assembly, together with all of the abstractions that it manufactured, was at one and the same time a laughable fiction and the product of (as well as the perpetrator of) horrible conceptual violence. What could be more appropriate, as Burke had said, than to laugh and cry at the same time? For Burke, as for so many of the Revolution's enemies, one could not help being horrified at the violence done to France's ancient bodily constitution or laughing at the absurd attempt to reconstitute a body from the dismembered parts:

> [Man] should approach to the faults of the state as to the wounds of a father, with pious awe and trembling solicitude. By this wise prejudice we are taught to look with horror on those children of their country, who are prompt rashly to hack that aged parent in pieces, and put him into the kettle of magicians, in hopes that by their poisonous weeds, and wild incantations, they may regenerate the paternal constitution, and renovate their father's life.[14]

Despite its relative obscurity, *Qu'est-ce que l'Assemblée nationale* serves, I think, as a kind of Rosetta stone, helping us to make sense out of the long-forgotten logic of the counterrevolution. What might otherwise seem to be the random and contradictory carping of an embittered and dispossessed aristocracy takes on its own logical coherence when viewed within the context of eighteenth-century attitudes toward metaphysical abstraction. The same worries within pre-Revolutionary philosophical discourse—that abstractions were indissolubly linked with the death of an organic whole, that man-made constructs might overwhelm the reality they were intended to represent—were now grafted onto contemporary political experience. With this key to understanding counterrevolutionary discourse in mind, then, I would like to read through a few examples of what might otherwise seem to be the colorful excesses of the Revolution's critics, to find at bottom this same logic of the fear and the ridicule of abstraction—a logic that we find not only on the right, but on the left as well.

Veiled Monsters: Rhetorical Similarities on the Left and Right Extremes

Recent studies have discussed a tendency on the part of the Jacobins to depict their enemies, from federalists to counterrevolutionaries, in monstrous form.[15] Somewhat less well known is the fact that the counterrevolutionaries were themselves drawn to precisely the same imagery.[16] Both counterrevolutionaries and Jacobins, for example, were taken with the image of the Hydra as the embodiment of evil. For the Jacobins, the multiheaded Hydra was a particularly effective means of conveying such varied themes as the omnipresence of aristocratic conspiracy, the coalition of foreign monarchies bent on the destruction of Revolutionary France, and the dangers of a federalist insurgency that hoped to divide France into many administrative centers. For the counterrevolutionaries, by contrast, the Hydra served as an apt metaphor for the National Assembly, that body of many heads which had replaced the one-headed body of the king as the political representation of the nation.

But even apart from the objects that the Hydra was made to represent, there were important differences between Jacobin and counterrevolutionary depictions of the Hydra. In Jacobin texts, the Hydra forms part of the retelling of the classic story of Hercules' victory over his many-headed adversary, a parable that nicely illustrated the inevitable victory of the French people united in one body by the general will vanquishing its multifarious enemies; the Hydra is invoked, therefore, so that readers might participate vicariously in its destruction.[17] Within texts hostile to the Revolution, however, the story is not quite so optimistic; far from being vanquished, the Hydra seems to stand unopposed. In the following passage from *Qu'est-ce que l'Assemblée nationale?* for example, the National Assembly is depicted as a Hydra with nary a Hercules in sight: "[The National Assembly] has substituted itself in the place of the laws of despotism, which it has gotten rid of only to take its place—a despotism that, like the Hydra, [has grown] a thousand heads for the one we have cut off" (265). Here the Hydra is invoked not, as in the Jacobin texts, as a prelude to its slaughter but as a description of the political status quo. If anyone or anything is in danger of being killed, it is certainly not the Hydra.

Within the texts of the counterrevolution, the image of the Hydra is joined by a veritable menagerie of monsters all of whom seem either poised for world domination or already celebrating the fruits of their victory. In short, counterrevolutionary texts are decidedly pessimistic; the monsters depicted within them are invariably running amok. And the monsters' adversaries seem rather pathetic when compared with the various incarnations of Hercules or dragon slayers that people the radical texts. A typical example of such defeatism is the counterrevolutionary pamphlet *Changement de décoration, ou Vue perspective de l'Assemblée nationale des Français* (Change of scenes, or Perspective view of the National Assembly of the French), which contains four "scenes" in which Revolutionary monsters go about their nefarious business unfettered by any effective opposition. In the following narrative, which accompanies a picture in which two monsters (Mirabeau and Sieyès) spar with a nameless knight, the outcome seems inevitable; the noble and valiant efforts of the latter are no match for the underhanded dirty tricks of the former:

> Look well . . . watch carefully. . . . Take a glance at the left [of the picture]; admire the noble knight [Valeureux]; how he fights with courage; how he cherishes the laws of honor. He despises his enemy, and even more the underhanded and shameful scheming [of his enemy]. If he had not disdained a cowardly and criminal defense, he would have overwhelmed his perfidious adversary a hundred times: firm in his principles, he defends himself with bravery; nevertheless he succumbs to the force of the two monsters united against him. . . . Oh what times! Oh what customs [*moeurs*]! Oh what a climax of horror![18]

In contrast to the omnipotent and victorious Hercules, the "hero" in this text is a decidedly more tragic, if not pathetic, figure. If a victory were to be had, it would not belong to the nameless knight. The only hope is a deus ex machina in the final act:

> The monster will pay well for the excess of his heinousness; it seems to me that I can already see him the prey of infernal furies; I see the laurels and roses with which an imbecile nation has crowned his head turning into brambles and thorns. I see flowing from his limbs in drops of blood the substance of the people he devoured with so much pleasure. (G–H)

If, for the moment, then, these monsters appear invincible, one could find some solace in the thought that their reign could not last forever. At some point, surely, good must triumph over evil; the French people, that "imbecile nation," would one day come to its senses.

But this complaint that the French people were acting like "imbeciles," with the implication that they could not perceive what any idiot could perceive, should detain us for a moment. Why were these monsters not seen for the horrid creatures that they truly were? The answer is that they had taken care to mask their true nature beneath a more agreeable and engaging exterior. These were hypocritical monsters, so dastardly that they did not even have the decency to appear as real monsters. In a scene entitled "Constitutional Committee," for example, the abbé Sieyès is pictured not in the virtuous human form he presented to the outside world but as the scheming monster he truly was, a half-clad beast seated on the floor of his den, scribbling furiously: "It is in this infernal hovel that the monsters, vomited up by the furies, hatched their odious plot. . . . Do you see this arrogant Vampire? . . . Underneath the veil of the most perfect hypocrisy, he dedicates everything to the success of his perverted designs. It is the execrable Sieyès" (F–G).

The monsters that lived in the counterrevolutionary imagination were *veiled monsters,* monsters whose monstrosity was all the more insidious because it needed to be unmasked. And, not surprisingly, there is a decidedly theatrical (or perhaps, more accurately, antitheatrical) quality to these unmaskings. These monsters were pretending to be something that they were not; they were hiding themselves behind an agreeable, even *entertaining* exterior. Thus, the pamphlet *Changement de décoration*—whose very title and manner of narration stress the theatricality of its subject—depicts the nefarious Lafayette as a singing and dancing monster who, after having danced "before princes and lords . . . is today deploying his talents before the eyes of the people." Here is a monster that vanquishes not by brute force but by charm: "[Y]ou must hear him speak! what softness in his speech! he knows how to win everything by his fake caresses; he is a great magician. . . . [H]e charms everyone; he makes everyone follow him: can you hear him?" (L–M).

Counterrevolutionary texts are not alone in their obsession with veiled monsters. Although radical texts are filled with images of obvious monsters who need only to be defeated, veiled monsters do have their place in the radical literature as well. In general, the more obvious monsters tend to be used to represent the more universally vilified figures such as Marie-Antoinette and the king's brothers, or more generic abstract categories such as "the aristocracy."[19] Veiled monsters, by contrast, tend to make their appearance in the radical literature as embodiments of those enemies of the Revolution who "posed" as Revolutionaries, those who needed to be unmasked precisely because they appeared to be doing the Revolution's work even as they undermined it. And here Mirabeau seems to have had pride of place. In the following passage from the radical pamphlet *La corruption de l'Assemblée nationale,* Mirabeau's monstrosity is unmasked in terms that bear a striking resemblance to the rhetoric by which the right-wing *Changement de décoration* unmasked Sieyès and Lafayette:

> This Mirabeau, this horrible *[affreux]* mixture of all vices, this revolting heart of putrid sentiments—do not allow yourself to be taken in by his verbose eloquence. . . . Credulous people, what error have you fallen into! You have allowed yourself to be seduced by the hypocritical mask of this hideous monster, & you have forgotten all of his vices; he has dazzled you so as better to slit your throat.[20]

So both the extreme left and the extreme right availed themselves of an almost identical rhetoric of veiled monstrosity; in fact, the rhetoric is often so similar that the historian is sometimes at a loss to distinguish between the two. It is possible to argue that there are subtle differences in tone, that the radical texts seem to be warning their readers to be more vigilant whereas counterrevolutionary texts seem to be lamenting a situation that has already come to pass. But, more often than not, the texts of the extreme left and right resemble one another so closely that the historian must look beyond the rhetoric for more tangible clues of the author's political orientation. Sometimes, after unmasking a host of veiled monsters and warning readers that no one can be trusted in a world of masks where nothing is as it seems, such texts will obligingly inform readers of those few individuals who *can* be trusted. Thus, for example, after unmasking Mirabeau as a monster in patriot's disguise, the author of *La corruption de l'Assemblée nationale* takes the trouble to let readers know the names of those deputies who can be trusted, whose patriotism is honest: such left-of-center deputies as Lameth, Armand-Desiré d'Aiguillon, Jacques-François Menou, Robespierre, Armand-Gaston Camus, and Barnave. And the pamphlet winds down with wide-ranging attacks on right-wingers like abbé Maury and Jacques-Antoine de Cazalès, who are so obvious in their enmity to the Revolution that there is no need to unmask them.[21]

This list of false patriots, true patriots, and enemies of the Revolution makes a very interesting contrast with a list offered in a counterrevolutionary pamphlet whose title also proclaims its antipathy toward the National Assembly, *Usurpations et attentats de l'Assemblée nationale*. Here, as the author seeks to make the French people see what monsters they have put in power, Mirabeau and Sieyès find themselves lumped together with many of the same deputies that *La corruption de l'Assemblée nationale* singled out as trustworthy, including Lameth, d'Aiguillon, Menou, Robespierre, Camus, and Barnave. All of these representatives are unveiled to the reader as the monsters they truly are:

> So you see, French people, to what kind of men you have entrusted your happiness, your interests, and the prosperity of your empire: a bunch of perverted

citizens without talent . . . and [who], like Harpies [winged monsters with the head of a woman and the tail, legs, and claws of a bird], infect and corrupt everything they touch and have not been able to destroy.[22]

But all is not entirely lost, the author of this pamphlet tells us. If only the French people could learn to differentiate between such evil monsters and those few representatives who have their best interest at heart, France might still be saved: "I know that all your representatives do not resemble the monsters whom I have just named. There are, among them, virtuous citizens, worthy Frenchmen who are sincerely penetrated with love for the people." And who are these virtuous citizens? They include some of the same individuals, like Cazalès and Maury, whom *La corruption de l'Assemblée nationale* considered so horrible that they did not even need to be unmasked.

Each side, therefore, vilified the trusted few named by the other, a confusing situation that no doubt made the task of unmasking all the more crucial and all the more desperate. But in the middle of this mayhem in which the left and the right bashed each other, we should not lose sight of something rather interesting: in virtually identical language, both the left and the right unmasked the veiled monsters who inhabited the political middle—individuals like Mirabeau who seemed too difficult to classify and whom both the right and the left denounced as an agent of the other.

But how are we to explain the specificity of the language of veiled monstrosity that the counterrevolutionaries and the Jacobins shared, these political groups that seemed such polar opposites that the mere fact that they shared anything at all strikes us as strange? Why, in short, paint the National Assembly as a body filled with horrible monsters who, rather than wreaking havoc, instead charm and "seduce" their victims? How can we make sense of a virtually identical rhetoric across a seemingly unbridgeable political divide? At times, one has the suspicion that these political adversaries are somehow reading from the same script. Take, for example, the following warning about certain untrustworthy representatives, contained within the pamphlet *La corruption de l'Assemblée nationale;* in its specific denunciation of veiled monstrosity, it might just as easily have been written by one side as by the other: "They have had the artifice to dazzle you *[l'art de t'éblouir],* to excite your enthusiasm, your admiration, in order to get hold of all the avenues to your soul; they have hidden the most shameful passions, the most monstrous vices beneath the veil of wisdom, of philosophy, and a love of the public welfare."[23]

Antoine de Baecque has suggested that the language of monstrosity is to a certain extent a replaying of an obsession with monsters, and in particular with the beast of Gévaudan, which preoccupied France in the 1760s, complete with numerous sightings and organized hunts for monsters. De Baecque's observation rings true with respect to many of the Jacobin pamphlets he cites; such pamphlets as *The Hydra of Despotism Laid Low, or The Patriotic Hunt of the Great Beast* no doubt played upon this preexisting fascination with "real" monsters, and it seems plausible enough, as he claims, that "revolutionary monsters are only a politicization of this narrative framework."[24]

But if we are speaking not of the obvious monsters but rather of those peculiar *veiled* monsters who hid beneath a mask of virtue, then the hunt for the beast of Gévaudan does not seem quite as relevant. Obvious monsters could be dealt with in obvious ways; but monsters masked beneath a charming facade—these were an entirely different creature. And rather than looking at the literature of strange beasts of the 1760s, we would do better to look once again at the pre-Revolutionary discourse on metaphysical abstraction, for it is there that one finds not only monsters but that peculiar breed of charming monsters that work by seduction and "dazzle" rather than by brute force.

In 1749, Etienne Bonnot de Condillac published *Traité des systêmes,* a work that contains a subsection entitled "On the abuse of abstract systems," in which Condillac warned that "[the abstract method] . . . *dazzles* the imagination with the boldness of the results to which it leads; it *seduces* the mind *[esprit]*, because one does not think *[réfléchit]* when confronted with imagination and passions; and, inevitably, it gives birth to and nourishes persistence in the most *monstrous* of errors."[25] One might, of course, argue that Condillac's claim that the abstract method "dazzles" and "seduces" and his warning against "monstrous" errors are mere figures of speech, and perhaps not quite the same thing as the vivid rhetoric of monstrosity that one finds during the Revolution. But Condillac's critique of abstraction is understandably figurative and intangible; he was, after all, speaking of a metaphysical process. A quarter-century later, in 1775, the self-proclaimed antiphilosophe Nicolas Gilbert would avail himself of more tangible images of monstrosity and seduction when he directly attacked those individuals who propagated meaningless abstractions in their literary and philosophical works:

> We see the hydra of idiotic rhymers once again reborn
> And the fall of the arts follows the loss of
>   manners *[moeurs]*.
> A monster is growing in Paris and getting stronger
> Who, at the ready with the hammer of philosophy—
> What am I saying?—with [philosophy's] name
>   falsely disguised,
> Smothers talents and destroys virtue.
> . . . .
> This monster nevertheless has nothing at all of
>   a ferocious air,
> And the name of virtues is always on his lips.[26]

Here, then, is a clear precursor to those counterrevolutionary and Jacobin texts that would later seek to unmask their opponents and reveal the true monstrosity lurking beneath the veil of charm and virtue. Like the political critics who came after him, Gilbert was primarily concerned with, as he put it, "unmasking our dangerous sages, [and] clarify[ing] the disastrous effects of their errors *[peign[ant] de leurs erreurs les effets désastreux]*."27

The Jacobin rhetoric of veiled monstrosity is virtually indistinguishable from counterrevolutionary rhetoric of veiled monstrosity because they are both rooted in the same anxiety that predates the Revolution itself—an anxiety about fictional forms that laid claim to a representation of reality. For pre-Revolutionary anti-abstractionists, these forms were categories of knowledge; for counterrevolutionaries, they were a variety of abstract representations foisted on France by the National Assembly, including paper money and a new system of *départements* to replace the historical regions of the country. And for counterrevolutionaries and Jacobins alike, the representative forms that were most troubling were those political representatives to the National Assembly who claimed to be transparently representing the general will of the nation but who in truth were bent on distorting and perverting it.

If counterrevolutionaries and Jacobins were similar in their denunciation of fraudulent monstrosity masking itself as charm and virtue, they differed of course with respect to those whom they singled out for unmasking. But they also differed in an even more fundamental way: they differed in the solutions that they posed to the problem at hand. For counterrevolutionaries, there could be no question of reforming the system; the entire enterprise of the Revolution was rotten to the core, privileging abstract ideas over historical precedent and fictitious and man-made bodies over the historical, political, and mystical bodies of the French nation. The Revolution was, for them, a horrible farce, and the only way to stop it was to stop the show. For Jacobins, by contrast, the problem lay not with the Revolution as it was conceived but rather with the manner in which it was practiced. If only the French people were careful to elect trustworthy representatives who would not be tempted to distort their will, but who instead could be relied upon to re-present the people's will transparently, the problem would be solved. The problem for the Jacobins, in short, was not with the show but with the actors.

"Let Us Bring Down the Curtain": Counterrevolutionary Responses to Revolutionary Representation

Most counterrevolutionary texts seem to teeter back and forth between utter despair and resignation on the one hand and outrage and a call to action on the other. A typical example of the former can be seen in the following lament by the notorious counterrevolutionary pamphleteer Antoine Ferrand:

> Shall I offer a portrait of the national assembly, . . . which applauds [regicide] monsters at the podium . . . ? Ah! better to avert our eyes from such scenes of horror and seek to rest them upon less distressing objects. But where to focus them? No matter where one looks, one sees in all of France only a people reduced to misery.[28]

But even Ferrand, who here seems to wallow in dejection, occasionally roused himself from his state of resigned helplessness. And indeed the above quotation comes from a pamphlet entitled *Les conspirateurs démasqués*— a title that would seem to suggest that, however hopeless he may have thought the situation was, Ferrand nevertheless believed that something could still be done to challenge the rule by these monsters in pleasant guise: at the very least, one could rip off the mask that hid their true countenance and reveal these monsters for who they truly were. And so, for example, in another of his pamphlets, entitled *Nullité et despotisme de l'Assemblée prétendue nationale* (Nullity and despotism of the so-called National Assembly), Ferrand departs from his usual resigned despair and instead exhorts the French people to join him actively in this critical task of unmasking: "You who for thirteen centuries were the most kind, the most lovable of peoples, come tear with me the veil with which [the National Assembly] strives to cover itself: examine to their very bottom these weak, perfidious and corrupt hearts!"[29]

Unlike Jacobin unmasking, however, counterrevolutionary unmasking was very much an end in itself. Unmasking was not the prelude to a purge but an action intended to reveal the state of things, to expose the "état actuel de la France [current state of France]," the title of yet another of Ferrand's pamphlets. Deep despair, then, often coexists side by side in counterrevolutionary pamphlets with an almost Pollyanna-like belief that if only the French people would "open their eyes," they would suddenly see the mess that they had gotten themselves into. In his rousing conclusion to the pamphlet *Nullité et despotisme de l'Assemblée prétendue nationale*, Ferrand declares the fundamental counterrevolutionary hope that to unmask is to destroy:

> Inhabitants of the countryside, inhabitants of the towns, inhabitants of the capital, citizens of all orders, . . . it is to you all that I address myself in conclusion. Error has blinded you. Open your eyes to the truth. Brandish *[secouer]* her flame with me: carry it from one end of the kingdom to the other: shed light on schemes, on intrigues, on the crimes of the Assembly, which overthrows such a flourishing empire! To unmask it is to destroy it; & [the Assembly] can say with

even more cause than the famous impostor of la Mèque: "My empire is destroyed if the man is recognized."[30]

For Ferrand, then, the legitimacy of the National Assembly depended entirely upon the willingness of the French people to believe in its legitimacy.
If only the people would refuse to accord it that legitimacy, the National Assembly, that fearsome monstrosity, would be rendered powerless, would
vanish into thin air like the fiction it truly was. As Ferrand declared in his
pamphlet *Les conspirateurs démasqués,* imagining—in an uncharacteristi-
cally optimistic mood—the moment when the truth was at hand, "[The National Assembly] is powerless; her power had only your confidence as a
foundation, and that confidence has been withdrawn."[31]

Historically, political representatives had always been able to point to
tangible proofs of their legitimacy. The form and content of their representation were spelled out respectively in the powers signed by their constituents and in the views expressed in the cahiers that they carried with
them and to which they had sworn a binding oath or mandate. But the representatives to the National Assembly had gone beyond the powers initially
accorded them, and they had tossed aside the cahiers in which they were
meant to find the stuff of their representation. For Ferrand, as for the counterrevolutionaries as a whole, these freewheeling representatives, whose
representation rested on no tangible basis of legitimacy, could be nothing
other than individuals *pretending* to be representatives: "[W]henever [a
representative] strays from [his mandate], it is no longer a representative
who acts but an individual. By himself, this individual can do nothing:
united with others who like himself have strayed from their mandate, . . .
can he do anything more?"[32]

Ferrand's answer was clearly "No." The National Assembly's legitimacy
had no basis in reality but rested entirely on the willingness of the French
people to regard this so-called—or *prétendu*—body as believable, hence the
"nullity" of the National Assembly in the title of the pamphlet from which
the above quote is taken.

For Ferrand, there were but two possibilities for the motives that lay behind this rule by a fraudulent body masquerading as legitimate: either these
representatives were fully conscious of their usurpation of power from legitimate authorities and were motivated by their own lust for power and
wealth, or they were themselves victims of their own deception, living in a
dreamworld along with the vast majority of the French people: "I declare
that if you are not usurpers, you are an assembly of lunatics who take
dreams for reality and who should be sent to form the republic of Morpheus.
But you are more than usurpers and lunatics; you are tyrants who deceive
one portion of the nation in order to persecute the other and reign despoti-
cally over both."[33] Much like the horrifying and yet fraudulent monsters,

like the real and dangerous effects of imagined abstract categories, the National Assembly is here portrayed as both horrible and unreal.

But if the National Assembly was a fictional entity behaving in a tyrannical fashion and entirely dependent upon the confidence of the French people for its very existence, then it made no sense to battle it with conventional weapons: one could not crush an enemy that did not exist. As Ferrand told his countrymen in his *Lettre à mes concitoyens* (Letter to my fellow citizens), in order to rid France of "your delegates *[mandataires]* who have turned themselves into your tyrants," the people need only "rattle your chains; the noise alone will dissipate the league, its leaders, and its schemes."[34] Or, as he wrote elsewhere, "Frenchmen, you have only to declare yourselves in order to send this phantom, which for eighteen months has been the bane of the kingdom, back into the abyss."[35]

Ferrand's belief in the ease with which the Revolutionary assembly could be defeated helps to explain the exasperation that is so characteristic of counterrevolutionary authors. The act of simply opening one's eyes would precipitate the downfall of these monsters who thrived on the apparent inability or refusal of the French people to see what lay right before them. Ferrand could not help chastising his countrymen, urging them to come to their senses before it was too late and telling them that they themselves were responsible for the horrors the representatives to the National Assembly had visited on the French nation:

> Your blind confidence [in them] is the sole cause [of these horrors]. Frenchmen! We have not ceased shouting at you to open your eyes; there is still time; come out of this stupor that will be your everlasting ruin. Open your eyes & see if you do not wish to lose forever those properties that you still have and that they have not yet been able to destroy.[36]

Ferrand, therefore, presents us with an image of the relationship between the French people and their *prétendu* representatives in which the former seem almost entranced, unable to perceive what is going on right before their very eyes, while the latter take advantage of this obliviousness to go about their business unhampered. Or perhaps we should put this somewhat differently: the French people see, but what they see is not the same thing that Ferrand sees; they see only the masks of their representatives, the charming exterior mouthing the words they want to hear. Ferrand, by contrast, cannot help seeing something very different—the monstrous actor behind the mask. By exhorting his fellow citizens to "open your eyes," he is essentially heckling the play of representation; he is placing himself between the actors and the spectators, unmasking the former so as to prevent the latter from successfully suspending their disbelief. As Ferrand himself declares, addressing his remarks to the representatives of the Assembly, "It is to you yourselves, it is before your very eyes that I shall unmask your criminal conduct, and from that very moment, I shall have stood myself between you and my compatriots."[37] By placing himself between the representatives and their constituency, between the political actors and political spectators who seemed content to exist in a "stupor," his aim was nothing other than to stop the show itself: "Let us bring down the curtain on this horrible bunch and on this execrable scene that has passed in the night."[38]

Here, I think, we begin to see how aspersions of theatricality were not simply epithets that linked political actors with their more universally disparaged theatrical counterparts. The logic of antitheatricality was related to the general fear of representative forms and of metaphysical abstractions that had existed before the Revolution and that continued to be articulated primarily by the political extremes during the Revolutionary period itself. In the same way that one could fear the effects of unbridled abstract categories that distorted the very reality they were meant to represent, so too were many counterrevolutionaries horrified by the havoc wrought by political representatives whose claim to legitimacy rested not on historical precedent or tangible powers but on the willingness of an all too gullible populace to suspend its critical faculties. The similarities between a stupefied theatrical audience that was manipulated by wily dramatic actors and a cowed political constituency in the thrall of political actors seemed all too clear to the Revolution's enemies. And it was this essential link between theater and politics, between a plausible and yet illegitimate government and believable dramatic fiction, that critics of the Revolution sought to make clear. This fundamental identity between political and theatrical vraisemblance was precisely what Louis-Abel Beffroy de Reigny (alias Cousin Jacques)—a notorious gadfly and self-declared anti-abstractionist—intended to expose when, from the safe distance of newly Napoleonic France, he reflected back on the Revolution. In his dictionary of Revolutionary neologisms, he offered the following definition of the word *comédien:*

> COMEDIEN . . . I have often seen the question hotly debated as to what differences exist between *comédien* and *acteur.* We say *les acteurs de telle révolution* [the actors of such and such a revolution]; but we do not say the *comédiens* [of such and such a revolution]. As for me, I think we can say the *comédiens* of the revolution.[39]

By intentionally theatricalizing the potentially neutral term of (political) actor, Beffroy de Reigny left no doubt as to his views on Revolutionary political representation.

Performance Anxiety: Jacobin Fear and Suspicion of Representatives

Like many counterrevolutionaries, Jacobin authors occasionally exhorted the French people to "open their eyes" and not be fooled by the charming masks of their representatives. In the left-wing pamphlet *La corruption de l'Assemblée nationale,* for example, immediately after unmasking Mirabeau's perfidious nature, the author urges his fellow citizens to "finally open your eyes & recognize the man whom you have exalted, whom you have carried in triumph at the very instant he was the center of the most execrable plots formed against you; look what has been and what still is the conduct of this infamous scoundrel."[40]

Despite certain similarities, however, there is a clear and fundamental difference between counterrevolutionary attacks on the nation's representatives and those undertaken by the left wing. At issue for the Jacobins were never the fundamentals of the Revolution itself or, more specifically, the theory of representation that the Revolution ushered into existence. Rather, what troubled them was the manner in which Revolutionary representation was carried out and in particular the choice of individuals who had been entrusted with putting this theory into practice: "The new foundations of the government are excellent; unfortunately, evil geniuses have seized hold of [positions at] the highest levels; the people, good but credulous, deceived by false appearances, have made great errors in the choices they have made."[41] And so, although the Jacobins had absolute confidence in the theoretical ability of representative democracy to re-present[42] transparently the general will of the people, at the same time they had a profound fear of the potential obstacles and distortions posed by the selection of representatives who would be charged with the performance of this task.[43]

Given both their acceptance of the premise of representative democracy and their anxiety concerning the manner in which such representation was performed, it is not surprising that the Jacobins tended to focus their attention on that precise moment when representative theory became practice—the moment of political election. Time and again, left-wing authors took it upon themselves to alert the public to the inherent—but often hidden—dangers involved in the selection of their representatives. The following excerpt from a left-leaning pamphlet entitled *Avis aux citoyens françois* is typical of such expressions of anxiety:

> Citizens,
> The day has finally arrived when, by free elections, you will give yourself administrators. . . . This moment must decide the fate of your newborn constitution; . . . by placing your sacred trust in a small number among you, you will name for yourselves officials *[magistrats]* to govern you, to look after the common interest & the safety of your homes.
> But these men may [also] be the enemies of your liberty and use the powers you have entrusted to them for the purposes of favoring the partisans of the old regime; they might be or might have been the courtesans, the slaves of your tyrants; they might be men devoted to seduction; in the end, instead of assuring your victory, they may condemn you to servitude, turn you over to your enemies, & shackle you with the same irons [from] which you have just broken [free].

A thousand traps will be set before you in order to get hold of your vote; the ambitious will appear disinterested; the former agents of despotism will appear your equals and your friends; . . . your most bitter enemies will take on the outward appearance of harmony and friendship; the egotist will show off his patriotism; the villain, his humanity; and the vile slaves of the court will pass themselves off as the apostles of liberty.[44]

Here, the greatest fear seems to be that by seduction and guile the people's enemies will manage to pass themselves off as the people's friends, that the people's representatives in name will not, in truth, represent anything but their own private interests. Such fears were apparently warranted, at least in the eyes of some. No sooner had the municipal elections of early 1790 been held than another radical pamphlet was published, chastising the French people for the choices they had made and warning them against future errors:

Citizens,
My sorrow equaled my surprise upon learning that in many parts of the kingdom you have elevated the enemies of the constitution to the highest municipal offices. Justly alarmed by the dangers to which this imprudence subjects public liberty, I have endeavored to find out which are the men who must appear suspect to us, and by which deceitful *[artificieuses]* maneuvers they succeed in fooling us. Let my reflections that I hurry to impart to you protect you against even more disastrous errors.[45]

The warnings of "disastrous errors *[erreurs funestes]*" in the above passage as well as the "thousand traps *[mille pièges]*" mentioned in the preceding one should be familiar to us: in strikingly similar terms the *Encyclopédie* had warned that abstractions, if not used with great care, could be "a disastrous source of futile disputes & dangerous errors *[une source funeste de disputes vaines & d'erreurs dangereuses]*" and had detailed the various "traps *[pièges]*" inherent in their use.[46]

This similarity of rhetoric between those who warned of the dangers of metaphysical abstraction and those who spoke of the potential pitfalls of political representation should not surprise us. In many respects, contemporary justifications of metaphysical abstraction and political representation were conceptually identical: both were rooted in the idea that it was impossible for a multitude of objects to make themselves known without some form of abstract representation. And so, for example, political representation was very often predicated upon the practical impossibility of direct democracy. A well-known pamphlet explained this concept in December of 1788: "The large number of citizens does not permit each individual citizen to have his own representative in the Estates General; it is necessary that several citizens gathered together have a single and identical representative who will carry their will to the national assembly."[47] And if we turn to justifications of abstraction, we can see that virtually the same logic was employed to rationalize its use: the multiplicity of phenomena did not permit the representation of each individual object but necessitated their representation by one of the attributes that they shared in common. Thus, in the following passage from the *Encyclopédie*, the practical necessity of linguistic signs is explained in terms that cannot fail to recall the justification for political representation:

> It is by means of . . . [abstraction] that, without overburdening tongues with all the necessary words to equal the number of individual [objects], we can signify *[désigner]* them all, & that, without having any idea of each one of them, we represent all of them to ourselves. . . . Without classifications, what would all of natural history do? And how, without metaphysical abstraction, would we be able to arrange our ideas according to categories? How would we be able to distinguish without [metaphysical abstraction] those common traits between beings of the same type or of the same species?[48]

How, in short, would we process the multiplicity of phenomena in the world around us were it not for abstractions? How could we express our thoughts if we did not have words to represent objects that bore a resemblance to one another? And how, by the same logic, in the realm of politics, could the multiplicity of citizens express their will if not by allowing themselves to be represented by political representatives who could actually assemble in one place for the purpose of articulating that will?

On a practical level, then, the Jacobins recognized the necessity of elections in much the same way that those who were wary of abstraction nevertheless recognized its inevitability. There simply was no other means by which the nation could form a political body. But this recognition of the necessity of elections posed a fundamental theoretical problem for the Jacobins: if there was one essential principle that united them, it was the idea that the sovereign body and the expression of the sovereign will were fundamentally holistic and collective entities; by contrast, the individual as well as individual expressions of will were meaningless abstractions of a collective whole.[49] And yet, at the same time, the Jacobins were forced to recognize that there were no means of forming a political body to re-present the collective body and will of the nation except through a momentary particularization of the collective. How else, in other words, could the body of the nation vote except as individual citizens?

The regrettable practical necessity of election, therefore, without which the nation would not be able to form a political body, was for the Jacobins a weak link in what would otherwise have been a perfect chain between the body of the nation and the political body. The moment of election was the moment when pure re-presentation encountered a host of possible distortions, necessitating great vigilance. As one wary author warned, the French people should not be overconfident; they should not assume that a Revolution that had been won in theory would effortlessly be translated into a practical victory:

> The grand scenes of 1789 and 1790 have inspired in the French nation an enthusiasm, a soaring [spirit] of liberty that, like a torrent of fire, has foiled all the schemes of despotism. But it is not true that one is free because one wishes to be [free] (Lafayette has said: In order to be free, it is enough to wish it). . . . [T]oo proud of its victory, which cost [the nation] only the price of saying "I wish it," [the nation] did not notice that the very same men who yesterday held it in slavery have come forward now, with an embittered heart and the language of patriotism on their lips, in order to bear the standard of the very liberty they cursed; [the nation] has not seen that schemers of all classes, allied by a common interest, have played all the roles, assumed all the masks necessary to influence [public] opinion in the elections (the only act of sovereignty the people can exercise individually).[50]

This last parenthetical phrase leaves no doubt that, at least as far as this author was concerned, elections were the root cause of anxiety in that they necessarily entailed the splintering of sovereignty into its constituent parts. If the people as a body could always be trusted to know what was best for them, they were somehow undeserving of that trust as individuals.

To the Jacobins, then, the greatest danger to the nation as a whole was the credulity of individual citizens, who might easily be taken in by the artifice of the people's enemies. As in a Jacobin pamphlet quoted above, the French people were "good but credulous, deceived by false appearances." Jacobin unmasking, therefore, in contradistinction to counterrevolutionary unmasking, primarily served to *protect* Revolutionary re-presentation rather than to undermine it. By ensuring that this crucial link in the chain between the national and political bodies was filled by individuals who could truly be trusted, the Jacobins believed themselves to be safeguarding the transparency of re-presentation. In the following passage from a speech on the subject of representative government, Robespierre speaks directly to this need to ensure what he calls the "purity" of the representative process against the potential distortions posed by elections:

> However necessary it may be to restrain elected officials *[magistrats]*, it is no less [necessary] to choose them well: it is upon this twin foundation that liberty must be based. Do not lose sight of the fact that in representative government there are no constitutive laws as important as those that guarantee the purity of elections.
> Here I see dangerous errors *[dangereuses erreurs]* pouring forth; here I catch sight of the fact that we are abandoning the first principles of good sense and of liberty in order to pursue vain metaphysical abstractions. For example, there are those who want citizens across the republic to vote for the nomination of

each delegate [*mandataire*] in such a manner that a man of merit and virtue who is known only in the region he inhabits could never be called to represent his compatriots; and [instead] that notorious [*fameux*] charlatans, who are not always the best citizens or the most enlightened of men, or schemers, put forth by a powerful party that would rule throughout the republic, would be forever after and exclusively the inevitable representatives of the French people.[51]

Robespierre here privileges those representatives "of merit and virtue" who are known directly by their constituents over those "notorious" representatives who are known only by their reputations—or, in other words, those representatives who are known by their physical persons over those who are known by word of mouth. Robespierre here betrays a desire to retain a certain physicality and concreteness that were in many ways more characteristic of pre-Revolutionary re-presentation. In short, he hopes that the tangible links of actual acquaintance between the representative and the represented, between two human bodies, might preclude the kinds of distortion that would otherwise threaten the purity of political re-presentation.[52]

For Robespierre, then, as for the Jacobins in general, the transparency of re-presentation hinged upon electing the right individual—hinged on the character of the representative himself. For this reason, unmasking was critical. Those individuals who were truly virtuous had to be winnowed from those who merely appeared to be virtuous. One needed to go beyond the masks of the various candidates to see who they truly were. This is precisely the intention of pamphlets like *Le véritable portrait de nos législateurs,* which, as the title suggests, promised to offer readers the "true" portrait of their representatives. As the author of this pamphlet declared, "My work has had but one goal: to rip off the mask from the schemers, and to put vice and virtue, without disguises, in the presence of the nation."[53]

For the anonymous author of *Le véritable portrait de nos législateurs,* then, as for many authors sympathetic to the Jacobin cause, the act of unveiling was indispensable to the success of the Revolution. If everyone spoke words of patriotism, then it was crucial to know who was speaking from the heart and who was merely speaking. And so, taking aim, as did Robespierre, at those who were well known as opposed to *truly* known, the author proclaimed that "it is in the *heart* of these famous [*célèbres*] men that I will dig; it is not in their ostensible actions." Perhaps not surprisingly, what "digging" revealed in the case of Mirabeau was that behind the "verbose eloquence" one found a "revolting heart," exposing him as not the patriot he claimed to be but rather a *"grand comédien."* Not stopping with Mirabeau, the pamphlet went on to unmask numerous others "with an embittered heart and the language of patriotism on their lips."[54] At the conclusion of the pamphlet, out of a total of 1,200 representatives, only 288 left-wing deputies were declared worthy of being entrusted with the people's will.

The Jacobins placed a premium on safeguarding the purity or transparency of the process by which the general will was re-presented in the political body. But the goal that they set for themselves and for French society was a virtual impossibility. It demanded purity when distortion seemed all but inevitable; it demanded concrete presence within a system of abstract representation. In short, it necessitated eternal vigilance and the incessant unveiling of fraudulence and veiled monstrosity.

The ever-present need to ring the two-sided tocsin of honest patriotism and suspicious denunciation, which was fundamental to the Jacobin mindset, explains in part the frequency with which conspiracies were unveiled and monsters unmasked during the Revolutionary period. Such was the price to be paid for the purity of representation. But there was an additional factor that transformed what might have been an extremely important pursuit into an overriding obsession: Jacobins and counterrevolutionaries were mouthing virtually *indistinguishable* rhetoric in which the unmasking of veiled monstrosities figured prominently. The very fact that mortal enemies were reading from the same script, desperately trying to unmask each other—not to mention everyone else—as duplicitous monsters, served to heighten the already formidable sense of confusion and anxiety.

The obsession with unmasking was therefore a function not only of ideological necessity but also of a political climate in which identical accusations were leveled from both the left and the right. Such accusations could be rebutted only by counteraccusations, for to answer such allegations with expressions of patriotic devotion was to exhibit the telltale signs of veiled treachery.[55] Unmasking was therefore imperative not only because it assured the purity of representation, or because it revealed how rotten things had already become, but perhaps most important because it became the only means by which honest patriotism could be expressed. In short, as the Revolution progressed, unmasking became one of the few activities in which one could engage without arousing suspicion.

The Jacobins' recognition of the inevitability of representation and their fear and suspicion of the representatives entrusted to perform the task were manifested not only in the political arena but also, and in precisely the same way, in their attitudes toward theatrical actors. As we have seen throughout this book, actors had been a source of anxiety for individuals on both the right and the left, from the earliest days of the Revolution. But there is no question that, coincident with the Jacobin rise to power, suspicions concerning actors took on a new urgency. Consider, for example, the ominous threats contained in the following letter addressed to the Théâtre-National in July of 1793 from an author whose play had been rejected:

Citizens,
   Your behavior toward patriotic authors . . . is very much worthy of a society
of counterrevolutionaries. . . . Citizens, believe me, purify your stage. . . . [T]he
time is ripe; do not delay. Your enemies are watching; be careful not to increase
their numbers by refusing [to perform] patriotic plays. . . . Those who still believe that all the rumors being spread about you are the fruit of envy or wickedness will end up believing [those rumors], and your [theatrical] society will then
not be far from its downfall.[56]

We might assume that these are simply the words of an embittered author,
who was mistaking the actors' judgment of his play's merits for a rejection
of the "patriotic" sentiments contained within it. And yet subsequent events
would suggest that the author of the above letter was not alone in his suspicions of the actors. Not two months after the above letter was written, the
entire troupe of the Théâtre-National was arrested and thrown in prison for
the better part of a year. Ostensibly, the reason for the arrest of the Comédiens-Français was their performance of *Paméla, ou La vertu récompensée.*
According to François de Neufchâteau, the author of the play, who was arrested along with the actors, the entire affair was a misunderstanding; one
of the spectators had taken the following line from the play to be a criticism
of political radicalism rather than the rebuke of religious fanaticism it was
intended to be: "Oh! the persecutors are the only ones to blame, and the
most tolerant are the most reasonable." And, as the author reminded the
representatives to the National Convention in his published appeal, the play
had been revised under the direct supervision of the Committee of Public
Safety only three days before the performance in question.[57] Despite such
protestations of innocence, however, both the author of *Paméla* and most of
the Comédiens-Français would not be released from prison until Thermidor.
   Clearly, however, the reason for the actors' arrest was not quite as simple
as their performance of the play *Paméla.* Jacobin suspicions of actors were
general and long-standing. The order to arrest the actors explicitly accused
the Comédiens-Français of having "given sustained proof of their pronounced lack of patriotism *[incivisme]* since [the beginning of] the Revolution and [of having] performed antipatriotic plays."[58] And as the *Gazette national* reported the following day, "The Théâtre de la Nation, which was
anything but *national,* has been closed."[59]
   But even this allegation of political treachery is less a reason in itself than
a manifestation of an underlying suspicion of actors in general. Actors were
perceived as counterrevolutionaries because actors were inherently untrustworthy, not vice versa. How else are we to explain not only the arrest of the
actors of the Théâtre-National but also the subsequent arrest of dramatic actors and theater directors in other theaters, not only in Paris but in the
provinces as well? Two weeks after the actors of the Théâtre-National had
been imprisoned, the directors of the Opéra were arrested.[60] And two

months after that, Mlle Montansier, the well-known director of the theater that bore her name, the same La Montansier who had undertaken the task of exporting a propaganda troupe of actors to recently conquered Belgium only a year earlier,[61] was arrested under the pretext of having plotted to set fire to the Bibliothèque nationale under instructions from the British government.[62] Two weeks after the arrest of Montansier, representatives of the people *en mission* in Bordeaux decided to arrest eighty-six actors and other employees at the Grand Théâtre de Bordeaux.[63]

The Jacobin government arrested actors not because they performed counterrevolutionary plays or because they were agents of the counterrevolution. They arrested actors because actors were inherently problematic. As individuals who made a living out of pretending to be something they were not, actors were the very antithesis of everything the Jacobins stood for—honesty, virtue, transparency.

All of this is not say, however, that the Jacobins despised the theater; on the contrary, they, perhaps more than any other political group, recognized the potential importance of theater as a means of propaganda. But if they reconciled themselves to the uses of theater, they could not help being suspicious of those who performed on the stage. It was in part because of this suspicion of professional actors that the Jacobins embraced Rousseau's ideal of the public festival. For the festivals, in principle, were the very opposite of professional theater: instead of actors fooling passive spectators within a darkened theater, the people themselves would take to the streets in open-air festivals of self-presentation. This contrast is well expressed in the reaction of the prominent Jacobin official Claude Payan to the suggestion, made by a theater entrepreneur, that the Festival of the Supreme Being ought to be turned into a play: "What stage, with its cardboard rocks and trees, its sky of rags, could claim to equal the magnificence of 1 prairial?"[64]

And yet, from a propagandistic point of view, the festival certainly had its practical drawbacks. No matter how carefully scripted, no matter how many speeches it included in its program, a festival lacked that seamlessness and that vraisemblance that made the professional theater so compelling. And so those who staged Jacobin festivals were not above taking certain minor liberties with the ideal of self-presentation. When the situation demanded, festivals were supplemented with a little theatricality. Actresses from the Opéra were hired to play the role of Liberty and her handmaidens, so as to ensure that the spontaneous festival went according to plan.[65] And the Festival of Reason proved so important that Jacobin officials decided it was a shame that it could be performed only once; an exception had to be made. The Festival of Reason would be re-presented several times in the form of a play entitled, appropriately enough, *La fête de la raison*, performed in the salle of the Opéra.[66]

And there were simply too many important points to convey to a largely illiterate populace without the occasional help of professional actors to give voice to otherwise mute ideas. Thus the Jacobins decided to grant several of the imprisoned actors an early release, on the condition that they perform in the newly renamed Théâtre du Peuple—a theater that epitomized the Jacobins' belief that abstract representation, if subject to rigid controls, might serve the interests of the state. The actors who performed in this theater (not only those who were on work-release from prison but also actors who were requisitioned on a rotating basis from other theater companies) were subject to strict controls: "No citizen will be allowed to enter into the Théâtre du Peuple if he does not have a particular mark that will be given only to patriots, [and of which] the municipality will oversee the distribution."[67]

In the end, the Jacobins considered theatrical representation, like its political counterpart, to be too essential to dispense with entirely. Just as Jacobin authors focused on the moment of election as the moment of greatest danger, so too did they focus on the selection of actors as the moment for vigilance. If the purity of political representation could be assured by close scrutiny of the candidates for office, then the purity of theatrical representation could be assured by careful surveillance and selection of the actors themselves.

Perhaps the ultimate form of Jacobin surveillance and control over actors took place in the city of Marseilles. *En mission* in that city, Etienne Maignet, representative of the people, along with Michot and Hainault, both *commissaires* of the Committee of Public Safety for the Regeneration of Theaters, issued the following proclamation in the year II:

> That the Administrative Committee of the Theaters of this commune will alone have the right to distribute roles to whatever actors it judges capable of filling them, without those actors having the right to refuse or to object to [any roles] . . . ; in the distribution of roles, [it will be] the task of the committee to take into consideration only the public welfare, and the more nearly perfect execution of the plays, & the benefit of national instruction.[68]

If one could exercise complete control over the selection of the representatives, the purity of the representation could be assured. The Jacobins, in short, were not averse to representation, provided that they were the ones who cast the play.

The Jacobins shared, then, with their political enemies the counterrevolutionaries a deeply felt mistrust of abstract representations. As I have suggested, it can often be very difficult to distinguish between left- and right-wing denunciations of the political center as a dangerous farce. Nevertheless, counterrevolutionaries and Jacobins proposed radically different solutions to the problem at hand. For the former, the only possible solution was to stop the entire Revolutionary spectacle as quickly as possible—a goal they endeavored to accomplish by calling upon the political audience to open its eyes, halt its suspension of disbelief, and see the Revolutionary charlatans for who they really were. The Jacobins, by contrast, although they found many aspects of the Revolution equally as disturbing, nevertheless believed that the distortions inherent in the representative process—whether political or theatrical—could be mitigated, if not erased entirely, if only the Jacobins themselves were in a position to exercise complete control over the process. All of this was, of course, to be in the people's best interest. But, as we shall see, on those occasions when "the people" seemed unwilling to accept the Jacobin version of what was best for them, the Jacobins would find themselves in the awkward position of enforcing strict controls not only over the actors but over the spectators as well.

8 Breaching the Fourth Wall

Spectators Storm the Stage, Actors Invade the
Audience

At the beginning of this book, I outlined the theoretical and practical aesthetic revolution in the middle of the eighteenth century whereby spectators, who were used to participating in theatrical representations with spontaneous performances of their own, suddenly found themselves seated in the darkness of the parterre. Unable to see one another, so the theory went, they would have little else to do but watch performers basking in the floodlights above them, on a stage entirely cleared of all those who were extraneous to the representation.

Of course, even the best laid plans hardly ever progress as their architects intend, and when one is dealing with the notoriously unpredictable parterre of the French theater, the uncertainty is all the greater. Theatrical reformers could remove the spectators from the stage physically, but their audible presence proved decidedly more difficult to do away with. From down below in the darkness, audience members continued to participate in (or at least interrupt) the representative process with a variety of whistles, comments, and criticisms, making full use of that time-honored privilege of French theatergoers—the *sifflet*.[1]

Needless to say, the sifflet presented a significant obstacle to the proper functioning of the differentiated, hermetically sealed representative space. Actors could do their best to imagine a fourth wall, but the fourth wall could not keep out the din of whistling and the snide comments emanating from the parterre, interruptions that did not exactly aid in the creation of an aura of vraisemblance. The only means by which this form of audience participation could be eradicated was the active repression of the spectators' sifflets. And it so happens that in 1751, a year after Riccoboni first published his innovative theories on theatrical representation, the royal government implemented a plan to quash the exuberance of Parisian audiences with the introduction of armed guardsmen into the theaters; soldiers were instructed

258

to load their weapons in full view of the spectators in order to impress upon the audience the serious nature of the government's intentions.[2]

Despite the best efforts of the authorities to police theater audiences, however, spectators continued to disrupt theatrical performances well into the latter half of the eighteenth century and into the Revolutionary period itself. In 1789, when *cahiers de doléances* from various orders and corporations throughout France were being submitted to the Estates General, a satirical pamphlet in the form of an apocryphal cahier of the royal actors of Paris included the following suggested legislation for the Estates General to enact: "That the parterre be expressly forbidden to tire our ears with their cries of *à bas* [down with so and so] and *paix-là* [shut up over there]."[3] In a similar vein, in 1790, while the National Assembly was occupied with the task of drafting a constitution, a satirical pamphlet put the following suggestion for a constitutional amendment into the mouths of actors: "[I]t will be forbidden to all citizens to make fun of us [actors], under penalty of giving us a lot of money."[4]

By the time of the Revolution, then, far from having been eradicated, the sifflet was alive and flourishing. Indeed, with the new spirit of liberty and freedom of expression that marked the first phase of the Revolution, there was even an increase in audience disruptions of performances. As one author declared in 1790, the tumultuous nature of theater audiences was a welcome sign that the reign of despotism was over:

> [A despotic government] must establish a severe order *[police]* in the theaters, for fear that these places of assembly might become a meeting place where resolutions are made against [the government's] interests. No one is permitted to raise his voice or speak in public except the actors. . . . Today, one makes motions from the parterre with impunity; if they are ridiculous, then the boos and sifflets [of one's fellow spectators] quickly put an end to them. The assembled public is tumultuous and impolite, but rarely is it unjust.[5]

The right of the audience to interrupt a play therefore became equivalent to the right of free speech and the legitimate expression of public opinion. Consequently, in 1791, as part of the January Decrees which granted authors property rights over their plays, theaters were demilitarized, and government censorship of both the play itself and audience behavior was abolished.[6]

As an expression of the audience's will, however, the sifflet was rather limited. Although a chorus of sifflets could force an actor from the stage or bring down the entire play altogether, the sifflet was essentially restricted to the act of negation, the antithesis of applause. But audiences had other means of enforcing their will than the simple vote of yes or no, applause or sifflets. When they felt that their will had been ignored, and that the actors on the stage were acting in violation of the express will of the parterre, Revolutionary theatrical audiences made their will known in more substantial, participatory ways, on occasion even daring to breach the fourth wall not simply audibly but physically.

Charles IX

No theatrical battle of the Revolutionary period was more viciously waged or more politically charged than the events surrounding the performance of *Charles IX,* an unflattering portrait of a murderous king written by the twenty-five-year-old Marie-Joseph Chénier. The question of whether or not to perform *Charles IX* not only pitted various combinations of actors and spectators against one another but also involved several of the most important political figures of Revolutionary France, including Mirabeau, Danton, Desmoulins, and Bailly.

The story of the audience revolt over *Charles IX* is rather complicated, and accessible mostly through vindictive denunciations and indignant self-justifications. Some of this textual evidence survives in various archives; some managed to find its way into print in contemporary periodicals and pamphlets. Although many of the sources conflict with one another as to which side was composed of malevolent schemers and which was composed of unwitting victims of a conspiracy, virtually all of the textual evidence betrays a fundamental preconception that is crucial to this study: neither side seemed to differentiate between the theatrical and the political stages. From this lack of differentiation followed several corollary assumptions: that the parterre was equivalent to the nation; that theatrical audiences possessed a general will; and that audiences had a fundamental right to demand that their theatrical representatives accede to the general will of the parterre, by force if necessary.

The story of the battle over *Charles IX* begins five days after the storming of the Bastille. After months of frustration with royal censors and the reluctance of the Comédiens du roi to do anything that might be seen as politically inflammatory, Chénier showed up at a formal meeting of the actors to request that his play finally be performed, "now that there is no censorship at all."[7] The actors, however, demurred, saying that they did not have the authority to invent a "new regime" for themselves and would wait until they received orders from whoever was now in a position of authority.

For a month, it would seem, nothing happened. Then, on the night of 19 August, during the intermission between two plays, printed copies of the following leaflet were suddenly dropped from the balconies onto the theater floor:

Brothers,
In this moment of the triumph of French liberty, will we stand idly by while dramatic genius succumbs to the latest efforts of despotism? . . . [We] demand

the representation of *Charles IX* as well as several other plays. . . . [L]et us unite our voices to demand, in the name of Liberty, the prompt representation of *Charles IX*.[8]

Meanwhile, outside the theater, a leaflet entitled *Adresse aux bons patriotes* (An address to good patriots) was being spread through the streets of Paris:

Frenchmen! The Theater of the Nation has for long enough been handed over to works tainted with banality and servitude. Your national plays offer only a model of slavery. There is a truly political, truly patriotic tragedy. It has been received [for consideration] by the Comédie-Française; its title is *Charles IX*. . . . The author is M. de Chénier. This work inspires the hatred of fanaticism, despotism, aristocracy, and civil wars. The enemies of M. Necker, that great minister, the savior of France, are afraid of the resemblance one will undoubtedly find between him and the Chancelier de l'Hôpital, one of the characters in the play. The actors do not dare to represent it at this moment.

If you think that such a subject is worthy of your attention in these first days of French liberty, then it is no longer for the Gentlemen of the Bedchamber to give orders [to the actors]; it is for you [to do].[9]

Perhaps still unaware of the forces mustering against them, the Comédiens du roi began the performance of the second play of the evening. An internal memo of the Théâtre-Français, written later that evening, would report that no sooner had the actors set foot onstage than voices were raised from different parts of the theater, calling out: *"Charles IX!* Chénier's play!"[10] Misunderstanding, at first, the meaning of the disturbance, one of the actors asked if the spectators were calling for the author of the previous play, perhaps to express their admiration. The cries of *"Charles IX!"* continued, and then one spectator stood up and spoke on behalf of the others: *"Charles IX,* the tragedy of M. de Chénier, was received [for consideration and] went into rehearsal; why isn't it being performed?"

The actors, apparently at a loss for a response, retired for a few moments to confer with one another, and then Fleury, one of the lead actors, came out to speak to the audience. The actors' memo reported the interchange between Fleury and the audience as follows:

"Gentlemen, the Comédie-Française has always made it its duty to fulfill your wishes. The tragedy *Charles IX* has not been in rehearsal. As soon as we have received permission. . . ."

Here, Fleury was interrupted by the public, which cried out: No permission!

The orator said: "We don't want to hear any talk of permission. For too long the public has suffered the despotism of censorship. We want to be free to hear—and to see represented—the works that please us, just as we are free in our thought." The orator was applauded.

The actors were clearly at a loss. For as long as anyone could remember, they had taken orders from the Gentlemen of the Bedchamber, the royal officials who were in charge of the administration of Paris's official theaters. The parterre had certainly attempted to dictate its will in the past, with varying degrees of success, but never had it so audaciously presented itself as the legitimate authority to be obeyed above all others. After several minutes of dialogue between Fleury and the audience, the actors finally agreed to request permission from the municipal government to perform *Charles IX*. This the spectators apparently accepted, as the municipal authorities were presumably *their* representatives, and therefore constituted the next best thing to their direct control over the actors. But the spectators demanded to know when the actors would contact the municipal authorities. Fleury responded to the audience: "Whenever you order us to do so, gentlemen." That was more like it. The spectators' spokesman responded on behalf of the parterre: "Tomorrow. And you will give us a reply the day after tomorrow." Fleury then bowed his head and said, "The Comédie-Française will always be eager to satisfy the wishes of the nation and to render itself worthy of [the nation's] indulgence." The memo reports that he was loudly applauded for this last statement. The actors, despite some initial difficulties, seemed to be catching on to the new order of things, and the audience made known its satisfaction.

If spectators had always exerted a certain influence over theatrical representations, they were clearly emboldened by political events taking place during that summer of 1789 to push for direct and unmediated control over the actors. As a newspaper would later report the events of that particular evening, the public had done something entirely unprecedented: "On 19 August, in the parterre of the Comédie-Française, the public exercised an authority never before seen in that location. . . . [The episode] serves as proof that the word liberty is today being applied in more than one genre."[11] Liberty, in this instance, meant that the effective control of theatrical representation had passed from the royal to the Revolutionary authorities. As the day-to-day control over political affairs was slowly ebbing from the king and gradually being invested in the National Assembly, the various government functionaries—actors as well as other professions that were considered part of the royal administration (including the actors' fellow outcasts the executioners)—had to strike a careful balance between two masters. In August of 1789, it was not entirely clear which master would prevail.

The day following the audience's revolt, the actors reported to the municipal government, which in turn demanded a copy of Chénier's play in order to decide for itself in the matter. The municipal government then published a copy of its request to see the play, no doubt so that citizens would see that their political representatives (in contrast to their theatrical representatives) could not be accused of thwarting the public's will.[12] Eventually the municipal government gave its permission, and the play was performed on 4 November 1789. Despite rumors of assassination attempts on the actors and the threat of general violence, the play was performed without incident. In attendance at the premiere were Mirabeau, Danton, Desmoulins, and Le Chapelier. Desmoulins reportedly declared, "This play furthers our cause more than the October days." And Danton apparently stated, "If *Figaro* killed off the nobility, *Charles IX* will kill off royalty.' "[13]

But the story of *Charles IX* did not end there. After squabbles between Chénier and the actors, Chénier withdrew his play from the repertoire of the Comédie-Française in May of 1790.[14] And then, two months later, as National Guardsmen and military officers from all over France began converging on Paris for the upcoming Festival of the Federation to be held on the first anniversary of the storming of the Bastille, Chénier apparently changed his mind. He requested that the Théâtre-Français—now renamed the Théâtre de la Nation[15]—perform *Charles IX* for the benefit of the provincial *fédérés*, fifty thousand of whom were expected to be in Paris over a period of eight days. The actors refused.

Rumors began to circulate once again that the actors of the Théâtre de la Nation were thwarting the people's will. The actors, defending themselves against such allegations, drafted a letter on 10 July, which was possibly intended for publication. The letter explains that it was Chénier himself who had withdrawn the play and that it was now impossible to rearrange their schedule, and concludes with the following comment: "Here, gentlemen, are the reasons against [Chénier's] demands; it is the patriotic wish of the actors concerned to represent to the eyes of the nation those kings who love their people, [and] people who love their kings." And then the following phrase is crossed out, the actors apparently having thought better of it: ". . . and not any longer to offer patriotic Frenchmen the frightening spectacle of a historical event that one should perhaps have covered forever with an impenetrable veil."[16] These words certainly lend credence to the allegations of the actors' critics, many of whom claimed that if the actors were not outright counterrevolutionaries, then at the very least they were determining for themselves what the public *ought* to see represented rather than doing the bidding of the public.

The above letter was, however, apparently never published. Instead, no doubt recognizing the danger of appearing to express their own opinions rather than merely acceding to the wishes of the public, the actors sent a matter-of-fact letter to Chénier on the impossibility of performing his play out of turn; they made no mention of the play's problematic content.[17]

Suspecting that the actors' refusal was politically motivated, Chénier and his allies once again set out on a campaign to intimidate the actors into performing his play. An article appeared in a newspaper claiming that "[t]he Comédiens-Français are refusing to perform the only national play that exists."[18] On 17 July, Mirabeau and Danton sent separate letters to the actors formally requesting, on behalf of the provincial *fédérés*, a performance of

Charles IX.[19] Still the actors refused. According to a pro-Chénier pamphlet, Mirabeau sent the actors a second letter, "warning them of the severe consequences of their stubbornness."[20] And several of the *fédérés* themselves personally contacted the actors, requesting a performance of the play, all to no avail.[21] In the eyes of many, the actors were stubbornly refusing to listen to the will of the people, almost as if their fourth wall existed not only during performances but as a permanent barrier between themselves and the public. Clearly, many individuals were infuriated by the thought that actors might be acting according to their own will rather than the general will of the public, the assumption being that the actors were onstage to do the bidding of the parterre.

The battle reached its climax on the evening of 22 July, when many of the *fédérés* had not yet left Paris to return to the provinces. During the intermission between plays, the cashier came backstage to inform the actors that Chénier's servant had just been spotted purchasing an enormous number of tickets to the parterre for the second play of the evening. When asked why she needed so many tickets in view of the fact that the evening's repertoire was already half finished, she responded that it was for a wedding party. The actors would later comment: "If it wasn't for a wedding party, it was for a party at any rate, . . . [and] Palissot, Talma, Chénier, Camille Desmoulins & others were in attendance."[22]

According to the actors' account of that evening, as soon as they had been apprised of the servant's purchase, they feared the worst, and those fears proved justified. No sooner did the curtain open on the second play of the evening than the parterre "filled with people and became agitated" and then erupted in "confused and tumultuous cries, among which could be discerned the request for *Charles IX.*"[23] The actor Naudet, who was not only a member of the troupe but also a lieutenant in the National Guard and thus—the actors no doubt hoped—perceived as something of a legitimate authority figure, stood up before the spectators and said:

> "Gentlemen, you should not doubt that the Comédie [-Française] is always eager to seize the opportunity to do that which is pleasing to you; but it is impossible"—(a great noise arose in response to this word); [the audience] calmed down; Naudet continued: "But it is impossible [for the Comédie] to perform *Charles IX* [because the actress] Madame Vestris is ill, and [the actor] M. Saint-Prix is detained by an erysipelas of the leg."[24]

Then, in true dramatic fashion, the young, flamboyant actor Talma (himself a member of the theater troupe) suddenly appeared from behind the curtain and, in a rush of apparent patriotic fervor, fraternized with those on the other side of the fourth wall:

> "Gentlemen, I will answer for Madame Vestris: she will perform; she will give you this ultimate proof of her zeal and patriotism; and someone will read the

part of the Cardinal [which Saint-Prix would have performed], & you will have your *Charles IX*."[25]

The actors' version of events continued as follows: Talma and his co-conspirators were silenced by the rest of the spectators, and the intended play was performed without further interruption. But no sooner had the play finished than a menacing crowd of approximately sixty people formed outside the theater, which "demanded in a very bitter fashion to see the actors, who themselves had run off to the mayor to apprise him of the situation."[26] Talma then greeted the crowd, leading Chénier by the hand, and declared: "You will have your play; I answer for Madame Vestris and myself; I give you my word of honor that I will perform no play before *Charles IX*, & if the Comédiens [-Français] persist in refusing you [the play], I will have you open the storeroom where the costumes are kept, & we will perform the play with you."[27]

This extraordinary invitation to the spectators to present for themselves that which their (theatrical) representatives refused to represent was followed, again according to the actors' account, by the spectators' taking to the streets in a spontaneous and boisterous demonstration not unlike those of the Revolutionary *journées*. The spectators, along with Talma and Chénier, went to Madame Vestris's house, where they all sang "Ça ira." After cheering Talma and Chénier, the crowd then began screaming, "The Comédiens are aristocrats who should be strung up on the lantern!"[28]

The following morning, an *Avis aux patriotes* was posted, urging the people of Paris to gather at four o'clock that afternoon to arm themselves and to set fire to the theater if any play other than *Charles IX* was performed.[29] At this point, the actors gave in. They would later claim that it was fear of provoking a general riot that decided them: "The fear of serving as a pretext to a riot, for which then as now one needed but an opportunity, immediately forced the Comédiens to come to a decision, and when, at eleven o'clock, a crowd gathered to find out [the actors'] response, [the response] was that they would perform *Charles IX*."[30] The play was performed without incident; although, after it was over, a confrontation broke out among spectators, swords were drawn, and the National Guard was called in to restore order.

Talma's role in this affair did not go unpunished. He had not only betrayed his colleagues by crossing over to the other side but actually incited the public to take the stage and perform the play for themselves. The actors of the Théâtre-National voted never again to perform with Talma.[31] Talma, for his part, would insist on his innocence, eventually begging Mirabeau to intercede on his behalf. Mirabeau obliged, composing the following public letter to Talma:

Yes, certainly, sir, you can say that it was I who requested *Charles IX* in the name of the provincial *fédérés*, and even that I firmly insisted; you can say it because it is the truth, and a truth of which I am proud. The kind of repugnance that the actors showed in this matter, at least if one believes the rumors, was very offensive [*désobligeante*] to the public. . . . [The actors] said in such explicit fashion that they simply wanted a pronounced will on the part of the public that I spread the word. That will was pronounced and poorly received, so I've been told. The public wanted to be obeyed; that is simple enough [to understand], there [in a place] where it pays, and I don't see why anyone should be surprised.[32]

And another public letter from the commander of the detachment from the district of Marseille also defended Talma on the grounds that it was not he but rather the will of the public that forced the actors to perform the play: "This truly national play . . . should not have suffered such difficulty in being performed; it should have been [performed] as soon as the will of the public was made known."[33]

Unlike the political actors of the National Assembly, who could claim to be representing (abstractly) the will of the public more purely and transparently than any (tangible) portion of the public could claim to do, the actors of the Comédie-Française never quite mustered the nerve to pull off this maneuver within the theater. One can tell from the letter that they decided not to send to Chénier, quoted above, that they thought they knew what was best for the public. Yet, faced with the physical presence of an irate public who threatened to storm the stage, theatrical actors—unlike their counterparts in the political sphere—thought better of telling spectators that they were nothing more than particularizations of a greater, general will, which could be perceived in its entirety only by professionals.

In the absence of any bold claim to be representing a will greater than that of the parterre, the foot-dragging of the actors looked suspiciously as if it were motivated by an antagonism toward the Revolution. One pamphlet insisted that the actors were "serving as the instrument of the aristocracy's wild schemes" and that they posed a grave threat to the future of the Revolution:

I am in no way exaggerating the dangers to which the actors have exposed you. They have raised the banner of rebellion; it is for you either to renounce a free constitution or to force these slaves of a vindictive court to chomp, in spite of themselves, at the bit of the fatherland. The public voice imposes upon them the necessity to obey, and they scorn the public voice! And you will put up with this, citizens! Oh! I do not believe that you have come to such a degree of political inertia. You have conquered the Bastille, you have undermined the very foundation of the palaces built by the nobility and the temples put up by a ruinous clergy; you have brought down the grandeur of kings; you have closed the abyss that the ministers filled in with the labors of the people, & you bow down before actors who insult you! . . . Friends, fly to the theater and teach these ignorant histrions that, if they call themselves the actors of the nation, they are criminals from the moment they obstruct [*heurter*] the will of that nation: punish the guilty who defy you.[34]

Here we see expressed in rather bold terms the principle that the people have the inherent right to take the stage and enforce their will directly, whenever they feel that the actors are defying the will of the nation. But we also see the important presupposition that the political and theatrical stages are somehow two sides of the same coin: it went without saying that if the people could make its will dominate on one stage, then it should necessarily make its will dominate on the other.

A Political Sifflet? Early Reflections on Audience Participation in Representative Democracy

If the actors' critics could cite political rebellion as the model for enforcing the people's will in the theater, then it should perhaps not surprise us that sometimes the analogy worked in the opposite direction, with spectator behavior serving as a metaphor for public participation in politics. Early in the Revolution, for example, the prominent Cordelier and future Jacobin Camille Desmoulins invoked two contrasting images of the French spectator to describe the choice that lay before the French people with respect to their active or passive participation in the Revolution. On the one hand, Desmoulins lauded the crowds of the Palais-Royal for *resisting* the role of spectators to the Revolution, claiming that they had transformed the Palais-Royal itself into "the seat of patriotism, the rendezvous of the finest patriots who have left their homes and their provinces in order to take part *[assister]* in the magnificent spectacle of the revolution of 1789, & not to be idle spectators to it."[35] Here the spectator, in contrast to the active citizen of the Palais-Royal, is "idle" or passive, sitting back and watching silently while others perform. On the other hand, Desmoulins praised the crowds of the Palais-Royal precisely because they behaved like spectators—not the passive, silent spectators who sat entranced by the play, but rather the active, loud spectators of the notoriously rebellious theatrical parterre who were always ready to *siffler* what they did not like.

At the Palais-Royal, claimed Desmoulins, there was no formal differentiation between actors and spectators such as one might find in the National Assembly or even in the many local assemblies of the various Parisian districts. Spectators at the Palais-Royal were always ready to take the stage themselves, providing the perfect model for direct democracy: "[At the Palais-Royal] you don't have to ask for the right to speak from a president, to wait your turn for two hours. You propose your motion; if it finds supporters, then the orator is put up on a chair. If he's applauded, he writes it up; if he is *sifflé*, he leaves."[36] Here, the wall between actors and spectators seems almost transitory: it is erected only as long as the actor is speaking, but even then it is continuously breached by the audible expression of the will of the spectators in the form of the sifflet, and the spectators seem to continuously threaten to take the stage themselves if ever the actor's will diverges from the will of the audience. Here was a perfectly transparent re-pre-sentation, with spectators unimpeded by a fourth wall from taking the stage, and once they had done so, kept pure by the threat of sifflets from the polit-ical parterre they had left behind. Here, in short, was the theoretical ideal of Jacobin rule (if not, as we will see, the manner in which it was actually de-ployed).

To elaborate upon the concept of the political sifflet, Desmoulins related the story of Grammont, an actor at the Théâtre-Français whom the Corde-liers district had just elected to the post of captain of the district detachment of the National Guard. Upon Grammont's election, the district assembly had reportedly considered issuing a decree that would forbid citizens from other districts to siffler their captain when he appeared on the stage, apparently re-garding the humiliation of the sifflet as incongruous with the authority of public office.[37] But, according to Desmoulins, the president of the district had intervened, expressing his admiration for the sifflet, not only on the dra-matic stage, but outside the theater as well:

> Gentlemen, I believe it would be tyrannical and contrary to the progress of the arts to forbid the parterre to siffler an actor or an author; but it should also be permitted to siffler both a barrister [*avocat*] and a captain, who are no more privileged [than the actor]. . . . You have seen the entire Parlement sifflé in many a session. . . . In such a happy nation, the first article of our liberty should be the liberty of the sifflet. As to me, gentlemen, I permit you to siffler your pres-ident if you so please.[38]

Desmoulins himself was clearly sympathetic to such views, regarding the presence of active spectators—spectators who were not only free to voice their approval and disapproval but who also, if the situation demanded, might become actors themselves—as a crucial guarantor of the purity of rep-resentation. Within the hall of the National Assembly, therefore, Desmoulins pointed to the spectator galleries as an indispensable bulwark against the tyranny of representatives: "Fortunately there are the spectator galleries, the incorruptible galleries, always on the side of the patriots: [the galleries] re-produce those tribunes of the people who, [seated] on a bench, attended the deliberations of the Senate [in ancient times], & who possessed the veto."[39]

Of course, there were many who did not find political spectators' inter-ference with the national representation (much less their threats to storm the stage) quite as heartening as did Desmoulins. The Englishman Arthur Young, for example, regarded the boisterous behavior of spectators in the galleries not as the guarantor of the proper functioning of representative de-mocracy but rather as an impediment to it.[40] And right-wing deputies seemed particularly incensed at the thought of being treated by spectators as if they were a bunch of second-rate actors who were there to amuse the pub-lic. As the abbé Maury pointedly observed when he exhorted the president of the National Assembly to exercise some control over the unruly galleries, "[T]he nation did not send *comédiens* here [to the National Assembly] to be handed over to the applause and the boos of the multitude."[41]

The abbé Maury was at the forefront of the group within the Assembly who hoped to deny actors a civil status in December of 1789 on the grounds that their profession was wholly out of keeping with the dignity of the active (and eligible) citizen.[42] It is not surprising, therefore, that the abbé should have bristled at the thought of being treated like an actor. On one occasion, he refused to return to the podium after having been heckled by the galleries: "[T]he character of a representative of the nation is so respectable that I do not wish to compromise it in this assembly."[43] As a representative of the nation, the abbé seemed to think that he was entitled to a modicum of respect. Politics, for him, was not and should not be brought down to the level of theater.

We should be careful to note, however, what the abbé Maury did not say: he was *not* objecting to the basic right of citizens to question his judgment. Indeed, most right-wing deputies continued to defend the theoretical rights of constituencies to exercise control over their representatives. If the abbé objected to the way he was treated, perhaps it was because he knew, having been originally elected to the Estates General by the clergy of Péronne, that these vocal spectators in the galleries of the National Assembly were most certainly *not* his constituents.

There were, however, quite a few politicians who did object to the right of citizens to exercise control over their representatives and who were always looking for opportunities to close off access to the political stage to those who might attempt to interfere in the representative process, either by their words or by their actions. These political actors were to be found not in the political wings but at center stage. For it was one of the most enduring characteristics of Revolutionary politics that those who were on the periphery of political power were forever urging political spectators to be more active and more vigilant, while those at center stage were forever searching for ways to limit the possibilities of audience participation.

Erecting the Political Fourth Wall, Spring and Summer 1791

As I discussed in the conclusion of part I of this book, the somewhat naive conviction expressed in the Declaration of the Rights of Man that "[a]ll citizens have the right to take part personally, or through their representatives" in the expression of the general will was rather quickly theorized away. Even before the Declaration of the Rights of Man was drafted, individuals within the National Assembly were formulating a conception of the general will's representation that was so totalizing in nature that it could not allow for any interference by individuals other than those who had been duly authorized to express the interests of the nation as a whole. As Sieyès put it, "[C]itizens who name representatives for themselves renounce and must renounce [the right] to make the law in an unmediated fashion themselves."[44]

Such a totalizing vision of the general will effectively rendered each individual citizen's will a meaningless abstraction of the whole. The general will of the nation came to be seen as something that was necessarily outside the purview of the citizen and was instead uniquely within the jurisdiction of the nation's representatives. This conception of the general will and of its representation was formally made part of the French political system with the Constitution of 1791, which stated very clearly that the nation could exercise its sovereign powers "only by delegation."

Even before the Constitution had been officially ratified, however, the various statements emanating from the constitutional committee in the spring of 1791 made it clear that moderates within the Assembly were attempting, once and for all, to eradicate any challenge to the Assembly's monopoly on the expression of the nation's will. In May of 1791, Le Chapelier, speaking on behalf of the constitutional committee, proposed a decree that was clearly intended to silence the voices of all collective bodies—clubs, sections, municipal authorities—that might present a threat to the Assembly's exclusive right to voice a corporate will. Ingeniously, Le Chapelier presented this attack on the expression of any collective will outside the Assembly as a spirited defense of the natural right of each individual to express his own will:

> Every active citizen has the right to present his will, whether it be to the legislative body or the king or administrative bodies. The petition *[plainte]* is a natural right of every man who believes himself to be wronged by any authority or individual. Each individual must exercise the right of petition by himself, in conformity with the principle that citizens must not delegate the rights that they can exercise. From this it follows that no body, no society, no commune can exercise the right of petition under a collective name, that the petition can be created only in the name of those who have signed it.[45]

The right to petition, therefore, was a natural right that pertained to all individuals, a right that they were fully capable of exercising on their own behalf and that they therefore were precluded from delegating to others. For if individuals could delegate their will to corporate bodies capable of speaking on their behalf, the rights of the individual would be unable to compete with the power of these corporate entities: "Let us then look upon the right of petition as one that is inherent in the quality of citizen, of a member of society. This is not to suppress [this right]; it is on the contrary to conserve it; because if corporate bodies take [this right] upon themselves, the petitions of simple citizens will seem less important" (10:2–3).

According to such logic, petitions signed by many people could never be anything more than the sum of individual petitions. To the National Assembly, and to it alone, was accorded the right to claim that its decrees represented something more than the mere sum of the individual members of its body. Exceptions could be made, of course, for the expression of nonnational collective wills. Citizens of a municipality, for example, could gather to form and express the will of that municipality, but only if the subject was municipal business. They could, as Le Chapelier put it, "assemble themselves in a family council, in order to deliberate on their private interests." But, if ever they sought to form a collective will on matters of national business, then their collective will could never be anything more than the views of several individuals who happened to agree with one another:

> [In matters that concern the general affairs of the nation] the citizens of each town cannot express anything but individual wills; the inhabitants can no longer meet as a family council, because they form a part of the great family [of the nation]; they cannot express a collective will, because each town would then be a corporation. (10:3)

If municipal bodies were to be prohibited from formulating and expressing collective opinions on matters of national interest, then it only stood to reason that *portions* of municipalities had, if anything, even less of a right to engage in such activity. And here Le Chapelier and his fellow moderates took aim at the growing political power of the radical Parisian sections and their increasingly turbulent assemblies.[46] As far as the constitutional committee was concerned, even if sections banded together to form common assemblies, their legitimacy as corporate bodies was limited to pronouncements on issues of mutual (and local) concern. On issues of national interest, by contrast, their pronouncements were meaningless. In such matters, "the power of the sections or of their deputies is nil" (10:3).

If, for Le Chapelier, the right to petition legislative or administrative bodies was a uniquely individual right, then the power to post one's petition in the form of a public notice must necessarily be expressly forbidden. If such a notice were posted in the name of a collective, then such postings were forbidden on the same grounds that any collective expression of will was prohibited. And if such notices were posted by individuals qua individuals, then such postings must be prohibited for the simple reason that the public sphere could not accommodate the expression of millions of individual wills: "If everyone had the right to post [notices], would one have the right to cover the notice of one's neighbor? Opposing the right of the first would be the right of the strongest. From this would arise brawls that would frequently bloody the public square" (10:4). He does not say it, but one can almost hear him whisper it: the raison d'être of the representative system—of the National Assembly itself—was the prevention of the chaos and disorder arising from the expression of a multiplicity of wills.

Virtually contemporaneous with Le Chapelier's speech in the National Assembly, political sympathizers within the public sphere took it upon themselves to denounce the arrogance of the sections in somewhat less restrained tones. At the end of April or early May 1791, an outraged pamphleteer, whose sympathies clearly lay with the moderates in the Assembly, denounced the practice whereby sections posted their collective will on the city streets. The author of the pamphlet was intent on informing the citizens who composed these sectional assemblies that, in the general scheme of things, their collective opinion was absolutely meaningless:

> [B]y what right can a section post a decree [arrêté]? What is the decree of a section? It is the will of a small portion of a city, which is itself a small [portion] of a department, which is a small portion of the kingdom; all of which relegates the poor section to the order of the infinitesimally small, which makes all those who compose [the section] and who believe themselves to be something in and of themselves an assemblage of Lilliputians.⁴⁷

For the anonymous author of this pamphlet, the fact that a group of citizens in a section of Paris should think that their collective will deserved to be posted on the street was as absurd as the idea that all the citizens of Paris should suddenly think their individual ideas worthy of posting on the street: "[E]veryone would think he had a useful idea; everyone would want to force the public to read what was going on in his head. There wouldn't be enough walls for so many posters, not enough hours in the day for so many readings. That which is not permitted to a simple individual is no more [permitted] to a small number of simple individuals."⁴⁸

Clearly, at least as far as the author of this pamphlet was concerned, the days in which individuals had the choice of expressing their wills "personally or through their representatives" were long gone. The particular wills of individuals or groups of individuals could be expressed only through their designated representatives, municipal or national depending upon the case:

> You will ask me what you must do with your will? This: You must bring it to the municipality, which is charged with assembling all the constituent parts [élémens], or to the national assembly, which having within itself the legislative and constitutional power, can with a single element [i.e., as one body] compose a law. But until that day when the municipality or the national assembly, depending on the matter, is done away with, your opinion is nothing other than a conjecture that certainly does not merit the trouble of being posted.⁴⁹

Sovereignty was indivisible: it could not be formed of constituent parts but had to be expressed in its totality. And as it was entirely impracticable that the millions of citizens in France could re-present their own wills, there was no alternative but for every citizen in France to recognize that he was not an actor on the political stage but necessarily a passive subject whose duty was to obey:

[I]n so much as the sovereign is indivisible, and as there exists in France no more a thousandth [of sovereignty] than there exists a quarter of sovereignty, as long as I am alone, I regard myself as being as null as the isolated [Parisian] section; together we can equal nothing. And so not being sovereign, I am nothing more than subject; I do not have the right to post notices, and I give the example of obedience. Sections, may you imitate me.[50]

This movement to expel all bodies—whether individual or corporate—from the national stage except for the nation's duly designated political representatives reached something of an apex with the so-called Le Chapelier law, which was ratified by the Assembly on 14 June 1791. Although the Le Chapelier law was ostensibly directed at journeymen's corporations (and was used for almost a century afterward to prohibit collective bargaining),[51] it effectively established the relative nullity of all expressions of nonindividual will other than by duly designated representative bodies. In other words, individuals were free to express their wills qua individuals, or collectively through their representatives, but they were forbidden from banding together with like-minded individuals in order to form a supra-individual will, a prohibition that, in the eyes of some, seemed to abrogate the right of assembly. In the following remarks, with which he prefaced the law that would forever after be associated with his name, Le Chapelier endeavored to tread the thin rational line between the taboo on corporate deliberations and the right of assembly:

It must of course be permitted to all citizens to assemble; but it must not be permitted to citizens of certain professions to assemble for their so-called [*prétendu*] common interests. There are no longer corporations in the state; there is no longer anything but the particular interest of each individual and the general interest. It is not permitted to anyone to inspire in citizens an intermediary interest, to separate them from the public interest [*la chose publique*] by a spirit of corporation. (10:194)

In many respects the Le Chapelier law's division between the representative body, endowed with the right to speak, and the social body, precluded from speaking except as isolated individuals, offers a striking parallel to the dynamic between actors and spectators that had been envisioned by the aesthetic revolutionaries of the theater in the decades before 1789. Much like the various innovations in the theater (such as immovable seats and a darkened parterre) that were intended to break up the noisy and disruptive coalitions of spectators into isolated and silent individuals, the Le Chapelier law was intended to remove all groupings other than the designated actors from the national stage and to dismember groupings within the political audience into the individuals who composed them. Citizens had little choice but to sit back and listen to the one corporation that had a legal right to exist—the

National Assembly, whose members were alone permitted to deliberate and voice their will as a body.

Was there, then, no recourse for the expression of wills outside of the National Assembly? In his speech before the Assembly on 9 May, Le Chapelier responded to anticipated objections that the inability to formulate collective wills and the consequent prohibition on the posting of notices would infringe upon freedom of expression: "They will say to me that posters can serve [the interest] of public instruction. I respond that it is not at the street corners that one instructs oneself; it is in books, in reading the law, in peaceful societies where one does not debate and where, as a result, one is removed from all passions" (10:4). Here, Le Chapelier seems to betray the fact that his conception of freedom of expression has to do more with the right of individuals to receive information than with their right to disseminate it. And as far as the former is concerned, why should the streets be littered with inflammatory and contradictory posters, when individuals could much more effectively gather information by looking through books, by quietly reading the law, and by quietly reflecting in "peaceful societies where one does not debate"?

One cannot help noting a certain similarity between Le Chapelier's vision of a turbulent Revolutionary society transformed into a nation of quiet readers and a vision put forward by Malesherbes some sixteen years earlier. Malesherbes had stressed the advantages of a political system in which the formulation of public opinion was left to "gifted" individuals, while the vast majority of citizens were consigned to "dispassionate and thoughtful reading." Such a clear and orderly division of labor had seemed to Malesherbes to be infinitely preferable to a system in which public opinion was formed in the midst of a "tumultuous assembly."[52] Needless to say, for both Le Chapelier and Malesherbes, there was not much of a role to be played by individual spectators or groups of spectators on the national stage.

Le Chapelier's dream of a peaceful society content to be led by expert, dispassionate representatives encountered something of a setback when, less than one week after the law that bore his name was ratified in the Assembly, the king attempted to flee France. The ensuing confusion and outrage within the population at large (not to mention within the Assembly itself) created a turbulent atmosphere that seemed very far removed from Le Chapelier's political mise-en-scène peopled by dispassionate actors and quiet spectators. The king's departure created something of a political vacuum in which many citizens felt emboldened to supersede the representatives to the Assembly and take matters into their own hands. Only hours after the king's departure had become known, the members of the Cordeliers Club dashed off a petition in which they chastised the nation's representatives for having squandered the authority that the nation had placed in their hands: "Legislators, you had distributed the powers of the nation that you represent; you had invested Louis XVI with a limitless authority" (10:416).

For the Cordeliers, Louis's departure seemed the perfect opportunity to call into question hereditary monarchy itself. In doing so, however, they resurrected a conception of representation that, if it had been somewhat in abeyance since the earliest months of the Revolution, had never quite died in the minds of the more popular and radical sectors of society: "[The Cordeliers] society believes that a nation must do everything, either by itself or by its chosen, removable officers" (10:416–17). Here, one discerns not only a forthright repudiation of hereditary monarchy but also the conviction that political representation, in whatever form it may take, is an expedient rather than a positive good. One also discerns, lurking in the subtext of the petition, the pointed reminder to the nation's representatives that they sat in the Assembly for the sole purpose of doing the nation's bidding and that they, like any other officers appointed to voice the will of the people, were "removable" if they failed to do so. The petition concludes with a demand that if the representatives could not bring themselves to abolish the monarchy in the name of the people, then the representatives should "at the very least wait [before making any decision] until all the departments and primary assemblies should have pronounced their will on this important question" (10:418).

Despite such objections that the representatives were not authorized to determine the status of the king without first consulting their constituents, the Assembly took up the question of the king's status on 13 July. In the midst of heated debate, a petition signed by "the people" arrived at the Assembly on the night of the fourteenth, warning the representatives "not to decree anything until the will of all the communes of the kingdom has made itself known." And "the people" admonished the representatives not to "forget that all decrees that are not contained within the limits of the power that has been confided in you are necessarily null" (11:21).

This petition was accompanied by a formidable crowd as well as by certain individuals who claimed to have been deputized by "the people" to present the petition. Neither the crowd nor the people's deputies were admitted to the Assembly on the night of 14 July, but the petition was accepted and read to the Assembly on the following day. On that day, 15 July, the crowd once again attempted to gain entry to the Assembly and was rebuffed. The crowd then made its way to the Champ-de-Mars, where commemorations of the taking of the Bastille were then under way and where the following petition to the Assembly was drafted and signed:

The citizens of Paris, having gathered together yesterday in great numbers, wanted to make known to you [i.e., the Assembly] its fears; [the citizens] were extraordinarily surprised at not being able to enter the national house. Profoundly distressed, although still confident, they decided that, without arms, and in the greatest order, they would go today, 15 July, to hurry to gather together in the bosom of the fatherland, in order to draft a petition to suspend all determinations on the fate of Louis XVI until such time as the clear will of the whole French empire had been effectively pronounced." (11:80–81)[53]

This petition was then accompanied to the National Assembly by an enormous crowd that was once again rebuffed. The nation's representatives then proceeded to do exactly what the petition had asked them not to do: they prepared articles declaring the inviolability of the king and announced the search for all those who might have "abducted" him.

Refused entry onto the political stage, ignored by political actors who seemed intent on acting as if they did not exist, the crowd of political spectators refused to return quietly to their seats. Rebuffed from one stage, the crowd turned its wrath on another: mobs of people invaded virtually every major theater in the city of Paris and shut them down. It was not quite the right stage, but apparently it would do to make a point.[54]

The point was taken. On the following day, 16 July, an incensed representative to the Assembly demanded that municipal officials be brought before the Assembly to explain their apparent inability to defend the theaters from public invasion. Only the National Guard, that force of order made up primarily of upstanding bourgeois, had actively resisted the unruly populace. Even as the theaters of Paris were falling to the mob, the guard had valiantly and successfully saved the Opéra from invasion: "Yesterday, . . . after having shut down several theaters, [these men] made their way to the Opéra as well for the same purpose. The detachments of the guard were so levelheaded *[sage]* that they succeeded in rebuffing the seditious" (11:90).

The general ferment in the capital provoked the nation's representatives to issue a series of decrees concerned with the surveillance of the populace in large cities. The decrees themselves, as well as several of the speeches surrounding their passage, betrayed an anxiety (older than the Revolution) concerning individuals without a profession or domicile, not to mention a particular uneasiness concerning foreigners. Addressing the leading authorities of the department and the municipality of Paris, the president of the Assembly enjoined them to "make use of all means that the law places at your disposal in order to put down the disorders, to discover the authors of them, and to go after them with all the rigor of the laws." In response, the president of the department assured the Assembly that "the most prompt and certain precautions will be undertaken in order to restore public tranquillity," and Bailly, mayor of Paris, likewise assured the Assembly that its decrees aimed at suspect persons within the populace would be put into effect immediately (11:92–93).

The battle between political actors and spectators, which had been temporarily displaced onto the stages of the Parisian theaters, was joined more directly only a few days later. This time, however, it was not the spectators who would storm the stage but rather the actors who would come down into the parterre to silence the audience. As we have seen, the authorities were already in a heightened state of alert, and the provocation for action was not long in coming.

The details of what happened on the morning of 17 July on the Champ-de-Mars will always remain shrouded in a certain amount of mystery and confusion. What seems clear, however, is that two men who had been hiding for unknown purposes beneath the staircase of the altar to the fatherland were discovered in the early morning hours. They were seized by the assembled crowd, who were deeply suspicious of their intentions. Depending upon the account one reads, these individuals intended either to sneak a peek at the legs of women who walked up the staircase or to blow up the altar and all the citizens who stood upon it with a barrel of powder that they had brought along for this purpose. In any event, the two individuals were in the process of being delivered over to the municipal authorities for questioning when they were apparently seized by a crowd of people. The two men were killed, and their heads were severed from their bodies and paraded on pikes around the streets of Paris and in particular around the Palais-Royal (11:103–6, 119–20).[55]

When news of these events reached the National Assembly, the two individuals beheaded by the crowd were, it seems, initially misidentified as members of the National Guard whose only crime had been to urge the assembled crowd to respect the execution of the law. Although this account was soon contradicted, at least one of the representatives confessed to being less concerned with the details of the events than with the need to restore order. As Michel Regnault de Saint-Jean d'Angely declared, "I also heard it said that [the two individuals who had been killed] were hanged for having preached the execution of the law. But whether it happened like this or otherwise, their death is still an attack that must be prosecuted according to the rigor of the laws." Regnault then urged his fellow representatives to consider a declaration of martial law in order to ensure the restoration of order. And finally he reminded his fellow representatives of the core issue that really underlay the events of the day:

[T]here is an offense that occurs very often, and this is the opposition of the individual will to the general will. There are as yet no precise laws in this matter; but now is the moment to explain yourselves. I ask that the Assembly declare that all persons who, in writings, whether individual or collective, should manifest the intent to interfere with the execution of the law and move the people to resist the constituted authorities be regarded as seditious, that they be arrested and prosecuted for the crime of treason *[lèse-nation]*. (11:107)[56]

No matter what the reason for the death of the two individuals on the Champ-de-Mars that morning, the central problem was the continued presence of this unruly crowd intent on drawing up collective petitions that were in and of themselves a flagrant challenge to the general will as formed and articulated by the designated representatives of the nation.

Even as these sentiments were being expressed within the National Assembly, the crowd at the Champ-de-Mars were busy actively defying the Assembly's monopoly of will. A new, bolder petition had been thrown together and was in the process of being signed by numerous members of the crowd, men as well as women and children. This petition went further than all the others in its indictment not only of the king but also of the representatives themselves:

> A great crime is committed: Louis XVI flees; he abandons his post in an undignified manner; the empire is two steps removed from anarchy. The citizens of Varennes arrest him; he is brought back to Paris. The people of this capital ask you insistently not to make any decision on the fate of the guilty party without having heard the expression of the will of the eighty-three other departments. You stall. A large number of addresses reach the Assembly; all sections of the empire demand simultaneously that Louis be judged. You, gentlemen, have decided beforehand that he is innocent and inviolable. . . . Legislators! This was not the will of the people, and we had thought that your greatest glory, that your very duty, consisted of being the organs of the public will. (11:114)

Just as Regnault's speech to his fellow representatives boiled down the events of the day to the essential question of the battle of wills between representatives and the people, so too did this petition locate the fundamental issue in the divergence of wills, or in the words of the petition itself, "the lack of harmony between the representatives and the represented" (11:115). The key difference between the two points of view, of course, is that whereas Regnault cast the National Assembly in the role of the general will, the petitioner cast "the people" in that role, relegating the deputies to the role of a collection of individual wills.

That afternoon, martial law was declared. At approximately seven o'-clock that evening, troops of the National Guard arrived on the Champ-de-Mars, accompanied by the red flag of martial law. Within minutes, some fifty people had been killed. After clearing away the crowd at the Champ-de-Mars, the guard then fanned out through the city, even invading the epicenter of public democracy, the Palais-Royal.

What had provoked this attack on the people? Was it the heads on pikes, the certain sign of the populace on the move that could not fail to recall the July and October days of 1789 when the people had been the leaders and the representatives had been forced to play catch-up? Was it the bold content of the petition that implied that the representatives were not acceding to the will of the people? Or was it the very form of the collective petition, which inherently implied a will outside the Assembly itself? Undoubtedly, it was all three.

PUBLICATION DE LA LOI MARTIALE AU CHAMP DE MARS
le 17 Juillet 1791

11. Martial law is declared on the Champ-de-Mars, 17 July 1791. Photo: Bibliothèque nationale de France, Paris.

In the aftermath of the Champ-de-Mars incident, the Assembly lashed out against the popular clubs and moved to restrict the electoral franchise. In the final days of the National Constituent Assembly, with the disturbances of the Champ-de-Mars relatively fresh in the minds of the representatives, Le Chapelier stood before his colleagues and urged them to finish the job. Speaking once again on behalf of the constitutional committee, Le Chapelier called for the effective end of all political clubs, those nests of extraparliamentary collective will from which so much of the popular agitation had emanated. Endeavoring to explain why the French people, who by taking to the streets at crucial moments were directly responsible for the success of the Revolution, should now be content to sit down and allow others to perform on their behalf, Le Chapelier argued that a dynamic that had been appropriate in the earliest days of the Revolution had outlived its usefulness:

> When a nation changes the form of its government, every citizen is a public official *[magistrat]*; everyone deliberates and should deliberate on matters of public import *[la chose publique]*; and everything that hastens, everything that en-

sures, everything that accelerates a revolution should be put into use. It is a momentary unrest *[fermentation]* that must be supported and even augmented, so that the revolution, leaving no doubt to those who oppose it, might encounter fewer obstacles and might reach its goal more promptly.

But, when a revolution is finished, when the constitution of the empire is fixed, when it has delegated all public powers, named all authorities, then it is necessary for the safety of this constitution that everything return to the most perfect order, that nothing hinder the action of the constituted powers, that deliberation and power exist nowhere but where the constitution has placed them, and that everyone respect sufficiently both his rights as a citizen as well as the responsibilities that have been delegated, so as not to exceed the former or ever infringe on the latter. . . .

There are no powers other than those constituted by the will of the people expressed by its representatives; there are no authorities other than those delegated by it; there can be no action other than that of its mandataires invested with public functions. It is in order to conserve this principle in all its purity that the constitution has made all corporations disappear from one end of the empire to the other, and that it no longer recognizes anything but the social body and individuals.[57]

Le Chapelier's words were warmly received by the majority of his fellow deputies, who voted in favor of the proposed decree that would have restricted the role of clubs in political life. The galleries, however, were in an uproar. It must have been a very interesting scene. Here were the deputies of the Assembly, in the final hours of their tenure as representatives, boldly declaring all political groupings outside of the Assembly itself to be illegitimate. And here, up above them, were the spectators in the galleries, the political parterre loudly decrying their representatives' actions, refusing to sit quietly while representatives put the final theoretical bricks in place for a political fourth wall that would render them meaningless. The galleries erupted into shouts as if to say that they *were* an important political entity and would not be ignored.

Into this confrontation stepped Robespierre. Four months earlier, he had denounced Le Chapelier's proposed restrictions on the right of petition as attacking a fundamental right that even "the most absolute despots have never dared to formally contest" (10:4). And now, Robespierre stood up in defense of the right of assembly. Addressing himself directly to the galleries, whom he referred to as "you" in contrast to his fellow deputies whom he referred to as "they," Robespierre shrewdly positioned himself as a defender of the people against the perfidy of their supposed representatives—a tactic that earned him the loud approbation of the galleries:

> They knew [in the report presented by Le Chapelier] how to speak the language of liberty and of the constitution in such a way as to destroy them and to

hide personal views and individual resentments under the guise of good, justice, and the public interest. . . . (Applause in the galleries. Several members of the Assembly: *Order!*)

I ask how they dare to tell you that a correspondence between a gathering of peaceful, unarmed men and other assemblies of the same nature can be forbidden by the principles of the constitution? . . .

But, they say, we no longer have any need for these clubs, because the Revolution is finished; it is time to break the instrument that has served us so well. (Applause in the galleries. The president of the Assembly: *I call the galleries to order—they must not interfere repeatedly with the deliberation.*)

And then, Robespierre turned his attention to his fellow deputies, admonishing them for their arrogance:

The Revolution is finished: I would like to suppose that to be the case along with you, although I do not understand very well the meaning you attach to this proposition that I have heard repeated with such ostentation *[affectation]*. But, accepting hypothetically [this to be the case], is it any less necessary to propagate knowledge, the principles of the constitution and the public spirit, without which the constitution cannot endure? Is it any less useful to form assemblies in which citizens can together occupy themselves in the most efficacious manner with these subjects, these interests which are the most cherished of their fatherland?[58]

Not unlike the actor Talma, who had expressed his solidarity with the parterre and had chastised his fellow actors for flouting the will of the people, Robespierre here fraternized with those on the other side of the fourth wall. While the moderate deputies and the president of the Assembly called for order and insisted that the spectators not interrupt the representative process, Robespierre told the audience that the true public spirit was to be found in them, rather than in the body of their supposed representatives. For many months to come, this would be a constant refrain of the rising left-wing opposition.

The events on the Champ-de-Mars and the ensuing repression of popular movements were, of course, only a stage in the ongoing battle between national representatives and more popular, less formal groupings of citizens and local political assemblies such as the sectional assemblies of Paris. By August of 1792, these extraparliamentary political bodies were sufficiently emboldened to achieve what they had tried and failed to achieve a year earlier: in early August, forty-seven out of Paris's forty-eight sectional assemblies—most of which had only weeks before admitted citizens previously classified as passive—voted to end the monarchy, a decision that was put into effect shortly afterward by armed citizens. Tired of waiting for the Assembly—now called the Legislative Assembly—to do what it apparently could not bring itself to do, the populace of Paris took matters into its own hands. Crowds armed with pikes stormed the Tuileries, and when Louis and his family fled to the Legislative Assembly for refuge, the crowds followed them there and forced the Assembly to suspend the king from his functions. The Legislative Assembly, as if recognizing that its hand had been played, voted to dissolve itself and to call for elections to a National Convention elected by universal male suffrage. Radical political spectators had, at least for the moment, taken the stage; and the political actors, who were for the most part too moderate to do what the people of Paris demanded of them, had voluntarily exited stage right.

Although the events of August undoubtedly resulted in the victory of the will of a significant part of the Parisian populace, the vexing questions had yet to be settled. To a great extent, the revolution of 10 August had bypassed the essential questions concerning the relationship between the representatives and the represented. The will of the people had triumphed. But the manner according to which that will would make itself known and would be put into effect on a regular basis had not been addressed. The people could hardly take matters into its own hands every time it wished to manifest its will. The new National Convention, which was assembled in September of 1792, would therefore be plagued by the same problems and questions as its predecessors. This assembly too would have to ask: Did the deputies rule in the name of the people or in strict accordance with the people's will?

Spectators Storm the Stage: The Purging of the National Convention

In April and May of 1793 the question of the relationship between the will of constituents and representatives once again came to the fore. Moderate deputies (Girondins) had attempted to quell popular radicalism by impeaching the radical (Montagnard) deputy Jean-Paul Marat and forming an antiradical Commission des Douze, which, soon after coming into existence, ordered the arrest of the popular leaders Jacques-René Hébert, Claude-Emmanuel Dobsen, and Jean-François Varlet. In response, several Parisian sections dispatched delegations to the Convention in protest; when not presenting petitions on the floor of the Convention, sectional radicals sat in the galleries, voicing their loud support of the Montagnard deputies and their hostility to the Girondins. The speeches of the Montagnards were so frequently punctuated by applause and shouts of approval from the galleries that one Girondin deputy denounced the unseemly theatricality of the Montagnard deputies who could not help playing to the crowd: "It is time that the assembly assume the dignity that is appropriate to it. We are not at Nicolet's [theatrical farce] here; we were not sent by our departments to hear the farces of a puppet like Marat" (27:212).

Whereas moderate deputies were accusing their radical colleagues of pandering to the audience like a bunch of boulevard actors, radical deputies retorted by accusing their more conservative colleagues of behaving, in a certain sense, like actors as well—not like the actors of the boulevard, but like the new, sophisticated, professional actors whose realistic performances depended on their behaving as if the public did not exist. On 10 May 1793, only weeks before popular insurrection would forcibly alter the political character of the National Convention, Robespierre accused unnamed intriguers of having constructed a representative space from which spectators had been removed so far that they could barely see or hear the proceedings. And so, Robespierre seemed to be suggesting, the political actors of the Convention did not even have to bother pretending that this public did not exist because, for all practical purposes, they did not:

> All observers have noticed that [the hall] has been laid out with great intelligence by the same spirit of intrigue [that has governed previous incarnations of the assembly], under the auspices of a perverted ministry, in order to remove the corrupt *mandataires* from the gaze of the people. Marvels have even been accomplished in this regard; the secret has at last been found, sought after for such a long time, of excluding the public while [at the same time] admitting it, such that [the public] can attend sessions, but they cannot hear if they are not in the small space reserved for *"honnêtes gens"* and journalists, with the result that they are both absent and present at the same time.[59]

As a remedy to this calculated "admission of a few hundred spectators, enclosed within a narrow and cramped space," Robespierre instead proposed a publicity of representation on a grand scale:

> It would be necessary, if it were possible, for the assembly of delegates of the people to deliberate in the presence of the entire people. A vast and majestic edifice, open to twelve thousand spectators, should be the site of the sessions of the legislative body. Beneath the eyes of such a great number of witnesses, neither corruption, nor intrigue, nor perfidy would dare to show itself; the general will alone would be consulted, the voice of reason and the public interest would alone be heard.[60]

With such rhetoric, Robespierre expressed the long-standing Jacobin conviction that abstract political representation could avoid distortion only through constant and careful vigilance. His words may also have been intended to appeal to the political sensibilities of the sansculotte militants in the Parisian sections, who had expressed an unwavering conviction in the rights of the people—as the true sovereign—to exercise control over and if necessary recall their elected officials.[61] We should be careful to note, however, that Robespierre's rhetoric stopped short of calling for the political counterpart to spectator participation. His call for twelve thousand spectators, for all its overtones of direct democracy, is still a call for *spectators*, not participants. The people at its most active can exercise vigilance—an extreme form of watching—and nothing more. We might contrast Robespierre's views to those of such popular leaders as Varlet and Jacques Roux, who urged citizens to be not simply vigilant but prepared to take the stage if necessary. As Varlet declared in May of 1793, "[T]hat which our mandatories cannot nor will not do, let us do it for ourselves."[62]

As tensions escalated toward the end of May, more moderate representatives within the assembly became increasingly anxious about the threat posed by the radical Parisian populace to the nation's representative body. With rumors afoot of a plot to invade the Convention, one deputy proposed immediate defensive and offensive countermeasures: dissolve the municipal bodies of Paris and move the Convention to Bourges for its own safety (27:129–30). A week later, tensions had reached fever pitch. Just as royalists in 1792 had threatened the people of Paris with severe retribution in the event that they harmed the bodies of the monarchs, now the moderates within the National Convention promised, in the name of the provinces, exemplary vengeance in the event that any harm should befall the body of representatives. Maximin Isnard, who was presiding over the Convention on 25 May, warned the assembled deputies and spectators that Paris must respect the National Convention or be prepared to suffer the consequences:

France has placed in Paris the depository of the national representation; Paris must respect it. . . . If by these ever-renewing insurrections it were to happen that the national representation were attacked, I declare to you in the name of the whole of France (interruptions: Cries of *No! No!* from the extreme left. The remainder of the assembly rose to its feet: *Yes, say in the name of France!*). I declare, in the name of the whole of France, Paris will be exterminated . . . (more interruptions). Soon they would be searching the banks of the Seine to see if Paris had ever existed. . . . (more interruptions). . . . [T]he blade of the law, which still drips the blood of the tyrant, is ready to strike the head of whosoever dares to rise up above the national representation. (Applause on the right.) (27:225)

The people of Paris were, it seems, relatively unfazed by this threat. Two days later, on 27 May, deputations from various sections of Paris crushed into the hall of the Convention in such great numbers that representatives complained that the representative space itself had been violated (27:258). Indeed, a vote by the Convention that evening to abolish the Commission des Douze and free the imprisoned Hébert, Dobsen, and Varlet would be overturned the following day on the grounds that, as one deputy put it, "the petitioners [from the Parisian sections] had mixed with the members [of the Convention] and had voted along with them" (27:277).

Even while the Convention desperately attempted to protect the sanctity of the representative space, outside the Convention several of the Parisian sections as well as the department of Paris set about organizing an insurrection against the Convention. On 31 May, the people were called to arms, and an enormous crowd accompanied sectional representatives to the Convention where they presented a petition calling for a variety of radical measures, most notably the expulsion of the Girondins from the assembly. It was in the course of this attempted insurrection that a united delegation representing various Parisian municipal bodies issued the following direct reply to Isnard's threat: "[Paris] would rather be overturned from top to bottom than to endorse tyranny; and if Paris were to disappear from the surface of the earth, it would not be for having been unworthy of its fatherland, but rather for having defended the indivisibility of the republic" (27:345).

Despite their differences, both the deputations of the radical populace of Paris and the moderate representatives of the nation claimed to be speaking in the name of the general will. Isnard, as we saw, dared to speak "in the name of the whole of France," a presumption that was immediately assailed by the left and applauded by the right.[63] For their part, the delegates from the Parisian municipal bodies laid claim to a representation of the general will of France in its entirety by arguing that Paris could be considered a microcosm of the nation: "We declare that we are proud of the fact that Paris, which is nothing in itself, is nevertheless the distillation *[extrait]* of all the departments, whose splendor consists of being the mirror of opinion and the meeting place of all free men" (27:346). On this basis, then, the delegates of the Parisian municipal bodies could speak in the name of the nation as a whole when they demanded of their legislators that they expel the likes of Isnard from the national representative body: "You [legislators] will take your revenge for us on Isnard and de Roland and all those impious men against whom public opinion rises up in such a striking manner. Legislators, give us this great example, deliver yourselves over to the will of a generous nation that honors you with its esteem" (27:347). And at the conclusion of their speech, as if to show that Paris was not only one with France but one with its representatives (or at least those representatives who sat on the left), the members of the delegation "merg[ed] fraternally with the members of the party of the left."

Although the crowds that had stormed into the Convention had come with several different demands, the National Convention somehow managed to appease them with a few concessions: the Commission des Douze was abolished (for the second time that week); the remaining demands, including the matter of the expulsion of the Girondin deputies, were referred to the Committee of Public Safety for further review. The insurrection fizzled, and both deputies and the assembled crowds dispersed peacefully. Two days later, however, on 2 June, events would take a different course. This time the organizers of the insurrection took no chances. Some eighty to one hundred thousand armed sansculottes and five thousand Parisian guardsmen under the command of François Hanriot surrounded the Convention.[64] Toward the beginning of the session, an orator from a delegation of the Revolutionary authorities of the department of Paris informed the deputies that the people of Paris had come to "reclaim from their mandataires the rights [they have] ignobly betrayed." This was, he warned the legislators, their last chance: "Citizens, the people are tired of endlessly putting off the moment of its happiness; [the people] leaves [its happiness] in your hands a moment longer; save it, or we declare to you that [the people] will save itself" (27:388).

Presented with this ultimatum, the deputies stalled. They were unwilling to expel the Girondin leaders from their ranks, but there seemed to be very little in the way of alternatives. The precariousness of their position was made clear to them when several deputies were refused permission to exit the hall by armed men, even to go to the bathroom. Other deputies were physically accosted. What was to be done? The representatives were reluctant to bow to the will of the crowd or to the force of arms. And yet it seemed clear that, in this instance at least, they were powerless to have their will respected as the force of law. Many of the deputies were—or at least claimed to be—outraged. Barère, a member of the Committee of Public Safety, angrily declared, "It is not for slaves to make laws; France will disavow those [laws] that emanate from a subjugated assembly. How can your laws be respected if you can make them only surrounded by bayonets?" (27:399).

We will perhaps never know Barère's true motives. He was a Jacobin closely tied to Robespierre, and not only had Robespierre loudly called for precisely such an insurrection against the Convention only a few days before,[65] but Barère was presumably in the know concerning the preparations for the events of the day. And yet he was perhaps embarrassed by the obvious and heavy-handed manner in which the insurrection was being carried out, leaving not even a pretense of free will to the assembled deputies.[66] A few minutes after these expressions of outrage, Barère rushed back to the podium, apparently having thought of a way in which the appearance of free will might be preserved: "Citizens," he shouted, "I repeat to you. Let us prove that we are free. I ask that the Convention go to deliberate in the middle of the armed force, which will undoubtedly protect it" (27:400).

Barère's suggestion was immediately approved. The majority of deputies got up from their seats, exited the hall, and went outside into the street. They stood face to face with the armed crowd and soldiers, and then they awkwardly marched around the perimeter of the building. Confirming that they were completely surrounded, they went back inside, where Georges Couthon, another Jacobin and member of the Committee of Public Safety, made the following speech to his colleagues:

> Citizens, all the members of the Convention must now be assured of their liberty. You have walked by the people; everywhere you found them good, generous, and incapable of attacking the safety of their mandataires, but indignant against the conspirators who want to subjugate [the people]. Now that you recognize that you are free in your deliberations, I ask . . . that the Convention decree that [the twenty-nine accused Girondin representatives] be placed under arrest in their homes, as well as the members of the Commission des Douze and the ministers Clavière and Lebrun." (27:401)

The decree was passed immediately.

How are we to interpret this ritual dance of the encircled deputies, who stiffly sashayed through the no-man's-land between the assembly hall and the heavily armed crowd that ringed the building before returning to their seats "assured of their liberty"? Undoubtedly they knew that the game had already been played. Armed men had invaded the hall itself, roughing up several of the deputies. Outside were massed at least eighty thousand more people. The only way for the deputies to retain their dignity was to pretend that the fourth wall had been removed by mutual consent. The people had come up on the stage and insisted that its will be heeded. Now, the representatives of the people would go down into the audience and show that they were one with the people, that there was nothing that separated the representatives from the represented. The bayonets were, of course, somehow inappropriate to the picture that the deputies were attempting to paint, but they had little choice in the matter. They "freely" strolled around the courtyard, returned to the hall, and "decided" to order the arrest of twenty-nine of their colleagues as well as two ministers.

Both the Jacobin deputies and the sansculottes of the sections characterized this invasion of the assembly as an effort to restore sovereignty to the people, its rightful owners.[67] As the Central Revolutionary Committee of the Paris Commune declared in its address to the Convention on the following morning, "The people . . . decided to do for you [i.e., the Convention] that which you could not do for [the people]."[68]

But what exactly had the people done? Yes, the radical populace of Paris had forced the National Convention to accede to its will, but to what end? Had they stormed the stage merely to replace a few of the actors and then return meekly to their seats to watch the rest of the play? Or had they breached the fourth wall of inviolability with the intention of altering the play of representation itself? Precisely on these questions, the temporary alliance between the Jacobin deputies and the radical populace of Paris would founder.

The Jacobins as Political Actors: Terrorizing the Audience

We will never know whether the Jacobin deputies truly believed the rhetoric that championed the people's will or whether instead they merely mouthed this rhetoric as a means of gaining the support of the Parisian radicals whose help they needed in order to do away with their political rivals the Girondins. What seems certain, however, is that this alliance between the Jacobins and the Parisian radicals known as the *enragés* was a marriage of convenience rather than of conviction. Underlying their common assault on the Girondin deputies lay two very different conceptions of political representation. For the Jacobins, the purge of the Girondins was an attack on the *content* of the representative body, to ensure that its representation might be a more nearly transparent reflection of the general will. For many of the sectional activists, by contrast, and particularly for individuals like Varlet and Roux and their supporters, the attack on the Girondins was an attack on the *form* of the representative system itself. By attacking the Girondins, they were attacking the arrogance of the political actors; they were launching an assault on the whole system of representation put in place in 1789, which had done away with the right of constituents to exercise control over their representatives. Morris Slavin, a historian of the enragés, writes,

> [T]he Enragés and other militants hoped to go beyond a simple removal of some two dozen Conventionnels: they aspired to replace the parliamentary system with one based on direct democracy under which representatives would become mere proxies or mandatories of the people's will (actually, of the primary assemblies). This doctrine was embodied in the term *mandat impératif*. The right to convoke primary assemblies without prior permission of higher authorities, embraced in the word *permanence*, was also the right of what we call initiative, referendum, and recall.[69]

With the Girondins disposed of, however, the Jacobins no longer needed to pay lip service to the ideals of the enragés. The same Robespierre who only a week earlier had called for an insurrection against the Convention and denounced the betrayal of the people by its mandataires now found such rhetoric distasteful. As far as Robespierre was concerned, the Girondins no longer sat on the Convention; therefore, the Convention no longer needed to be criticized.

The enragés, however, seemed not to understand that the representative body, now cleansed of the Girondin leadership, had once again assumed the mantle of the irreproachable arbiter of the general will. On the evening of 25 June, Roux read his famous petition to the Convention, in which he warned the assembled deputies that "the people remembers that it has already been betrayed two times by two legislatures. It is now time that the sansculottes, who have shattered the scepter of the tyrants, bring down all manner of tyrannies" (28:217). Although Roux went on to talk about economic oppression, the implied threat to the nation's representatives could not have gone unnoticed. Even before Roux had finished reading his petition, some were calling for his immediate arrest. And no sooner had he finished than he was denounced by the Jacobin Thuriot as a "vile orator of anarchy" (28:218). Robespierre, too, denounced "the perfidious intentions of the orator" and accused him of wanting to "taint patriots with moderatism so that they would lose the confidence of the people" (28:219). Although many called for Roux to be punished, the Convention resolved to follow the wisdom of Louis Legendre, who suggested that Roux simply be thrown out of the assembly: "There are patriots in the section [where he comes from]; they will mete out justice themselves" (28:219). The *Moniteur*, in its recounting of Roux's speech, gave little indication of how it was received by the audience (apart from the repeated *murmures* and even *murmures violents* that presumably emanated from the assembled deputies); Roux himself, however, would claim that he was wildly applauded by the spectators in the galleries.[70]

Some two months later, Roux helped to orchestrate one last movement by the people against its representatives. On 5 September 1793, crowds gathered from the various sectional assemblies and marched on the Convention. But this incursion proved very different from the one of 2 June. The Jacobin deputies remained levelheaded, acceding enthusiastically to many of the demands of the people. To all appearances, the people had been the victors: among other decrees pushed through that day, a maximum would be declared on food and incomes, perhaps the most important demand of the radical working classes; and workers who attended sectional assemblies would receive forty sous in compensation.

But the representatives achieved much from 5 September as well: Terror was officially declared the "order of the day"—a concept that would necessarily be interpreted and executed by the central powers. And if the now Jacobin-dominated Convention appeared to embrace the marchers, they nevertheless ordered the immediate arrest of Roux, whose writings and rhetoric had inspired many of those who had marched on the Convention. And finally, if the National Convention decreed that those who attended sectional assemblies would be compensated for their participation, the deputies would clarify in a subsequent addendum, issued four days later, that such assemblies could no longer meet continuously but would be limited to two sessions per week. The people in assembly would therefore meet henceforth by the permission of and on the payroll of their representatives.

If the Jacobins had up until this point championed the voice of the people as the voice of the nation, after 2 June they began to sound a lot more like Le Chapelier, who had endeavored to achieve for the nation's political representatives a monopoly on the articulation of the general will. The voice of the people was no longer something that needed to be heard. The Jacobins, now that they themselves occupied center stage, did their best to limit the heckling of the audience. As the *Journal de la Montagne* declared on 19 September 1793, there was no need for popular movements now that the government had the people's interests at heart: "Popular movements are just and defensible only when they are made necessary by tyranny . . . ; the rascals who have advocated the formation of ferocious irregular movements, whether to serve our enemies or to satisfy their own special interests, have always incurred shame and obloquy."[71]

The Jacobin deputies had never intended to challenge the fundamentals of the representative system. For all the problems they may have had with the concept of representation, they could not bring themselves to consider scrapping it entirely. In fact they were as critical as anyone else of the concept of direct democracy. Robespierre even attempted a kind of redefinition of the term *democracy*, arguing that a true democracy was really a particularly virtuous form of representative democracy:

> Democracy is not a state in which the people, continually assembled, regulates by itself all public affairs; even less is it a state in which one hundred thousand fractions of the people, [acting] by isolated, precipitous, and contradictory measures, would decide the fate of the whole of society: such a government has never existed, and it could exist only to lead the people back to despotism.
>
> Democracy is a state in which the sovereign people, guided by laws that are of its making, does by itself all that it can do well, and by delegates all that it cannot do by itself.[72]

In these criticisms of direct democracy, the Jacobins shared more with their Girondin colleagues than they did with the sansculottes and the enragés with whom they had temporarily allied themselves. As Slavin puts it, "[T]he introduction of direct democracy would have ended the system of representation, which is why both the Girondins and the Montagnards feared the Enragés and why the revolutionary government ultimately suppressed them."[73]

If one were to look only at the rhetoric of the Jacobins, one would think that they advocated a system of representation that was more like the embodied, nonabstract re-presentation of old. Indeed, the politicians of the Terror were forever insisting that they did not represent in the modern sense of the word but rather transparently reflected the will of the nation. In a speech on the subject of political representation in May of 1793, for example, Robespierre described the task of the public official in terms that resemble the way in which the actor's craft was conceived in the prerealist theater: "[T]o be good, it is necessary for the public official [*magistrat*] to immolate himself to the people."[74] Any individual entrusted with public functions must forget himself, must immolate himself—literally sacrifice his own body—for the purposes of the representation. Like actors who performed in the days before Riccoboni's and Diderot's reforms had swept the French stage, political actors were called upon to undergo a kind of bodily metamorphosis in which they were meant to forget their own private passions and take on the passions of their re-presentation. As Robespierre declared in February of 1794, "[T]he public official *[magistrat]* is obliged to immolate his interest to the interest of the people . . . ; it is therefore necessary that the representative body begin by submitting all the private passions within it to the general passion for the public welfare."[75]

Their rhetoric notwithstanding, the Jacobins were no throwback to an earlier age. Unlike the premodern actors, who mixed familiarly with spectators and who knew no fourth wall dividing them from their audience, the Jacobins had achieved the most hermetically sealed representative space that the Revolution had yet known—a space where spectators were not welcome because everything that they could possibly say worth listening to was being said for them. Despite their claims to the contrary, the Jacobin leadership did not in reality "forget" themselves while taking on the character of the nation that they claimed to re-present; they were keenly aware of their role as leaders and were forever looking for ways to *instill* the correct view of things into the people, rather than simply reflecting the people's will.[76]

And so, if the political actors of the Terror were not really like the actors of old who endeavored to forget that they were re-presenting so that they could become the object of their re-presentation, what precisely were they? By every criterion, they were consummate political actors—but the *new* kind rather than the old. For is it not the ideal of the modern actor to act while at the same time convincing the audience that he is not acting? The Jacobins, for all their rhetoric of transparency and all their criticism of theatricality, were putting in place an unparalleled system of political vraisemblance. As in the theaters, the believability of their representation ultimately depended upon a clear differentiation between actors and spectators. As in the theaters, the audience's suspension of disbelief necessitated that the actors be the only ones to speak. As in the theaters, the heckling had to be silenced if the play was to succeed.

I conclude this final chapter of the book, then, with a story—a story played out simultaneously on two stages. It is the story of an actor who, when confronted with the sifflets of his audience, came down off the stage, hunted down the offending spectators, and killed them. It is the classic tale of the Terror, the story of a member of the Committee of Public Safety and former theatrical actor who, so the story goes, simultaneously did away with his political and theatrical critics.

In the autumn of 1793, when the people of Lyon flirted with federalism and called into question the validity of the central government's representation, the government responded by virtually destroying the city. The government official in charge of repressing the rebellion was Collot d'Herbois, an influential member of the Committee of Public Safety. Collot d'Herbois had been both an actor and a director of the Théâtre de Lyon prior to the Revolution. And inevitably, the story came to be told that Collot, in so viciously punishing Lyon, was seeking retribution not only for the metaphoric political sifflet of federalist rebellion but for the actual theatrical sifflets that he had been subjected to by the Lyon parterre.

Several pamphlets were published, each claiming to expose the "real" reason behind Collot's hatred for Lyon. One pamphlet claimed that Collot had not only been made to endure sifflets during his tenure at the theater of Lyon, but had actually been forced to his knees by spectators—an act that so humiliated him that he devoted the rest of his life to seeking retribution. His election to the National Assembly, his membership in the Committee of Public Safety, were all nothing more than the means by which he could re-

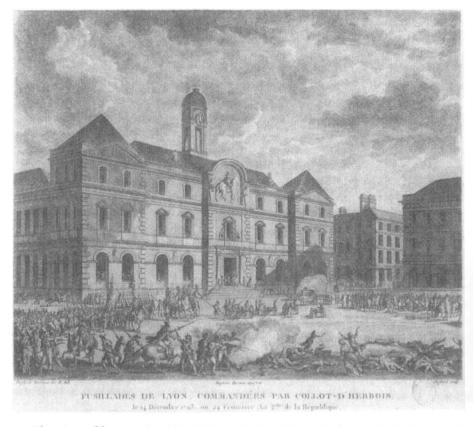

FUSILLADES DE LYON COMMANDÉES PAR COLLOT-D'HERBOIS,
le 14 Décembre 1793, ou 24 Frimaire An 2.me de la République.

12. Shootings of Lyon, ordered by Collot-d'Herbois. Engraving by Duplessis-Bertaux. © Photothèque des Musées de la Ville de Paris/negative: Ladet.

turn to Lyon and repay his humiliation by forcing the entire city to *its* knees, "not pausing for breath until he had eaten of the city's ashes."[77] There was even a play published, entitled *Collot in Lyon,* which reaches its dramatic climax when Collot, in a monologue, confesses the real reason behind the sacking of Lyon:

> . . . Collot [he says to himself], in your perversity,
> Can you hide from yourself the horrible truth? . . .
> . . . .
> You wanted to punish. . . . Can you still recall?. . .
> Where am I? . . . Horrible walls that witnessed the affront,
> Tremble, I shall wash the shame from my forehead.
> People of Lyon, bow to my omnipotence;
> Insolent city, shudder from my vengeance.[78]

The story seemed such a neat fit, the wreaking of vengeance for a political and a theatrical sifflet all at once, that it found its way into the official documents of Collot's trial after Thermidor. One of the accusations made against him during his trial was that in the midst of the horrors of the rape of Lyon, Collot actually took the time to search out individuals who had been in the

13. Collot's victims, lined up before the cannon. Engraving by Vinkeles. © Photothèque des Musées de la Ville de Paris/negative: Jean-Yves Trocaz.

294 | *Representation in the Revolution*

parterre on that fateful day, years earlier, when he had been forced to endure the audience's sifflets; having found them, he lined them up before a cannon and exacted his revenge.[79] And a letter drafted by "the people of Lyon" for the purposes of his trial left no doubt as to Collot's real motives:

> Legislators, glance if you will at our city . . . ;
> You will see ruins, and mounds of corpses; . . .
> You will see two hundred and thirteen unfortunates, [who] without interrogation, without a hearing, were gunned down and hatcheted all at once . . . ; [and] you will hear in the midst of this bloody day, Collot d'Herbois shouting in the throes of a rabid joy: "Now I have exacted vengeance for the sifflets to which I was subjected at the theater of Lyon."[80]

And finally, there was the satirical pamphlet congratulating Collot for his bloodthirsty success. Explicitly drawing the parallel between the theatrical and the political sifflet, the author pretends to understand and to sympathize with Collot's actions: "With real and palpable examples, you wanted to captivate the incredulity of the rebel sifflets." And then the final lament; Collot and his cronies have done everything for the benefit of the nation they loved: "Oh! Ungrateful fatherland, you forget what we have done for you."[81]

In this evocative metaphor of the Terror, the actor has come down from the stage, murdered the very spectators for whose benefit the play is performed, and claimed that it is all in the spectator's best interest.

Conclusion

The French Revolution changed the form in which political representation was practiced. If the theoretical elaboration of this change had been prepared over the course of several decades, the practical shift itself occurred virtually overnight. In June of 1789, the National Assembly dispensed with the notion of political re-presentation as literal embodiment and put in its place a conception of representation that rested not on the ability of the political body to incarnate the nation but rather on its ability to speak on behalf of the nation in a manner that public opinion regarded as legitimate. Or, to put it in the theatrical terms in which this book is written, the French Revolutionaries ushered in an era in which the legitimacy of representation depended not upon the physical identity between the actor and the object of representation but upon the political audience's willingness to accept the representative body as vraisemblable.

The French Revolutionaries also changed the content of political representation. Again acting upon theoretical innovations that had been decades in the making, the Revolutionaries killed the corpus mysticum—that living body made up of qualitatively different organs and members which had defined France for centuries. And in its place the Revolutionaries posited a metaphoric body made up essentially of separate male citizens who, if they differed from one another at all, differed only in their economic stake in society.

These innovations in the process and the object of representation ushered into existence a host of new possibilities: a more egalitarian sociopolitical order that rejected the qualitative distinctions so important to the old regime; the inclusion of profane outcasts previously excluded from the sacred politico-religious corpus mysticum; the invention and the valorization of the individual citizen and of the inviolable rights that he (for it was, ultimately, he) was deemed to possess.

But these innovations also gave rise to certain anxieties that were to plague the new regime. Abstract representation did not provide for the occasional spectacles of embodiment (such as monarchical spectacles of entry or the *processions générales* of the Estates) that had, during the old regime, served to reassure all concerned that the political bodies truly *were* that which they re-presented. Even if the National Assembly had declared itself to be the nation for all practical purposes regarding the formulation of sovereign will, the National Assembly could never *be* the nation in that concrete, embodied sense in which pre-Revolutionary political bodies had historically incarnated the corpus mysticum. A system of political representation that relied upon vraisemblance rather than physical embodiment rested upon a comparatively unstable foundation, depending ultimately upon the willingness of the political audience to accept the representation as legitimate. And just as the practitioners of vraisemblance in the theaters seized upon the importance of visual aids such as costume and scenery to aid spectators in their suspension of disbelief, so too did the political actors of the Revolution discover the importance of costume, scenery, and the festival as tools in the fabrication of an aura of legitimacy.[1]

But the vacuum of tangible legitimacy could not be overcome by costumes and festivals alone. The very nature of abstract representation seemed to contain the seeds of a new form of disillusionment, as if spectators, even while they appreciated the heightened illusion of the new theater, nevertheless yearned deep down for the concrete embodiment of old. Nowhere could the object of the representation *actually* be seen; it was almost as if it were vaguely promised at some point in the future, like a Messiah who would never actually come.[2] In the meantime, one was left with these actors, who if they seemed plausible enough for the time being, were always a moment away from implausibility—if they forgot their lines, if they were heckled by the parterre, or even if the audience lost interest.

On the political stage, in particular, the actors were continuously threatened with the presence of rival actors, who seemed to be purporting to play the same role, only better. And how, really, was one supposed to distinguish between two political actors, each of whom claimed to be speaking on behalf of the nation? Each faction accused the others of being *merely* actors, frauds, while claiming for themselves the mantle of true representatives. And yet, deep down, they were all actors. And no matter how often or how insistently they claimed to be speaking from the heart, there was always the suspicion that their protestations of honesty and transparency had been practiced in front of a mirror. They were not, and they could never truly be, that which they claimed to represent. And this is why denunciations of imposture and fraudulence were so crucial to Revolutionary discourse: in the end, it was perhaps the only thing that political actors could say that seemed to have an air of truth about it.

And so, since such trappings of political vraisemblance as cockades and liberty trees could get one only so far, and since assurances of transparency and honesty were perhaps doomed from the outset by the very fact that the relationship between actor and object was not, in truth, transparent, political actors increasingly turned to denunciation in their efforts to garner legitimacy. But there was one other, somewhat more desperate method by which legitimacy could be achieved. If all else failed, the legitimacy of representative bodies could be forced upon the audience: those spectators who failed to see the light could be forcibly silenced.

The final pages of the pamphlet *Evénemens remarquables & intéressans, à l'occasion des décrets de l'auguste Assemblée nationale, concernant l'éligibilité de MM. les comédiens, le bourreau, & les Juifs*—the pamphlet with which I began this book and which is largely responsible for having inspired it—recount the aftermath of a troupe of actors' election to political office in a provincial town. In gratitude for their election, the actor-politicians decide to put on a show for the townspeople (doubling the ticket prices, now that they are not only actors but public officials). No sooner do they begin their performance, however, than they are interrupted by the usual boisterousness of the parterre. But the actors, now emboldened by their new status, will not tolerate this insubordination from the parterre, and they order the spectators to be quiet. The parterre, indignant that the actors have dared to tell them what to do, erupts in revolt. The actors do their best to intimidate the parterre with their authority, and finally the actor-mayor Crispin calls upon the commanding officer of the town guard to put down the revolt: "Sir, I order you, in my capacity as mayor of the city, to lend me the [force of arms], and to have your troops advance with the red flag, in order to put martial law into effect, & to disperse the parterre or else to kill it, according to the law." When the commanding officer balks at these orders to slaughter the parterre, the actor-mayor threatens to hold the officer and his troops responsible for the sifflets to which they have been subjected and threatens to write his fellow actor Mirabeau: "He will protect us, & everyone knows his power."[3] At this point, the entire theater erupts in laughter, and the crisis is diffused. And so the standoff between political actors and the parterre comes to an end when the spectators finally see that the words of their newly elected officials are empty threats and that the officials on the stage are the same jokers they have always known and never taken seriously.

This story, as unserious and playful as it may be, is nevertheless remarkable for its insights into the new actor/spectator dynamic. And it is also remarkable for its prescience. Writing late in 1789 or very early in 1790, the anonymous author of the pamphlet already glimpsed the potential threat of violence that lay just beneath the surface of the new, Revolutionary representative system.[4] Political actors were just beginning to search for ways to limit audience participation in the representative process, just as their theatrical counterparts had been attempting to do for decades. And just as in the theater it had been universally determined that "the actor must . . . be alone with his character upon the stage,"[5] so too were politicians beginning to conclude that political representation precluded spectator participation. If the Declaration of the Rights of Man and of the Citizen seemed to promise a certain degree of direct participation, the Constitution of 1791 would make very clear that the nation could exercise its authority "only by delegation." No one was more concerned with the dangers of spectator interference in the representative process than Le Chapelier, who declared that if there had perhaps been a role for the people on the political stage in the earliest days of the Revolution, that time had now passed, and the appropriate role for all those who were not legislators was to resume their seats in respectful silence.

What is fascinating about this desire to render the political audience passive is that it cut across conventional political lines. Moderates such as Le Chapelier and Sieyès may have defended the sanctity of representation on grounds that can justifiably be termed elitist, but were they really all that different from the Jacobins of the Terror when it came to the defense of the representative system itself? The Jacobins, for all their democratic rhetoric prior to their accession to power, were quick to quash all calls for greater democracy once they held the reins of power firmly in their grasp. And despite all their ostensible differences, the moderates of 1791, the Jacobins of the Terror, and the Thermidorians alike were, like the fictional actor-politicians in the satirical story above, not averse to resorting to violence to defend the political stage. The massacre on the Champ-de-Mars, the destruction of Lyon, and the suppression of the uprising of Prairial were each perpetrated by profoundly different political factions against a populace with a range of different agendas, and yet they share a common logical thread: political actors, when they felt their representation to be in jeopardy, would do what was necessary to silence the parterre. The Thermidorians may have been the only ones to translate this threat of violence into explicit legislation when, at the instigation of Sieyès, they pushed through the *loi de grande police* promising death to all those who uttered premeditated, seditious words against the representative body; yet the sentiment behind this legislation was common to all political actors through all of the various Revolutionary regimes.

I do not think that I have made a secret of the fact that the argument I have been constructing here is not simply about Revolutionary France. A world was created—a political and cultural world—in eighteenth-century France that no doubt reflected changes happening elsewhere but that also, through the sheer violence and exuberance of its spectacle, stamped its own character on the change that was underway. And we, as citizens of the early twenty-first century, are still living in the world that they helped to bring into existence.

I should say very clearly that my intention here is in no way to advocate some sort of nostalgic return to the days in which the corpus mysticum reigned supreme; I could not be farther from suggesting this. My intention is simply to point out the basic fact that Western civilization embarked upon a particular path at the end of the eighteenth century, and it has since characterized that turning point as the straightforward choice between tyranny and liberty, arbitrary injustice and the inalienable rights of the individual. Because of the Manichaean terms in which this shift has been described, both by the Revolutionaries themselves and by many of the subsequent historical accounts, we have been blind to the innumerable possibilities that still existed at the end of the eighteenth century; the peculiar form of representation that they stumbled upon has come to define the limits of our conception of political possibility. Indeed, virtually all of our efforts at reforming the system seem to lie in tinkering with the content of the representative body[6] rather than rethinking the nature of representation itself.[7] Does the world wish to free itself from the tyranny of communism or dictatorship? We have a ready-made system that we can bestow upon them: representative democracy, that gift which the West would like to give to the entire world and which we so often euphemistically refer to simply as "democracy." But we never stop to ask, as did many of the Revolution's critics, whether in replacing tyranny with representative democracy—rule by representative bodies—we have not replaced one form of tyranny with another. For representative democracy is *not* democracy. And what is perhaps even more remarkable than this simple truth itself is our collective determination to elide this truth in everyday thought. After all, the distinction is not particularly difficult to grasp; and yet somehow, even if it is occasionally made mention of, it invariably slips back into a conceptual blind spot. Only a decade or so after 1789, Pierre Louis Roederer already seemed to sense a kind of mass suspension of critical faculties when it came to the subject of Revolutionary representation. In particular, he seemed struck by the extent to which distinctions between democracy and representative democracy had been blurred. For Roederer, who was not at all an opponent of the system, the very term "representative democracy" seemed a bit misleading, in that the government that it described was perhaps more properly defined as an aristocracy than a democracy:

> We must say, at the risk of causing great sadness to the modern politicians who believe that they have invented representative government, that the elective aristocracy of which Rousseau spoke fifty years ago is that which we today call representative democracy. . . . Pure democracy is a government in which all citizens, without regard to distinctions in birth, play an unmediated role in the formation of the law and the greater part in its execution. Representative democracy is that in which a portion of citizens chosen by another portion makes laws and executes them.[8]

I have resisted the temptation to make any connection between the process described in this book and contemporary political culture. As a historian of the eighteenth century, I feel myself on more solid ground speaking about events two hundred years ago than I do about events in the world today. (And if my only claim to expertise in the field of twenty-first-century political culture is the fact that I am a citizen of the present, then I am no more qualified than anyone else to pronounce judgment on it and a good deal less qualified than many; and there are also, of course, the difficulties of extrapolating across considerable chronological and geographical distances.) And yet I am convinced that we in Western culture at large inhabit the same world that the French Revolutionaries helped to bring into existence. But I will leave it to the reader to draw whatever connections she or he might care to between contemporary political culture and the world that burst into existence with the French Revolution, with respect not only to the merging of theatrical and political forms but also and more specifically to the rigorous imposition of the actor/spectator divide.

One might argue that the passivization of the audience, whether theatrical or political, has always encountered resistance, and that I have overstated my case here. Perhaps. After all, there were certainly occasions when spectators on both stages successfully enforced their will on the actors. Politically, the events of 10 August 1792 and late May and early June of 1793 would seem to be moments that contradict the general trend that I have outlined here. But what exactly did these popular uprisings accomplish? Did they substantially change the *form* of representation? Or did they rather substitute certain actors on the stage for different ones? I am convinced that, such popular incursions notwithstanding, the general trend—for both theatrical and political audiences—is toward spectators' silence and toward their separation from the representative stage. Try standing up and speaking out loud during the performance of a play anywhere in the Western world, much less getting up on the stage and touching the actors. Try walking into the assembly hall of a national political body of a representative democracy anywhere in the world and informing the representatives that you are there to exercise your right (as expressed in the Declaration of the Rights of Man and of the Citizen) to participate *personally* in the formation of the law. You may not be shot, as were the citizens on the Champ-de-Mars in 1791, but at the very least you will be escorted from the stage and asked to return to your seat. "Democracy," as we define it, means that actors act and spectators watch.

Like the contemporaries of the French Revolution, we are not oblivious to the strange theatricality of our own political culture (although it must be said that we are often content simply to marvel at it, as if it required no explanation). But the unequal dynamic that lies at the heart of this actor-spectator relationship seems to evade our critical gaze. We may criticize the actors in the play; we may even criticize the entire play. But it rarely seems to occur to us to question the representative form itself.

Notes

INTRODUCTION

1. [P. Ph. Gudin de la Brenellerie], *Observations sur la dénonciation de la corporation des auteurs dramatiques* (n.p., [1791?]), 1.

2. Most accounts set the number of Parisian theaters in 1789 at somewhere between ten and twelve. By 1791, there were some thirty-five theaters in Paris.

3. [Louis-Abel Beffroy de Reigny et al.], *Almanach général de tous les spectacles de Paris et de la province, pour l'année 1792* (Paris, 1792), 276. (The second part of this quotation, after the ellipsis, is cited as a quotation from *Nouvelles lunes* of "Cousin Jacques," otherwise known as Beffroy de Reigny. The author was therefore most probably quoting himself.)

4. As I use the terms, the quality of *theatricality* is as different from *drama* as artifice is different from truth, as representation is different from reality, and as orchestration is different from spontaneity. *Drama*, for example, might refer to the inherent pathos or historical import of an event. The spontaneous scene in which the king and queen were forced from Versailles to Paris by a mob of their subjects, accompanied all the way by the heads of the royal guards, impaled on pikes—this is clearly a dramatic event in every sense of the word. *Theatricality*, in contrast, describes the conscious staging of an event for the purposes of producing a particular effect, the intentional grafting of theatrical elements onto "real" life. The speeches of Mirabeau, for example, or the festivals of the Terror are *theatrical* in the sense that they are carefully scripted, choreographed, and performed, leaving little to spontaneity.

For works that have explored the theatricality of the Revolution, see Angelica Goodden, *Actio and Persuasion: Dramatic Performance in Eighteenth-Century France* (Oxford: Clarendon Press, 1986), as well as Goodden's article "The Dramatising of Politics: Theatricality and the Revolutionary Assemblies," *Forum for Modern Language Studies* 20, no. 3 (July 1984): 193–212. See also Susan Maslan, "Resisting Representation: Theater and Democracy in Revolutionary France," *Representations* 52 (fall 1995): 27–51; and Joseph Butwin, "The French Revolution as Theatrum Mundi," *Research Studies* 43, no. 3 (1975): 141–52. Most important, see the following works by Marie Hélène Huet: *Rehearsing the Revolution: The Staging of Marat's Death, 1793–1797*, trans. Robert Hurley (Berkeley: University of California Press, 1982); "Performing Arts: Theatricality and the

Terror," in *Representing the French Revolution: Literature, Historiography, and Art,* ed. James A. W. Heffernan (Hanover, N.H.: Dartmouth College, University Press of New England, 1992), 135–49; and *Mourning Glory: The Will of the French Revolution* (Philadelphia: University of Pennsylvania Press, 1997).

5. *Evénemens remarquables & intéressans, à l'occasion des décrets de l'auguste Assemblée nationale, concernant l'éligibilité de MM. les comédiens, le bourreau, & les Juifs* (n.p., 1790), 25.

6. The classic articulation of this approach is Robert Darnton's claim that "[w]hen we cannot get a proverb, or a joke, or a ritual, or a poem, we know we are on to something. By picking at the document where it is most opaque, we may be able to unravel an alien system of meaning. The thread might even lead into a strange and wonderful world view." Darnton, *The Great Cat Massacre and Other Episodes in French Cultural History* (New York: Basic Books, 1984), 5.

7. *Réimpression de l'ancien Moniteur* (Paris, 1857), 1:261 (Montmorency, 1 August 1789).

8. Jules Michelet, *History of the French Revolution,* trans. Charles Cocks, ed. Gordon Wright (Chicago: University of Chicago Press, 1967), 163–64.

PROLOGUE: A PARABLE

1. On the official decrees, see [Pierre-Ambroise-François Choderlos de Laclos], *Questions sur l'état des comédiens françois* (Paris, 1789), 14–15. One of the most important royal declarations was that of 16 April 1641, which stipulated that as long as actors offered spectacles that had been purified of indecencies, "the exercise [of their profession] . . . cannot be a basis for blame or prejudice to their reputation in public dealings." Cited in Simone de Reyff, *L'église et le théâtre: L'exemple de la France au XVIIe siècle* (Paris: Cerf, 1998), 42. On the strange conflict between government support of the theater and official religious hostility, see Henry Phillips, *The Theatre and Its Critics in Seventeenth-Century France* (Oxford: Oxford University Press, 1980), 204–20.

2. "Bossuet au P. Caffaro, Théatin" [9 mai 1694], in *L'église et le théâtre,* ed. Ch. Urbain and E. Levesque (Paris, 1930), 126. This same passage can also be found in Bossuet's "Maximes et réflexions sur la comédie" (see Urbain and Levesque, *L'église et le théâtre,* 180–81). Similar indictments of the content of the passions presented on the stage can be found in the works of the prince de Conti as well as in the writings of the Jansenist Jean Barbier d'Aucour. See Armand de Bourbon, prince de Conti, *Traité de la comédie et des spectacles* [1669], ed. Karl Vollmöller (Heilbronn, 1881), 21–22; on Barbier d'Aucour, see Urbain and Levesque, *L'église et le théâtre,* 19–20.

3. Bossuet, "Bossuet au P. Caffaro, Théatin," 125–26. A slightly different version of this passage appears in "Maximes et réflexions sur la comédie," 179. Similar worries about the influence of actors on the audience can be found in the pamphlet *Lettre écrite par un séculier à son amy. Sur les désordres qui se commettent à Paris, touchant la comédie. Et sur les représentations qui s'en font dans les maisons particulières* (Paris, 1710), 18–19.

4. Bossuet, "Maximes et réflexions sur la comédie," 212. See also p. 125. Jonas Barish compares this passage from Bossuet to a similar statement some thirty years earlier by the antitheatrical Jansenist Nicole. See Barish, *The Antitheatrical Prejudice* (Berkeley: University of California Press, 1981), 194.

5. "Bossuet au P. Caffaro, Théatin," 131.

6. Jean-Marie Apostolidès, *Le prince sacrifié: Théâtre et politique au temps de Louis XIV* (Paris: Minuit, 1985), 50.

7. Samuel Chappuzeau, *Le théâtre françois* (Paris, 1875), 89 [reprint of the 1674 edi-

tion]. See also abbé Parisis, *Questions importantes sur la comédie de nos jours* (Valenciennes, 1789), 63–64.

8. "Sur la Passion de Jésus-Christ," in *Bossuet: Textes choisis et commentés par H. Bremond* (Paris, 1913), 1:157–58.

9. Jonas Barish writes that this parallel between Christ's Passion and theatrical re-presentation underlay much of Jansenist antitheatricality as well: "But to [the Jansenists] the actor's sincerity was worse than hypocrisy. It sprang from an unholy pact between his conscious self and his own darkest impulses. It created a debased version of the passional existence, which competed, in the minds of spectators, with the passion of Christ." Barish, *Antitheatrical Prejudice*, 197.

Another manner in which actors' re-presentations seemed to compete with Christ's uniqueness was in the ability to perform metamorphoses. Several of the miracles performed by Christ involved changing the nature of objects and people (from water to wine, from sick to healed, from death to life). As Ernst Kantorowicz has suggested in a little-known essay, this power to change the nature of things, which had been credited to Jesus, had by the thirteenth century become the exclusive province of the pope. By the fifteenth century it had come to be shared with the secular power of kings, who were "emperors in their realms." Kantorowicz, "The Sovereignty of the Artist," in *Selected Studies* (Locust Valley, N.Y.: J. J. Augustin, 1965), 358–59. Artistic creation, then, not only seemed to compete with Christ himself but also seemed to infringe upon this power vested in popes and kings.

10. Jean Savaron, *Traité contre les masques* (Paris, 1611), 9.

11. [Abbé Mahy], *La comédie contraire aux principes de la morale chrétienne; ouvrage extrait des Saint Pères, & de MM. Bossuet & Nicole. . . .* (Auxerre, 1754), 4.

12. Cited in [Alex Tournon de la Chapelle], *L'art du comédien vu dans ses principes* (Amsterdam, 1782), 21.

13. On Greek rhetoric, see Joseph R. Roach, *The Player's Passion: Studies in the Science of Acting* (Newark: University of Delaware Press, 1985), 26.

14. Georges de Scudéry, *Apologie du théâtre*, cited in Phillips, *Theatre and Its Critics*, 185. The translation is mine.

15. Abbé d'Aubignac, *La pratique du théâtre* (Amsterdam, 1715), 299.

16. [De Brize], *L'art du théâtre, ou Le parfait comédien. Poème en deux chants* (n.p., [1744]), 9. See also [Pierre-Alexandre Lévesque de la Ravalliére?], *Essay de comparaison entre la déclamation et la poésie dramatique* (Paris, 1729), 43–44, which expresses a similar conception of acting.

17. Pierre Rémond de Sainte Albine, *Le comédien* (Paris, 1747), 32.

18. François Riccoboni, *L'art du théâtre* (Paris, 1750), 37.

19. Jean-François Cailhava de l'Estendoux, *De l'art de la comédie, ou détail raisonné des diverses parties de la comédie, et des différents genres* (Paris, 1772), 16.

20. [Jean-Charles Levacher de Charnois], *Conseils à une jeune actrice, avec des notes nécessaires pour l'intelligence du texte. Par un coopérateur du Journal des théâtres* (n.p., 1788), 21. See also [Alex Tournon de la Chapelle], *L'art du comédien*, 21–36, for similar criticisms of the new theories of theatrical representation.

21. Denis Diderot, *Paradoxe sur le comédien* (Paris: Garnier-Flammarion, 1967), 132. Although the *Paradoxe* was not actually published until 1830, Diderot circulated various drafts of the work as early as 1769, and several of its most important concepts can be found in earlier works such as the *Discours sur la poésie dramatique* (1758). See Roach, *Player's Passion*, 117–69.

22. Diderot, *Paradoxe*, 132–33.

23. Ibid., 133–34.

24. I use the term *carnivalesque* here in the specific sense in which Bakhtin used it in contradistinction to the prescripted, orderly nature of the modern theater. See Mikhail Bakhtin, *Rabelais and His World*, trans. Hélène Iswolsky (Bloomington: Indiana University Press, 1984), 7: "In fact, carnival does not know footlights, in the sense that it does not acknowledge any distinction between actors and spectators. Footlights would destroy a carnival, as the absence of footlights would destroy a theatrical performance. Carnival is not a spectacle seen by the people; they live in it, and everyone participates because its very idea embraces all the people."

25. Barbara G. Mittman, *Spectators on the Paris Stage in the Seventeenth and Eighteenth Centuries* (Ann Arbor: UMI Research Press, 1984), 29–32. See also John Lough, *Paris Theater Audiences in the Seventeenth and Eighteenth Centuries* (London: Oxford University Press, 1965), 115–18.

26. Cited in Adolphe Jullien, *Les spectateurs sur le théâtre, établissement et suppression des bancs sur les scènes de la Comédie-Française et de l'Opéra, avec documents inédits extraits des Archives de la Comédie-Française* (Paris, 1875), 8.

27. James Johnson provides wonderful details about spectator inattentiveness at the Opéra in a chapter entitled "Opera as Social Duty" in his book *Listening in Paris: A Cultural History* (Berkeley: University of California Press, 1995). See also the book by Jeffrey Ravel which is sure to become the classic text on the eighteenth-century French parterre: *The Contested Parterre: Public Theater and French Political Culture, 1680–1791* (Ithaca: Cornell University Press, 1999).

28. Montesquieu, *Lettres persanes* (letter 28).

29. Perhaps the most extensive account of the existence of spectator benches on the theatrical stage and their subsequent removal can be found in Jullien, *Les spectateurs sur le théâtre*. See also Pierre Peyronnet, *La mise en scène au XVIIIe siècle* (Paris: A.-G. Nizet, 1974), 59; Mittman, *Spectators on the Paris Stage*, 97; Jules Bonnassies, *Comédie française: Notice historique sur les anciens batiments* (Paris: Aubry, 1868), 21–22; and *Le théâtre à Paris au XVIIIe siécle. Conférences du musée Carnavalet* (Paris, 1929), 121. It should be noted that Voltaire had suggested the removal of spectator seating on the stage as early as 1730 in his *Discourse on Tragedy*. Apparently, however, no theaters were willing to put his ideas into practice, no doubt reluctant to forgo the comparatively high revenues earned from stage seating. See Jullien, *Les spectateurs sur le théâtre*, 16.

30. Jullien, *Les spectateurs sur le théâtre*, 23. See also Richard Sennett, *The Fall of Public Man* (New York: Knopf, 1977), 80.

31. Bonnassies, *Comédie française*, 24. Bonassies cites de Mouhy as his source. See also Gösta M. Bergman, *Lighting in the Theatre* (Totowa, N.J.: Rowman and Littlefield, 1977), who writes that already by the late 1750s "[t]he light in the auditorium had been dimmed, whereas the light on the stage had been considerably increased. . . . Stage and auditorium were being separated into two worlds" (171). By 1759, Bergman argues, "The actor had become sovereign of the stage" (175).

32. Peyronnet, *La mise en scène*, 67.

33. *Réimpression de l'ancien Moniteur* (Paris, 1860), 17:372. I owe this reference to Beatrice Hyslop's article "The Parisian Theater during the Reign of Terror," *Journal of Modern History* 17, no. 4 (December 1945): 332–55. See also the review of the first play to be produced on the newly cleared stage: "What is most remarkable is the proscenium, which, instead of being filled with little spectator boxes and benches, as at all the other theaters, is an area decorated with statues and bas-reliefs, which form a very pronounced line of demarcation between the stage and the spectators. . . . The illusion is maintained by not seeing the characters in the spectator boxes mixed up with those in the play." *Réimpression de l'ancien Moniteur*, 17:515. Again, I owe this citation to Hyslop.

34. *Discours de la poésie dramatique*, cited in Michael Fried, *Absorption and Theatricality: Painting and Beholder in the Age of Diderot* (Chicago: University of Chicago Press, 1980), 95. I have modified his translation somewhat.

35. [Cl. Jos. Dorat], *La déclamation théâtrale, poëme didactique en trois chants, précédé d'un discours* (Paris, 1766), 23–24. For additional statements on the importance of realistic costumes, see Jean-François de La Harpe, "Eloge de Lekain," in *Oeuvres de La Harpe . . . accompagnées d'une notice sur sa vie et sur ses ouvrages*, ed. Saint-Surin (Paris, 1821), 4:453. On the actor Talma's obsession with costumes, see C. G. Etienne and A. Martainville, *Histoire du théâtre français, depuis le commencement de la révolution jusqu'à la réunion générale* (Paris, [1802]), 2:114–16.

36. Charles-Joseph, prince de Ligne, *Lettres à Eugénie* (Paris, 1774), 99–100. On the rise of bourgeois dramas that seemed to fulfill this vision, see Scott Stewart Bryson, *The Chastised Stage: Bourgeois Drama and the Exercise of Power*, Stanford French and Italian Studies, vol. 70 (Saratoga, Calif.: Anma Libri, 1991). See also Sarah Maza, *Private Lives and Public Affairs: The Causes Célèbres of Prerevolutionary France* (Berkeley: University of California Press, 1993), 61–63.

37. See de Ligne, *Lettres à Eugénie*, 100. See also Cailhava, *De l'art de la comédie*, 425–48; and Dorat, *La déclamation théâtrale*, 54. As far as ridding the French theater of verse was concerned, the classics presented something of a problem for the practitioners of the realistic theater. An acting textbook from 1782 simply advised actors to do their best to deemphasize the rhyme: "Speak in a tone that most approaches ordinary conversation. . . . As there is in reality and in nature, and above all in theater, [no practice] of speaking in cadenced words, the actor must take as much care in making rhyme and measure disappear as an author may have taken in making [them] appear." Du Fresnel, *Essai sur la perfection du jeu théâtral . . .* (Liège, 1782), 4–5. One might almost credit the decline of opera as a popular art form to this new obsession with vraisemblance. As an anonymous author declared, also in the year 1782, "I have never been able to get used to the idea of seeing a man die while singing. This is such an affront to vraisemblance that unless you have no taste you should blush for the author as well as for the actor." *Lettres d'un solitaire sur le théâtre, ou Reflexions sur le tableau du spectacle français* (n.p., 1782), 23.

CHAPTER 1. EMBODIMENT

1. On the representative nature of the monarchy in France, see Ernst Kantorowicz, *The King's Two Bodies: A Study in Mediaeval Political Theology* (Princeton: Princeton University Press, 1957); Louis Marin, *Portrait of the King*, trans. Martha M. Houle (Minneapolis: University of Minnesota Press, 1988); Peter Burke, *The Fabrication of Louis XIV* (New Haven: Yale University Press, 1992); Ralph Giesey, *Cérémonial et puissance souveraine: France, XVe–XVIIe siècle* (Paris: Armand Colin, 1987); and Jean-Marie Apostolidès, *Le prince sacrifié: Théâtre et politique au temps de Louis XIV* (Paris: Minuit, 1985), as well as Apostolidès' *Le roi machine: Spectacle et politique au temps de Louis XIV* (Paris: Minuit, 1981).

2. The following description of different forms of government by Thomas Hobbes illustrates not only that early modern political theorists characterized monarchy as a form of representative government but also that they drew much sharper distinctions than modern theorists between democracies and representative democracies, the latter of which would seem much closer to Hobbes's definition of aristocracy than democracy: "When the Representative is One man, then is the Commonwealth a MONARCHY: when an Assembly of All that will come together, then it is a DEMOCRACY, or Popular Common-

wealth: when an Assembly of a Part onely, then it is called an ARISTOCRACY." Thomas Hobbes, *Leviathan*, edited with an introduction by C. B. Macpherson (New York: Penguin, 1986), 239 (chap. 19).

3. Kantorowicz, *King's Two Bodies*, 18.

4. Ibid., 209. Ralph E. Giesey, "The French Estates and the Corpus Mysticum Regni," in *Album Helen Maud Cam, Studies Presented to the International Commission for the History of Representative and Parliamentary Institutions*, vol. 23 (Louvain, 1960), 157; and E. H. Kantorowicz, "Mysteries of State: An Absolutist Concept and Its Late Mediaeval Origins," *Harvard Theological Review* 48(1955): 65–91.

5. Jean Gerson, "Pour la réforme du royaume (vivat rex, vivat rex, vivat rex)," in Jean Gerson, *Oeuvres complètes*, introduction, textes et notes par Mgr Glorieux (Paris: Desclée, 1968)[7 nov. 1405 Discours vivat rex], 7:1013. Gerson is here offering an interpretation of Nebuchadnezzar's dream of a statue with a head of gold, finding a contemporary political parallel to each part of the statue.

6. Guy Coquille, "Discours des estats de France, et du droit que le duché de Nivernois a en iceux. Par Maitre Guy Coquille sieur de Romenay, procureur general audit duché," in *Les oeuvres de Maistre Guy Coquille, Sieur de Romenoy . . .* (Paris, 1666), 1:328. How the clergy, as the brain, might be distinct from the king, as head, is an issue Coquille does not broach.

7. Terre Rouge, quoted in Giesey, "French Estates," 164. Giesey argues, "The *corpus mysticum* was the chief element [of Terre Rouge's political writings], and more than any other writer known to us Terre Rouge tested—or taxed—its mettle as a concept of the state." Giesey, "French Estates," 157. By Giesey's estimate (ibid., 163), Terre Rouge refers to the concept of the mystical body some one hundred times in the third tract of his *Tractatus de iure futuri successoris legitimi in regiis hereditatibus.*

8. Gerson, "Pour la réforme du royaume," 1155–56.

9. As Bossuet wrote, "Being persuaded by the Scriptures that we are but one body by charity [i.e., through man's love of his fellow man], we must look at ourselves not as individuals *[en nous-mêmes]*, but in the unity of the body, and direct all our actions with respect to others according to this thought." Bossuet, quoted in Pierre Ronzeaud, *Peuple et représentations sous le règne de Louis XIV* (Aix-en-Provence: Université de Provence, 1988), 286.

10. [Pierre Matthieu], *Histoire des derniers troubles de France. Soubs les regnes des Rois Tres-Chrestiens Henry III. Roy de France & de Pologne; & Henry IIII. Roy de France & de Navarre . . .* , 2d ed. (n.p., 1600), 111a–112b; Coquille, "Discours des estats de France," 333; *De la puissance des roys, et droict de succession aux Royaumes; contre l'usurpation du Titre & Qualité de Roy de France . . .* (Paris, 1593), 30–31; "La Forme, et Ordre de l'assemblée des Estats tenus à Blois, sous le Tres Chrestien Roy de France & de Pologne, Henry III, du nom, és années 1576 & 1577," in *Le cérémonial françois . . .* , ed. Theodore Godefroy and Denys Godefroy (Paris, 1649), 2:299–301; and "Harangue prononcée à l'ouverture de la session des Etats généraux assemblée à Orléans le 13 décembre 1560," in *Oeuvres complètes de Michel L'Hospital . . .* (Paris, 1824), 1:379. Several of these texts also suggest that civil and foreign wars constitute another situation in which the convocation of the Estates General is necessary.

11. I borrow this term from Otto von Gierke, *Political Theories of the Middle Age*, trans. F. W. Maitland (Cambridge, 1927), 65.

12. Certificate of the sworn-crier, cited in Georges Picot, *Histoire des Etats généraux* (Paris: Hachette, 1888), 5:253–54. Details on the notification of the convocation of the Estates can be found in Picot, *Histoire des Etats généraux*, as well as in J. Russell Major, *The Deputies to the Estates General in Renaissance France* (Madison: University of Wisconsin Press, 1960), 10–11.

13. Raymond Carré de Malberg gave a very apt description of the task of a delegate to the Estates General when he wrote, "[The delegates] are ambassadors, sent to the king so that he might hear the voice of the nation; [they are] plenipotentiaries. . . . In all of this, the idea of representation is quite clear: the manner in which the Estates General represents the diverse elements of the nation before the king resembles, in a sense, the manner in which a diplomatic agent represents his country before a foreign sovereign." Carré de Malberg, *Contribution à la théorie générale de l'état* (Paris, 1922), 239.

14. Major, *Deputies to the Estates*, 8–9. Elsewhere, Major wrote that "[deputies who] acted on their own initiative . . . were subject to recall and perhaps severe punishment. In neighboring Switzerland even the death penalty was inflicted." Major, *Estates General of 1560* (Princeton: Princeton University Press, 1951), 73.

15. L'Hospital, "Harangue prononcée à l'ouverture . . . des Etats généraux . . . 1560," 1:379–80.

16. Major, *Deputies to the Estates*, 11. Picot mentions the participation of women and minors in provincial assemblies of the nobility but suggests that they could participate only by proxy. Picot, *Histoire des Etats généraux*, 261.

17. The letter of convocation for the Estates General of 1560 was vague in stipulating the number of deputies to be sent, declaring that "at least one deputy" be sent from each estate in every region of France. *Recueil de monuments inédits de l'histoire du tiers état* (Paris, 1853), 2:670. At the Estates General of Pontoise in 1561, by contrast, the crown stipulated that only one delegate be sent from each estate, but apparently only half of the thirteen *gouvernements* of France respected this directive. J. Russell Major, "The Third Estate in the Estates General of Pontoise, 1561," in *The Monarchy, the Estates, and the Aristocracy in Renaissance France* (London: Variorum Reprints, 1988), section 4, 466. See also Picot, *Histoire des Etats généraux*, 5:248; Major, *Deputies to the Estates*, 5. See also Godefroy and Godefroy, *Le cérémonial françois*, 303, for a listing of the varying number of deputies sent by each of the estates to the Estates General of 1576.

18. On the changing manner in which deputies of the first two estates were selected before and after the fifteenth century, see J. Russell Major, "Royal Initiative and Estates General in France," in *The Monarchy, the Estates, and the Aristocracy in Renaissance France*, section 8, 254–55.

19. "Ordre et séance gardés en la convocation et assemblée des trois états du royaume de France . . . [1560], in *Recueil de pièces originales et authentiques, concernant la tenue des Etats généraux . . .* , ed. Lalourcé and Duval (Paris, 1789), 1:32.

20. [Matthieu], *Histoire des derniers troubles*, 114.

21. Journal de Guillaume de Taix, "Ordre de la procession aux premiers états de Blois" in Lalourcé and Duval, *Recueil de pièces originales*, 2:33–34.

22. [Matthieu], *Histoire des derniers troubles*, 114. This same account is given in Godefroy and Godefroy, Le *cérémonial françois*, and reprinted in Lalourcé and Duval, *Recueil de pièces originales*, 4:35.

23. "Déliberation du parlement pour la procession," in Lalourcé and Duval, *Recueil de pièces originales*, 5:88 (no. 79).

24. "Ordre que le roi veut être gardé en la procession générale des Etats généraux du royaume, tenus en la ville de Paris," in Lalourcé and Duval, *Recueil de pièces originales*, 5:91–94 (no. 82).

25. Lalourcé and Duval, *Recueil de pièces originales*, 5:94–97 (no. 83).

26. "The two sides of the street were bordered by the king's guards in order to prevent confusion resulting from the multitude of people [who had come] to see this procession, from the streets as well as the windows." "Registres du parlement de Paris."

Procès-verbal de la procession," in Lalourcé and Duval, *Recueil de pièces originales,* 5:106 (no. 84).

27. "La procession générale, suivant l'ordre donné cy-dessus par le Roy Louys XIII," in Godefroy and Godefroy, *Le cérémonial françois,* 2:338.

28. "Mémoires de l'ouverture des estats, faites par le Roy Louys XIII en la grande salle de Bourbon, à Paris le lundy 27 Octobre 1614," in Godefroy and Godefroy, *Le cérémonial françois,* 2:346. The chancellor acceded to the demands of the Estates and, over the objection of the Gentlemen of the Council, had a bench placed in front of them for the clergy and the nobility.

29. See the discussion of the "flowering" of this royal spectacle in Ralph E. Giesey, *The Royal Funeral Ceremony in Renaissance France* (Geneva: E. Droz, 1960), 77. See also Lawrence M. Bryant, *The French Royal Entry Ceremony: Politics, Society, and Art in Renaissance Paris* (Ann Arbor: University Microfilms, 1978).

30. This conception of the Estates General as an occasional political body that on rare occasions re-presents an ever-present mystical body comes close to Giesey's reading of Terre Rouge's conception of the Estates General: "[The mystical or civil body of the realm] cannot be precisely correlated with the Estates, for the mystical or civil body, as the fictitious body which is ever the holder of the dignities of the realm, must be in existence at all times. It is the omnipresent metaphysical form of the whole nation, it seems, and the Estates is a sort of contingent institutional form which the civil or mystical body of the realm sometimes assumes for the purposes of deciding upon fundamental law." Giesey, "French Estates and the Corpus Mysticum Regni," 162.

31. This reading of premodern symbols is very much indebted to Norbert Elias's discussion of identity in court society of the seventeenth century as a function of display rather than vice versa. See, in particular, the chapter entitled "Structure of Dwellings and Social Structure," in Elias, *The Court Society,* trans. Edmund Jephcott (New York: Basil Blackwell, 1983), 41–65.

32. As Louis XIV would later say with respect to his own obsession with rank and with visual re-presentations of his own preeminence, "Those who imagine that claims of this kind are only questions of ceremony are sadly mistaken. There is nothing in this matter that is unimportant or inconsequential. Since our subjects cannot penetrate into things, they usually judge by appearances, and it is most often on amenities and on ranks that they base their respects and their obedience." *Louis XIV King of France and of Navarre: Mémoires for the Instruction of the Dauphin,* trans. Paul Sonnino (New York: Free Press, 1970), 144.

33. Jean Masselin, "Harangue de monseigneur le chancelier," in *Journal des Etats généraux de France tenus à Tours en 1484 . . . ,* ed. and trans. A. Bernier (Paris: Imprimerie Royale, 1835), 63.

34. Coquille, "Discours des estats de France," 323. See the very useful discussion of Coquille in William Farr Church, *Constitutional Thought in Sixteenth-Century France: A Study in the Evolution of Ideas* (Cambridge: Harvard University Press, 1941), 272–302.

35. For a discussion of the religious, economic, social, and intellectual context in which the Estates General of 1560 was convened, see Major, *Estates General of 1560,* 16–41.

36. L'Hospital, "Harangue prononcée à l'ouverture . . . des Etats généraux . . . 1560," 1:404. Church quotes L'Hospital as comparing his role to that of a sailor, changing the position of the sails as the winds changed. Church, *Constitutional Thought in Sixteenth-Century France,* 205.

37. L'Hospital, "Harangue prononcée à l'ouverture . . . des Etats généraux . . . 1560," 1:389.

38. Innocent Gentillet, *Anti-Machiavel; édition de 1576 avec commentaire et notes*, ed. C. Edward Rathé (Geneva: Droz, 1968), 76–77.

39. J. G. A. Pocock, *The Ancient Constitution and the Feudal Law: A Study of English Historical Thought in the Seventeenth Century* (Cambridge: Cambridge University Press, 1957), 17. On Hotman's historically based argument, see Ralph E. Giesey, "The Juristic Basis of Dynastic Right to the French Throne," *Transactions of the American Philosophical Society*, n.s., 51, part 5 (1961): 30, and André Lemaire, *Les lois fondamentales de la monarchie française, d'après les théoriciens de l'ancien régime* (Paris, 1907), 92–101.

40. Théodore de Bèze, *Du droit des magistrats*, ed. Robert M. Kingdon (Geneva: Droz, 1970), 44.

41. *De la puissance des roys*, 32 (originally published in 1590).

42. Kantorowicz characterizes the execution of Charles as follows: "Parliament succeeded in . . . executing solely the king's body natural without affecting seriously or doing irreparable harm to the King's body politic—in contradistinction with the events in France, in 1793." Kantorowicz, *King's Two Bodies*, 23.

43. See Julian H. Franklin, *Jean Bodin and the Rise of Absolutist Theory* (London: Cambridge University Press, 1973), 26, 41, 49.

44. Other advocates of absolute royal sovereignty include Jean de Tillet, Grégoire de Toulouse, and Charles Loyseau. A useful discussion of all three as well as of Bodin can be found in Lemaire, *Les lois fondamentales*, 82–84, 114–22, 128–33, and 152–53.

45. Jean Bodin, *Les six livres de la république* (Paris, 1583; reprint, Aalen: Scientia, 1961), 141.

46. Ibid., 137–38.

47. Carré de Malberg, *Contribution à la théorie générale de l'état*, 239.

48. Giesey, *Cérémonial et puissance souveraine*, 85.

CHAPTER 2. A NEW POLITICAL AESTHETIC

1. Quoted in Jean-Marie Apostolidès, *Le roi-machine: Spectacle et politique au temps de Louis XIV* (Paris: Minuit, 1981), 13.

2. On re-presentations of the king's actual body see Lawrence M. Bryant, *The French Royal Entry Ceremony: Politics, Society, and Art in Renaissance Paris* (Ann Arbor: University Microfilms, 1978). Sarah Hanley has written a masterful study of the *lit de justice;* see *The Lit de Justice of the Kings of France: Constitutional Ideology in Legend, Ritual, and Discourse* (Princeton: Princeton University Press, 1983). On iconographic re-presentations of the king's body, see Louis Marin, *Portrait of the King*, trans. Martha M. Houle (Minneapolis: University of Minnesota Press, 1988); Jean-Marie Apostolidès, *Le Roi-machine;* and Apostolidès, *Le Prince sacrifié: Théâtre et politique au temps de Louis XIV* (Paris: Minuit, 1985).

3. Jürgen Habermas, *The Structural Transformation of the Public Sphere: An Inquiry into a Category of Bourgeois Society*, trans. Thomas Burger with the assistance of Frederick Lawrence (Cambridge: MIT Press, 1989), 29, 43.

4. Sarah Maza writes that "most of the hundreds of plays of the later eighteenth century that can be classified as *drames* revolve around familial crises, social tensions, or both. Many playwrights, taking their cue from Diderot and Beaumarchais, included the words *époux, épouse, fils, mère, père*, and so on in their titles." Maza, *Private Lives and Public Affairs: The Causes Célèbres of Prerevolutionary France* (Berkeley: University of California Press, 1993), 62. On the subject of the bourgeois drama, see also Scott Stewart Bryson, *The Chastised Stage: Bourgeois Drama and the Exercise of Power*, Stanford

French and Italian Studies, vol. 70 (Saratoga, Calif.: Anma Libri, 1991). On novels, see Habermas, *Structural Transformation of the Public Sphere*, 49–51. And on absorption in painting, see Michael Fried, *Absorption and Theatricality: Painting and Beholder in the Age of Diderot* (Chicago: University of Chicago Press, 1980).

5. Habermas, *Structural Transformation of the Public Sphere*, 40.

6. Habermas sees the rise of realism in literature as essentially analogous to the rise of vraisemblance within the theater: "The reality as illusion that the new genre created received its proper name in English, 'fiction': it shed the character of the *merely* fictitious. The psychological novel fashioned for the first time the kind of realism that allowed anyone to enter into the literary action as a substitute for his own, to use the relationships between the figures, between the author, the characters, and the reader as substitute relationships for reality. The contemporary drama too became fiction no differently than the novel through the introduction of the 'fourth wall.' " Ibid., 50.

7. La Font de Saint-Yenne, quoted in ibid., 40. On La Font and the concept of the public, see also Thomas E. Crow, *Painters and Public Life in Eighteenth-Century Paris* (New Haven: Yale University Press, 1985), 6.

8. Habermas, *Structural Transformation of the Public Sphere*, 29.

9. Habermas writes, "The criteria of generality and abstractness characterizing legal norms had to have a peculiar obviousness for privatized individuals who, by communicating with each other in the public sphere of the world of letters, confirmed each other's subjectivity as it emerged from their spheres of intimacy." Ibid., 54.

10. Recently, Jeffrey Ravel has raised some interesting questions about this trend within present-day historiography to privilege print culture over theatrical culture. See especially the introduction to Ravel, *The Contested Parterre: Public Theater and French Political Culture: 1680–1791* (Ithaca: Cornell University Press, 1999). I too find the hypothesis of a shift from theatrical to print culture somewhat problematic. For example, although it is certainly true that old regime court culture was frequently derided by its critics as a feminine and theatrical milieu, it is also true that aspersions of theatricality would be used by enemies of the *new* regime as a prime method, if not *the* prime method, of casting doubt on the legitimacy of the various Revolutionary governments. Despite certain superficial similarities, however, there are important differences in the ways in which the old and new regimes were characterized by their respective critics as theatrical. The theatricality of the old regime was a theatricality that inhered in its extravagance, its ostentatiousness, and its almost complete unbelievability; critics derided the court culture of the old regime because they no longer found it a credible source of authority. By contrast, the theatricality of the new regime was, not unlike the *drame bourgeois*, eminently believable and yet utterly fictitious; people criticized the new regime for its theatricality precisely because it was so skilled at passing itself off as something that it was not—namely, the *real* (as distinct from the *believable*) re-presentation of the French nation.

11. Roger Chartier, *The Cultural Origins of the French Revolution*, trans. Lydia G. Cochrane (Durham: Duke University Press, 1991), 158.

12. For general accounts of parlementary opposition to *Unigenitus*, see Jean Egret, *Louis XV et l'opposition parlementaire, 1715–1774* (Paris: Armand Colin, 1970), 17–33 and 50–68. See also the excellent study by Dale Van Kley, *The Religious Origins of the French Revolution: From Calvin to the Civil Constitution, 1560–1791* (New Haven: Yale University Press, 1996), as well as Van Kley, *The Damiens Affair and the Unraveling of the Ancien Régime, 1750–1770* (Princeton: Princeton University Press, 1984). Other works that touch upon the subject include Jeffrey W. Merrick, *The Desacralization of the French Monarchy in the Eighteenth Century* (Baton Rouge: Louisiana State University Press, 1990), chap. 3; and Jules Flammermont, introduction

in *Remontrances du parlement de Paris au XVIIIe siècle* (Paris, 1888; repr., Geneva: Mégariotis, 1978).

13. Egret, *Louis XV*, 53.

14. Voltaire, quoted in ibid., 58.

15. David A. Bell, *Lawyers and Citizens: The Making of a Political Elite in Old Regime France* (New York: Oxford University Press, 1994). See in particular chaps. 3 and 4. Although Bell points out that "French barristers had hardly remained aloof from political activity before 1713" (73), he argues that the promulgation of *Unigenitus* "marked the point at which barristers went beyond . . . occasional ventures to engage in what can only be called systematic campaigns of publicity" (75).

16. Ernst Kantorowicz, *The King's Two Bodies: A Study in Mediaeval Political Theology* (Princeton: Princeton University Press, 1957), 415–16. See also Ralph Giesey's discussion of the relationship between the parlement and the king in *The Royal Funeral Ceremony in Renaissance France* (Geneva: E. Droz, 1960), 185.

17. Montesquieu's analysis of the English system of government, written during the 1730s, was ahead of its time with respect to its familiarity with and possible advocacy of a system of government based upon the abstract (nonembodied) representation of the nation by a group of privileged individuals. Well before anyone else had begun to speak of such issues in France, Montesquieu was speaking of a government in which "distinguished" elected representatives might decide on behalf of their constituency without any specific instructions or cahiers to guide them in their thinking. On the advantages of a representative system over pure democracy, see Montesquieu, *De l'esprit des lois*, vol. 1 (Paris: Garnier Frères, 1973), 171–73 (book 11, chap. 6) and 347 (book 19, chap. 27). For Montesquieu's seeming repudiation of the need for specific instructions to the representatives, see p. 172.

Unlike almost all of the political theorists discussed in this book, however, Montesquieu was not advocating any specific practical reforms for the French government; his thinking tends to be on a very abstract, hypothetical plane, and when he does descend to the level of concrete experience, most of his references are to the English system of government, not the French. We should also be careful not to take Montesequieu's analysis of the English system for a sign of unqualified acceptance. As Keith Baker argues, "Montesquieu presented his readers with a kind of political prodigy: a bizarre, disturbing, even dangerous phenomenon, not one that was necessarily to be imitated." Keith Baker, *Inventing the French Revolution: Essays on French Political Culture in the Eighteenth Century* (Cambridge: Cambridge University Press, 1990), 178.

18. Flammermont, *Remontrances*, 1:528 (9 April 1753). See Keith Baker's discussion of the "double claim" being made by this statement (Baker, *Inventing*, 228–29). Keith Baker's citations of key passages in the remonstrances, as well as Jeffrey Merrick's, were enormously helpful to me.

19. Egret, *Louis XV*, 61. Flammermont, *Remontrances*, 1:609.

20. See Baker, *Inventing*, 170–71.

21. Flammermont, *Remontrances*, 2:iv.

22. Merrick, *Desacralization*, 88.

23. Baker, *Inventing*, 44. On Le Paige's general influence on the parlementaires, see pp. 36–37, 41–44. See also Bell, *Lawyers and Citizens*, chap. 4.

24. Flammermont, *Remontrances*, 2:32. See also 29–30.

25. Ibid., 2:430 (18 Jan. 1764). See also the remonstrance of 9 April 1753, which also referred to the dual aspects of the parlement's representation, and which asserted that "Your Majesty, by the organ [of the parlements] hears the complaints [*plaintes*] of every last citizen" (Flammermont, *Remontrances*, 1:529). See Baker's discussion of the symbolic

and performative nature of parlement's claim to represent the king to the nation and vice versa. Baker, *Inventing*, 229–30.

26. Flammermont, *Remontrances*, 2:431.

27. Baker, *Inventing*, 232.

28. Flammermont, *Remontrances*, 2:557–59.

29. See Keith Baker's article "Controlling French History: The Ideological Arsenal of Jacob-Nicolas Moreau," in *Inventing*, 59–85. With respect to the government's propaganda campaign, Baker writes (in a different article from the same collection), "In the course of subsequent decades [after 1760], the preambles to important decrees grew longer and more explicit in their explanations and justifications of government policies; ministers proved adept in the strategic proliferation of pamphlets and anonymous brochures; apologists for absolute government sought to deploy the ideological resources of the monarchy in its own defense. Reluctantly, inconsistently, yet with an increasing sense of urgency as successive pre-revolutionary crises became more acute, agents of the monarchy found themselves presenting their briefs before the tribunal of the public" (171).

Moreau and his researchers amassed thousands of historical records, which they hoped would lend the weight of history to their public claims on behalf of the monarchy. Baker writes that "it will give a sense of the scope of the ideological arsenal [Moreau] was eventually able to build . . . to say that by 1789 it contained some 50,000 documents, drawn from 350 different archives, an inventory of 41,000 pieces, and many other volumes of manuscripts" (40).

30. "Edit pour règlement," reprinted in Jules Flammermont, *Le Chancelier Maupeou et les parlements* (Paris, 1883), 117–18.

31. Quoted in Flammermont, *Le Chancelier Maupeou*, 133, 135.

32. Ibid., 207. Egret, *Louis XV*, 178.

33. Egret, *Louis XV*, 178–79.

34. Comtesse d'Egmont in a letter to the king of Sweden, quoted in ibid., 217.

35. Elie de Beaumont, quoted in ibid.

36. Quoted in Baker, *Inventing*, 139. See also p. 49.

37. Ibid., 140.

38. Abbé Galiani, quoted in Egret, *Louis XV*, 218.

39. Baron de Bésenval, quoted in Maza, *Private Lives*, 55.

40. David Bell claims that "well over a hundred pamphlets and broadsides, ranging from calm, closely argued constitutional treatises to quasi-obscene lampoons emerged from hidden presses." In turn, according to Bell, "Maupeou sponsored a counter-offensive of at least ninety pamphlets." Bell, *Lawyers and Citizens*, 141. Keith Baker counts more than four hundred oppositional pamphlets from the time of the Maupeou coup until the parlements were restored. Baker, *Inventing*, 77.

41. "Très humbles et très respectueuses remontrances de la cour des aides de Paris, du 18 février 1771, sur l'édit de décembre 1770, et l'état actuel du parlement de Paris," in Elizabeth Badinter, *Les "Remontrances" de Malesherbes, 1771–1775* (Paris: Union Générale d'Editions, 1978), 153, 164.

42. Ibid., 156–57.

43. Quoted in Badinter, *Les "Remontrances" de Malesherbes*, 79. See also p. 93 for a letter from Condorcet praising the remonstrances, as well as Egret, *Louis XV*, 190.

44. Shanti Marie Singham, " 'A Conspiracy of Twenty Million Frenchmen': Public Opinion, Patriotism, and the Assault on Absolutism during the Maupeou Years, 1770–1775" (Ph.D. diss., Princeton University, 1991), 124–25.

45. Quoted in Flammermont, *Le Chancelier Maupeou*, 308. Dale Van Kley provides

several relevant page numbers in Flammermont pertaining to provincial parlementary re-monstrances. Van Kley, *Damiens Affair,* 330 n. 101.

46. Flammermont, *Le Chancelier Maupeou,* 315.

47. Singham, " 'Conspiracy of Twenty Million Frenchmen,' " 79.

48. Baker, *Inventing,* 49.

49. Mably, quoted in ibid., 45.

50. Malesherbes, "Remontrances relatives aux impôts, 6 mai 1775," in Badinter, *Les "Remontrances" de Malesherbes,* 264–65. Further references in parentheses in the text.

51. Van Kley, *Damiens Affair,* 192–93. Bell, *Lawyers and Citizens,* 148–49. Egret, *Louis XV,* 219. Singham, " 'Conspiracy of Twenty Million Frenchmen,' " 132.

52. On Le Paige, Mey, and Maultrot as authors of parlementary pamphlets and *mémoires,* see Bell, *Lawyers and Citizens,* 112–17. On the *Maximes du droit public français* and its claim for national self-convocation, see Egret, *Louis XV,* 218–19; Singham, " 'Conspiracy of Twenty Million Frenchmen,' " 137–38; and Baker, *Inventing,* 330 n. 50, and 334 n. 48.

53. See the previous chapter.

54. Guillaume-Joseph Saige, *Catéchisme du citoyen, ou élémens du droit public français, par demandes & par réponses* (Geneva, 1775), 18–19; further references in parentheses in the text. I am grateful to Keith Baker for graciously supplying me a micro-film of Saige's text.

55. See also pp. 24 and 81.

56. Rousseau, of course, was famous for insisting that the general will could not be rep-resented. As he wrote in the *Social Contract,* "Sovereignty cannot be represented, for the same reason that it cannot be alienated; it consists essentially in the general will, and will does not represent itself: it is itself, or it is something else; there is no middle ground. The deputies of the people are not therefore and cannot be its representatives; they are only its emissaries; they cannot conclude anything definitively. All laws that the people have not rat-ified in person are null; they are not laws." Jean-Jacques Rousseau, *Du contrat social; ou Principes du droit politique* (Amsterdam: Marc-Michel Rey, 1763), 137–38 (book 3, chap. 15). A somewhat softer view of representation, and one that is similar to Saige's, can be found in Rousseau's *Considérations sur le gouvernement de Pologne,* where he seems to sug-gest tacit approval of a system in which the general will could make itself known through deputies tightly bound to their constituents' will—although Rousseau undoubtedly would have been reluctant to refer to this as "representation." See, in particular, chap. 7.

A very interesting discussion of Saige's intellectual debt to Rousseau can be found in Keith Baker, "A Classical Republican in Eighteenth-Century Bordeaux: Guillaume-Joseph Saige," in *Inventing,* 128–52. Here Baker argues that Saige "considere[d] immediate is-sues of French politics, and the fundamental character of the French constitution, within an essentially Rousseauian framework. If not the first, it is surely one of the most thor-oughgoing of such efforts" (142).

57. Here, too, Saige seems to owe an intellectual debt to Rousseau, who wrote, "The law being but the declaration of the general will, it is clear that the people cannot be rep-resented by legislative power; but it can and must be [represented] in executive power, which is but the applied force of the law." Rousseau, *Contrat social,* 139.

58. My comparison of Malesherbes's political public opinion to prepolitical forms of public opinion owes much to Roger Chartier's discussion of Malesherbes's remonstrances in general, and his interpretation of this passage in particular. See Chartier, *Cultural Ori-gins,* 30–32.

59. Chartier, *Cultural Origins,* 32.

60. Ibid., 31.

61. See Mona Ozouf's discussion of Beaumarchais's *Essai sur le genre dramatique*

sérieux, in which, according to Ozouf, "Beaumarchais held the [theatrical] public to be a fiction that did not hold up under examination and a collective being permanently threatened with dissolution and dispersion, constrained to give way to 'the judgement of the smaller number'—to intrigue and to influence." Mona Ozouf, " 'Public Opinion' at the End of the Old Regime," *Journal of Modern History* 60, Supplement (September 1988): s17.

62. In this speech, Malesherbes compared "men of letters" to orators in the assemblies of Rome and Athens: "[I]n an enlightened century, in a century in which each citizen can speak to the entire nation by means of print, those who have the talent for instructing men and the gift of moving them—men of letters, in a word—are, among the dispersed public, what the orators of Rome and Athens were in the midst of the public assembly." Malesherbes, *Discours prononcé dans l'Académie française le jeudi 16 février [1775]*, quoted in Ozouf, " 'Public Opinion,' " s9.

63. The *élus* were officials who in earlier times had been elected by inhabitants of areas designated as *pays d'élection* to oversee the distribution of tax revenues in their respective provinces. Gradually, these offices lost their representative character. The *élus*, despite their name, were eventually appointed by and responsible to the king, and the *pays d'élections* (in contrast to the *pays d'état*) became those provinces in which provincial estates did not meet, and officials were appointed directly by the crown. Malesherbes, "Remontrances relatives aux impôts," 208, 227, 232–34.

64. Turgot's entry in the *Encyclopédie* under the heading "Foundation" (originally published in 1757), in *The Old Regime and the French Revolution*, ed. Keith Baker (Chicago: University of Chicago Press, 1987), 94. For a comparison of Malesherbes, Turgot, and Saige, see Baker, *Inventing*, 120–27.

65. Turgot, "Foundation," 96. For other texts that emphasize the importance of the individual, see the writings of Target and Augeard, both of whom were members of Malesherbes's circle, and both of whom were at the forefront of the assault on corporatist conceptions of the French nation. See Singham, " 'Conspiracy of Twenty Million Frenchmen,' " 80, 154–55.

66. Cited in Maza, *Private Lives*, 29.

67. D'Alembert and Condorcet, cited in Ozouf, " 'Public Opinion,' " s9. See also Ozouf's article "Public Spirit" in *A Critical Dictionary of the French Revolution*, ed. François Furet and Mona Ozouf, trans. Arthur Goldhammer (Cambridge: Harvard University Press, 1989), in which she writes, "Public Opinion, the opinion of enlightened men, was therefore not the passive, untamed, divided opinion of the multitude. Sieyes, and with him Condorcet, Necker, and Mirabeau, held firmly to this distinction, which was destined to enjoy a remarkable future. They knew that taking opinion into account would lead logically to the conclusion that one individual is just as good as another. It was this conclusion that the adjective public exorcized; the public was not a people, and public opinion was not common sense" (772).

68. See Ozouf, " 'Public Opinion,' " s16.

69. Keith Michael Baker, *Condorcet: From Natural Philosophy to Social Mathematics* (Chicago: University of Chicago Press, 1975), 324–25. See also pp. 228–31.

70. [Anne-Robert-Jacques Turgot], *Des administrations provinciales, mémoire présenté au roi, par feu M. Turgot* (Lausanne, 1788), 29. Further references in parentheses in the text.

ENTR'ACTE: PUBLIC OPINION AND THE THEATER

1. Nina Rattner Gelbart writes that Mercier's drama *Olinde et Sophronie*, which came out within days of the exile of the parlements, was "specifically designed to infuriate Mau-

peou." Gelbart, *Feminine and Opposition Journalism in Old Régime France: Le Journal des Dames* (Berkeley: University of California Press, 1987), 214. According to Sarah Maza, Mercier also seized upon the causes célèbres as an appropriate subject for drama, suggesting that "the great court cases be reenacted on stage so that the public could witness them and then 'confirm by cheering . . . the triumph of the law.' " Maza, *Private Lives and Public Affairs: The Causes Célèbres of Prerevolutionary France* (Berkeley: University of California Press, 1993), 64.

2. Cited in Frederick Brown, *Theater and Revolution: The Culture of the French Stage* (New York: Viking, 1980), 45.

3. Norbert Elias, *The Court Society*, trans. Edmund Jephcott (New York: Basil Blackwell, 1983), 82–86.

4. The privilege of the Comédie-Française, also known as the Théâtre-Français, was actually rather narrowly defined, although it was an extremely important one: the Comédiens du roi possessed the exclusive right to perform five-act plays, within the boundaries of Paris, in the French language, but with neither music nor dance. The exclusive right to perform operas, not only in Paris but in all of France, was reserved to the Académie royale de musique et de danse. And a third troupe, the Théâtre-Italien, enjoyed the exclusive privilege of performing all theatrical representations not performed by the other troupes—namely, plays in Italian, musical sketches, or plays that included farcical characters, such as Harlequin, whose representation was generally considered to be beneath the Théâtre-Français. Furthermore, the right to represent a character who died or who killed himself on stage was reserved to the actors of the Théâtre-Français; the characters represented on the stage of the Théâtre-Italien were, however, entitled to faint or wound themselves, providing they did not actually expire on stage. A. L. Millin, *Sur la liberté du théâtre* (Paris, 1790), 49–50. Over the course of the eighteenth century, more narrowly defined privileges not already possessed by the three main theaters were accorded to several smaller theaters. For example, the Théâtre de Monsieur had the right to perform only Italian operettas; the Comédiens de la cour could not approach within two leagues of Paris; the Théâtre des Variétés could perform only three-act plays. In addition to these, there were those theaters whose theatrical niches are perhaps more accurately described as loopholes than privileges. The Théâtre de M. Audinot, for example, managed to get around the monopoly of the Théâtre-Français on plays in French by putting mute actors on the stage accompanied by marionettes who spoke fluent French and translated for their live, mute colleagues. And in later years, this theater obtained the permission for a more practical circumvention of the Théâtre-Français monopoly: it replaced its marionettes with children. And whereas the Théâtre des Beaujolois did not have the right to allow singers on its stage (a privilege whose various permutations had already been reserved by other theaters), the Beaujolois managed to overcome this obstacle by presenting actors who mouthed the words and performed the gestures, while the real singers remained hidden from view. Perhaps the most interesting method of circumventing the monopoly of the privileged theaters was employed by the Théâtre des Bleuettes, which not only adopted the innovations of the Théâtre des Beaujolois, but sidestepped the Beaujolois privileges by placing a thin veil between the actors and the audience. This device was copied by the Théâtre de Délassements, which managed to circumvent the privileges of the Théâtre de M. Audinot by placing a veil between its marionettes and the audience. Ibid., 50–52. Within this confusing array of privileges, therefore, there was but one theater that had the exclusive right to perform spoken, nonfarcical plays in French, with live actors in the direct presence of an audience, and that was the Théâtre-Français.

5. *Mémoire pour les Comédiens du Roy [contre Charles Dolet, & autres]* (n.p., 1680), 10.

6. *Mémoire pour les Comédiens-Français, contre les entrepreneurs du Spectacle du faubourg Saint-Antoine* (Paris, 1789), 12, 15–16.

7. Mercier, *Du théâtre,* quoted in Gelbart, *Feminine and Opposition Journalism,* 216–17.

8. Ibid., 218, 225. Gelbart devotes an entire chapter, entitled "Theater Criticism," to the feud between Mercier and the comédiens, and her account is an extremely thorough and insightful reconstruction of the events.

9. Ibid., 226.

10. Quoted in [Pierre-Paul-Nicolas Henrion de Pansey], *Requête au roi, pour le Sr Mercier, défendeur. Contre MM. les premiers gentilshommes de la chambre de Sa Majesté, demandeurs. Question. La législation & la police des spectacles appartiennent-elles, exclusivement, à MM. les premiers gentilshommes de la chambre du roi?* (n.p., 1775), 8.

11. *Le voeu des auteurs, lettre à messieurs les Parisiens, sur les Comédiens-Français & sur d'autres objets de littérature* (n.p.,n.d.), 12–13. Pierre Peyronnet, in *La mise en scène au XVIIIe siècle* (Paris: A-G. Nizet, 1974), credits this pamphlet to André Charles Cailleau and suggests that it was written around 1772; however, the pamphlet's references to Mercier's legal actions against the Comédiens indicate that the pamphlet was published in or around 1775.

12. *Mémoire à consulter, et consultation pour le sieur Palissot de Montenoy; contre la troupe des Comédiens-François* (Paris, 1775), 4–5.

13. [Henrion], *Requête au roi, pour le Sr Mercier, défendeur,* 14.

14. Gelbart, *Feminine and Opposition Journalism,* 226–28. According to Gelbart, Malesherbes "took special protective charge of Mercier's case. . . ." On Henrion's oration, see also David A. Bell, *Lawyers and Citizens: The Making of a Political Elite in Old Regime France* (New York: Oxford University Press, 1994), 156; the oration was published under the title *Discours prononcé à la rentrée de la conférence publique de messieurs les avocats au parlement de Paris, le 13 janvier 1775* (Lausanne, Paris, 1775).

15. Mercier, *Du théâtre,* quoted in Marie-Hélène Huet, *Rehearsing the Revolution: The Staging of Marat's Death, 1793–1797,* trans. Robert Hurley (Berkeley: University of California Press, 1982), 36. As Huet observes, "[T]his remark fits squarely in the ideological tradition of the *Social Contract,* with Rousseau's definition of the relationship between the citizen and the sovereign, the particular will and the general will."

16. Jean-François Marmontel, "Parterre," in *Nouveau dictionnaire, pour servir de supplément aux dictionnaires des sciences, des arts, et des métiers . . .* (Paris, 1777), 4:241. I am grateful to Jeffrey Ravel for signaling to me the importance of this article.

17. Jean-François Marmontel, "Apologie du théâtre, ou analyse de la lettre de Rousseau, citoyen de Genève, à d'Alembert, au sujet des spectacles," in *Oeuvres complètes de J.-J. Rousseau* (Brussels, 1828), 13. This is a reprint of Marmontel's "Extrait critique de la lettre à M. d'Alembert," which was printed in the *Mercure de France* in November 1758–January 1759.

18. Jean-Jacques Rousseau, *Contrat social,* book 2, chap. 3.

19. Marmontel, "Parterre," 242.

20. Jeffrey Ravel, *The Contested Parterre: Public Theater and French Political Culture, 1680–1791* (Ithaca: Cornell University Press, 1999), 192–93. Ravel cites, as one example of this phenomenon, an account from the *Anecdotes dramatiques* of the first visit of Louis XVI and Marie-Antoinette to the Comédie-Française at which, by the king's request, the Comédie performed the *Siège de Calais.* In the course of the performance, as the *Anecdotes* related the story, the parterre acted, through its exclamations and applause, as a kind of tangible embodiment of the French nation: "There were moments in the perfor-

mance when a sort of dialogue seemed to form between the future King and the Nation. All the French hearts repeated energetic expressions of love, zeal, and fidelity for the Prince which the author had put in the mouth of the Calais heroes" (208).

21. Ravel does not claim this. I am speaking more of a general trend within the historiography of the Revolution to read theater and theatricality through a political lens.

22. La Harpe, quoted in Jeffrey S. Ravel, "Seating the Public: Spheres and Loathing in the Paris Theaters, 1777–1788," *French Historical Studies* 18, no. 1 (spring 1993): 187–88.

23. Ledoux, quoted in ibid., 183.

24. See the previous chapter.

25. See Ravel's discussion of a 1771 drawing by the architect Charles de Wailly of a proposed interior for the new Comédie-Française: "He removed the multitude which previously occupied the pit to the third balcony, out of the view of spectators who purchased expensive first- and second-balcony seats. . . . The architect offered his patrons . . . a sanitized image of the social world of the theater, one where the tumult of the standing parterre would be hidden from sight in the third balcony and the *paradis*." Ravel, "Seating the Public," 183–85. See also La Harpe's and Levacher de Charnois's pronouncement along the same lines (ibid., 188, 190).

26. See the previous chapter.

27. Marmontel, "Parterre," 242.

28. Ibid., 241.

29. See Ravel, "Seating the Public," 190.

30. *Coup d'oeil sur le Théâtre-Français depuis son émigration à la nouvelle salle,* quoted in ibid., 198.

31. James Johnson, *Listening in Paris: A Cultural History* (Berkeley: University of California Press, 1995), 1.

32. Huet, *Rehearsing,* 35.

CHAPTER 3. THE RESURRECTION AND REFASHIONING OF THE ESTATES GENERAL

1. "Arret du conseil d'état du roi concernant la convocation des Etats généraux du royaume," in *Receuil de documents relatifs à la convocation des Etats généraux de 1789,* ed. Armand Brette (Paris, 1894), 1:19.

2. De Landine, *Des Etats généraux, ou Histoire des assemblées nationales en France, des personnes qui les ont composées, de leur forme, de leur influence, & des objets qui y ont été particulièrement traités* (Paris: Cuchet, 1788), vi. See also the preface to *Des Etats généraux, de la forme qu'on pourroit établir pour les convoquer, leur faire opérer le bien que le roi & la nation ont le droit d'en attendre* . . . (n.p., [1788]), 2: "This [text] was only intended as the first chapter of a much larger work; but the author believed it necessary to shift his attentions, in order to publish it at this moment, as a result of the circumstances that are holding public interest."

3. *De la formation des Etats généraux* (n.p., [1788]), 1–3.

4. De Landine, *Des Etats généraux,* 2. For a similar conception of the value of history, see *Des Etats généraux, de leur forme, et de la cause de leur convocation* (n.p., 1788), 1–2.

5. For another text that stresses the importance of historical precedent, see *Des Etats généraux, et de leur convocation* . . . (Villefranche, 1788).

6. Comte d'Antraigues, *Mémoire sur les Etats généraux* (n.p., 1788), 20.

7. *Instruction sur les assemblées nationales, tant générales que particulières, depuis le*

commencement de la monarchie, jusqu'à nos jours; avec le détail de cérémonial, observé dans celle d'aujourd'hui (Paris, 1787), 14–15, 43.

8. De Landine, *Des Etats généraux*, iii. The same distinction between the body of the king and the body of the nation is expressed in a somewhat more belligerent manner in another text, written shortly before the announcement that the Estates would be convened: "This supposed right [of the king's] to prevent all assemblies of the Estates is not given to the king by any express consent on the part of the nation. [The nation] would never have accorded rights against itself." *Dissertation sur le droit de convoquer les Etats généraux, tirée des capitulaires, des ordonnances du royaume, & des autres monuments de l'histoire de France* (n.p., 1787), 23.

9. D'Antraigues, *Mémoire sur les Etats généraux*, 226–27.

10. Comte d'Antraigues, *Mémoire sur les mandats impératifs* (Versailles, [1789]), 11–12. A similar if slightly different version of the story is offered in *Dissertation sur le droit de convoquer les Etats généraux*, 21. This insistence on the nation's retention of all aspects of sovereignty that it could not directly exercise was a fundamental tenet of a range of eighteenth-century political theorists as far back as Montesquieu: "Because, in a free state, all men who are supposed to have a free soul must be governed by themselves, it is necessary that the people as a body have legislative power. But as this is impossible in large states, and subject to many inconveniences in small ones, it is necessary that the people do through its representations all that it cannot do by itself." Montesquieu, *De l'esprit des lois*, ed. Robert Derathé (Paris: Garnier Frères, 1973), 1:171 (book 11, chap. 6).

11. Roger Barny puts the number of editions at thirteen, while Colin Duckworth cites fourteen. Barny, Duckworth, Jacques Godechot, and Jacqueline Chaumié all suggest that the book may have actually been as popular in its day as Sieyès's pamphlet. See Barny, *Le comte d'Antraigues: Un disciple aristocrate de J.-J. Rousseau: De la fascination au reniement, 1782–1797* (Oxford: Voltaire Foundation, 1991), 125; Duckworth, *The D'Antraigue Phenomenon: The Making and Breaking of a Revolutionary Espionage Agent* (Newcastle: Avero, 1986), 174; Chaumié, *Le réseau d'Antraigues et le contre-révolution, 1791–1793* (Paris: Plon, 1965), 30; and Godechot, *Le comte d'Antraigues, un espion dans l'Europe des émigrés* (Paris: Fayard, 1986), 33.

12. D'Antraigues, *Mémoire sur les Etats généraux*, 20.

13. Ibid., 125–26.

14. In this sense, I agree with Jacques Godechot when he writes, "The political theorists of the counterrevolution were for the most part revolutionaries in their own fashion." Godechot, *La contre-révolution: doctrine et action, 1789–1804* (Paris: Quadridge/Presses Universitaires de France, 1984), 2.

15. D'Antraigues, *Mémoire sur les Etats généraux*, 250–52.

16. Ibid., 246.

17. These viewpoints were certainly present; see, for example, Godechot's discussion of Moreau (Godechot, *La contre-révolution*, 18–19).

18. D'Antraigues, *Mémoire sur les mandats impératifs*, 23.

19. The logic of counterrevolutionary thought as well as its relationship to Rousseau's thought are discussed more fully in chap. 7.

20. Epigraph to d'Antraigues, *Mémoire sur les mandats impératifs*. The quotation is from Rousseau's *Considerations on the Government of Poland*. D'Antraigues paraphrases the same principle within the body of the text itself; see pp. 9–10.

21. "Considérations sur le gouvernement de Pologne," in Jean-Jacques Rousseau, *Ecrits politiques*, ed. Gérard Mairet (Paris: Librairie Générale Française, 1992), 434.

22. D'Antraigue, *Mémoire sur les mandats impératifs*, 10.

23. Rousseau, "Considérations sur le gouvernement de Pologne," 435.
24. D'Antraigues, *Mémoire sur les mandats impératifs,* 4. Rousseau, "Considérations sur le gouvernement de Pologne," 435–36. They were joined in this particular view by Saige, whose *Catéchisme du citoyen* is discussed in chap. 2.
25. Honoré-Gabriel Riquetti, comte de Mirabeau, *Discours sur la représentation illégale de la nation provençale dans ses Etats actuels, & sur la nécessité de convoquer une Assemblée générale des trois ordres, prononcé par le comte de Mirabeau, dans la quatrième séance des Etats actuels de Provence. Le 30 janvier 1789* (n.p., [1789]), 8.
26. *Principes sur la constitution de la France et des Etats généraux,* quoted in Mitchell Bennett Garrett, *The Estates General of 1789: The Problems of Composition and Organization* (New York: Appleton-Century, 1935), 187. For other examples of pamphlets that refer explicitly to the "purity" of France's earliest government (in contrast to the impurity of recent centuries), see Garrett's summaries of pamphlets on pp. 83, 130–31.
27. [J. P. Rabaut Saint-Etienne], *Considérations sur les intérêts du tiers état, adressées au peuple des provinces. Par un propriétaire foncier* (n.p., 1788), 13. Despite his repudiation of history, Rabaut, like many of his fellow revolutionaries, was not averse to romanticizing the age of Pharamond and Clovis (see p. 14).
28. Ibid., 15.
29. Cited in Garrett, *Estates General,* 82.
30. Pierre-Louis Lacretelle, *De la convocation de la prochaine tenue des Etats généraux* (n.p., 1788), 8.
31. Ernst Cassirer, *The Philosophy of the Enlightenment,* trans. Fritz C. A. Koelln and James Pettegrove (Princeton: Princeton University Press, 1951), 13–14.
32. Constantin-François Volney, "Des conditions nécessaires à la légalité des Etats généraux," in *Oeuvres,* ed. Anne Deneys and Henry Deneys (Paris: Fayard, 1989), 1:70–72.
33. Garrett, *Estates General,* 127.
34. [Jean-Jacques Duval d' Epréménil], *Réflexions impartiales sur la grande question . . .* (n.p., 1788), 6.
35. Volney, "Des conditions nécessaires," 70.
36. On the different meanings of the word *constitution,* see Keith Baker, *Inventing the French Revolution: Essays on French Political Culture in the Eighteenth Century* (Cambridge: Cambridge University Press, 1990), 254.
37. *Sur cette question: Est-il nécessaire ou utile que les Etats généraux de 1789 soient convoqués dans la forme de ceux de 1614* (n.p., [1788]), 6. Garrett's book (*Estates General*) was enormously helpful in directing me to all three of the quotations relating to the Reason of proportionality that I examine here.
38. Joseph-Ignace Guillotin, *Pétition des citoyens domiciliés à Paris. Du 8 décembre 1788* (Paris, 1788), 11–12, 15.
39. Louis Louchet, *Le tiers état au roi* (n.p., 20 December 1788), 42–45.
40. One did not have to return to the sixteenth century, however, to find individuals who found this new logic difficult to comprehend. The comte de Lauraguais warned those who sought to disrupt the traditional constitution that their efforts would end in chaos: "A political body is formed of several organs, as a machine is composed of diverse parts; each [part] has a particular effect, the ensemble of which produces the general and desired effect. But should you wish to change the function for which each of these organs is particularly destined by the nature of its existence, you will throw everything into the most horrible confusion." Comte de Lauraguais, *Lettre sur les Etats généraux convoqués par Louis XVI et composés par M. Target* ([Paris], 1788), 7–8.

41. Guy Target, *Suite de l'écrit intitulé "Les Etats généraux convoqués par Louis XVI,"* cited in Garrett, *Estates General,* 143.

42. *Le tout est-il plus grand que la partie? ou Réponse à cette question: Que doit faire le tiers état, si les ordres privilégiés refusent de délibérer par tête?* . . . (n.p., 1789), 21. See also p. 4: "Is it not to disrupt the order of nature to want to equate twenty-four million with three hundred thousand individuals?"

43. Cited in Garrett, *Estates General,* 90.

44. In addition to complaints about disproportional representation with respect to population and wealth, there were also complaints about geographic equity. See Garrett's discussion of a pamphlet by Jacques Augustin Mourgue entitled *Vues d'un citoyen sur la composition des Etats généraux* (Garrett, *Estates General,* 97–98).

45. Mirabeau, *Discours sur la représentation illégale,* 19.

46. Pierre Louis Roederer is something of an exception here, in that he seems to advocate an assembly that does not recognize any qualitative distinction between the orders in his 1788 pamphlet *De la députation aux Etats généraux* (n.p., 1788), esp. 72–76. Sieyès, too, although he ostensibly accepted the idea that the third might settle for double representation, was clearly opposed in principle to any division of the nation by orders. See the discussion of Sieyès later in this chapter.

47. *Le tout est-il plus grand que la partie?* 38.

48. See chap. 1.

49. Lauraguais, *Lettre sur les Etats généraux,* 4–5.

50. Ibid., 6.

51. Quoted in Garrett, *Estates General,* 79–80.

52. See chap. 1.

53. Rabaut Saint-Etienne, *Considérations sur les intérêts du tiers état,* 30.

54. Quoted in Garrett, *Estates General,* 163.

55. *Plan pour la formation des états provinciaux de la Lorraine et du Barrois, et pour l'élection des députés aux Etats généraux* (published in December 1788), quoted in Garrett, *Estates General,* 191.

56. [A. Morellet], *Projet de réponse à un mémoire répandu sous le titre Mémoire des Princes. 21 décembre 1788.* (n.p., [1788]), 32.

57. See the preface by Jean-Denis Bredin to Emmanuel Sieyès, *Qu'est-ce que le tiers état?* (Paris: Flammarion, 1988), 13; further references to Sieyès's pamphlet in parentheses in the text. Bredin quotes the work of Eugène Spuller, who suggested that the pamphlet may have had more than one million readers.

58. Sieyès declares the clergy to be members of a profession rather than an order (38).

59. Mirabeau, *Discours sur la représentation illégale,* 14.

60. See also *Le tout est-il plus grand que la partie?* which does not spare the clergy in a similar characterization of the true organic constitution of the nation:

Is it not evident that the privileged orders cannot exist by themselves? That they are in the nation, but they are not the nation? Is it not evident that the third estate contains within itself all that is necessary to form a complete nation; & that, if one removed the privileged classes, far from being something less, [the third estate] would be more free and more prosperous? That ivy which the oak supports . . . , is it the oak tree itself? This parasitic plant, is it necessary to the existence of the oak tree, or does it not finish by suffocating it? (3–4)

61. William H. Sewell Jr., *A Rhetoric of Bourgeois Revolution: The Abbé Sieyès and What Is the Third Estate?* (Durham: Duke University Press, 1994), 43.

62. *Le tout est-il plus grand que la partie?* 4.

63. See Garrett's discussion of pamphlets by the marquis de Serent, Antoine Lévrier,

and the comte de Serrant, all of whom insisted that the Estates General must meet before the constitution could be altered in any way. Garrett, *Estates General*, 83, 85, 127–28.

64. Target, quoted in ibid., 89–90.

65. It should be noted that Roederer had articulated a similar position several months before Sieyès's pamphlet was published: "We conclude that the deputies, in order to represent the nation truly, must have nonlimited powers and must answer only to themselves for their opinions." Roederer did caution, however, that this authority did not mean that the representative was relieved of the burden of at least articulating the views and complaints of his constituents, even if he himself did not share them. Roederer, *De la députation aux Etats généraux*, 14.

66. See Sewell, *Rhetoric of Bourgeois Revolution*, 68–69, 88–94, 149–52, and Baker, *Inventing*, 245–46. See also Jean Roels, *Le concept de représentation politique au dix-huitième siècle français* (Louvain: Nauwelaerts, 1969), 112–16.

67. Mona Ozouf includes Condorcet, Necker, and Mirabeau in this list along with Sieyès. See Ozouf, "Public Spirit," in *A Critical Dictionary of the French Revolution*, ed. François Furet and Mona Ozouf, trans. Arthur Goldhammer (Cambridge: Harvard University Press, 1989), 772. Roels writes, with respect to Sieyès's political "technocracy," that, "Sieyès situates himself in the direct line of two great philosophers of the eighteenth century: Montesquieu and the abbé de Mably." Roels, *Le concept de représentation politique*, 116.

Chapter 4. Praxis

1. *Règlement fait par le roi pour l'exécution des lettres de convocation du 24 janvier 1789*, in *Recueil de documents relatifs à la convocation des Etats généraux de 1789*, ed. Armand Brette (Paris, 1894), 1:66.

2. Article 26, in ibid., 1:77–78.

3. Article 20 in ibid., 1:75.

4. Article 39 in ibid., 1:82.

5. On the complicated procedures by which the election of deputies took place, see Ran Halévi, "Estates General," in *A Critical Dictionary of the French Revolution*, ed. François Furet and Mona Ozouf, trans. Arthur Goldhammer (Cambridge: Harvard University Press, 1989), 45–53. See also Patrice Gueniffey, *Le nombre et la raison: La Révolution française et les élections* (Paris: Ecole des hautes études en sciences sociales, 1993), 32–36.

6. *Réglement . . . du 24 janvier 1789*, 67.

7. See chap. 1.

8. Marquis de Ferrières, *Correspondance inédite (1789, 1790, 1791)*, ed. Henri Carré (Paris: Armand Colin, 1932), 27–28.

9. Gouverneur Morris, *A Diary of the French Revolution*, ed. Beatrix Cary Davenport (Boston: Houghton Mifflin, 1939), 1:67.

10. Gouverneur Morris to Mrs. Robert Morris, cited in ibid., 1:68.

11. Ibid., 1:68–69.

12. Ferrières, *Correspondance*, 47.

13. *Archives parlementaires de 1787 à 1860* (Paris, 1875), 8:109. Unless otherwise stated, all quotations in this chapter from debates in the Estates General and the National Assembly are from volume 8 of this collection.

14. These are the comments of Target. See also the comments by Nicolas Bergasse (117) as well as those by Jacques-Guillaume Thouret (118).

15. "Assemblée des représentants du peuple de France, vérifiés par les co-députés, au-

torisés par leurs commettants à s'occuper de leurs intérêts, et aptes à exécuter les mandats dont ils ont été chargés."

16. Isaac René Guy Le Chapelier offered an edited version of Sieyès's proposal, which simply replaced "known and verified" with "legally verified" (118). Alexis-François Pison du Galland proposed: "Assemblée active et légitime des représentants de la nation française" (Active and Legitimate Assembly of the Representatives of the French Nation) (122; see also 126). And Mounier suggested an edited version of his earlier proposal: "Assemblée composée de la majorité en l'absence de la minorité" (Assembly Comprising the Majority in the Absence of the Minority) (123).

17. [Antoine Ferrand], Les conspirateurs démasqués. Par l'auteur de Nullité et despotisme . . . (Turin, 1790), 59.

18. See the comments of Barère, on 7 July, who reminded his fellow representatives that "it is not only with the particular interest [of individual constituencies] that the general assembly must concern itself, but with the general interest." Archives parlementaires, 8:205.

19. "Déclaration du roi, concernant la présente tenue des Etats généraux," in Réimpression de l'ancien Moniteur (Paris, 1857), 1:93.

20. See Claude Soule, Les Etats généraux de France (1302–1789): Etude historique, comparative, et doctrinale (Heule, 1968), 209–10.

21. Ran Halévi, "La révolution constituante: Les ambiguités politiques," in The French Revolution and the Creation of Modern Political Culture, vol. 2, The Political Culture of the French Revolution, ed. Colin Lucas (Oxford: Pergamon, 1988), 76.

22. Moniteur, 1:95. This account should be taken with something of a grain of salt, as it was most likely derived from Mirabeau's own rendition of the events, published in his Lettres de Mirabeau à ses comettants. (See the note in the Moniteur, 1:1.)

23. See the previous chapter for a discussion of the concept of a "theoretical mandate" according to which deputies were bound to the nation as a whole rather than to the particular constituency that they served.

24. Moniteur, 1:113. Although the règlement was dated 27 June, it was apparently not posted until the thirtieth.

25. Déclaration de l'ordre de la noblesse aux Etats généraux pour la conservation des droits constitutifs de la monarchie française, de l'indépendance et de la distinction des ordres (July 5, 1789), Moniteur, 1:133–34.

26. Ibid., 1:134.

27. See Beatrice Fry Hyslop, French Nationalism in 1789 according to the General Cahiers (New York: Columbia University Press, 1934), 19–20. According to Hyslop, "the deputies used [the cahiers] as general guides," and in particular the committee on the constitution seemed to think it necessary to consult them, at least at first. On 27 July 1789 Clermont-Tonnerre gave a summary of the cahiers to the Assembly, which Hyslop sees as "a tacit acceptance of the cahiers as guides for business." But, she writes, the authority of the cahiers waned significantly as time went on: "After July 27, occasional reference was made to the cahiers in the deputies' speeches on the constitution, but less frequently as time passed. Thereafter, although interest in the cahiers continued, they ceased to exert a direct influence upon the course of events."

28. For an extraordinarily insightful discussion of the debates on the mandats impératifs, from June to September, see R. Carré de Malberg, Contribution à la théorie générale de l'état (Paris, 1922), 2:247–59. See also Halévi, "La révolution constituante," 74–81.

29. What Sieyès was no doubt referring to was the fact that the National Assembly, in constituting itself, had declared that "it belongs to [the National Assembly,] and it belongs

to it alone, to interpret and to voice the general will of the nation; there can exist no *veto* nor any negative power between the throne and this Assembly." *Archives parlementaires,* 8:127. Such a declaration, although it left undecided whether a royal veto was permissible, presumably left no room for any *other* interference in the Assembly's formulation of the general will.

30. Emmanuel Sieyès, *Qu'est-ce que le tiers état?* (Paris: Flammarion, 1988), 69. See previous chapter.

31. See chap. 1.

32. Sieyès, unpublished note, quoted in Patrice Gueniffey, "Les Assemblées et la représentation," in Lucas, *Political Culture of the French Revolution,* 235.

33. *Qu'est-ce que le tiers état?* 136. See previous chapter.

34. The emphasis in the final sentence is mine.

35. See also article XIV, which states, "All citizens have the right to determine, by themselves or through their representatives, the necessity of the public contribution [i.e., tax], to consent to it freely, to follow up on the use it is put to, and to determine its amount, its basis, its means of collection, and its duration."

36. Constitution of 1791, title 3, article 1.

37. Ibid., title 3, article 2.

38. Ibid., title 3, chap. 1, section 3, article 7.

39. *L'Assemblée nationale, traitée comme elle le mérite* (n.p., [1789?]), 1.

40. Critics of the National Assembly often referred to it as the *Assemblée prétendue nationale* (The so-called National Assembly) in order to highlight its illegitimate and non-representative nature. Antoine Ferrand was particularly fond of doing this in the titles to his pamphlets: *Le dénouement de l'Assemblée prétendue nationale* (Paris, 1790); *Tableau de la conduite de l'Assemblée prétendue nationale, adressé à elle-même, par l'auteur d'un ouvrage intitulé: Nullité et despotisme, &c* (Paris, 1790); and *Nullité et déspotisme de l'Assemblée prétendue nationale* (n.p., 1790). See also the anonymous pamphlet *Grands tableaux magiques des fameuses supressions faites par la très-grande et très-infaillible Assemblée prétendue nationale. Par l'auteur de La trahison contre l'état ou Les jacobins dévoilés, de la joyeuse semaine; &c., &c* (Paris, n.d.).

41. Comte Murat de Montferrand, *Qu'est-ce que l'Assemblée nationale? Grande thèse en présence de l'auteur anonyme de Qu'est-ce que le tiers? Et dédiée au très-honorable Edmund Burke, comme à un véritable ami de la vraie liberté* (n.p., 1791), 10.

42. The similarities between counterrevolutionary and radical discourse are discussed in chap. 7.

43. *La corruption de l'Assemblée nationale, et les crimes de membres; par un ami de la vérité* (Paris, 1790), 38–39.

44. Decree of the National Assembly (23 June 1789) in *Histoire parlementaire de la Révolution française, ou Journal des assemblées nationales, depuis 1789 jusqu'en 1815,* ed. P.-J.-B. Buchez and P.-C. Roux (Paris, 1834), 2:25.

45. [Antoine Ferrand], *Ambition et égoïsme de l'Assemblée nationale* (Paris, 1790), 9. For other counterrevolutionary attacks on inviolability, see Montferrand, *Qu'est-ce que l'Assemblée nationale?* 54; *Grands tableaux magiques,* 6; *Usurpations et attentats de l'Assemblée nationale, pour servir de parallèle à la conduite de Louis XVI* (Geneva, 1790), 10; and [Antoine Ferrand], *Etat actuel de la France* (Paris, 1790), 45–46.

46. Tuileries section, 10 April 1793 (Germinal year I), quoted in Albert Soboul, *The Sans Culottes: The Popular Movement and Revolutionary Government, 1793–1794,* trans. Rémy Inglis Hall (Princeton: Princeton University Press, 1980), 111–12. For another example of left-wing criticism of inviolability, see *La corruption de l'Assemblée nationale,* 9–10: "[The representatives] will make off with your property if they have any-

thing to gain from it; & no tribunal will dare to infringe upon their inviolability by giving you the justice that you might have had the right to expect."

CHAPTER 5. *MÉTISSAGE*

1. Throughout this chapter I occasionally retain the French word *comédiens*, which is
usually translated into English simply as "actor," but which in French retains the overtones of someone who cannot be taken seriously—a concept lost in its usual translation.

2. *Quelques lettres inédites de Collot-d'Herbois*, ed. M. A. Preux (Douai, 1869), 16.

3. The word and the concept of a historical "site," where seemingly unrelated concepts
find a historically specific common ground, are from the preface to Michel Foucault, *The
Order of Things: An Archaeology of the Human Sciences* (New York: Vintage, 1973).

4. For this portion of the chapter, I am indebted to the work of several theater historians, many of whom wrote the better part of a century ago, but whose studies remain the
most authoritative, factual accounts of the actors and the theaters of Revolutionary
France. Above all, I have relied extensively on Henri Lyonnet's "Comédiens révolution-
naires," which I consulted both in its manuscript form (in the Rondell Collection at the
Bibliothèque de l'Arsenal) and in the serialized version in *La nouvelle revue*. Other ac-
counts of Revolutionary theater that have proved extremely useful include Paul d'Estrée,
Le théâtre sous la Terreur: Théâtre de la peur, 1793–1794 (Paris, 1913); A. Pougin, *La
Comédie-Française et la Révolution* (Paris: Gaultier, Magnier, [1902]); Henri Welschinger,
Le théâtre de la Révolution: 1789–1799 (Paris: Charavay Frères, 1880); and Jacques
Hérissay, *Le monde des théâtres pendant la Révolution: 1789–1800* (Paris: Perrin, 1922).
In addition, the more recent book by Noëlle Guibert and Jacqueline Razgonnikoff, *Le
journal de la Comédie-Française, 1787–1799: La Comédie aux trois couleurs* (Paris: Sides,
1989), although intended as a popular history, has proved invaluable in many respects.

5. *Réponse de M. Naudet, Comédien du roi, aux injures répandues contre lui dans différens journaux* (Paris, 1790), 1–2.

6. Naudet gives the information concerning his own appointment and that of Saint-
Prix in his *Réponse;* however, two letters contained in the archives of the Bibliothèque de
la Comédie-Française (Naudet file), written on 19 September and 3 October 1789, are
signed: "Naudet, Lieutenant de la garde nationale parisienne." A letter written on 28 Jan-
uary 1790 indicates that he was a *capitaine de grenadiers.* The information regarding
Grammont's rank is contained in *Les Comédiens commandans MM. Naudet, Grammont,
St-Pry* [sic]*, Marcy, Dugazon, Chamville, tous Comédiens français. A Messieurs les
Parisiens* (Paris, 1789), 5.

7. For information on Saint-Prix's military service, see Archives nationales (A.N.), F[17]
1294, dossier 4. Talma's National Guard identity card can be found in the Talma file of
the archives of the Bibliothèque de la Comédie-Française (B.C.-F.). De Boizi—possibly a
pseudonym for the playwright Charles Palissot de Monlenay—reported in *Considérations
importantes sur ce qui se passe, depuis quelques tems, au prétendu Théâtre de la Nation,
et particulièrement sur les persécutions exercées contre le Sieur Talma* [1790], that Talma
"had had the honor of being admitted to the *compagnie des chasseurs volontaires de l'ancien district des Cordeliers,*" although he gave no precise date. On the military rank of the
others mentioned here, see *Les comédiens commandans.* See also Lyonnet, "Comédiens
révolutionnaires" (MS), 27. Lyonnet also mentions that Fusil and Michot from the
Théâtre de la rue de Richelieu were in the National Guard, and that Baptiste Cadet from
the Théâtre Montansier was in the Grenadiers.

8. Archives of the B.C.-F., "Feux," vol. 20.

9. These negative reactions to the soldier-actors are discussed in the following chapter.

10. *Les Comédiens commandans,* 11. This pamphlet will be discussed in greater detail in the following chapter. See also [Ducroisi], *L'homme aux trois révérences, ou Le comédien remis à sa place; étrennes à ces messieurs: Pour l'année 1790. Par un neveu de M. l'abbé Maury* (n.p., [1789]), 10, who comments on the "hasty choice" of the actors and expresses the conviction that they will shortly be sent back to the theaters.

11. See de Boizi, *Considérations importantes,* 12: "Will you forgive Mr. Naudet . . . [for his] abuse of the grenadiers which he has the honor of commanding, in making use of them to impose silence upon those among you [in the parterre] who would [otherwise] like to force him to show the respect which he owes you? Is this the kind of work that suits a National Guard? Does [the guard] wish to be brought down to the vile functions of the old regime's satellites?"

Naudet defended himself against this charge (as well as a similar allegation leveled by Camille Desmoulins in no. 39 of his *Révolutions de France et de Brabant*) in his *Réponse de M. Naudet,* in which he included a letter written by the grenadiers whom he commanded, assuring Parisians "that Mr. Naudet has never made use of the individuals who compose [his troop] for service at the Théâtre-Français" (9). For another defense of Naudet, see [J.-B. Laborde], *Justification des comédiens français. Opinions sur les chefs d'oeuvre des auteurs morts, & projet de décret portant règlement entre les auteurs dramatiques & tous les comédiens du royaume* (Paris, 1790), 8–9.

12. Cited in Lyonnet, "Comédiens révolutionnaires," in *La nouvelle revue* (15 January 1924): 179.

13. My information on Grammont's career is derived from the following sources: Richard Cobb, *The People's Armies,* trans. Marianne Elliott (New Haven: Yale University Press, 1987), 68–70; d'Estrée, *Théâtre sous la Terreur,* 298–99; Lyonnet, "Comédiens révolutionnaires" (MS), 51–52; and C. G. Etienne and A. Martainville, *Histoire du Théâtre-Français, depuis le commencement de la Révolution jusqu'à la réunion générale* (Paris, 1802), 2:178. I have also relied upon references to Grammont contained in Guibert and Razgonnikoff, *Le journal de la Comédie-Française.* Perhaps the most detailed, if not the most rigorously footnoted, biography of Grammont can be found in the chapter entitled "Un comédien révolutionnaire," in Pougin, *La Comédie-Française,* 295–332.

14. On Ronsin's military career and his relationship with Grammont and the other actors of the Théâtre Montansier, see Cobb, *People's Armies,* 62–70. Cobb writes that Grammont hired Folleville, Gaillard, and Lavault onto the general staff and remarks that Grammont had but one adjunct who was not an actor (69).

15. Lyonnet, d'Estrée, and Guibert all seem certain of this fact. See also Pierre Frantz, "Pas d'entracte pour la Révolution," in *La Carmagnole des muses: L'homme de lettres et l'artiste dans la Révolution,* ed. Jean-Claude Bonnet (Paris: Armand Colin, 1988), 383.

16. The Théâtre-Français possessed the exclusive privilege to perform virtually all of France's dramatic masterpieces.

17. Lyonnet, "Comédiens révolutionnaires" (MS), 54. Lyonnet writes that Fusil was booed off the stage for his Jacobin ties when he first returned to the theater after Thermidor.

18. Ibid., 53.

19. Cobb, *People's Armies,* 230. According to Cobb, Dufresse's enthusiasm for the Terror was more "playacting" than real conviction, thus accounting for his acquittal by the Thermidorian court.

20. Most of the theaters of Paris formed such troops in response to the general alarm. On the troop formed by the Théâtre Montansier, see A.N., C. 163 (micro), no. 372, piece 25 (3 September 1793). See also Lyonnet, "Comédiens révolutionnaires" (MS), 31–34. For information on troops assembled by the Théâtre de la Liberté, Théâtre de l'Egalité,

and the Théâtre du Palais, see A.N., C. 163 (micro), no. 374, f. 69, piece 24 (7 September 1792). See also the document cited in Alexandre Tuetey, *Répertoire général des sources manuscrites de l'histoire de Paris pendant la Révolution française* (Paris: Imprimerie nouvelle, 1890–1914), 4:239 (no. 1918), which refers to the troops formed by the Théâtre de la rue Richelieu and the Théâtre du Palais (Tuetey gives his source as A.N., C. 167, no. 405). And a document contained in the archives of the B.C.-F. details the formation of the troop of actors of the Théatre de la Liberté et de l'Egalité (box labeled 1791–1793).

21. My source for Saint-Preux's military career is an undated archival document, apparently in Saint-Preux's own hand, with the heading "Conduite civique du citoyen Auvray dit St. Preux depuis l'année 1789." A.N., F¹⁷ 1294, dossier 4.

22. A.N., AA 40, dossier 1300. Lyonnet mentions another actor-soldier by the name of Maillot who similarly strutted the stages in enemy territory. Lyonnet, "Comédiens révolutionnaires," *La nouvelle revue* (1 May 1924): 59.

23. See the following chapter.

24. *Le paysan magistrat* was performed at the Théâtre-Français (newly renamed Théâtre de la Nation) on 7 December 1789. Guibert and Razgonnikoff, *Le journal de la Comédie-Française*, 72.

25. The almanac of Parisian theater for the year 1792 gave the following review of Collot's play *Les deux porte-feuilles*: "This little play, full of gaiety, and an analogy to current events, is one of the plays that has had the most success in the [Théâtre de Monsieur]." [Louis-Abel Beffroy de Reigny et al.], *Almanach général de tous les spectacles de Paris et de la province, pour l'année 1792* (Paris, 1792), 74. The almanac also referred to Collot as one of the "authors who are justly appreciated by the sane portion of the public" (35).

26. By 1792 Collot had become active on the Committee of Correspondence, which the historian François Furet has called "the most important of the [Jacobin] Club's internal organs . . . [and] the heart of the Jacobin apparatus." François Furet, "Jacobinism," in *A Critical Dictionary of the French Revolution*, ed. François Furet and Mona Ozouf, trans. Arthur Goldhammer (Cambridge: Harvard University Press, 1989), 707.

27. Testimony of Marie Jeane Elizabeth Brocard Jolly, 26 ventôse II. A.N., W 78, plaq. 2, piece 131.

28. This incident and these claims are discussed more fully in chap. 8.

29. Cobb, *People's Armies*, 68.

30. Ibid., 373, 580.

31. Dorfeuille, quoted in R. R. Palmer, *Twelve Who Ruled: The Year of the Terror in the French Revolution* (Princeton: Princeton University Press, 1973), 170–71. On Dorfeuille's theatrical and political career, see Lyonnet, "Comédiens révolutionnaires," in *La nouvelle revue* (15 August 1924): 373–74. In addition to his role as the president of the Commission de justice in Lyon, Dorfeuille had also been the *commissaire des représentants du peuple* in Roanne.

32. [Louis-Abel Beffroy de Reigny], *Dictionnaire néologique des hommes et des choses, etc par le cousin Jacques* (Paris, year VIII), 3:392–95. On Collot's motivation for his role in the siege of Lyon, Beffroy de Reigny wrote, "Collot d'Herbois, [when performing as an actor in pre-Revolutionary Lyon] . . . seeing that the Lyonnais persisted in their irreverence by greeting him with boos [when he appeared on the stage], swore that sooner or later he would avenge himself upon them. . . . Chance played only too well into his plans and desires!"

33. For the theatrical background on Fabre d'Eglantine, I have relied primarily on Lyonnet's short biography in "Comédiens révolutionnaires," *La nouvelle revue* (15 August 1922): 90–94 and (1 September 1922): 276–81.

34. *Arrêté du district des Cordeliers, du 5 mars 1790. Extrait des registres des délibérations de l'assemblée du district des Cordeliers. Du 5 mars 1790* (n.p., [1790]).
35. See the favorable notice in [L.-A. Beffroy de Reigny et al.], *Almanach général de tous les spectacles de Paris et des provinces, pour l'année 1791* (Paris, [1791]), 146. It is also worth noting that both Fabre and Collot are included among the twenty-five most prestigious playwrights in Paris who signed a document in support of authors' property rights to their plays. See *Réponse aux observations pour les Comédiens-Français* (n.p., 1790), 56. Despite this fact, both Collot and Fabre were singled out by the actors and theater directors of Lyon as two out of four "justly famous" playwrights who, in contradistinction to the rest of their colleagues, treated actors in a considerate fashion. See *Mémoire pour les comédiens du spectacle de Lyon; contre les auteurs dramatiques* (n.p., n.d.), 48.
36. See *Almanach général . . . 1792*, 240.
37. See above. Both Lyonnet and Guibert and Razgonnikoff (*Le journal de la Comédie-Française*, 352) make reference to this relationship.
38. Lyonnet, "Comédiens révolutionnaires" (MS), 279.
39. Robespierre, "Rapport sur les principes de morale politique qui doivent guider la Convention nationale dans l'administration intérieure de la république" (delivered to the National Convention in the name of the Committee of Public Safety, 5 February 1794), in *Oeuvres de Maximilien Robespierre*, ed. Laponneraye (New York: Burt Franklin, 1970), 3:565.
40. See also the comment Billaud-Varenne made to Danton when the latter attempted to defend his friend: "Woe betide the man who has sat by the side of Fabre-d'Eglantine and who is still duped by him." Cited in Albert Soboul, *The French Revolution: From the Storming of the Bastille to Napoleon*, trans. Alan Forrest and Colin Jones (New York: Vintage, 1975), 368.
41. Boursault to Danton and others, dated 3 September 1792. A.N., F^{17} 1069, dossier 2.
42. Arthur Pougin, "Un original: Boursault-Malherbe, fondateur du Théâtre Molière en 1791," extracted from the *Revue d'art dramatique* (and contained in the collection of the Bibliothèque de l'Arsenal Rt 3159), 195. Lyonnet notes that this article was also printed in *Bulletin de la Société de l'histoire du théâtre* (2d year [1903], no. 6).
43. A.N., F^{17} 1069, dossier 2.
44. A.N., F^{17} 1069, dossier 7 (5e division. Théâtres ans IV–VII).
45. Pougin, "Un original," 197; Lyonnet, "Comédiens révolutionnaires" (MS), 25.
46. *Réponse des citoyens . . . A un écrit . . . intitulé: Réflexions nécessaires à l'intelligence de l'état actif et passif, présenté par le citoyen Boursault à ses créanciers . . .* (n.p., [1792]), 4–5.
47. Lyonnet, "Comédiens révolutionnaires" (MS), 52–53. See also Frantz, "Pas d'entracte pour la Révolution," 383.
48. According to Lyonnet, Beaulieu, an actor at the Variétés amusantes, was present at the taking of the Bastille and was later named a captain in the National Guard. Lyonnet, "Comédiens révolutionnaires," in *La nouvelle revue* (1 May 1924): 54–55. Lyonnet mentions another actor by the name of Ribié, employed at the Théâtre de Nicolet, who also was present at the taking of the Bastille and also was later named a captain in the National Guard. Ibid. (15 July 1924): 170.
49. See Boursault's comments above on his activity in Marseille during the Revolutionary *journées*. In addition, the provincial actor Brisse, who was later to become mayor of Nancy, claimed that he took part in Revolutionary events in Rouen during the summer of 1789. A.N., F^{17} 1216.
50. See the following chapter.

51. *Le petit almanac des grands spectacles de Paris* (Paris, 1792), 157.

52. Much of the biographical background on Lacombe can be found in Lyonnet, "Comédiens révolutionnaires," in *La nouvelle revue* (1 September 1924): 83–90.

53. Claire Lacombe, *Discours prononcé à la barre de l'Assemblée nationale, par Madame Lacombe, le 25 juillet 1792, l'an 4e de la liberté* (Paris, [1792]), as translated by Darline Gay Levy, Harriet Branson Applewhite, and Mary Durham Johnson, *Women in Revolutionary Paris: 1789–1795* (Urbana: University of Illinois Press), 156.

54. Lyonnet, "Comédiens révolutionnaires" (MS), 86; and *Women in Revolutionary Paris*, 144.

55. Cited in *Women in Revolutionary Paris*, 183.

56. D'Estrée, *Théâtre sous la Terreur*, 268. On Vergniaud's eloquence, as well as his writing and possibly acting in plays, see also Jean-Denis Bredin, "Vergniaud, ou Le génie de la parole," in François Furet and Mona Ozouf, *La Gironde et les Girondins* (Paris: Payot, 1991), 369–70.

57. *Dispatches from Paris, 1784–1790*, excerpted in *The Old Regime and the French Revolution*, ed. Keith Baker (Chicago: University of Chicago Press, 1987), 188–89.

58. Arthur Young, *Travels in France during the Years 1787, 1788, and 1789*, ed. Constantia Maxwell (Cambridge: Cambridge University Press, 1950), 144.

59. Cited in Lynn Hunt, "The 'National Assembly,' " in *The French Revolution and the Creation of Modern Political Culture*, vol. 1: *The Political Culture of the Old Regime*, ed. Keith Michael Baker (Oxford: Pergamon Press, 1987), 412.

60. Cited in Angelica Goodden, "The Dramatising of Politics: Theatricality and the Revolutionary Assemblies," *Forum for Modern Language Studies* 20, no. 3 (July 1984): 204. See also a similar example cited by Goodden in which the *Mercure* reported that a proposal by the abbé Maury, on the floor of the Assembly, could not be heard because it was drowned out by "a general brouhaha, and the applause of the galleries . . . which either think of themselves as the representatives of France or believe that they are attending the Comédie-Italienne" (ibid.).

61. Alain-Charles Gruber, *Les grandes fêtes et leurs décors à l'époque de Louis XVI* (Geneva: Droz, 1972), 141–42.

62. Ibid., 144–45.

63. Young, *Travels in France*, 254. For the dates on which the National Assembly moved into its various salles, I have relied on the list provided in Colin Jones, *The Longman Companion to the French Revolution* (London: Longman, 1990), 166.

64. Mercier, quoted in Marie-Hélène Huet, *Rehearsing the Revolution: The Staging of Marat's Death, 1793–1797*, trans. Robert Hurley (Berkeley: University of California Press, 1982), 2.

65. Joseph Butwin, "The French Revolution as Theatrum Mundi," *Research Studies* 43, no. 3 (1975): 144.

66. Maximilien Robespierre, "Sur le gouvernement représentatif [Prononcé à l'Assemblée nationale, séance du 10 mai 1793]," in *Robespierre: Textes choisis* (Paris: Editions Sociales, 1957), 2:151.

67. Edmund Burke, *Reflections on the Revolution in France*, ed. Conor Cruise O'Brien (New York: Penguin, 1981), 161.

68. See Goodden, "Dramatising of Politics," 199, 210. See also Butwin, "French Revolution as Theatrum Mundi," 148.

69. See, for example, the pro-Jacobin pamphlet *Le véritable portrait de nos législateurs, ou Galerie des tableaux exposés à la vue du public depuis le 5 mai 1789, jusqu'au premier octobre 1791* (Paris, 1792), which brands Mirabeau a "Grand Comédien" (9) and claims that the bulk of his speeches were scripted by others (14). See also *Evénemens*

remarquables & intéressans, à l'occasion des Décrets de l'auguste Assemblée nationale, concernant l'éligibilité de MM. les comédiens, le bourreau, & les Juifs (n.p., 1790), in which a fictional Mirabeau not only confesses before the National Assembly that he is an actor but also unmasks a good number of his political colleagues as fellow thespians.

70. Cited in Goodden, "Dramatising of Politics," 206.

71. Etienne and Martainville, *Histoire du Théâtre-Français*, 1:195–96. See also Hérissay, *Le monde des théâtres*, 85.

72. It is interesting to note that a mid-nineteenth-century bibliography seemed so confused by the title that it branded this work a satire. A reading of the play reveals quite plainly, however, that the work is not a satire. See Joseph de Filippi, *Essai d'une bibliographie du théâtre: ou, Catalogue raisonné de la bibliothèque d'un amateur, complétant le catalogue Soleinne* (Paris: Tresse, 1861).

73. For example, the phrase "seal of the magistrates" (p. 17) of the 1786 version is replaced with "seal of the nation" in the 1791 version (p. 9). In addition, a reference that might have explicitly excluded individuals outside the theater in the 1786 version—"The stage represents the foyer of the Théâtre-Français, where the busts of the great men of this theater are arrayed in relief" (p. 5)—was transformed in the later version to "The theater represents the foyer of the Théâtre de la Nation, where the busts of great men are arrayed" (p. 2). De Valigny, *Le poëte au foyer, ou L'éloge des grands hommes du Théâtre François, scène lyrique nouvelle en prose* (Paris, 1786); De Valigny, *Le poëte au foyer, ou L'éloge des grands hommes du Théâtre de la Nation; y compris celui de Mirabeau. Scène lyrique nouvelle* (Paris, 1791).

74. De Valigny, *Le poëte au foyer* (1791), 11–12.

75. *Almanach général . . . 1792*, 225.

76. Bibliothèque nationale de France (B.N.F.), MSS, nouv. acq. fr. 2665, fol. 266 (15 juin 1790).

77. Ibid., fol. 267.

78. *Almanach général . . . 1791*, 1:266–68.

79. Ibid., 258.

80. Ibid., 258–59.

81. Cited in J. Charrier, *Claude Fauchet: Evêque constitutionnel du Calvados, député à l'assemblée législative et à la Convention (1744–1793)* (Paris, 1909), 169.

82. *La bouche de fer* no. 3 (October 1790): 17.

83. *La bouche de fer* no. 1 (October 1790): 15.

84. Cited in Charrier, *Claude Fauchet*, 169.

85. Cited in Goodden, "Dramatising of Politics," 204.

86. Etienne and Martainville, *Histoire du Théâtre-Français*, 1:156–57.

87. This topic is discussed more fully in chapter 7.

88. For background information on La Montansier, which I have occasionally made use of in this chapter, see Ch. Gailly de Taurines, "Une campagne en Belgique," in *Revue des deux mondes* (April 1904): 670–83; Lyonnet, "Comédiens révolutionnaires" (MS), 31–36; and Marie-Laurence Netter, "Theatres and Their Directors," in *Theatre, Opera, and Audiences in Revolutionary Paris: Analysis and Repertory*, ed. Emmet Kennedy, Marie-Laurence Netter, James P. McGregor, and Mark V. Olsen (Westport, Conn.: Greenwood Press, 1996), 70–71.

89. Montansier to Minister of Foreign Affairs Lebrun, 26 November 1792. A.N., F1c 11, dossier 5.

90. Dufresse had been Moreton's ordinance officer at Jemappes. Lyonnet, "Comédiens révolutionnaires" (MS), 34. According to Montansier's letter, he was now Moreton's aide-de-camp.

91. See the description of Grammont's career above.

92. Montansier to Minister of Foreign Affairs Lebrun, 26 November 1792. A.N., F^{ie} 11, dossier 5.

93. Ibid.

94. Ibid. Gailly de Taurine wrote (in 1904) that Montansier's list was appended to her first letter. "Une campagne en Belgique," 675. By the time I consulted these documents, however, the repertory was loose in the folder, without a date.

95. Chépy to Lebrun, 18 November 1792 (received the twenty-first). A.N., F^{ie} 11, dossier 2.

96. Lebrun to La Montansier, 27 November 1792. A.N., F^{ie} 11, dossier 5.

97. Lebrun to La Montansier, 29 November 1792. A.N., F^{ie} 11, dossier 5.

98. Montansier to Lebrun (n.d.). A.N., F^{ie} 11, dossier 5.

99. Lebrun to the administrators of the Opéra, 1 December 1792. A.N., F^{ie} 11, dossier 7.

100. Ibid.

101. Montansier to Lebrun, 4 January 1793. A.N., F^{ie} 11, dossier 5.

102. Ibid.

103. Montansier to Lebrun, 8 January 1793. A.N., F^{ie} 11, dossier 5.

104. *Pierre le cruel* was performed at the Théâtre de la Citoyenne Montansier four times over the course of October and November 1791. In addition to *Pierre le cruel*, Montansier's theater had performed two other plays by Belloy from July to December of 1791: seven performances of *Zelmire* and two performances of *Gabrielle de Vergy*. This information comes from an extraordinary database entitled "The Parisian Stage during the French Revolution," compiled by Emmet Kennedy, Marie-Laurence Netter, James P. McGregor, and Mark V. Olsen; it can be accessed at http://barkov.uchicago.edu/mark/projects/theatre/ (June, 2001). This datebase is a more complete version of findings that were partially published in *Theatre, Opera, and Audiences*.

105. Montansier to Lebrun, 4 January 1793. A.N., F^{ie} 11, dossier 5.

106. Ibid.

107. Bill [from Montansier] to the [Executive] Council. A.N., F^{ie} 11, dossier 7.

108. Report of Deshacquets to the minister of foreign affairs, cited in Gailly de Taurines, "Une campagne en Belgique," 681.

109. Ibid.

110. Bill [from Montansier] to the [Executive] Council. A.N., F^{ie} 11, dossier 7.

CHAPTER 6. THEATER CRITICS

1. Estimates of the number of actors in France in 1789 range from 100,000 to 200,000. See abbé Bonnefoy de Bouyon, *La civilisation des comédiens, ou La demande que personne n'a faite à la nation assemblée* (Paris, 1789), 7; and Jean-Louis Laya, *La régénération des comédiens en France, ou Leurs droits à l'état civil* (Paris, 1789), 31. By comparison, the number of Jews is estimated at between 40,000 and 50,000. Robert Badinter, *Libres et égaux . . . : L'émancipation des Juifs, 1789–1791* (Paris: Fayard, 1989), 18. The other group denied a civil status in the old regime simply on the basis of their profession was the relatively small number of executioners in the kingdom.

2. See the previous chapter.

3. [De Lavaud], *Réflexions sur la garde bourgeoise en général, et en particulier sur l'organisation de la garde nationale parisienne* (n.p., [1789]), 4.

4. Ibid., 17.

5. *Les comédiens commandans MM. Naudet, Grammont, St-Pry, Marcy, Dugazon,*

Chamville, tous comédiens français. A Messieurs les Parisiens (Paris, 1789), 4. Further references in parentheses in the text.

6. The practice of putting the definite article before the names of actors was often considered to be inherently demeaning and implied, in the eyes of many, an objectification of the actor in his relationship to the audience (a theme I discuss below). As a supporter of actors would declare a few months later, within the context of the debates on the actors' civil status in the National Assembly, "We used to say *la Duménil, la Doligni* [two well-known Parisian actresses]: This word *la* was invented only to imprint a stain on the name of the actor; consequently, it must be blotted out of our dictionaries, and never again made use of in our language." Bouyon, *La civilisation des comédiens,* 14.

7. [O. Ducroisi], *L'homme aux trois révérences, ou Le comédien remis à sa place; étrennes à ces messieurs: Pour l'année 1790. Par un neveu de M. l'abbé Maury* (n.p., [1789]), 10.

8. On the concept of the actor as the plaything of spectators, Rousseau wrote the following in his *Letter to d'Alembert on the Theater:* "But a comédien on the stage, displaying sentiments that are not his own, saying only what he is made to say, often represents a chimerical being, and annihilates himself, so to speak, loses himself in his hero; and, in this forgetting of the man, if anything remains, it becomes the plaything of spectators." J.-J. Rousseau, *Lettre à Mr d'Alembert sur les spectacles,* ed. M. Fuchs (Lille: Droz, 1948), 108.

9. Camille Desmoulins, *Discours de la lanterne aux Parisiens* (Paris, 1789), 39.

10. Georges Lefebvre claims that the Rouen incident is more a part of the long-standing fear of brigands than of the Great Fear itself. See Georges Lefebvre, *The Great Fear of 1789: Rural Panic in Revolutionary France,* trans. Joan White (New York: Schocken, 1989), 202.

11. *La mort subite du sieur Bordier, acteur des Variétés. Lettre d'un négociant de Rouen, à M. Guillaume, Marchand de Draps, rue Saint-Denis, du 22 août 1789* (n.p, [1789]), 1. Further references in parentheses in the text.

12. *Bordier aux enfers, comédie en un acte* (Paris, 1789), 11–12. The catalogue of the Bibliothèque nationale de France lists the author of this text as Beffroy de Reigny, a prolific critic of Revolutionary representative forms, both political and theatrical. Further references in parentheses in the text.

13. See also a play entitled *Jugement de Bordier, dans l'empire des morts,* which also portrays Bordier as ranting on in the afterworld. In this text, Bordier arrives in the empire of the dead, where he tries to join the ranks of France's great dead actors. These luminaries are so disgusted by his uncultured manner and his endless jabbering that they consider sending him back to the land of the living to be hanged again—clearly an extremely popular solution. When this proves impossible, they issue the following sentence: "Bordier, a bad, histrionic actor, [is condemned] . . . in order to atone for crimes against the French language, . . . to chew until the end of time the same works with which he corrupted and gave cause to corrupt the language of his country." As in the other pamphlets, Bordier is condemned to a perpetual sentence that seems to have the added benefit of stopping the incessant flow of words from his mouth. *Jugement de Bordier, dans l'empire des morts, ou Lettre de Lekain aux amateurs* (Paris, [1789]), 6.

14. *Les iniquités découvertes, ou L'innocence reconnue des sieurs Bordier et Jourdain. Démontrée par les dépositions des témoins, sur lesquelles néanmoins le sieur Flambart, lieutenant de la maréchaussée de Rouen, a prononcé la peine infamante de leur mort. Dédié aux destructeurs des aristocrates, par ordre des ennemis du despotisme* (Paris, 1789), 11.

15. Ibid.

332 | Notes to Pages 209–218

16. [Dumaniant], *Mort de Bordier, acteur des Variétés* (Paris, n.d.), 6.

17. Archives of the Bibliothèque de la Comédie-Française (B.C.-F.), from a box labeled "XVIIIe s. 1789–1791."

18. Letter dated 24 September 1789 (archives of the B.C.-F.).

19. *Suite du procès-verbal de l'Assemblée nationale de samedi 26 septembre 1789, au matin [don de la Comédie-Française de 23,000 livres à l'Assemblée]* (Paris, n.d.).

20. The general dossier "XVIIIe s. 1789–1791" in the archives of the B.C.-F. contains a significant number of such records.

21. Brousse Desfaucherets, *Compte rendu à l'assemblée générale des représentans de la commune de Paris, le huit février 1790, par M. Brousse Desfaucherets, lieutenant de maire au département des etablissemens-public* ([Paris], 1790), 18.

22. Archives of the B.C.-F., XVIIIe s. 1789–1791.

23. See *Cahier plaintes et doléances de messieurs les Comédiens-Français* (n.p., 1789), 9–12, for an apparently half-serious, half-satirical portrayal of the debate within the ranks of the comédiens on what the name of the theater should be. See also *Défense des comédiens françois, contre les auteurs dramatiques, adressée au comité de Constitution* ([Paris], [1790]), 8–9, for a criticism of the actors' political fence straddling.

24. Archives of the B.C.-F., "Feux," vol. 20, 1789–90.

25. [Ducroisi], *L'homme aux trois révérences*, 3.

26. [Duchosal], *Dénonciation des Comédiens-Français* (n.p., 1790), 3.

27. A. L. Millin, *Sur la liberté du théâtre* (Paris, 1790), 34–35.

28. *La critique de la tragédie de Charles IX; comédie* (Paris, 1790), 4.

29. My discussion here is necessarily limited to male actors, as the question of the actress's civil status was subsumed under the general question of the civil and political status of women in the new regime. The civil status of actresses, in short, was a moot question, as their sex necessarily precluded their consideration for civil and political eligibility. It should be noted, however, that the supporters of the actors were not above attempting to shift problematic moral stereotypes against actors onto their female colleagues as a means of rehabilitating the image of male actors in the eyes of the public. See Paul Friedland, "Representation and Revolution: The Theatricality of Politics and the Politics of Theater in France, 1798–94" (Ph.D. diss., University of California at Berkeley, 1995), chap. 4.

30. [Ducroisi], *L'homme aux trois révérences*, 7.

31. Palissot, cited in ibid., 9.

32. Ibid., 4.

33. Ibid., 11–12.

34. Ibid., 13.

35. *Révolutions de Paris* 23 (December 1789): 6–7.

36. Laya, *La régénération des comédiens en France*, 19.

37. Bouyon, *La civilisation des comédiens*, 5.

38. In the decade before the Revolution, numerous texts were published which, in their portraits of the private life of actors, aimed either to excite or to scandalize their readers (perhaps both). A typical example of such pamphlets is [François-Marie Mayeur de Saint-Paul], *Le désoeuvré, ou L'espion du boulevard du Temple* (London, 1781), which detailed the sexual exploits of the comédiens of Paris's boulevard theaters.

39. Letter from the comédiens of the Théâtre-Français to the representatives of the National Assembly, contained in a folder labeled "Ecrits relatifs à l'état civil du comédien et aux différentes préjuger [sic] detruits ou à détruire," in the archives of the B.C.-F.

40. M. J. Chénier, "Courtes réflexions sur l'état civil des comédiens, 6 septembre, 1789," in *Oeuvres de M. J. Chénier* (Paris, 1825), 4:448–49.

41. *Archives parlementaires de 1787 à 1860* (Paris, 1875), 10:694. Unless otherwise stated, all quotations from debates in the National Assembly are from this collection.

42. The original of this letter can be found in Archives nationales, AA 40, dossier 1300.

43. On the actors' monitoring of the debates, see below, the letter from Dazincourt addressed to Mlle La Chassaigne, reporting the outcome of the debates that same night. On the lobbying efforts of the actors' supporters, see below, the letter from the abbé Bouyon to Florence, an actor and administrative officer at the Théâtre-Français.

44. This logic, according to which the Assembly might declare a question moot, or already decided, rather than dare to decree something that might not play well in public opinion, recalls Sieyès's logic according to which the National Assembly was spared the unpleasantness of abolishing the binding mandate. By declaring that the binding mandate had already been annulled de facto, the Assembly could declare that there were no grounds to deliberate on the question. (See chap. 4.)

45. Dazincourt to La Chassaigne, 24 December 1789, in the archives of the B.C.-F., XVIIIe s. 1789–91.

46. Bouyon to Florence, an actor and administrator at the Théâtre-Français, 24 December 1789, in the archives of the B.C.-F., XVIIIe s. 1789–91.

47. *Evénemens remarquables & intéressans, à l'occasion des décrets de l'auguste Assemblée nationale, concernant l'éligibilité de MM. les comédiens, le bourreau, & les Juifs* (n.p., 1790), 9–10.

48. Rousseau, *Lettre à Mr d'Alembert sur les spectacles*, 164–65.

49. *L'homme aux trois révérences*, 12–13. These words, expressed through the character of the elderly gentleman, were purportedly added as a postscript to the pamphlet after the news of the Assembly's decree had been announced.

CHAPTER 7. THE FEAR AND RIDICULE OF REVOLUTIONARY REPRESENTATIONS

1. Edmund Burke, *Reflections on the Revolution in France and on the Proceedings in Certain Societies in London Relative to that Event*, ed. Conor Cruise O'Brien (New York: Penguin, 1969), 92–93.

2. I use the term *Jacobin* loosely to mean the radical left in general and to comprise (not exclusively, but perhaps most characteristically) the Jacobins and the Cordeliers after the purging of the Feuillants.

3. [Comte Murat de Montferrand], *Qu'est-ce que l'Assemblée nationale? Grande thèse en présence de l'auteur anonyme de Qu'est-ce que le tiers? Et dédiée au très-honorable Edmund Burke, comme à un véritable ami de la vraie liberté* (n.p., 1791), 93–94. Further references in parentheses in the text.

4. *Encyclopédie, ou Dictionnaire raisonnée des sciences, des arts, et des métiers* (Paris, 1751), 1:45.

5. *Encyclopédie*, 1:45.

6. *Supplément à l'Encyclopédie, ou Dictionnaire raisonné des sciences, des arts, et des métiers* (Amsterdam, 1776–77), 1:70.

7. Rousseau was perhaps the most determined of eighteenth-century anti-abstractionists. For a few examples of Rousseau's anti-abstractionism, see his condemnation of political representation in book 3 of *Du contrat social*, especially chapters 14 and 15; and for Rousseau's critique of theatrical representation and the arts in general, see the entire texts of the *Lettre à M. d'Alembert* and *De l'imitation théâtrale*. In the latter text, Rousseau brands dramatic authors "the people's corrupters" and compares theatrical representation to the painting of a palace built by an architect, regarding

20. *La corruption de l'Assemblée nationale, et les crimes de ses membres; par un ami de la vérité* (Paris, 1790), 10–11.

21. Ibid., 29–38. See also *Le véritable portrait de nos législateurs,* which takes the trouble to unmask several members of the Assembly as disguised enemies of the people, but which passes over the people's more obvious enemies, declaring, "I did not think it necessary to speak of the *noirs* or aristocrats; they are known." *Le véritable portrait de nos législateurs, ou Galerie des tableaux exposés à la vue du public depuis le 5 mai 1789, jusqu'au premier octobre 1791* (Paris, 1792), 163.

22. *Usurpations et attentats de l'Assemblée nationale, pour servir de parallèle à la conduite de Louis XVI* (Geneva, 1790), 22.

23. *La corruption de l'Assemblée nationale,* 6–7.

24. De Baecque, *Body Politic,* 166–67.

25. Etienne Bonnot de Condillac, "Traité des systêmes," in *Oeuvres de Condillac* (Paris, 1798), 130. Emphasis is mine.

26. Nicolas-Joseph-Laurent Gilbert, "Le dix-huitième siècle," in *Oeuvres de Gilbert* (Paris: Garnier Frères, 1859), 29–30.

27. Ibid., 51.

28. [Ferrand], *Les conspirateurs démasqués,* 57.

29. [Antoine Ferrand], *Nullité et despotisme de l'Assemblée prétendue nationale* (n.p., [1790]), 16–17.

30. Ibid., 34–35.

31. [Ferrand], *Les conspirateurs démasqués,* 59.

32. [Ferrand], *Nullité et despotisme,* 5.

33. [Ferrand], *Tableau de la conduite de l'Assemblée prétendue nationale,* 64–65.

34. [Antoine Ferrand], *Lettre à mes concitoyens . . .* ([Paris], [1790]), 16.

35. [Ferrand], *Les conspirateurs démasqués,* 60.

36. [Antoine Ferrand], *Ambition et égoïsme de l'Assemblée nationale* (Paris, 1790), 13–14.

37. [Ferrand], *Tableau de la conduite de l'Assemblée prétendue nationale,* 3.

38. [Ferrand], *Les conspirateurs démasqués,* 48.

39. [L.-A. Beffroy de Reigny], *Dictionnaire néologique des hommes et des choses, etc par le cousin Jacques* (Paris, an VIII), 3:411. Beffroy de Reigny was by no means a counterrevolutionary in the conventional sense of the word. In many respects he supported the Revolution, but he remained critical of the system of representation that it had brought into existence. But in the sense that he challenged the very theory of representation itself, his writing is perhaps more typical of counterrevolutionaries than of Jacobins.

40. *La corruption de l'Assemblée nationale,* 11

41. Ibid., 4.

42. I am using the hyphenated form of the word *representation* here to imply that the Jacobins struggled for a literal embodiment of the general will rather than the more abstract representation of the moderates. In this sense, then, the Jacobin re-presentation retains certain elements of the pre-Revolutionary system of re-presentation, with the important difference that actual physical embodiment did not play a part in the Jacobin system, as it had in the pre-Revolutionary system.

43. I am here borrowing the terminology of "obstruction" and "transparency" that Jean Starobinski coined in his masterful study of Rousseau, *Jean-Jacques Rousseau: Transparency and Obstruction,* trans. Arthur Goldhammer (Chicago: University of Chicago Press, 1988), and that was later employed by Lynn Hunt and François Furet (among others) in their studies of left-wing Revolutionary rhetoric.

44. *Avis aux citoyens françois, sur le choix des officiers municipaux, des membres des*

assemblées de districts et de départemens. Par l'auteur de L'adresse au peuple breton (Paris, [1790]), 1–2.

45. *Avis aux citoyens sur la prochaine formation des assemblées de département et de district* (n.p., [1790]), 3–4.

46. *Encyclopédie,* 1:45.

47. Joseph-Ignace Guillotin, *Pétition des citoyens domiciliés à Paris. Du 8 décembre 1788* (Paris, 1788), 11–12.

48. *Supplément à l'Encyclopédie,* 1:69.

49. Jacobin conceptions of the general will are discussed in the following chapter. See, in particular, the discussion of the Jacobin pamphlet *Oh! elle est bien nommée la section du Théâtre-Français, car elle nous donne la comédie,* which was dedicated to challenging the notion that the general will was in any sense divisible and that the sectional government—as a mere abstraction of the general will—could act independently of the nation as a whole.

50. *Le véritable portrait de nos législateurs,* 4–5. The parenthetical sentence quoting Lafayette is contained in a footnote in the original text.

51. "Sur le gouvernement représentatif," a speech delivered before the National Assembly in the session of 10 May 1793, in *Robespierre: Textes choisis* (Paris: Editions Sociales, 1957), 2:154.

52. One might compare Robespierre's thoughts on re-presentation to those of Malesherbes, as expressed in his remonstrances of 1775, in that both cling to the idea that a personal and concrete relationship between the representative and the represented, within a system of abstract representation, might assure a certain transparency of representation. See the discussion of Malesherbes's remonstrances in chap. 2.

53. *Le véritable portrait de nos législateurs,* 163–64.

54. Ibid., 2 (my emphasis), 9, 4–5. This last quote was cited earlier. It is interesting to compare this denunciation of individuals with "the language of patriotism on their lips" to Gilbert's denunciation of the monster of abstraction for whom "the name of virtues is always on his lips."

55. See the interesting document "Extract from the Register of Deliberations of the General Council of the Commune of Paris, Twentieth Day of the First Month, Year II of the French Republic (11 September 1793)," which contains a list of "distinguishing characteristics of suspected persons," including the following, rather interesting telltale sign of treachery: "[t]hose who have the words *Liberty, Republic,* and *Patrie* constantly on their lips, but who consort with former nobles, counterrevolutionary priests, aristocrats, feuillants, moderates, and show concern for their fate." In *The Old Regime and the French Revolution,* ed. Keith Baker (Chicago: University of Chicago Press, 1987), 338.

56. Letter signed "Daumale," dated 21 July [1793], contained in the archives of the B.C.-F., 1791–93.

57. Nicolas Louis François de Neufchâteau, *Auteur de Paméla à la Convention nationale* (Paris, 1793), 3.

58. Arrest order dated 2 September 1793, contained in the archives of the B.C.-F.

59. Cited in Henri Welschinger, *Le théâtre de la Révolution: 1789–1799* (Paris: Charavay Frères, 1880), 60.

60. Ibid., 65.

61. See chap. 5.

62. See Henri Lyonnet, "Comédiens révolutionnaires," in *La nouvelle revue* (15 July 1924): 163.

63. A.N., F^{17} 1069, dossier 4, Comité d'Instruction publique; see also Lyonnet, "Comédiens révolutionnaires," in *La nouvelle revue* (15 January 1924): 51. Lyonnet men-

tions several other actors arrested during these months of what he calls "this rage to imprison actors and singers [of the Opéra]."

64. Cited in Mona Ozouf, *Festivals and the French Revolution*, trans. Alan Sheridan (Cambridge: Harvard University Press, 1988), 208. One might compare these words to those of Rousseau in his *Letter to d'Alembert on the Theater*: "But let us not adopt these exclusive spectacles that sadly confine a small number of people in some obscure cavern; which keeps them timid and immobile in silence and inaction. . . . No, happy people, these are not your festivals. It is in the open air, it is underneath the sky that you must assemble and give yourselves over to the sweet sentiment of your happiness." J.-J. Rousseau, *Lettre à Mr d'Alembert sur les spectacles*, ed. M. Fuchs (Lille: Droz, 1948), 168.

65. Jean Starobinski, *The Invention of Liberty, 1700–1789* (New York: Rizzoli, 1964), 102.

66. Judith Schlanger, *L'enjeu et le débat: Les passés intellectuels* (Paris: Hachette, 1979), 123.

67. "Extrait des registres du Comité de Salut public de la Convention nationale, du vingtième jour de ventôse l'an deuxième de la République française une et indivisible." A.N., F^{17} 1294, dossier 2.

68. Comité d'Instruction publique, "Autre arrêté du représentant du peuple et des commissaires du Comité de Salut public, chargés de la régénération des théâtres." A.N., F^{17} 1069, dossier 4.

CHAPTER 8. BREACHING THE FOURTH WALL

1. The French verb *siffler*, which literally means "to whistle," referred in general to any act by which audience members expressed their disapproval of an actor or the play itself.

2. See Jeffrey Ravel, *The Contested Parterre: Public Theater and French Political Culture, 1680–1791* (Ithaca: Cornell University Press, 1999), 159ff. See also Jules Bonnassies, *Comédie-Française. Notice historique sur les anciens bâtiments* (Paris: Aug. Aubry, 1868), 20.

3. *Cahier de doléances, remontrances, et instructions de l'assemblée de tous les ordres des théâtres royaux de Paris* (n.p., [1789]), 10.

4. *Défense des Comédiens-François, contre les auteurs dramatiques, adressée au comité de Constitution* ([Paris]: Laillet & Garnéry, [1790]), 9.

5. A. L. Millin, *Sur la liberté du théâtre* (Paris, 1790), 4. The second part of the quotation is from an intervening footnote that appears on p. 43.

6. See Isaac René Guy Le Chapelier, *Rapport fait par M. Le Chapelier, au nom du Comité de Constitution, sur la pétition des auteurs dramatiques dans la séance du jeudi 13 janvier 1791, avec le décret rendu dans cette séance* (Paris: Imprimerie nationale, 1791).

7. Report of the Assembly of the Comédiens du roi, Sunday, 19 July 1789. Archives of the Bibliothèque de la Comédie-Française (B.C.-F.), XVIIIe s. 1789–91.

8. Letter dated 19 August 1789. Archives of the B.C.-F., XVIIIe s. 1789–91. The information regarding the pamphlet's means of dissemination is given in Noëlle Guibert and Jacqueline Razgonnikoff, *Le journal de la Comédie-Francaise, 1787–1799: La Comédie aux trois couleurs* (Paris: Sides, 1989), 58.

9. [Ducroisi], *Adresse aux bons patriotes par Du Croisi* ([Paris], [1789]).

10. Internal memo of the Théâtre-Français, written in the hand of Delaporte, and dated the evening of 19 August 1789. Archives of the B.C.-F., XVIIIe s. 1789–91. The remainder of the details of the night of 19 August are from this memo.

11. *Courrier d'Avignon*, no. 7 (Wednesday, 2 September 1789): 291–92.

12. *Extrait de procès-verbal de l'assemblée des représentans de la commune de Paris du 20 août 1789* (n.p.,n.d.).

13. The information on the premiere, as well as the quotations from Desmoulins and Danton, are from Guibert and Razgonnikoff, *Le journal de la Comédie-Française,* 66–67. Danton's statement is also quoted in an article by André Tissier entitled "Les Comédiens-Français pendant la période révolutionnaire (1789–1799)," *Revue d'histoire du théâtre* (1980–81): 143. Neither of the texts offers a source for these quotations.

14. Chénier wrote a letter dated 18 May 1790 in which he demanded that the Comédiens-Français stop performing his plays. Archives of the B.C.-F., XVIIIe s. 1789–91.

15. See chap. 6 for the controversy surrounding this change of name.

16. Letter dated 10 July 1790. Chénier file in the archives of the B.C.-F.

17. This letter, which they sent to Chénier, was reprinted by the actors in their *Exposé de la conduite et des torts du sieur Talma, envers les Comédiens-Français* (Paris, 1790), 11–12.

18. Ibid., 12.

19. Henry Lyonnet, "Comédiens révolutionaires," MS contained in the Rondell Collection, Bibliothèque de l'Arsenal, 14.

20. De Boizi, *Considérations importantes sur ce qui se passe, depuis quelque tems, au prétendu Théâtre de la Nation, et particulièrement sur les persécutions exercées contre le Sieur Talma* (n.p., [1790]), 7. Note that the title refers to the theater as the *prétendu* (so-called) theater of the nation. The qualifying adjective *prétendu* was also applied to the National Assembly by several pamphlets that challenged its representational legitimacy.

21. On 19 July, a letter arrived at the Théâtre-Français from a *fédéré* names Toussent, requesting, on behalf of the Department of the Pas-de-Calais, a performance of *Charles IX* for all of its *fédérés*. Letter dated 19 July 1790 in the Chénier file at the archives of the B.C.-F. Also, on 22 July, Sarrasin, a member of the federation of Marseille, publicly requested, on behalf of the provincial *fédérés*, a performance of the play. See De Boizi, *Considérations importantes,* 7–8.

22. *Exposé,* 15.

23. Ibid., 16. Lyonnet claims that a political representative, who many said was Mirabeau, read a written demand in support of the performance of *Charles IX* at this point in the evening. I have found no independent verification of this claim. See Lyonnet, "Comédiens révolutionaires," 14.

24. *Exposé,* 16–17.

25. Ibid., 17.

26. Ibid., 18.

27. Ibid., 19.

28. Ibid., 20.

29. Ibid., 20–21.

30. Ibid., 21.

31. Signed document dated 2 August 1790 in the archives of the B.C.-F., XVIIIe s. 1789–91.

32. Mirabeau to Talma dated 27 July 1790, reprinted in De Boizi, *Considérations importantes,* 15–16.

33. Letter from Barthelemy, commander of the detachment of the National Guard of the district of Marseille, reprinted in De Boizi, *Considérations importantes,* 16–17. Both this letter and Mirabeau's were also reprinted in *Réflexions de M. Talma, et pièces justificatives sur un fait qui concerne le Théâtre de la Nation* (Paris, [1790]).

34. [Duchosal], *Dénonciation des Comédiens-Français* (n.p., 1790), 6–7.

35. [Camille Desmoulins], *Discours de la lanterne aux Parisiens* (Paris, 1789), 49.

36. Ibid.

37. At the time in which Desmoulins was writing, the sifflet was held up as one of the primary reasons why actors should not be considered eligible for public office. See the statement quoted in chap. 6 on the ridiculousness of a Parisian bourgeois being commanded by an individual whom he could, "for the sum total of forty-eight sous, applaud or siffler at his whim."

38. Desmoulins, *Discours de la lanterne*, 39–41. For another reference to the political sifflet, see Laya, *La régénération des comédiens en France, ou Leurs droits à l'état civil* (Paris, 1789), 40–41. Laya asks, "Will it be said . . . that there is something degrading in coming forth and being sifflé in public? . . . What! my friends, is not everyone here on earth sifflé . . . ?" Laya then proceeds to give a list of occupations subject to the sifflet, and concludes that "I could give a thousand more examples: but it will be enough for me to send those who do not believe me to the Assembly of our representatives: let them tell me upon their return if their ears aren't ringing from the sound of 1,199 sifflets against one orator."

39. Desmoulins, *Discours de la lanterne*, 27.

40. See chap. 5, where I have quoted Young referring to the noisy clapping and hissing of the spectators in the galleries as "an indecorum which is utterly destructive of the freedom of debate."

41. Cited in Angelica Goodden, "The Dramatising of Politics: Theatricality and the Revolutionary Assemblies," *Forum for Modern Language Studies* 20, no. 3 (July 1984): 203. Goodden also quotes Mallet du Pan complaining of representatives being "subject like histrions to the boos of spectators" (204).

42. See chap. 6.

43. Quoted in Goodden, "Dramatising of Politics," 202. The translation is mine.

44. See chap. 4.

45. *Histoire parlementaire de la Révolution française, ou Journal des assemblées nationales, depuis 1789 jusqu'en 1815*, ed. P.-J.-B. Buchez and P.-C. Roux (Paris, 1834), 10:2. All parenthetical citations in this chapter relating to the proceedings of the various incarnations of the National Assembly refer to this collection.

46. On the composition and workings of these sectional assemblies, see Albert Soboul, *The Sans Culottes: The Popular Movement and Revolutionary Government, 1793–1794*, trans. Rémy Inglis Hall (Princeton: Princeton University Press, 1980), 164–79.

47. *Oh! Elle est bien nommée section du Théâtre-François, car elle nous donne la comédie* (n.p.,n.d.), 1. The subject matter of the pamphlet makes clear that it was written in April of 1791.

48. Ibid., 2.

49. Ibid., 2–3.

50. Ibid., 8.

51. See William H. Sewell Jr., *Work and Revolution in France: The Language of Labor from the Old Regime to 1848* (Cambridge: Cambridge University Press, 1980), 86–91.

52. See chap. 2.

53. According to Buchez and Roux, the editors of *Histoire parlementaire*, this petition was drafted by the same individuals who had drafted the "people's petition" of 14 July.

54. See the official report of the *corps municipal* in *Histoire parlementaire*, 11:81.

55. See also the account of these events by Madame Roland in *The Old Regime and the French Revolution*, ed. Keith Baker (Chicago: University of Chicago Press, 1987), 276–78.

56. See also *Réimpression de l'ancien Moniteur* (Paris, 1857), 9:152.

57. Le Chapelier, speaking on behalf of the constitutional committee (29 September 1791), *Archives parlementaires de 1787 à 1860* (Paris, 1875), 31:617.

58. Robespierre (29 September 1791), ibid., 31:619–20.

59. Robespierre, *Sur le gouvernement représentatif [Prononcé à l'Assemblée nationale, séance du 10 mai 1793]*, in *Robespierre: Textes choisis* (Paris: Editions Sociales, 1957), 2:151–52.

60. Ibid., 150.

61. See Soboul, *Sans-Culottes*, 106–14.

62. Quoted in Morris Slavin, "Left of the Mountain: The Enragés and the French Revolution" (Ph.D. diss., Western Reserve University, 1961), 220.

63. See also the interruptions to Danton's speech, which followed soon after Isnard's, with respect to whether he could speak of the municipality of Paris as a whole or merely of the majority or "near totality" of Paris. *Histoire parlementaire*, 27:229.

64. For details on the events of 2 June, see Morris Slavin, *The Making of an Insurrection: Parisian Sections and the Gironde* (Cambridge: Harvard University Press, 1986), 110–26.

65. See Robespierre's speech before the Jacobin Club on 27 May 1793, in *Histoire parlementaire*, 27:243–44.

66. Barère would later report in his memoirs that Robespierre whispered to him, "What are you doing? You're making a mess of it." Quoted in Slavin, *Making of an Insurrection*, 115.

67. It should be pointed out that the Girondins undoubtedly believed themselves to be safeguarding the very sovereignty that the radicals claimed to be restoring. They thought of themselves as defenders of the general will of the nation against the particular will of radical groups, which were disproportionately powerful within the city of Paris, and which were endeavoring to make use of this tactical advantage in order to intimidate the Assembly and subvert the national will.

68. *Moniteur*, 16:562.

69. Slavin, *Making of an Insurrection*, 127.

70. See Roux's speech to the Cordeliers Club in *Histoire parlementaire*, 28:219.

71. Quoted in Albert Soboul, *The French Revolution 1787–1799: From the Storming of the Bastille to Napoleon*, trans. Alan Forrest and Colin Jones (New York: Vintage, 1975), 338.

72. Maximilien Robespierre, "Rapport sur les principes de morale politique qui doivent guider la Convention nationale dans l'administration intérieure de la république" (delivered to the National Convention in the name of the Committee of Public Safety, 5 February 1794), in *Oeuvres de Maximilien Robespierre*, ed. Laponneraye (New York: Burt Franklin, 1970), 3:543.

73. Slavin, *Making of an Insurrection*, 127.

74. Maximilen de Robespierre, "Sur le gouvernement représentatif," in *Robespierre: Textes choisis*, 2:142.

75. Robespierre, "Rapport sur les principes de morale politique," 548.

76. See Lynn Hunt's insightful discussion of the tension between didacticism and transparency. Hunt, *Politics, Culture, and Class in the French Revolution* (Berkeley: University of California Press, 1984), 72–77.

77. Francastelle, *Tableau des noms, âges, qualités et demeures des principaux membres des Jacobins, avec l'état de leur fortune, avant et depuis la Révolution, ainsi que l'état des services qu'ils ont rendus à la République. Par une société de Jacobins* (n.p., [1794]), 4–5.

78. Fonvielle aîné, *Collot dans Lyon, tragédie en vers et en cinq actes, dédiée aux membres de la Convention, victimes de la tyrannie, au 31 Mai 1793, & rendus aux voeux de la France après le 9 thermidor, an 2e de la République* (n.p., [1794]), 19–20.

79. Archives nationales (A.N.), F⁷ 4438, plaq. 7, pièce 4.

80. *Le peuple de Lyon à la Convention nationale* (n.p, [1794]), 2. This printed pamphlet can be found at A.N., F7 4438, plaq. 7, pièce 6.

81. *Le nouveau testament de J. B. Carrier en faveur de Collot-d'Herbois, Billaud de Varennes, Barrère de Vieuzac etc. et sa grande aventure aux enfers* (n.p., [1794]), 3.

CONCLUSION

1. Lynn Hunt, perhaps more than anyone else, has argued the importance of these trappings of legitimacy. See in particular the chapter "Symbolic Forms of Political Practice," in her book *Politics, Culture, and Class in the French Revolution* (Berkeley: University of California Press, 1984), 52–86, as well as her chapter "Freedom of Dress in Revolutionary France," in *From the Royal to the Republican Body*, ed. Sara E Melzer and Kathryn Norberg (Berkeley: University of California Press, 1998), 224–49.

2. Jacques Derrida seems to hint at this dissatisfaction and nostalgia for concrete presence in his essay "Différance," which explicitly mentions modern political representation within the context of other abstract signs: "When we cannot take hold of or show the thing, . . . then we signify, we go through the detour of signs. . . . The sign would thus be a deferred presence. Whether it is a question of verbal or written signs, monetary signs, electoral delegates, or political representatives, the movement of signs defers the moment of encountering the thing itself, the moment at which we could lay hold of it, consume or expend it, touch it, see it, have a present intuition of it. . . . [T]he sign (which defers presence) is conceivable only *on the basis of* the presence that it defers and *in view of* the deferred presence one intends to reappropriate." Derrida, "Différance," in *Speech and Phenomena, and Other Essays on Husserl's Theory of Signs*, trans. David Allison (Evanston: Northwestern University Press, 1973), 138.

3. *Evénemens remarquables & intéressans, à l'occasion des décrets de l'auguste Assemblée nationale, concernant l'éligibilité de MM. les comédiens, le bourreau, & les Juifs* (n.p., 1790), 25.

4. Marie-Hélène Huet comes close to this argument when she speaks of the development during the Revolution of a "tradition that consists in repressing by means of spectacle." See my discussion of her views on the actor-audience dynamic in the Entr'acte.

5. See the passage from the *Moniteur* that I quoted in the Prologue.

6. We are forever being told that politics can be changed by changing the political actors, by voting for a different party. In addition, within the United States at least, there is occasionally talk of term limits, as if somehow the longer a political actor stays on the stage, the less she or he seems capable of representing constituents transparently. In France, meanwhile, the *parité* movement promises a more transparent representation of the French nation, not by altering the form of representation, but by attempting to alter the content of the representative body.

7. Lani Guinier's probing questions on the nature of representative democracy within the American context are something of an exception to this rule. See Guinier, *The Tyranny of the Majority: Fundamental Fairness in Representative Democracy* (New York: Free Press, 1994).

8. Pierre Louis Roederer, "Discours du 13 ventose an IX," quoted in Jean Roels, *Le concept de représentation politique au dix-huitième siècle français* (Louvain: Nauwelaerts, 1969), 120.

Index

CPSIA information can be obtained at www.ICGtesting.com
Printed in the USA
LVOW07s2238240714

395887LV00003B/22/P

9 780801 488092